GOLFF NEFYN YN GANT
A HUNDRED YEARS' VISION FULFILLED

Researched and compiled / *Ymchwiliwyd ac ysgrifennwyd*
by / *gan*

T GARETH GRUFFYDD
and / *a*
SHAN E GRUFFYDD

Designed / *Dyluniwyd*
by / *gan*

DAFYDD E GRUFFYDD

Golff Nefyn yn Gant
A 100 Years' Vision Fulfilled

First Published in 2009 by
Nefyn and District Golf Club
Lôn Golff
Morfa Nefyn
Pwllheli
Gwynedd

© Nefyn and District Golf Club

All Rights Reserved

No part of this publication may be reproduced,
stored in a retrieval system, or transmitted
in any form or by any means,
without the prior permission
of the Copyright holder.

All aerial photographs of the Course are © Crown copyright (2009) Visit Wales

All telescopic photographs are © copyright (2009) Nefyn Golf Club

Paperback: ISBN: 978-0-9563005-0-8
Hardback: ISBN: 978-0-9563005-1-5

Printed and bound by
The Printing House Ltd
Marshfield Bank Employment Park
Crewe

This history of Nefyn Golf Club is dedicated to the memory of
Captain Charles Wynne-Finch (January 1929 - April 2008), former President and Captain,
and a staunch supporter of our Club for many years.

We owe an enormous debt of gratitude to the Wynne-Finch family.
Without their generous and enlightened patronage this Club would not exist in its present form.

*Cysegrir yr hanes yma o Glwb Golff Nefyn er cof am
Capten Charles Wynne-Finch (Ionawr 1929 - Ebrill 2008), Cefnamwlch,
cyn Lywydd, Capten a chefnogwr pybyr o'r Clwb am nifer fawr o flynyddoedd.*

*Mae ein dyled i deulu Wynne-Finch yn enfawr.
Heb eu cefnogaeth hael a goleuedig, ni fuasai'r Clwb yn bodoli fel y mae heddiw.*

RHAGAIR A CHYDNABYDDIAETHAU

Wrth ysgrifennu'r llyfr yma, ein bwriad oedd cynhyrchu hanes deniadol a llawn gwybodaeth o Glwb Golff Nefyn, hanes a fuasai'n apelio at ystod o ddarllenwyr, Aelodau ac ymwelwyr. Bydd rhai yn ei ddarllen o glawr i glawr, ambell un yn dewis darnau er gwybodaeth ac i ennyn difyrrwch, tra bydd eraill yn mwynhau'r ffotograffau a'r darluniadau. Hyderwn y bydd y llyfr yn profi i fod yn deyrnged deilwng iawn i bob person sydd wedi cynorthwyo i wneud ein Clwb a'n Cwrs yn fangre hollol arbennig.

Rydym wedi defnyddio sillafiadau modern i drefydd a phentrefi'r ardal yn yr hanes, er y gwelir yr hen sillafiadau mewn dyfyniadau. Gwelir dyfyniadau o gofnodion y Clwb ar femrwn brown tra bod dyfyniadau o gofnodion Pwyllgor y Merched i'w gweld ar femrwn glas.

Diolchwn i Bwyllgor Gwaith y Clwb am ryddhau Cofnodion y Clwb, i nifer fawr o gyn-Aelodau ac Aelodau presennol, eu teuluoedd a'u ffrindiau am eu gwybodaeth a'u hatgofion ac am fenthyg ffotograffau.

I'r canlynol, rydym yn hynod o ddyledus:
- Chris Gaskell (Cadeirydd y Clwb), Arwel Jones (cyn-Bennaeth Ysgol Botwnnog) a William L Griffith (cyn-Bennaeth Adran Gymraeg Ysgol Brynhyfryd, Rhuthun) am eu sylwadau a'u hawgrymiadau ynglŷn â'r testun
- ein cartwnydd, Tony Connolly, am greu darluniadau i ysgafnhau'r testun
- Dewi Wyn Pwllheli, Llinos Lanini Yr Wyddgrug, ac Alex Brown am eu cyfraniadau ffotograffig
- ein mab Dafydd sydd wedi gweithio'n drylwyr ar ddyluniad y llyfr gan lwyddo i gael canlyniadau nodedig o amrywiaeth o ffotograffau a dogfennau
- ein ffrindiau am eu hanogaeth a'u cefnogaeth ar hyd y daith.

Gareth a Shan Gruffydd, Pasg 2008.

FOREWORD & ACKNOWLEDGMENTS

In writing this book our aim has been to produce an informative and attractive history of Nefyn Golf Club that would appeal to a range of readers, whether Members or visitors. Some may read it from cover to cover; some will 'dip in' for information and amusement; others may simply enjoy the photographs and illustrations. We hope the book proves a worthy tribute to all who have helped make our Club and Course such a special place.

We have used the modern spelling of town and village names in the narrative, although the older spellings may appear in quotations. Excerpts from the Club's Minutes appear on brown parchment, while those from the Minutes of the Ladies' Committee appear on blue.

We would like to thank the Executive Committee for allowing us access to the Minute Books, and the many past and present Members, their families and friends, who loaned photographs and provided valuable information and recollections.

In particular we are indebted to:
- Chris Gaskell (Club Chairman), Arwel Jones (former Head of Botwnnog School) and William L Griffith (former Head of the Welsh Department at Brynhyfryd School, Ruthin) for their comments and suggestions regarding the text
- our cartoonist, Tony Connolly, for adding light relief
- Dewi Wyn Pwllheli, Llinos Lanini Mold, and Club Member Alex Brown, who added to our photographic contributions
- our son Dafydd, who has painstakingly worked on the design of the book and produced remarkable results from a miscellany of photographs and documentation
- our friends for their encouragement and support throughout.

Gareth and Shan Gruffydd, Easter 2008.

LLYWYDDION 2007 — THE 2007 PRESIDENTS

Anrhydedd o'r mwyaf yw cael bod yn Lywydd Clwb Golff Nefyn a'r Cylch ar achlysur ei Ganmlwyddiant.

Mae'n rhaid diolch i'r Sylfaenwyr am ddechrau'r Clwb a thrwy waith trylwyr y Staff ac Aelodau'r holl bwyllgorau a fu, i roi inni heddiw gwrs golff nad oes ei debyg yn unman.

Mae ein diolch yn fawr i Gareth a Shan Gruffydd a phawb arall a fu'n gysylltiedig, i gyflwyno inni y llyfr arbennig hwn. Gobeithio y bydd i chwi i gyd ei fwynhau.

It was a great honour to be elected President of Nefyn and District Golf Club on the occasion of the Club's Centenary.

Thanks are accorded to the Club's Founders for establishing the Club and through the conscientious work of the Staff and all Committee Members, we have today a golf course second to none.

We are grateful to Gareth and Shan Gruffydd and everybody else concerned in producing this unique book. I sincerely hope you enjoy reading it.

I R Williams

Fel un a gafodd y fraint o fod yn Llywydd y Merched am flwyddyn Canmlwyddiant y Clwb, edrychaf ymlaen at ddarllen am hynt a helynt y Clwb a'i Aelodau dros y can mlynedd diwethaf. Mae'n siŵr pan sefydlwyd Clwb yr adeg honno, nid oedd gan y Sylfaenwyr amcan o'r hyn a fyddai'n digwydd i'r Clwb yn y dyfodol.

Rwy'n siŵr y caf finnau a phawb sydd â chysylltiad gyda'r Clwb fwynhau bodio'r tudalennau am yr holl hanesion a ffeithiau nad ydym yn gyfarwydd â hwy, a hefyd dwyn atgofion o'r amseroedd a'r bobl sydd wedi gadael eu hoel ar y Clwb.

Hoffwn ddiolch yn bennaf i Shan a Gareth am y gwaith ymchwil trylwyr a wnaethant ar ddechrau'r dasg yma, hefyd i bawb sydd wedi cyfrannu at wneud y gyfrol yn ddiddorol a deniadol. Anodd yw gwasgu hanesion di-ri, digwyddiadau a lluniau ond rwy'n siŵr fod yr awduron wedi ystyried y rhain yn fanwl cyn cyhoeddi'r llyfr.

Hoffwn ddiolch i bawb sydd yn gwneud Clwb Golff Nefyn a'r Cylch yn unigryw, sef yr Aelodau, Gwŷr y Lawntiau, Gwasanaethwyr y Tŷ ac Aelodau'r Pwyllgorau, pawb yn cyd-weithio i edrych ar ôl ein hetifeddiaeth. Gai i ddymuno'n dda i'r Clwb yn y blynyddoedd sydd i ddod.

As one who is honoured to be Ladies' President in the Centenary Year, I look forward to reading about the Club and its Members during the last hundred years. The Founders would have no inkling of what was to come when they established the Club all those years ago.

I am certain that I, along with all who are associated with the Club, will enjoy browsing through the pages for the stories and facts that have come to light, and also to remember the many occasions and the people who have left their mark on the Club.

I wish to primarily thank Shan and Gareth for the thorough research undertaken at the start of this project and also to all who have provided information or materials enabling the production of this attractive and interesting book. It is a difficult task to précis all the stories, events and photographs but I am sure the authors have given great thought to this.

I would like to thank everyone who contributes to make Nefyn and District Golf Club quite unique. I refer to the Members, the Greens' Staff, the House Staff and Members of Committees – all of them pulling together to safeguard our heritage. May I take the opportunity to wish the Club all the best for the future.

Carys Wyn Jones

CONTENTS / CYNNWYS

1 - 16	THE DEVELOPMENT OF THE CLUB DATBLYGIAD Y CLWB	
17 - 38	THE DEVELOPMENT OF THE GOLF COURSE DATBLYGIAD Y CWRS GOLFF	
39 - 114	THE CAPTAINS Y CAPTEINIAID	
115 - 198	THE LADY CAPTAINS AND DEVELOPMENTS WITHIN THE LADIES' SECTION CAPTEINIAID Y MERCHED A DATBLYGIADAU YN ADRAN Y MERCHED	
199 - 212	THE JUNIOR SECTION AND CADDIES YR ADRAN IAU A CHADIS	
213 - 252	I REMEMBER... DWI'N COFIO...	
253 - 262	CLUB PROFESSIONALS 'Y PROS'	
263 - 288	CUPS AND COMPETITIONS CWPANAU A CHYSTADLEUTHAU	
289 - 294	MEMBERS' GOLFING SUCCESSES DURING THE CENTENARY YEAR LLWYDDIANNAU GOLFFIO AELODAU YN YSTOD Y CANMLWYDDIANT	
295 - 300	MEMORABLE GOLFING OCCASIONS DYDDIAU GOLFF COFIADWY	
301 - 304	COURSE RECORDS COFNOD O'R SGORIAU GORAU AR GWRS NEFYN	
305 - 310	TEAMS AND GROUPS TIMAU A GRWPIAU	
311 - 314	HELPING OTHERS HEPLU ERAILL	
315 - 320	SOCIAL EVENTS OVER THE YEARS DIGWYDDIADAU CYMDEITHASOL DROS Y BLYNYDDOEDD	
321 - 326	OUTINGS TEITHIAU	
327 - 336	PHOTOS COMMEMORATING CENTENARY EVENTS AND GREETINGS LLUNIAU O DDIGWYDDIADAU'R CANMLWYDDIANT A CHYFARCHION	

THE DEVELOPMENT OF THE CLUB
DATBLYGIAD Y CLWB

Ymddengys yr arferid chwarae golff ar drwyn Porthdinllaen cyn sefydlu Clwb Golff Nefyn a'r Cylch ym mis Mai 1907. Roedd John Wales yn un o sylfaenwyr chwarae golff ar y Penrhyn. Talwyd rhent i Mrs Williams, Fferm Porthdinllaen, am gael chwarae ar y trwyn yn ystod misoedd yr haf. Cyn y chwarae ar drwyn Porthdinllaen bu gwŷr o Nefyn yn teithio i Bemprys, ger Pentreuchaf mewn ceffyl a throl i chwarae. Yn nes ymlaen ceisiwyd chwarae yn nes adref ar dir Botacho Wyn. Yn ogystal, ystyriwyd chwarae golff ar dir Hirdrefawr (ar y ffordd i Dudweiliog). Fe chwaraewyd golff ar werni glas yn y Gors yn Edern yn ail ddegawd y ganrif ddiwethaf ac, o bosib, cyn hynny. Ond ym 1907, cynigiwyd Penrhyn Porthdinllaen i chwarae arno gan Mrs Wynne-Finch a sefydlwyd Clwb Golff Nefyn a'r Cylch.

The Royal and Ancient Game arrives in Llŷn

Before the turn of the twentieth century and prior to playing on Porthdinllaen Headland, men from Nefyn used to travel to play golf by pushbike or by Tŷ Cerrig's waggonette to Pemprys, near Pentreuchaf [on the way to Y Ffôr/Fourcrosses]. This was a small nine hole course and jam-pots were used for holes and sticks for flags. Although the Founder Members are believed to have been the Rev Wynne Lewis, the Baptist Minister and William Thomas, Iorwerth, Nefyn, there is no recorded date for the opening of this course but it is believed it was in existence at the turn of the century.

Later on, an attempt was made at opening a course nearer home on the land at Botacho Wyn which extended from Dyffryn to Bryncynan in Morfa Nefyn. The attempt failed. One of the reasons given for the failure was that a Telephone Relay Office had opened in the Cecil Hotel [originally Ashdene] which was nearby and that there were too many engineers digging the road in the area, ruining the peace and quiet required for tranquil golf! Consideration was also given to playing golf on land belonging to Hirdrefawr Farm [on the way to Tudweiliog]. It is known that golf was also played on swampy ground in Y Gors (Marsh) at Edern in the second decade of the twentieth century and may very well have been played there for some time prior to this.

Golf comes to the Headland at Porthdinllaen

It appears that golf was played on the Headland at Porthdinllaen before Nefyn and District Golf Club was established in May 1907. John Wales was one of the founders of playing golf on the Point. He was involved with the new telegraphy network being installed throughout the country and particularly with the laying of submarine telegraph cables between Morfa Nefyn [Abergeirch] and Newcastle, south of Dublin.

A very early photograph of Abergeirch [Cable Bay], showing the telegraph relay station on the right and 'Old Siani's Cottage' on the left. To the right of the estuary is the rock on which the present 5th Tee is sited.

John Wales first approached the Cefnamwlch Estate in September 1903, for a suitable piece of land on which to play golf. In April 1905, a contract was finally signed which enabled golf to be played on the Headland during the summer months for an undisclosed rent paid to Mrs Williams, Porthdinllaen Farm. After advice from a Professional from Hoylake, a nine hole links course was laid out and was called the Porthdinllaen Golf Club. [This Professional may very well have been (Young) Tom Morris from Hoylake, previously a 17 year old Winner of the British Open at Prestwick in 1868 and designer of Pwllheli Golf Club at the turn of the Century.]

John Wales

The initial work and the subsequent maintenance of the fairways and greens were undertaken by John Wales, his friends and local enthusiasts.

Documentation exists showing disagreement with Mrs Williams in June 1906. In a letter to George Bovill, Cefnamwlch Estate Agent, dated 09.06.1906, John Wales wrote:

'I think it right to inform you that we [Porthdinllaen Golf Club] have, somewhat summarily and unceremoniously, been deprived of the use of the grounds, or the greater part of them for some reason not quite apparent to me, save that Mrs Williams objects to visitors on the headland. The rent was paid six or seven weeks ago and nothing was then said to any possibility of the golf not being allowed to continue this year. The land has not during the two years of its existence been played upon more than seven or eight weeks in the 12 months. This Easter I certainly placed the boxes etc on the ground a little earlier I admit of the tour of Mrs Wynne-Finch going over the course, and I was surprised to find they were removed on the following day and thrown on one side without any apparent reason or warning to me.

I think you will agree that this is very shabby treatment.'

George Bovill replied on July 25th 1906 stating that Mrs Wynne-Finch 'consented to golf being played at Hirdrefawr Farm, Tudweiliog, known as Rhosfawr, but only up to September 15th and only with favourable arrangements being made with the tenant, Mr Owen Williams'. A week later, John Wales replied thanking Mrs Wynne-Finch for the offer but 'deciding to let the matter lapse for the present'. He continued 'If however an opportunity should arise of taking up the Porthdinllaen grounds again, either direct from you or by arrangement less interferable than the last one, I should be glad of your kind office'.

All this may account for the fact that when an offer was later made, John Wales appeared to have not been involved in any way and did not join Nefyn and District Golf Club until May 1910, three years after the Club's inception. The Club nevertheless recognises and acknowledges his vision and is indebted to him for his promotion of golf in those early days on the Headland.

THE DEVELOPMENT OF THE CLUB - DATBLYGIAD Y CLWB

The Origin of Nefyn and District Golf Club

Although no documentary evidence is to hand, it is almost certain that Mrs Wynne-Finch of the Cefnamwlch Estate reconsidered and offered the headland at Porthdinllaen to form a golf club prior to the spring of 1907. A far more amicable relationship between the Estate and the Golf Club was established and was to be nurtured and developed even further over the years. Lt Col Robin Parry, writing in the Club's 75 Year Anniversary Booklet, while recognising that the Club was unable to act in the early days without the Estate's authority and certainly not in financial matters, nevertheless acknowledged that the relationship was more avuncular than that of Landlord and Tenant. It would appear 'almost certain that the Club would have ceased to exist had it not been for the sound advice and generosity offered by the Estate over the years'.

The inscription inside the front cover of the Club's First Minute Book in the handwriting of Harold Hinton, (Secretary 1911-1918) states quite simply 'Club Commenced 7th May 1907'.

(Right) *Letter dated April 1907 to recruit members for the Golf Club at Subscriptions of: Gentlemen £1-1-0, Ladies 10/6 and Non-playing Members also 10/6.*

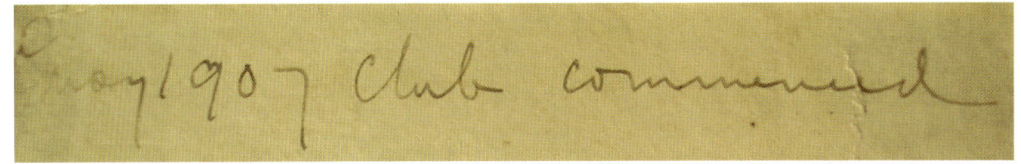

Inscription inside front cover of Minute Book

However, a letter in the name of 'Nevin and District Golf Club Porthynlleyn' (sic) had been written to prospective members in April 1907 and signed by a Hon Secretary, B Ryman-Hall and a Hon Treasurer, Wm Thomas. This in itself is evidence that a Committee had already been formed and the contents of the letter show that work had already been undertaken on a course that had previously existed in John Wales' era.

The first actual recorded Committee Minutes of Nefyn and District Golf Club were dated March 14th 1908. The early Committee Meetings took place at the Tŷ Coch Inn in Porthdinllaen Harbour and during the first few months, there was as much negotiation with the Porthdinllaen Farm regarding the grazing rights of animals as there was discussion regarding golf competitions and matches! A Handicap Committee and a Greens' Committee were set up in the early

THE DEVELOPMENT OF THE CLUB - DATBLYGIAD Y CLWB

meetings, Rules of Golf and of the Club were drafted for approval at the first AGM in August and an Open Meeting was planned for the same month.

The self-appointed Committee Members listed during the meetings of 1908 were: John Beaumont, Captain; B Ryman-Hall, Secretary; Wm Thomas, Treasurer; Arthen Owen, Rev R C J McCurdy, H Hinton, J C Lloyd, Capt Lloyd, the Vicar (Cynfelin Jones) and W Savidge.

W O Hughes of the Metropolitan Bank in Pwllheli was asked to audit the Accounts and he presented the first Balance Sheet in April 1908.

The first Clubhouse was a large portable bathing cabin situated at the head of the road that leads down to the Beach and the Tŷ Coch Inn. Golf was played from this spot towards the headland and back presumably utilising some, if not all of the original holes. In 1909, when the new wooden clubhouse was built, at the site of the present greenkeeper's shed, a purpose built nine hole golf course was designed. (See Chapter on Development of the Course)

Membership

The very first entry in the Minute Book is a list of Members at the inauguration of the Club.

GENTLEMEN:			LADIES:
E Abney*	T J E Hughes	W Thomas	Mrs Abney*
H Beaumont*	Rev R C Jones	J Ward*	Mrs Beaumont*
J Beaumont	Rev R T Jones	(E Wallis)	Mrs Colleton*
J Briggs*	(Kennan)	F Whitworth	Miss Cook
(F Brummitt)	E A Lakey	A H Wheeler*	Miss Cooper
(Thurston Cook)	(Rev D W Lewis)	J E Williams	Miss Francis
H Cook	Rev D W Lewis	(Dr Williams)	Mrs Garnett
Gerald Carter*	(Capt Lloyd)	(Capt Williams)	Mrs Hinton*
Sir R Colleton*	J T Little	(Rev Ll Williams)	Mrs Hudson
(W R Davies)	J C Lord	H Edeyrn Williams*	(Mrs Jones)
(Rev J Eastwood)	J N McCurdy	R Williams*	Mrs Lakey*
T Ellis*	J E Millar	Capt William, Pwll Parc*	Mrs Little
(Capt O Evans)	(Rev J Morgan)	Willis*	Mrs McCurdy
(W A Findley)	T W Owens	J C Wynne-Finch	Miss Roberts
W Fitzhugh	Arthen O Owen	W H Wynne-Finch	(Mrs Rowlands)
Cpt G Fitzhugh*	O H Parry		Mrs Silvester*
F Garnett	(Rev Roberts)	HON MEMBERS:	Mrs Williams
Rev A W Gough	H G Roberts	Walter Davies	Mrs Wynne-Finch
Dr R Griffith	E A Ryman-Hall	Capt Jones Sportsman	Mrs E Ward*
(A Hines)	B R Ryman-Hall*	C Jones	
H Hinton	W Savidge	R Jones Glynllifon	
J H Hudson	H Silvester	F M Owen	
Dr Hughes	P Smith	Tom Williams	
		Rich Davies*	

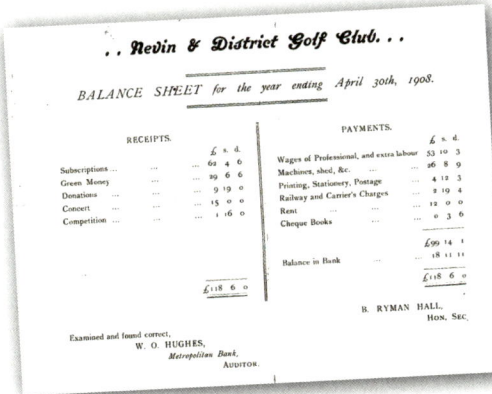

1st Recorded Balance Sheet, April 1908

List of Members at the Inauguration of the Club 1907.
(*New Members 1908: Bracketed Members withdrew in 1908)

THE DEVELOPMENT OF THE CLUB - DATBLYGIAD Y CLWB

In those early days, the Members were very much a cross-section of locals, holiday visitors and those temporarily employed in the area. The Lady Members were largely spouses of the Gentlemen Members.

At the 1st ever held AGM, on August 3rd 1908, at the Nanhoron Hotel, the Officers and Committee for 1908-1909 were formally elected and the Vicar and J Beaumont were elected Trustees.

In 1909, Pwllheli and Abersoch Golf Clubs were approached as to the feasibility of mutual honorary membership during the months of October to April inclusive and in August 1910, a new category of membership was approved – non-playing members. The Club decided to start advertising further afield. £1-5-0 was paid to John Wales in June 1911, to advertise in his 'Second Guide to Nevin and District'. A photo of the Clubhouse and running-advert was put in the 'North Wales Guide' at the same time at a cost of £1-0-0.

In 1920, there was a proposal that 'Members of the Parish of Nevin and Edeyrn and Members of the Caernarvonshire Golfing Union be admitted as Local Members'. Over the years there were many different borders discussed and approved for 'Local' Membership as opposed to 'Country' Membership. It is unclear how and when these were approved and what difference, if any, there was in subscription rates. What is certain is that the Membership increased steadily from the 20s onwards.

The records are decidedly unclear as to how many Members were on roll at any given time. The Minutes each month list new Members who were proposed and accepted. There is never any mention of resignations. Between the months of January 1920 and January 1937, for example, 456 new Members were listed as being accepted. These were in addition to any registered Members from 1907 onwards. However, on January 13th 1937, it was stated that there were only 299 Members on roll!

In November 1948, it is reported that the Roll of Members was as follows:

Local Gents:	104	Local Ladies:	109
Country Gents:	99	Country Ladies:	57
Juniors:	23		

It is difficult to understand how these figures are calculated!

Committee of 1956
Standing Left to Right: *Henry Parry, Richard Williams, Alec Smart, John Evan Roberts, S R Knowles, Captain Hugh Roberts, Richard Glyn Williams, Unknown and Peter Lane.*
Seated: *D A Williams, Brig William Wynne-Finch and Owen Roberts*

In 1963, the Vice President (H Buckley) proposed the following increases in subscription. Entry Fee for Local Members was to be £3-3-0 but for Away Members, the Entry Fee was double, at £6-6-0. The annual Subscription for both Local and Away Members was to be the same and the Executive Committee reserved the right to define 'a Local Member.'

Shortly afterwards there was a concern that the Membership was increasing too rapidly.

Committee in the Mid 60s
Standing from Left to Right: *Albert Portlock (Senior), G I Pritchard-Ellis (Treasurer), Richard Williams, Henry Fitzpatrick.* **Seated:** *Owen Roberts, Alec Smart, G I Hughes, Alf Whalley, Peter Lane and John Ogwen Jones.*

Committee and Past Captains in 1984
Standing Left to Right: *Ken Fitzpatrick, Richard Edgar Jones, G I Hughes, Richard Williams, R M Williams, Stanley Cresswell, Cliff Kilner, Captain Will Roberts, R Frank Evans, John Williams, Evan Hughes, Henry Fitzpatrick, G T Roberts, Harry Fray, Jim Bentley, Ioi Williams.*
Seated: *Wil Hughes, Captain Dan W Jones, Ivor E Williams, Owen Roberts, Lt Col Robin W Parry, Laurence A Barbet, Richie Glyn Williams.*

Committee and Past Captains in 1994
Standing Left to Right: *T Graham Owen (Secretary Manager), G Ifor Jones, Will Lloyd Jones, David Cooper, Lt Col Robin W Parry, Hugh D Jones (Treasurer), Dennis Humpherson, Captain Will Roberts, Laurence A Barbet, Stanley Cresswell, John Williams, Richard Edgar Jones, Ieuan M Ellis, Jim Bentley, Robin Moi Williams, Evan Hughes, Cliff Kilner, Gresham T Owen, Ioi Williams, T Gareth Gruffydd.*

A ceiling was set at 500 in January 1967, with a maximum of 300 Local and 200 Away Members. In 1969 there was a block on new membership for a while and the Minutes confirm that no new Members were proposed from July 1969 until January 1970.

In January 1973, the ceiling of membership was raised to 800 from 500, with equal weighting of Home and Away Members. However in the 1973 AGM this was changed to 500 Local Members (within the line drawn from Trefor Pier to Afonwen Station, except Borough of Pwllheli) and 300 Away Members. (It was not until 1988, that the Joining Fee was made one uniform fee for both Home and Away Members.)

Some 33 resignations were apparent by March 1976, due to increases in subscriptions (see Chart, P.8 on Fees). However, many were Members who played very little golf.

In October 1976, the Executive agreed that Members of 10 years' standing (Men 65 and Women 60) could elect to be Senior Members for one half of the normal subscription. (The age was increased subsequently to 65 for Ladies.) 103 Members took advantage of this offer.

The Club ran into financial difficulties in the Autumn of 1976. Green fees and bar takings had suffered due to the long dry and very hot weather of '76. The Club was overdrawn by £7,500 at the bank and Members were asked to help with Interest Free Loans. By May 1977, 37 Members (out of a total of 800 Members) had raised £5,050 in debenture loans (£50 units).

In 1995, the Ladies' Section looked seriously at the prospect of Ladies becoming Full Members. The motion was not put to the AGM until 1996 however, whereupon several rule changes were made to enable Lady Members to become

Full Members of the Club. The Ladies were to pay the same subscription fee as the Men and at the AGM of 1997, the Ladies attended for the first time.

In March 1999, the Welsh Golfing Union wrote expressing concern at a 7% drop in Nefyn Ladies' Membership between 1991 and 1998. The Ladies were asked to respond. They explained (a) the 7% drop was due to the increase in subscription following the change in membership status and Ladies were now paying the same Subscription as the Men and (b) the fact that the Ladies' Section had an ageing membership.

Various initiatives were put forward in an attempt to increase membership. In 2001, Junior Members were allowed to become Intermediate Members on their 18th Birthday and pay a proportionately lower fee than the Full Subscription until the age of 24. They were precluded from attending AGMs and could not be elected on to the Committee of the Club.

The AGM of 2001 saw the ceiling for Membership raised from 800 to 1000. In the AGM of 2002, R J Spud Taylor successfully proposed a new category of membership – Overseas Membership.

In Dec 2002, the Match & Handicap Committee proposed yet another new category of membership named 'Newcomer Members' to attract more members who lived locally. This membership allowed restricted rights for 2 years before deciding on Full Membership or not. This was put to the AGM of 2003 as 'Introductory Membership' and passed unanimously. In 2005 E L Evans was successful in proposing that the Intermediate Membership for young people aged 18-24 should now include voting rights and they should be allowed to participate in the running of the Club the same as Full Members. In 2007, the AGM gave powers to the Executive Committee to increase the age range of the Intermediate Members to 32 or such age as the Committee deemed appropriate, in an effort to recruit or keep young people over the age of 24. As seen in the Table on Categories of Membership below, this has proved effective.

By 2006, there was a national concern regarding the decline of ladies' golf. Thus, in the Autumn, Shan Gruffydd put forward a 'Taster Ladies' Scheme' in conjunction with Golf Development Wales. The scheme began in early Spring 2007 and had the full support of the Executive Committee. Initially, 34 non-playing ladies joined the scheme and paid for group lessons run by the Pro assisted by Members of both the Ladies' and Gent's Sections. Many of these ladies were local and many were somewhat younger than the sadly ageing membership of our Ladies' Section!

A Ladies' Taster Group is shown how to grip the club correctly by John Froom, the Professional, on April 1st 2007

25 of these ladies then continued to the second stage where they paid £50 for an extended Green Fee of 3 months while receiving more group lessons, this time paid for by Golf Development Wales. The Executive then agreed to offer these Taster Ladies an introductory annual fee

(£150 - one year only). This allowed them full membership rights other than not being allowed to attend AGMs or stand for Committee. The intention was and is to encourage them to procure a CONGU handicap so they may enter Club Competitions. The scheme has proved to be wholly successful and by the end of the Centenary Year, March 2008, 20 ladies have taken up the offer and have become Members of the Club.

Categories and Numbers of Members

Category of Membership	2004	2005	2008
Full	425	400	372
Joint	117	114	114
(Spouse)	117	114	114
Senior (Ladies and Gent)	102	101	109
Non-Playing	19	17	23
Intermediate	46	37	70
Special Category Junior *	3	3	*
Junior	96	93	117
Reciprocal	30	30	30
New Schemes **			28
Total	955	909	977

* Disbanded 2007 ** New Schemes e.g. Taster Ladies (20) and Extended Green Fee (8)

Subscription Rates for Junors

Year	Juniors	Special Category	Student Gents	Student Ladies	Int* (18-24)	Int* (25-30)
1920	3/-					
1936	10/6					
1969	£1					
1973	£2					
1975	£2.20					
1978	£5.00					
1982	£7.50					
1984	£15		£45	£27.50		
1987	£17.50	£27.50	£52.50	£32.50		
1989	£30	£40	£65	£45		
1991	£40	£55	£87.50	£58		
1998	£20	£55				
2008	£25	2007*			£122	£244

* Dispanded

Subscription Rates

These are presented in tabular form to allow ease of comparison. (Please note, little information is documented in the Minutes. Subscription fees are often grouped together in the AGM Balance Sheet.)
Subscription Rates over the years where documented in the Minutes. (L= Local; A= Away Members – over 6 miles)

Year	Subs Men	Subs Ladies	Entrance Fee Men	Entrance Fee Ladies	Joint	Senior Men(65)	Senior Ladies(60)	Non Playing
1907	£1-0-0	10/6						10/6
1920	£1-10-0	15/-	£3-3-0	£1-11-6				
1934	£1-5-0	12/6	£2-2-0	£1-1-0				
1951	£2-2-0	£1-5-0						£1-1-0
1963			L £3-3-0 A £6-6-0					
1969	£6	£4	L £6 A £12	L £4 A £8				
1974	£10	£8	L £10 A £25	£8				
1975	£20	£12	L £20 A £40	L £12 A £24				
1976	£30	£20				50% (10 yrs+)	50%	
1981	£60	£30						
1984	£90	£55			£125	£45	£25	
1986	£105	£65			£145	£52.50	£32.50	
1990	£130	£90	£110	£75	£180	£65	£45	
1992	£175	£116	£175	£116	£250	£116	£77	
1994	£204	£136	£204	£136	£302	£136	£90	
1998	£220	£220	£220	£220	£396	£147	£147	
2004	£294	£294	£10	£10	£529	£196	£196	
2007	£333	£333	£10	£10	£599	£222	£222	
2008	£366	£366	£10	£10	£680	£244	£244	£61

Green Fees ('Green Money' in the Early Days)

Year	Per Round	Day Round	W/E Round	W/E Day	Week	2 Weeks	Month
1912		2/6		7/6	£1	£1-10 Season	
1934		3/-		15/-	£1-5-0	£1-15-0	
1951		6/-		£1-5-0	£2	£2-2-0	
1976	£2.25		£3	£9.00	£15.50		
1980		£4		£5	£20.00	£35.00	
1990		£12.50		£15	£60	£100	
1991	£16	£20	£22.50	£30	£80	£150	
1994	£20	£25	£25				
2004	£29	£36	£36 Fri/Sat £33 Sunday	£42 Fri/Sat £38 Sunday			

THE DEVELOPMENT OF THE CLUB - DATBLYGIAD Y CLWB

Management

For virtually 90 years the Club's management lay in the hands of the Gentlemen Members. The Ladies had formed their own Committee in 1928 'to see to their own affairs' but since they were not Full Members with full voting rights, they were very much under the complete control of the 'Men's Committee'! There are many amusing anecdotes relating as to how the ladies had to ask the 'Men's Committee' for all their needs from waste bins and nail brushes to the increase in the amount of food served for afternoon tea and even how much filling was to be put in the sandwiches!

For many years, the Executive Committee was generally chaired by the Captain, ably supported by an Hon Secretary and Hon Treasurer. These were the Officers of the Club. There were very few Members on the Committee but this number increased over the decades.

On the retirement of Hon Sec Robin Parry in 1994, T Graham Owen was appointed Secretary/Manager and a motion was carried at the AGM to delete any reference to the Hon Secretary being an Officer of the Club.

Barry Owens, Secretary/Manager, shortly before his retirement in 2006 after serving the Club for 11 years.

Graham Owen resigned in May 1995 and in July, J Barry Owens was appointed the new Secretary/Manager.

In 1996, Ladies were accepted as Full Members of the Club and 2 ladies represented the Ladies' Section on Greens' and House Committees. At the AGM of 1998, Mrs Muriel Entwistle was elected to serve on the Executive Committee. She was the first Lady Member to ever take her seat on the ruling Committee of the Club.

Neville Ingman, at the AGM of 1999, in his retiring speech as Captain, put forward some sound reasons as to why the 'Members of the Executive Committee should seriously consider a radical review of the management and administration of the Club'. The incoming Captain, S B Murray, in his first Executive Meeting as Captain, following on from Neville Ingman's comments, suggested that a new streamlined management system should be considered. This would be led by a Chairman who would be elected every 3 years. It would mean the Club Constitution would have to be re-written and to this end, he called an EGM in October 1999 to gauge Members' opinions. It is reported that 'Members expressed their views and eventually the whole issue was thrown out even though the idea of a Chairman was well supported'.

Will Lloyd Jones (Right) enjoying the companionship of Captain Will Roberts outside the Clubhouse in the late 90s

At the AGM of April 2000, S B Murray successfully proposed the creation of a Club

Chairman to be implemented in the AGM of 2001 and on April 14th 2001, Will Lloyd Jones was elected as the Club's first Chairman and an Officer of the Club.

In January 2006, a Special Meeting was convened to again discuss the re-organisation of the Club's Management Structure. This meeting was attended by 65 Members and as a consequence the following resolutions were passed at the AGM of 2006:

1. The President and the Lady President to serve for 1 year;
2. The Officers of the Club were to be the Captain, the Ladies' Captain, the Chairman, the Vice-Captain, the Ladies' Vice-Captain, the Hon Treasurer (6 in total);
3. The number of Committee Members reduced from 9 to 8;
4. The Executive to delegate powers to sub-committees;

Thus in April 2006, there was an historic Executive Meeting when the Officers, Ladies' Captain and Ladies' Vice-Captain, Mrs Megan Roberts and Miss Fiona Vaughan Thomas, took their elected places on the Executive Committee for the first time.

The Executive Committee 2007-2008
Standing Left to Right: *Secretary Manager Simon Dennis, Duncan Smith, Chairman of Greens Richard Harris Roberts, Mrs Rhiannon Ingman, Chairman of Match and Handicap Ian Hamilton, Graham Reynolds, H Eirwyn Jones and Treasurer Richard Rimmington* **Seated:** *Chairman of House Howard Dennett, Ladies' Vice-Captain Janet Brown, Ladies' Captain Fiona Vaughan Thomas, Chairman Chris Gaskell, Club Captain Emyr L Evans and Vice-Captain Gordon Smith.*

THE CLUBHOUSES

Y Clwb

Cyfeirir at Dŷ'r Clwb gan yr Aelodau Lleol fel Y Clwb a chyfeirir at y maes golff ei hun fel Y Golff. O gwt newid bychan ar ben Lôn Tŷ Coch yn 1907 i'r Clwb presennol gyda'i gyfleusterau cyfoes a'i olygfeydd ysblennydd dros Borthdinllaen a Bae Caernarfon, ardystiwyd nifer fawr o ddatblygiadau. Yn dilyn tannau erchyll yn 1909 a 1928, llosgwyd dau Glwb i'r ddaear a bu rhaid ail-adeiladu. Erbyn 2007 mae gennym Glwb mae'r Aelodau oll yn ymfalchïo ynddo, ond dros y ganrif ddiwethaf rhaid oedd goresgyn sawl anhawster wrth symud ymlaen.

The Clubhouse in 2007

Today, the Club is proud of its Clubhouse which consists of a spacious and comfortable lounge and 80 seater dining room, both offering superb views overlooking the Course. A smaller but equally comfortable spike-bar with television leads to a snooker room. Both Gent's and Ladies' Locker Rooms are modernised and the first floor houses offices, a committee room and the caterer's accommodation. A separate building houses the trolley shed and the Pro's shop. Excellent kitchen facilities ensure quality catering and one fully stocked bar serving both lounge and spike bar, is available to quench the golfer's thirst. The progress to reach the standard of excellence we now have has been slow and sometimes fraught with problems.

The First Clubhouse

The first Clubhouse was little more than a large bathing hut and was situated at the top of the road leading down to the Tŷ Coch Inn and the Beach. It was used only for changing and all refreshments were taken at the Tŷ Coch. Committee Meetings were held at the Tŷ Coch but larger meetings, like AGMs, were held in the Nanhoron Arms Hotel in Nefyn.

The 1909 Clubhouse

The first purpose built Clubhouse was situated where the Groundstaff's Machinery Shed is situated today and was built by the Cefnamwlch Estate. It was opened on May 1st 1909 and rent became due when water was connected! Facilities included a 'Dressing Room', a Club Room which housed tables and chairs and a kitchen. A coalhouse, mower shed and Pro's shop were added as lean-tos. Committee meetings were immediately transferred from the Tŷ Coch!

(See Photo of the original Clubhouse in the Captain's Chapter, 1909 Ryman-Hall)

There was a constant water supply problem for many months and both the Club and the Estate realised the problem would not be solved until the Clubhouse was connected to the main Nefyn Water Supply.

This wooden Clubhouse had a thatched roof and this became the seat of a serious fire in July 1910 which completely destroyed the Clubhouse and the adjacent buildings. Some Members' effects were salvaged together with some crockery etc. The Estate agreed to rebuild if the Insurers agreed to their claim and in the meantime it was proposed to put up an 18' by 12' building with brick flue as a temporary Clubhouse. [The intention was to use this later as the Pro's shop and store room.] This temporary Clubhouse was opened on July 23rd 1910, the insurance claim was met and building began on the new Clubhouse.

The 1911 Clubhouse

On July 21st 1911, the New Clubhouse was informally opened to Members – with 6 buckets of water hung in suitable places! Jane Jones was appointed the first Stewardess *(although no note is made of the appointment – but see Annette Jones' reminiscences in Chapter 'I remember…')* but it is minuted she asked to leave at the end of September 1911 and was re-appointed in April 1912.

The 1911 Clubhouse, Sept 1923; *General Meeting at Nefyn (Note the Pro's 'workshop' on the right hand side – separate from the main Building)*

In 1923, the Estate was approached and a proposed plan to enlarge the Clubhouse was put forward. The Estate refused to finance the proposal.

On December 19th 1928, another serious fire completely destroyed the Clubhouse, including the outbuildings and Members' effects. On January 4th 1929, the Club asked the Estate to build a larger, better Clubhouse costing £400 to £500 and to erect it near the parking ground [present site]. A temporary hut 'with suitable lavatory accommodation' was to be erected on the site of the Pro's old workshop and would serve the Members until the new Clubhouse was built.

The 1929 Clubhouse

In February 1929, a new 15 year lease was produced by the Estate. The Golf Club was to hand £775 to Major Wynne-Finch (amount obtained for buildings allowance from the insurance company). Major Wynne-Finch would find the balance including the architect's fee and the Golf Club would pay him 5% per annum on this sum. The rental was £88 per annum plus 2/- per annum for right of way, etc. The Golf Club was to insure the building for the full cost against fire.

In the same month, the Hon Sec was asked to distribute subscription letters to Members and seek financial aid to tide the Club over this difficult period. Nothing is minuted as to the response to this request. In June, the Offices in the Clubhouse were completed and furniture was bought with the intention of officially opening in July. Mrs Wynne-Finch's unavailability however led to a postponement and the Clubhouse was officially opened by her in August. A Commemorative Open Competition with a 1st Prize of £10-10-0 was played on the same day.

The 1929 Clubhouse

Some interesting developments over the years follows, as reported verbatim in the Club's Minutes.

May 1921: Introduction of Intoxicating Liquor (but 'no Juniors to be allowed intoxicating liquor').

Dec 1936: Installation of electricity discussed and idea abandoned due to cost.

Feb 1938: Decided to reserve the Bar for 'Men Only'.

Sept 1945: Extension of Clubhouse to include a billiards room to be considered.

Nov 1947: Wiring of the Clubhouse by Robert Jones...and in December, a Lighting Plant was bought 'for the needs of the Club'.

Jan 1952: Resolved that no action be taken in respect of the request of Messrs D Roberts & Co, Pwllheli, that Members of Committee visit their Bottling Works. This request resulted from the incident of a member finding a dead mouse in his Bottle of Stout. (sic)

'...finding a dead mouse in his bottle of Stout.'

Oct 1956: Lighting plant regarded as condemned. Club buys second-hand Diesel TVO Lighting Plant.

Mar 1958: Clubhouse and Bar to open on Sundays.

Apr 1959: £5 paid for connection fee to Manweb.

The Clubhouse in the 50s

Sept 1961: Clubhouse extension (to Men's Locker Room) contract given to R G Parry, Arddol, Morfa (£3,894).

Feb 1969: Extension to Clubhouse – lounge with flat roof. J Jones Llanaelhaearn awarded the contract (£18,253). Gas Heating System installed at the same time.

Mar 1970: Official Opening of Extension to the Clubhouse (see Photo in Captain's Chapter, 1969, Captain Dan W Jones).

Feb 1972: Roof leakages 1st reported... [and were to continue for the next 35 years!]

Mar 1975: Clubhouse extension [upstairs] proceeding with very little inconvenience to administration.

Mar 1984: Snooker Room extension completed (tender by W Ambrose Griffith accepted at £15,728).

The Snooker Room (2007)

Jul 1985: Dress rule to be relaxed. No need for jacket and tie in lounge in the evening but Dress must be of a reasonable standard.

Oct 1987: Extensive renovations to Lounge – wooden panels removed from walls, re-plastering and full redecorating and re-furbishing.

Winter 1987: Ladies allowed in Men's Bar while the Lounge was renovated.

Mar 1988: Concert to officially open the new Lounge after extensive renovations.

Nov 1990: The Secretary reported that office accommodation needed to be upgraded. Resolved that Secretary's Office move upstairs to Ladies' Lounge and Ladies move to Lounge underneath this room.

Feb 1994: Club informed Porthdinllaen Village and Uwch-y-Don Car Park to be sold to National Trust.

Apr 1994: New bar completed.

Sept 1994: Strict Dress Code enforced: Course – no trainers, no straps, no jeans, no leggings, tailored shorts only and all shirts to have collars. Clubhouse: No jeans, no tailored shorts at any time, no leggings, no trainers.

Dec 1994: A sum of £38,197 received from Customs and Excise in respect of VAT repayment and £11,204 in calculated interest. Decision made to carry out further extensions and improvement to the Clubhouse (March 1995).

Mar 1995: Extensive alterations to Clubhouse planned but many objections from the National Trust. [Took several months to resolve]

Oct 1996: Smoking banned in the main lounge on formal Club Presentation Nights.

Late 1997: Building work began. Alterations included new entrance hall and stairs, new central heating system, new kitchen, improvements to locker rooms and upstairs dining room. The contract was given to Cheshire Contracts for an estimated £230,000 + Vat. This was to include carpets throughout and curtains for the lounge.

April 1998: Work completed. [Many defects apparent over ensuing months and legal issues involved with contractors.]

May 1998: Concern re lack of use of Dining Room upstairs and by June, area downstairs was designated as additional dining room.

Sept 2001: Club inherits the sum of £1500 from the will of a Member, Mr Keith Welsh. Quality patio furnishings to be purchased to permanently benefit the Members. Part of the trolley shed to be partitioned off to create an area where Members could charge their trolley batteries on payment of a fee.

Feb 2003: Executive Committee vote in favour of changing the men's bar to an 'open bar'.

Jul 2004: Total ban on smoking in the Clubhouse and Pro's Shop.

Nov 2004: An analysis of a questionnaire sent to Members revealed widespread dissatisfaction about the piecemeal development of the Club, the poor standards, layout, locker rooms and space allocation. Members felt that the Clubhouse was not consistent with a Course ranked in the UK's top hundred. Catering was felt by almost everyone to be inadequate in quality, variety and opening hours and lacked the staff capable of delivering the services required.

Jan 2005: New Caterer appointed.

(Left) Front entrance to the Club in the late 90s with the Ladies' Powder Room, left of front door, converted to additional dining room.

Feb 2005: Work on Ladies' Locker Room progressing satisfactorily. New Captains' and Honours Boards to be renewed.

May 2005: Dining Room extension to cost £75,000 + £15,000 for soft furnishings.

Dec 2005: H E Jones awarded the contract for the Dining Room extension at a cost of £106,740. Delays on start due to planning and grant considerations and then programme delayed again due to structural problems!

Part of the spacious new Dining Room, completed June '06.

June 2006: Extension completed in less than two months in readiness for the Ryder Cup Challenge Tour.

H E Jones and son, John, at work on the new Dining Room Extension

June 2005: House Chairman recommending relaxing of dress code to include jeans and trainers. Juniors would therefore be made to feel more welcome.

Members and Guests listen to Rod Taylor, the Guest Speaker at the Ladies' Captain's Evening, August 2007. (Note the advantage of being able to use both the Lounge and Dining Room for large gatherings.)

June 2006: New electricity supply to be connected on June 30th. Dress Rule relaxed: Smart jeans and trainers could be worn.

June 2007: Executive gives go-ahead for complete re-furbishment of kitchen subject to planning consent. Locker rooms to be adapted accordingly.

June 2007: New PA System up and running. Spike Bar Opened in the old Men's Bar.

The Spike Bar is opened 2007. Note the new Honours Boards.

Jan 2008: Building contract awarded to H E Jones and kitchen and locker rooms in use by mid-Feb 2008. Estimate for work approx £25,000 and all work to be in full compliance with all current and pending legislation.

THE CLUB LOGO
LOGO'R CLWB

Lluniwyd Logo Clwb Golff Nefyn o arfbais bwrdeistref Nefyn sy'n deillio o'r ddeunawfed ganrif. Yn sgil datblygiad Nefyn fel porthladd penwaig enwog, mabwysiadwyd arwydd y tri phennog ar Logo'r Clwb o'r pumdegau ymlaen.

In the 18th century around 120 shipping vessels were built in Nefyn and fishing, particularly for herring, became a prime trade. The Coat of Arms of the Borough of Nefyn proudly displayed the three herrings as a sign of the town's importance as a major herring-fishing port. The Golf Club adopted the three herrings sign and the Club Logo appeared for the first time in the mid-50s. (1)

The Lady Captain's Brooch, presented in 1960 is still worn today by the Ladies' Captain in office and has the herrings facing right. (2)

For many years the famous herrings faced right on the Captains' Blazer Badges. (4 & 5 - 1990 and 2005)

1 One of the earliest examples of the Club Logo, mid-50s

2 Lady Captain's Brooch, 1960

3 Glenmuir Sweater with embroidered Logo (mid 80s)

4 Captain's Blazer Badge 1990

5 Captain's Blazer Badge 2005

6 The Club's Centenary Logo 2007

Glenmuir however, had the Logo with the herrings facing left on all their sweaters and shirts! (3) Other suppliers followed suit but some faced the herrings the opposite way and soon we had a complete mix of logos!

For the Centenary Year, it was decided to have a specific Club's Centenary Logo. (6) This was formally adopted in 2006 with an amended version for 2008 onwards. (7) Club Member, Tony Connolly, designed the logos and consulted with a leading archivist who confirmed that the herrings should be represented facing the 'dexter', the senior left hand side of a shield of arms, as opposed to the 'sinister' right hand side.

7 The Club's Logo 2008 onwards

THE DEVELOPMENT OF THE CLUB - DATBLYGIAD Y CLWB

The Development of The Course - Datblygiad Y Cwrs

THE DEVELOPMENT OF THE GOLF COURSE
DATBLYGIAD Y CWRS GOLFF

Dyma ddechrau can mlynedd o olffio ar gwrs naw twll i ddechrau, cyn gweld sawl datblygiad a goresgyn nifer o stormydd nes cyrraedd 2007 a safiad cadarn y Cwrs ymysg mawrion Prydain.

The Course in 2007 as introduced on the Club's Website

The Old Course opens with three Par 4s and a Par 5 which run along the coastline before turning inland to a series of six holes which provide the golfer with the spectacular backdrop of the surrounding mountains. The remaining eight holes are played on the Point, a narrow peninsula with the sea on one side and sandy beaches on the other. Every hole calls for accurate shot making and in a few cases, some spectacular carries across coves and inlets.

Alternatively, after 10 holes of The Old Course, the golfer can continue on The New, with an opening par 3 which, depending on the wind, can be a wood or a medium iron. Thereafter, a series of longish Par 4s and a Par 5 around a coastal inlet brings the golfer back to the 18th tee with its panoramic view of the entire course.

It has taken 100 years to develop this unrivalled piece of coastline into the spectacular 26 hole golf course of today.

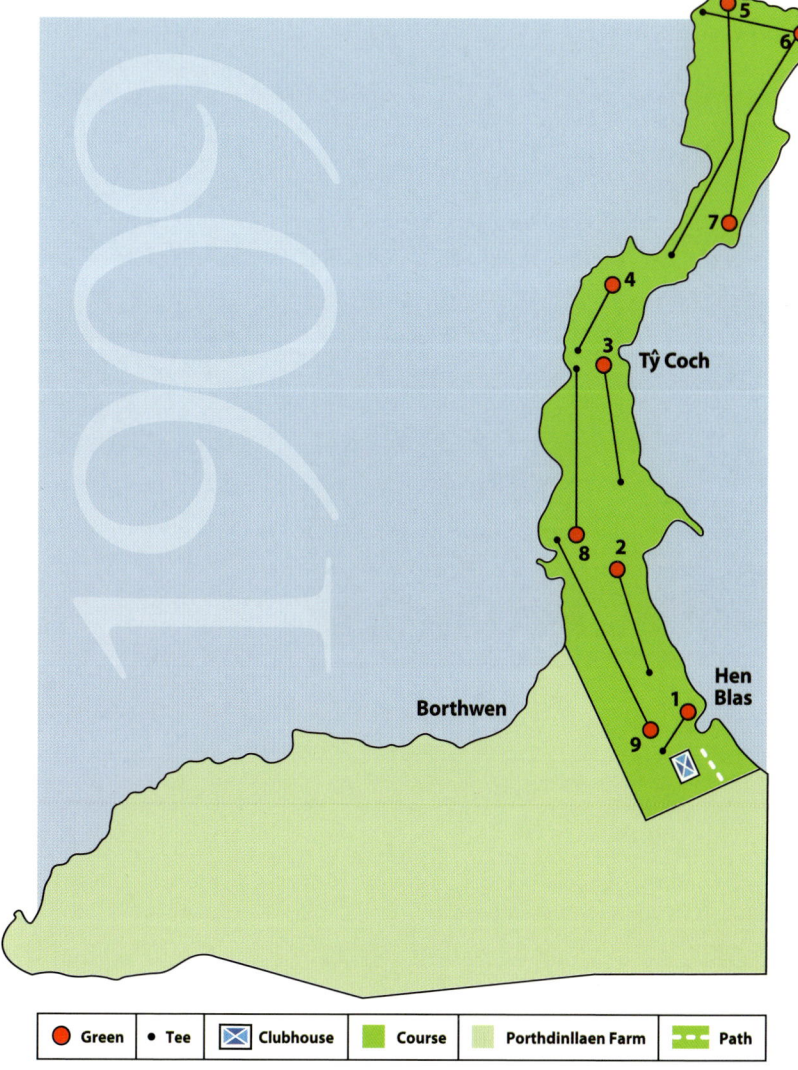

The 1909 Course

1st Hole

This was a Par 3, played from the Clubhouse [Greenkeeper's Shed today] to the present 11th Green of the Old Course. This was a very difficult shot - the land rising some 30 to 40 feet.

The site of the 1st Tee in 1909 before the development and extension of 1912 when it became the 3rd Tee. (See Photo of Winifred Janion playing the 3rd hole in April 1913 in Chapter on Captains.) The Tee can be seen to the right of the Original Clubhouse.

The purchase of a coconut mat for the 1st Tee in June 1911 would appear to verify that this was indeed a Par 3. In July of the same year, wire netting was erected at the back of this green, presumably to prevent balls running through the green and over the cliff [by the public footpath that runs down to Henblas].

A letter sent by the Secretary, Harold Hinton on 27th November 1912 to a Mr Jones, a member of the Cefnamwlch staff, refers to the back of this first hole:

> **November 1912:**
> Dear Mr Jones,
> There has been a land slide at the back of our number one green. The Henblas path has disappeared. Perhaps you could have a look at it if you are Edeyrn way. I am writing to Mr Bovill [Cefnamwlch agent] on another matter and have mentioned this.
>
> Yours faithfully,
> Harold Hinton

2nd Hole

This was also a Par 3, played from a Tee very close to the cliff edge [around present 12th Tee of the Old Course] down to the valley ahead. This Tee has eroded by today. The path leading to this Tee had wire netting on the seaward side, presumably to prevent golfers from tripping over the dangerous cliff edge.

3rd Hole

The 3rd Hole was played from a point half way along the present 12th Hole to the 12th green by Tŷ Coch. It is minuted that a coconut mat was purchased for this Tee, again implying it was a Par 3.

4th Hole

The 4th Hole was a short hole uphill. [This became the 12th Hole, 93 yds in length, on the pre-1977 Course.]

5th Hole

The 5th Hole was the present 13th Hole on the Old Course. It is stated in the minutes that 'the fairway was cut by horse mower in Aug 1911.'

The 5th Hole during this time, looking towards the green with the flag pole in the distance. This was in the days before the Coastguard Lookout was erected.

Holes 6 - 9

The 6th, 7th, 8th and 9th were the present 14th – 17th Holes of the Old Course.

Apart from Holes 5 [13th], 7 [15th] and 9 [17th] the holes were quite short Par 3s. This seems typical of Courses at the turn of the last century.

Extension of the Course to 18 Holes, 1912

As early as Easter Saturday 1908, the Committee 'had discussed 9 v 18 holes' [sic] – nothing more recorded! The question was then asked periodically until September 1911 when a firm decision was undertaken to move forward.

> *September 1911* '...and agreed that we extend the Course to 18 holes and that James Braid of Walton Heath Golf Course be asked to lay out the Course' and 6 Committee Members were asked to 'arrange the matter with the Estate'.

James Braid replied saying he could not give an early date, and Fred Collins, the Pro of North Wales Golf Club, Llandudno, was approached. He subsequently visited Nefyn and put forward his recommendations. The 'Extension Sub-Committee' (as the 6 Committee Members were called) had full powers to proceed with the new development but were not allowed to exceed an expenditure of £80 before submitting a statement of expenses. In October 1911, the estimated cost of the work rose to £165 and a £100 loan was secured from Mrs Wynne-Finch of the Cefnamwlch Estate, to be repaid 'in annual amount which the Club could afford'.

On Fred Collins' recommendation, John Henry Jones was appointed as a Greenkeeper at 27/- a week and together with Griffith Davies, commenced work on the new tees and greens. In order to proceed with the alterations to the holes on the Point, a request was made to Mrs Williams, Porthdinllaen, to remove horses but to leave sheep and cattle. A horse was bought for £9 for use on the links. Apparently it was a 'jibber' and a new grey horse was bought which worked well. During the winter of 1911/12, five men were employed to assist J H Jones on the new development and it was hoped the Course would be available for play in June 1912. In March 1912, the lease as drafted for the new land was finally agreed and accepted. Mr Bovill, the Cefnamwlch Agent, walked over the new Course and was pleased with Fred Collins' plan. However, he did recommend as much gorse and rough grass as possible was to be left, to keep the natural appearance of the links.

A satisfactory arrangement was made between the Estate and Mrs Williams, Porthdinllaen, in reference to sub-letting of the new portion of land. 'A rebate of £40 per annum was to be made in Mrs Williams' rent, which amount the Club should pay in rent to the Estate, plus rates.' Mrs Williams, in turn, was to pay the Club £30 per annum for sheep grazing.

Harold Hilton, twice Amateur British Open Champion (1892 and 1897), was contacted to officially open the Course in March 1912. On his failure to respond, John Ball of Hoylake, eight times British Amateur Champion and Open Champion was approached but he was unable to agree to the request. Four club professionals were therefore contacted - Gadd of Caernarfon, Ball of Bangor, Walker of Harlech and Bowman of Pwllheli - to play an official Opening Match at the Club and this took place on May 23rd 1912. Different pairings' Foursomes were played morning and afternoon and Bowman secured a Hole in One on the 3rd!

The actual holes on the Point were not altered in the new development but were re-arranged. It was decided to erect 'a two foot high wire netting right round the 'Pot'. This would improve that formidable bunker!'

In July 1913, it was resolved to purchase a Bamford Single horse grass cutting machine to cut the rough on the course at a cost of £9-10-0 from Davies and Jones, Pwllheli and the Secretary was asked to send a horse and cart for the mower. In September 1913, due to the poor condition of the Course, especially the greens after a very wet spring, it was resolved to ask Collins of Llandudno to visit the Course and advise.

Collins duly visited and made recommendations on each hole. These are documented in the Minutes. Collins recommended opening drainage here and there, enlarging some greens, making 2 new greens, erecting netting in certain areas, moving a few tees, raising areas around some greens and all greens to be weeded and dressed with sand or lime and manured. His recommendations were accepted with the one exception of not moving the 3rd green for the time being.

1914 - 1920

There were obvious financial concerns during the war.

> **August 1915:** Concern re prospective deficit in club's income to meet expenditure.
>
> **October 1915:** Due to financial constraints, decided not to purchase a horse to replace the one that had died in August, but to hire one from Porthdinllaen Farm as rarely as possible.
>
> **December 1916:** [Reported] ...excess of Liabilities over assets of £33-1-7. This will be the first time the assets failed to cover the liabilities.

As a consequence of the above, the Course was closed in 1916 until the end of the war (See Captains' Chapter) and the land was leased out as pasture to a Mr William John Turner and a Mr Richard Jones (of Glynllifon, Nefyn).

In February 1919, the Greens' Committee, consisting of Cynfelin Jones, O H Parry, Capt J D Griffith and Henry Williams were charged with getting the Course up to pre-war standard by August. The Course reopened in April 1919 with Jack Jones (J H Jones, the 'Pro', see Chapter on the Pros) being re-appointed as the 'Groundsman' with his wife as Stewardess. John Owen Jones and Arthur Parry were appointed 'groundsmen' to work on the Course on the understanding that Jones was in charge! The grass was cut by Tom Roberts (Twm Sara) Tŷ Mawr, Nefyn 'with the support of his horse'. In October, it was exceptionally agreed 'to keep the 3 present Greens' staff for winter work, Jones (again) in charge'. However, throughout these months, all work on the Course was carefully monitored by the Greens' Committee.

Sequence of the First 18 Holes (1912)

The sequence of the 1912 holes can be seen in the Scorecard of Braid and Taylor when they played an Exhibition Match on July 29th 1920. It is fairly easy to follow the first nine holes. (Note a Bogey was the term used in the old days for a Par.)

1st Hole: 255 yds Bogey 4: Penyrhiw [Top of the Hill]

This was played from an area by the present 9th Tee, up past the present 9th Green to a Green near the marker post on the present 10th Hole. [We assume this was a Double Green shared with the 12th.]

2nd Hole: 220 yds Bogey 4: Valley

This was played from the previous Green to the bottom of the valley on the present 1st Hole.

Putting out on the 2nd Green. Note the tall flag held Left of picture and, in the background, the pathway up the hill to the 3rd Green. The 3rd Tee is hidden by the crowd.

3rd Hole: 110 yds Bogey 3: Spion Kop

This was the original starting hole from the 1909 Clubhouse up to the present 11th Green on the Old Course.

The ensuing holes follow today's Old Course:

4th Hole: 440 yds Bogey 5: Henborth [Old Port] [present 12th]

5th Hole: 92 yds Bogey 3: Punch Bowl [old 12th hole – pre-1977]

6th Hole: 366 yds Bogey 5: Landsend [13th]

7th Hole: 112 yds Bogey 3: Life-boat [14th]

8th Hole: 304 yds Bogey 5: Hafan [Haven] [15th]

9th Hole: 153 yds Bogey 4: Pot [16th]

THE DEVELOPMENT OF THE COURSE - DATBLYGIAD Y CWRS

10th Hole: 425 yds Bogey 5: Rocket [present 17th]
The 'Rocket' was so named because it was on this hole that the big gun was located which was used to send ropes out to ships in distress. The gun was at the top of a high pole which had steps leading up to the top where the launching of the rope took place.

The ensuing holes were not as easily followed.

11th Hole: 360 yds Bogey 5: Corner
This hole was the equivalent of the 18th Hole on the Old Course today. It was played to the corner of the field, before the present Clubhouse was built.

12th Hole: 374 yds Bogey 5: Double green
This was a hole which took a westerly direction from the present Clubhouse, over the old practice ground, to a double green.

13th Hole: 249 yds Bogey 4: Caenewydd [New Field]
This returned to the area where the Clubhouse stands today. [The area which is occupied by the 10th hole today was not part of the Golf Club at this time.]

14th Hole: 155 yds Bogey 3: The Rocks
This was a shorter version of the present 1st Hole, looking out to sea.

15th Hole: 289 yds Bogey 4: Golygfa
A short hole was then played to the present 1st Green from a Tee placed behind the present Greenkeeper's Shed. [The name 'Golygfa', meaning 'view', is given to the 1st Hole today.]

16th Hole: 120 yds Bogey 3 Borth Wen [White Cove]
This went in the direction of today's 2nd hole

17th Hole: 120 yds Bogey 3: The Gorse
This was another short hole, played from a Tee at the side of the previous green to an area below the hill where the 18th tee stands today.

18th Hole: 249 yds Bogey 4: Home
The last Hole came back towards the Old Clubhouse, in the direction of today's 8th Hole.

Course Improvements 1923 - 1933

In December 1923 and February 1924, 'Mr Fred Collins of Llandudno was again invited to Nevin for the purpose of instructions as to the possible improvements on the Links, and while here, the consideration of lengthening the holes' (sic). Slight alterations to the sequencing of holes were made in August 1928. The old 3rd Hole was now to be Hole 1 and the old 1st and 2nd Holes were to be Holes 17 and 18 respectively.

1928 Course (with 1912 holes in brackets)

1st Hole: 110 yds Bogey 3 (Spion Kop)	(3)
2nd Hole: 440 yds Bogey 5 (Henborth)	(4)
3rd Hole: 92 yds Bogey 3 (Punch Bowl)	(5)
4th Hole: 366 yds Bogey 5 (Landsend)	(6)
5th Hole: 112 yds Bogey 3 (Life-boat)	(7)
6th Hole: 304 yds Bogey 5 (Hafan)	(8)
7th Hole: 153 yds Bogey 4 (Pot)	(9)
8th Hole: 425 yds Bogey 5 (Rocket)	(10)
9th Hole: 360 yds Bogey 5 (Corner)	(11)
10th Hole: 374 yds Bogey 5 (Double green)	(12)
11th Hole: 249 yds Bogey 4 (Caenewydd)	(13)
12th Hole: 155 yds Bogey 3 (The Rocks)	(14)
13th Hole: 289 yds Bogey 4 (Golygfa)	(15)
14th Hole: 120 yds Bogey 3 (Borth Wen)	(16)
15th Hole: 120 yds Bogey 3 (The Gorse)	(17)
16th Hole: 249 yds Bogey 4 (Home)	(18)
17th Hole: 255 yds Bogey 4 (Penyrhiw)	(1)
18th Hole: 220 yds Bogey 4 (Valley)	(2)

Golf attire came under discussion at this time and the Secretary was asked (07.04.28) 'to place a notice on the Board calling the attention of the ladies to the damage caused to Greens by wearing high heels' (sic).

'...attention to the damage caused by high heels.'

During this period, the Club bought a 30" Dennis Mower to cut the fairways and two hand mowers to cut the greens. Prior to this, all fairway cutting was by horse mower. The rough area was cut by two scythemen from Edern.

It was Proposed and Seconded (26.07.27) that two men be engaged to cut all the rough with scythes for a fortnight. (sic)

In 1929 a 'Best Course Improvement Competition' was launched and a prize of £3-3-0 was given to the winner, Mr Tom Jones of Maesdu Golf Club, Llandudno. It is not reported what conclusions were to be drawn from Tom Jones' recommendations.

However, it appears that the holes were re-numbered to co-incide with the re-positioning of the new Clubhouse in 1929. Holes 1 and 2 were played as the previous 10th (Double Green) and 11th, back to the Club House. There then followed a loop of 7 holes, 3-9 played from the Clubhouse following the previous 12th – 18th. Holes 10 – 18 were played on the point in the familiar sequence.

In December 1930, it was reported that Capt O G Owen had secured 3 loads of Leafmold (sic) from Boduan but it was stressed 'this would not be suitable for the Greens this year'. The Committee accepted Capt Watkin Williams' offer to lend his tank to spray the Greens with a solution of sulphate of ammonia and it was reported that a Testing Outfit had been purchased for the Greens.

September 1931: Complaints had been received about a Raven that was continually on the Course, taking and hiding Members' Golf Balls. The Hon. Sec. was asked to write to Mrs O'Farrell, [the owner of the said Raven] asking her to take the necessary measures to prevent the Bird returning to the Course and annoying members! (sic)

It would appear that the letter had no effect and in the Meeting of 28.10.31 the Chairman of the Committee (W H Cowburn) 'kindly promised to interview Mrs O'Farrell of Porthdinlleyn'. The Raven was neither seen nor mentioned again!

THE DEVELOPMENT OF THE COURSE - DATBLYGIAD Y CWRS

'...necessary measures to prevent the bird...'

In June 1932, a Sub-Committee decided 'to purchase 1 Cwt of Carters' Summer Compost and 1 Cwt of ICI fertiliser for stimulating the 'backward greens': half the greens to be treated with one kind and half with the other. The respective results to be reported in due course!'

One month later, Riley (Pro) reported that better results had been obtained from the ICI fertiliser than from Carters' so it was decided to purchase another 1 Cwt of ICI for use on the greens.

It had been reported in December 1932 that 'the man from the Lifeboat House' made a practice of riding his cycle over the 15th Green and the Chairman had agreed to interview him. This practice was reported for many years and in March 1937, it was stated that 'the Lifeboat employee was still riding over and damaging 15th Green. The Lifeboat authorities to again be written to saying that if the trespass does not cease, the Committee will consider prosecuting the individual concerned for trespass and damage'(sic).

'...riding his cycle over the 15th green'

Many complaints were received about the condition of the Course in 1931. W Cradoc Davies, Secretary of the Caernarvonshire and District Golfing Union had written to the Club regarding the poor state of the Course in 1931 and in March 1932, he wrote again giving his observations and particularly criticising the very poor state of the greens. L A A Riley, the Pro, was consequently dismissed in September 1932 and A D Grace appointed Pro (see Chapter on Pros).

Extra Land and J H Turner's Alterations 1933

In September 1933, there was a meeting with Mr Bovill (Cefnamwlch Agent) on the Course to discuss a request for extra land to improve the Golf Course. By November, Colonel Wynne-Finch had agreed to rent new land (c.18 acres) at £30 extra per year within the same lease arrangement. Colonel Wynne-Finch was asked to write off the debt of honour in respect of rent during the period of the War, viz £131-10-6, because of the increased rent. There is no report of the Colonel's reply but in Sept 1934, a flat sum of £50 was offered by the Club to pay off any outstanding debt from the War Years.

In December 1933, J H Turner, the Golf Professional from Frilford Heath Golf Club, was approached and asked to recommend alterations and proposals for the use of the new ground which had been acquired. [J H Taylor, like James Braid, had been a five times Open Champion and since 1922, had gone into partnership with Fred Hawtree and had designed and produced many golf courses in the United Kingdom as well as several in Europe.]

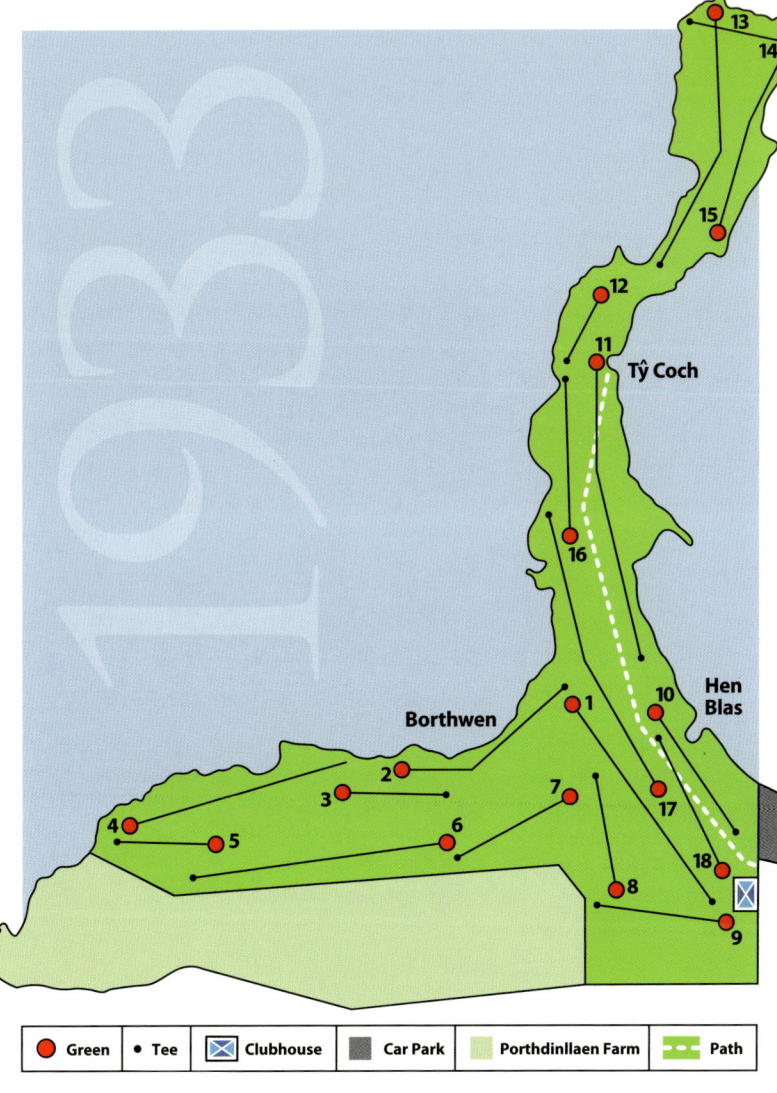

The new ground was the area occupied by the present 3rd Hole, part of the 4th Hole and the 7th Hole.

> *January 1934:* While explaining his proposals in January 1934, Turner was quoted as saying, 'Your course is situated upon one of the most beautiful sites I have ever seen...'

Turner was very impressed with the new acquisition which he claimed enabled him 'to extend and spread out the first 9 Holes so that when completed there will not be a blind hole or crossing...and in my opinion gives excellent golfing holes'. He also made proposals for alterations to the 11th and the 12th Holes. Turner's new design was considered for a few months.

1934 - 1939

However, in September 1934, J H Turner's scheme for the first half of the Course was withdrawn and a modified scheme suggested by J E Pontefract (Member of Committee) was substituted.

The scheme was to develop the Course, starting from the new Clubhouse [where it stands today]. The new development was the onset of the Old Course pre-1977 with the exception of the 8th and 9th Holes [present 9th and 10th]. The 8th was played (as was the 1st Hole in the 1920 plan) to a Green by the marker post on the 10th Hole. The 9th Tee was right of the marker post by the Lôn Penrhyn Bach Footpath. The 9th Hole was played to a Green close to the site of the putting green today.

THE DEVELOPMENT OF THE COURSE - DATBLYGIAD Y CWRS

In 1934 the Pro's Shop and the Caddies' shed was much closer to the Clubhouse than at present and there was no putting green.

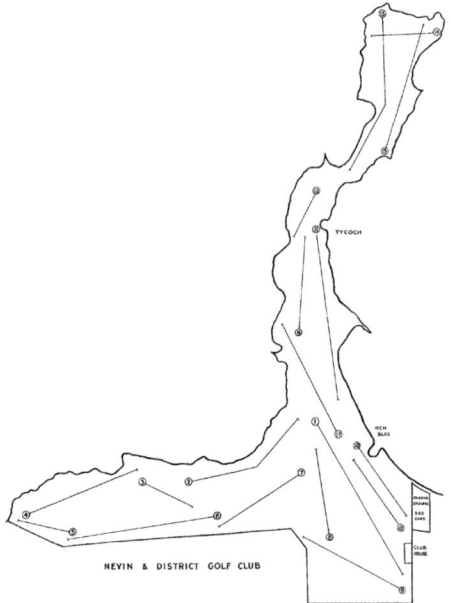

Plan of Course as appeared in Browning's Booklet on Nevin and District Golf Club (1936)

The 1st 9 holes were as follows:

Holes 1 and 2: Golygfa and Borthwen, were played as today.

Hole 1: This was 450 yds, Bogey 5
Hole 2: This was 367 yds, Bogey 4

Hole 3: Dyffryn [Valley]
This was a new 175 yds Bogey 3 from the present 3rd Tee to a Green near the present fairway ditch [and was actually played in the Winter of 2006/7 while present 3rd Green was being re-built.] This was the beginning of the newly acquired land.

Hole 4: Abergeirch
This was a new 425 yds Bogey 5 from a Tee to the side of the 3rd Green. [which is still visible today, in the semi-rough, just short of Pwll Gwlyb.] The fairway extended over the present 3rd Green to an area some 100 yds in front of the present 4th Tee. [This Green is still visible today.]

Hole 5: Porthdinllaen
A new 144 yds Bogey 3 was played from a Tee on the cliff side of the 4th Green in the direction of the Clubhouse. On the right-hand side of this hole was the perimeter wall with Porthdinllaen Farm. [This wall can be seen today on the right-hand side of the present 7th fairway.]

Hole 6: Yr Eifl [The Rivals]
This was a new 393 yds Bogey 4, [the present 7th Hole].

Hole 7: Penrhyn Bach [Small Promontory]
This was a 327 yds Bogey 4 [today's 8th].

The 7th Green in the foreground and the 10th Green [11th on the Point today] can just be seen at the top of the hill in the background. [Note the Old Clubhouse has been raised to the ground on the Right of the picture.]

Hole 8: Madryn
This was a 267 yds Bogey 4. [This was a longer version of today's 9th with the Green near today's guide post on the 10th Fairway.]

Hole 9: Cae Gwynt [Windy Field]
This was a 310 yds Bogey 4 [part of today's 10th] back to the Clubhouse.

Outward Half: Bogey 36, Length 2858 yds.

Hole.	HOME. Length.	Bogey.
10	299	4
11	443	5
12	93	3
13	413	5
14	157	3
15	290	4
16	150	3
17	500	5
18	243	4
	2588	36

Inward Half: Bogey 36, Length 2588 yds.

Holes 10-18 were played on the Point, including the short Par 3 12th [not used today] and the Holes were named as follows: Henblas, Tŷ Coch, Niblick, Land's End, Lifeboat, Pen Cei, Pot, Long and Adref (Home).

By March 1937, due to the damage caused by sea spray during storms, heavy rains and cold winds, growth had practically stopped and the greens, on the headland particularly, were in a dire state. The 9 holes on the Point were closed as a result.

Even in these early days, agronomy reports were available from the The Board of Greenkeeping Research at St Ives Research Station, Bingley, Yorks, [the forerunner of STRI]. Analysis of soils from the greens on the headland by the Research Station showed no deficiency in the soil and it was agreed to bring an expert down to visit as a matter of urgency. This was Dr Alun Roberts, Principal of the School of Agriculture, Bangor University and he visited in April 1937.

He agreed with the findings of the Board of Greenkeeping, although he admitted the severe attacks by leather-jackets suffered over the last few years may have accounted for some soil deficiency. However, he put the blame firmly at the door of the 'Salt Spray washed from the sea'. Briefly, his report stated that the salt spray on the greens was acting in the same way as a prolonged drought, drying the vegetation and causing it to wilt. The concentration of salts in the spray was so much stronger than the sap of the vegetation, that water was drawn from it at a much higher rate than the roots could take in, especially as the soil water itself was salty. In his view, the correct remedy was to avoid cutting in the autumn. He pointed out that some of the surrounding grass and neighbouring tees had escaped owing to the fact that the longer grass blades were able to discharge sufficient moisture to dissolve the salt without becoming exhausted.

Dr Roberts made many recommendations e.g. the resting of the holes from mid-September onwards, establishing a nursery on the headland made of a combination of Red Fescue and a sown sward and many other scientific recommendations beyond the scope of this narrative! Dr Roberts was of the opinion that any attempts made the following autumn to increase the drainage would have an adverse effect rather than a salutary effect, as the supply of moisture to the grass roots would therefore be lessened.

Many of Dr Roberts' recommendations were accepted and the Greens' Staff were instructed to carry them out. The 9 Holes continued to be closed for many weeks and during the next 18 months much remedial work was undertaken.

1939-1945

During the Second World War (1939-45) very little golfing activity was apparent. In fact, golf balls were in short supply and the Secretary was asked in 1943 to try and find a monthly quota of golf balls from various companies. He was successful and procured 3 dozen in 1944 (1 dozen Spaldings 'Topflite' Balls and 2 dozen Dunlop 'Flag-hi 1' Balls) A draw was made for their distribution!

In February 1942, it was resolved that the Morris Commercial Motor Vehicle be not sold at present and that when not in use the vehicle be jacked up to preserve the tyres. (sic)

Discussions took place on the use of the Course during the early war months. Finally it was decided that a small Sub-Committee of J E Roberts and Capt Price be authorised to purchase sheep, and fence the Course at a total cost of no more than £250. [This was later called the 'Sheep Committee' and it was considered quite an honour to serve on this Committee'!] It was further agreed that J P Hughes (Groundsman / Club Repairer should look after the sheep when they arrived.

> *September 1939: Due to present emergency it was decided to employ one man – J P Hughes. Duties: to look after the sheep on weekdays and Sundays. Keep the first 9 holes in playing order and maintain the mowers and other implements in good condition. He will be supplied with a dog to be purchased by the Sub-Committee (at a cost not exceeding £10) and his wages will be increased by £2 a week to cover cost of feeding the dog.*

Sixty sheep were initially bought at a cost of £1-6-6 each in September 1939. In November 1939, when blackouts came into being, Wing Commander Sleigh attended a meeting of the National Golf Clubs' Protection Association in London. The Ministry of Agriculture was reported not in favour of digging up golf courses. The Club however still had a visit in February 1941 from Mr W R Williams representing the Caernarfonshire War Agricultural Executive Committee. He met with the Committee and was satisfied that we had no available land which could be utilised for producing crops.

Mid-1950s – 1966

It was not until February 1956 that the new 8th Green [Present 9th] was laid by the end of Lôn Penrhyn Bach [Present position]. Mr A J Holton (Bob Holton's Father and Ex-Professional Golfer) was in charge of this project in conjunction with A D Grace.

Course in the mid 50s looking from the old 11th Tee on the Point [now 12th]. Centre background can be seen the newly built 8th Green [now 9th]. Note the ROC observation hut on the brow of the hill, at the side of Lôn Penrhyn Bach.

Course again in the 50s, looking back from the approach to the 10th Green [now 11th on the Point] towards the Clubhouse and Garn Fadryn.

In 1961 arrangements were made to pipe water on to the Course. 6,000 feet of polythene tubing was ordered by G I Hughes (Captain in 1963) and was laid by the Groundstaff.

1963 saw the introduction of Tiger Tees on the Course (painted black and yellow) and David Williams, Porthdinllaen, was approached regarding the possibility of releasing land to add to the Course. This land was Cae Penabergeirch, a large field occupied by the 4th, 5th and 6th Holes today. ['Tiger Tees' is a slang term for tee boxes but the Club always referred to the 'Back Tees' as 'Tiger Tees'!]

In August 1965, an invitation was sent to Mr Smith of Carters to inspect the Course and seek estimate of fees for two top ranking Golf Architects to add character to the links, and if at all possible, eliminate blind shots and some short holes. Later on, a Mr Beaver of Rigby Taylor (Bolton) was engaged for the course inspection instead of Smith of Carters.

In September 1965, it was decided to bring the Top Green of the 12th Hole on the point into play. This Green was some 30 yds further up the slope towards the 13th Tee. However, since most of the Green and the flagstick were not visible from the Tee, it was decided to revert to the original Green.

In 1966, the Club successfully bought the Course from the Cefnamwlch Estate for £15,000. This was apparently quite a low evaluation and was seen by many in reality to be a generous gift from the Wynne-Finch Family. The Club received a grant of £7,552 from the Ministry of Education and Science towards the purchase of the land.

THE DEVELOPMENT OF THE COURSE - DATBLYGIAD Y CWRS

Mid-1960s – Mid-1970s

In May 1967, Capt Will Roberts (as Head of Greens' Committee) proposed the replacement of the machine shed. The contract was awarded to William Williams, Bron y De, Nefyn, and the project was completed in the Spring of 1968. This machine shed, with some minor additions, still stands today.

In January 1970, saplings were ordered to be planted behind the 1st Tee, on the left hand side of the First Hole and on the left hand side of the Second Hole, just past the dogleg.

In the period between the appointment of J H Jones as Head Greenkeeper in 1911 and 1971, the incumbent Professional was always put in charge of the Greens' Staff. In December 1971 however, Donald Williams, after serving on the Greens' Staff for several years, was appointed as Head Greenkeeper on condition that he attended a course at Bingley at the Club's expense.

In October 1970, consideration was given to purchasing Tŷ Mawr, Edern, from the Estate at an auction, with a view of being able to offer an exchange for part of Porthdinllaen Farm at a future date. The President, Captain Charles Wynne-Finch, declared that there was no land available from Porthdinllaen Farm at that particular time for Course extension, but should the occasion arise, 'the needs and requirements of the Club would be first and foremost in his mind'.

During the winter of 1971, considerable damage was reported to greens and fairways (especially 12th and 13th Greens on the Point) due to very severe gales. The spring and summer saw little improvement and in September, reports were requested and received from both Bingley and Fisons stating that the poor condition of the greens was attributable to a lack of water at the material time – late spring and summer periods. It was decided to seek particulars for course irrigation schemes from Wright Rain Co. [Pop-up Sprinklers] and purchase a hollow tining machine. Bingley also stated that the Greens suffered from excess thatch.

In March 1974, Richard Cook from Bury, Lancs. was appointed Head Greenkeeper. Captain Charles Wynne-Finch kindly found accommodation for Richard Cook on the Cefnamwlch Estate.

The 1977 Extension of the Course at Abergeirch

In 1974, Captain Charles Wynne-Finch agreed to discuss the possibility of acquiring more land for the Club with David Williams, the tenant of Porthdinllaen Farm. Negotiations proceeded for the release of Cae Penabergeirch which was around 13 acres in size. No apparent progress was made.

Once again, in June 1975, Mr Wood, the Cefnamwlch Agent and David Williams, Porthdinllaen, were in discussion with the Club regarding the purchase of Cae Penabergeirch. Charles Hawtrey, Golf Course Designer, was invited to submit plans for developing this field. The purchase of this land was finally completed on December 17th 1975. The Course Architect was Mr Jiggins of F W Hawtree & Co, Chester, and Jones & Evans from Llanddulas carried out the contractual work.

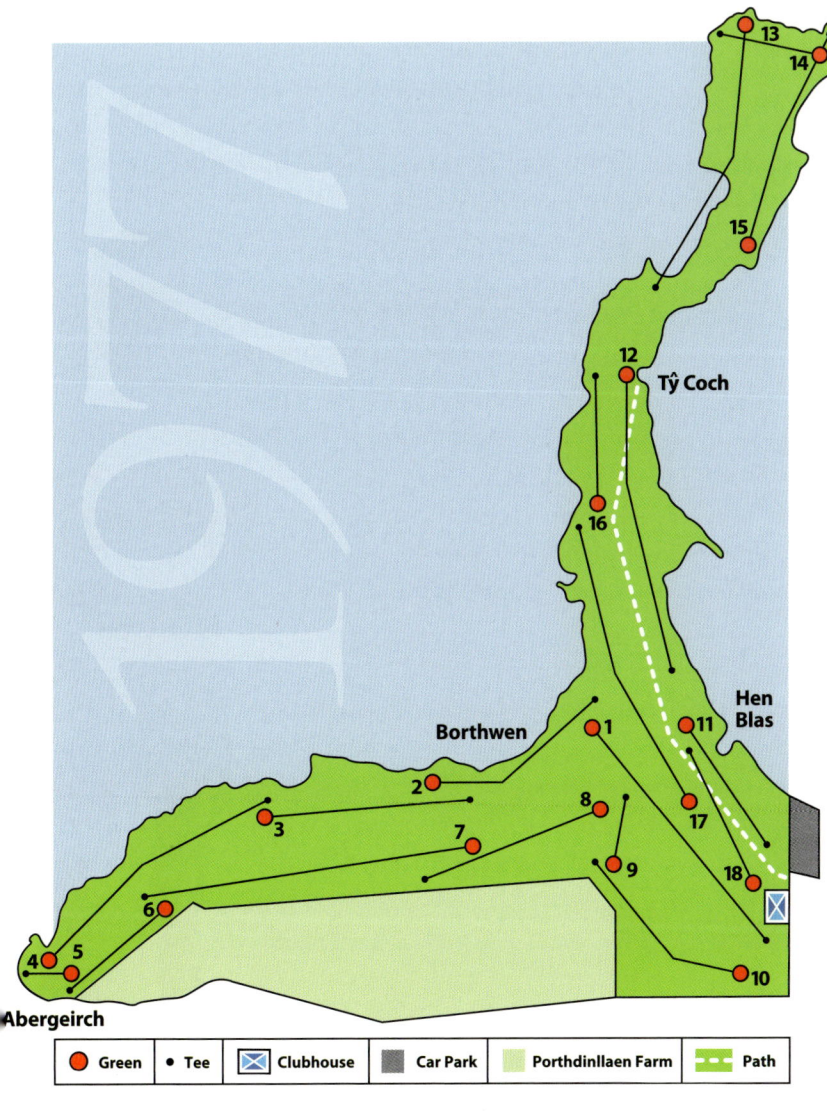

The newly purchased land at Abergeirch was developed to incorporate 3 new holes (4th, 5th and 6th). This was achieved by omitting the 3rd, 5th and 12th Hole (on the Point) from the 1933 Course. This meant that the New Course, instead of having six Par 3s and 2 Par 5s, was to have 4 Par 3s and 4 Par 5s. The standard scratch score (SSS) of the Course changed from 69 (Par 68) to 71 (Par 72). The new 3rd Hole was changed from a 170 yds Par 3 to a 396 yds Par 4, with a new green built at the top of the hill. The new 4th Hole was a 477 yds Par 5 directly to Abergeirch into the prevailing wind; the new 5th a 156 yds Par 3 downwind and uphill and the 6th a short Par 4, measuring 310 yds, returning parallel to the new 4th Hole. This brought the Course back to the old layout. Instead of playing the original short 5th hole, the 5th Tee was moved forward some 50 yds and, combined with the 6th Hole, created the new 7th Hole, a 532 yds Par 5. The Course then continued as previously, except that each hole was numbered one ahead of the old Course, e.g. the new 8th was previously the 7th. The old 12th Hole on the Point (93 yds Par 3) was omitted. Consequently, the front loop of holes from the Clubhouse amounted to 10 holes while the remainder on the Point amounted to eight. This Course remained as above until the latest redevelopment initiated in 1992.

On June 21st 1976, under the supervision of Mr Jiggins, the Groundstaff undertook some of the ground work. (In July 1976, Steven R Griffiths was appointed as Head Greenkeeper.) By December, the turfing programme was completed, with Jones & Evans returning in April to cultivate and seed the scarred areas. A very wet winter delayed the progress of the Course improvements. Play was initiated on June 1st 1977 and an Exhibition Match was organised for July 31st to celebrate the Official

THE DEVELOPMENT OF THE COURSE - DATBLYGIAD Y CWRS

Opening of the new Course. The 4 players selected were to include T G Gruffydd, J R Pilkington (the Pro) & two Professional Celebrities. Unfortunately, the match was later cancelled due to the state of the Course.

Drainage Problems

Later on in 1977, an initial quote of £20,000 was secured to complete the laying of a pop-up sprinkler system. The Stafford Irrigation Company was contracted to lay the system at a cost of £20,500. Messrs Jiggins and Hawtree were invited back in 1978 regarding the poor drainage of the 3rd Green.

In May 1980, G T Williams of Pwll Parc, Edern, was contracted to carry out drainage on the 4th and 6th Fairways at a cost of £720. In addition, the area between the 6th Green and the cliff edge was drained in the spring of 1980. David Williams of Porthdinllaen Farm was often quoted saying 'You will never drain the field at Penabergeirch!'

Because of the early problems with drainage on the three new holes in the winter, a contingency plan was brought into play, affording 18 holes. This was achieved by bringing into play the Practice Green as the 1st Hole [now the 18th Fairway on the New Course]. The 2nd Hole was then played from the Practice Green Area to the 1st Green. In addition, the old 3rd (170 yds) and the old 12th (93 yds on the Point) were brought into play. However, in extremely wet conditions, the three holes at the far end of the Point (13th, 14th and 15th) were also closed in the winter, reducing the Course to 15 holes.

Some Modifications in The Eighties

In 1981, bunkers were built across the front of the 8th Green in order to block off ground level approaches. In addition, under the Greens' chairmanship of Mr G T Owen, the grassy mound on the left hand side of the 10th Green was removed at this time.

In the autumn and winter of 1986, two projects were undertaken to develop two greens on the Point. The 12th Green was lengthened and developed into a two tier green while the 15th Green was levelled and a protective bank built on the right hand side.

In October 1987, Steven Griffiths tendered his resignation as Head Greenkeeper to take on a position in Merseyside. Patrick McAteer was offered a probationary period as Head Greenkeeper while attending the College of Agriculture at Reaseheath. Mr John Pilkington, the Professional, became Acting Advisory Head Greenkeeper. In October 1989, Pat McAteer was offered the Head Greenkeeper's position as a result of his College examination results and his probationary period. The Pro was relieved of his temporary position. [P McAteer was presented with a special award for outstanding work at the College.]

Patrick McAteer on the Course, Sprimg 2008

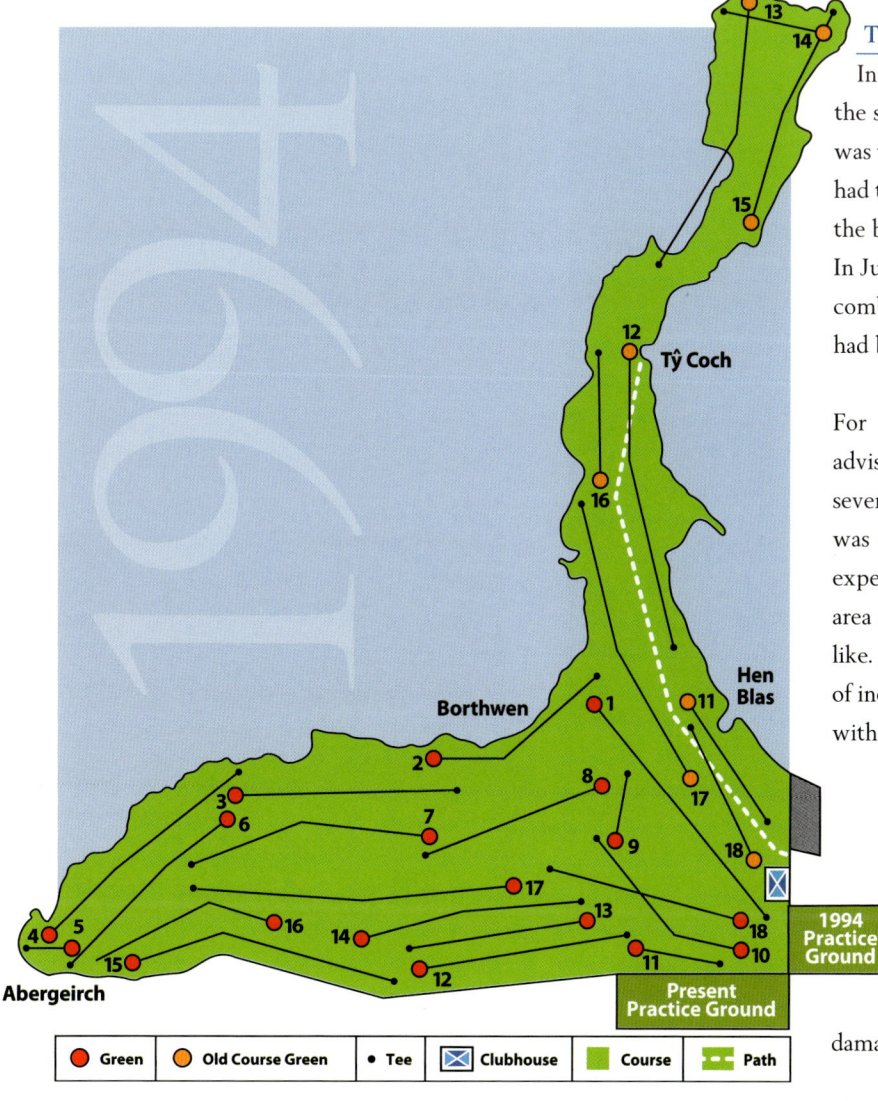

The Nineties

In February 1990 the whole Course suffered from severe storms and the sea washed completely over the Point. The recovery from the storms was very slow, mainly due to prevailing weather conditions. Consideration had to be given to re-turfing some damaged greens. The 13th Fairway took the best part of 3 years to recover through various reseeding programmes. In July 1990, a report from STRI praised the work of the Greens' Staff in combating the effects of the February storm damage but a total of £8,000 had been spent on the recovery programme.

For many years, there had been regular discussions regarding the advisability of purchasing new land to avoid playing the Point with its several blind shots in the busy summer season. Further frustration was caused by increased visitors on the road and footpaths. Also the expenditure for maintenance on the Point was disproportionate to the area of land involved, especially considering storm damage and the such like. At the AGM of 1990, the Treasurer had reported a £54,068 surplus of income over expenditure and this prompted serious and extensive talks with the Cefnamwlch Estate regarding the purchase of additional land.

In February 1991, the Estate finally agreed to sell the 45 acres of additional land for £180,000 with a 'no frills' arrangement. Originally, the Estate had wanted to purchase the Point and rent it back to the Club. The Club was unsuccessful in claiming a purchase grant from the R & A but at the AGM of 1991, it was reported that a £52,000 surplus of income over expenditure (inspite of storm damage) was added to the Money Market Investment held by the Club,

(Above-Left) The Urdd Camp Field in the 1930s looking towards Abergeirch. (Above-Right) The same view in 2007 showing the 15th White and Blue Men's Tees on the 'New Course'.

Building the 1st Fairway Bunker on 16th (New Hole)

16th Hole (New Course) today

Building the 16th Green (New Hole)

bringing that total up to a healthy £190,000. The Club applied for a loan from Midland Bank and received £150,000 at 2 per cent above bank rate to finance the reconstruction work.

The new land was developed to provide an alternative finish to the initial 10 holes and was to be called The New Course. Mr Wishart of STRI (Bingley) was invited to design and oversee the work of the contractor (Mr Palmer). The cost of constructing the new holes amounted to £125,000. New equipment was bought e.g. a top-dressing machine at £2,965; a slitter at £1,780 and a Toro 3000D at £13,000.

Shrubs at a cost of £7,000 were planted after advice from STRI and by October 1992, the Course Development costs had escalated to £468,644.

The New Course

The New Course was opened for play in April 1994 and at the AGM of the same year, the Treasurer reported that £60,000 had been paid by the RNLI for an access road to the Lifeboat Station. This £60,000 enabled the bank loan for the development of the new land to be fully repaid. From start to finish, in approximately four years, a half million pound project had been undertaken and paid in full – an extraordinary feat!

(Please refer to Mark Pilkington's New Course Record of 1998 (Course Records' Section) for details of yardage and Pars of these new Holes.)

Included in the purchase of the land was the field immediately behind the Professional's Shop, facing the village of Morfa Nefyn. This was intended to be used as a practice ground. However, Cyngor Dosbarth Dwyfor instructed the Club not to use this field.

In 1993 a project to construct a new green for the 12th Hole on the Point (removing the bank and building a new green to the right of the road) at a cost of £18,000 was tabled. This project had been discussed on numerous other occasions. The plan never saw daylight, primarily because of erosion problems near the cliff edges.

In March 1994, the Committee resolved to adopt a 3 nine-hole layout devised by T G Gruffydd on a trial basis. The formal opening was to be on the AM-AM weekend of June 4th and 5th. However, when it was trialled one week earlier, the first players out did not follow the planned course and confusion followed! The scheme was abandoned. Over the following years, other suggestions were made. One scheme converted the 7th and 8th Holes into one long hole on the front loop to create 9 holes instead of 10 and added a new par 3 hole between the present 16th and 17th Holes on the back loop to make another 9 holes. However, new schemes were never adopted.

In March 1995, granite stones from Nanhoron Quarry were selected and placed by tees and new metal tee marker plates were attached to them.

In June 1997, P McAteer was nominated for the National Torro Head Greenkeeper of the Year Award after an Assessor had visited the Club to carry out a Course Inspection.

1998 saw a temporary extension of the 2nd and 15th Men's Tees (put back 35 yds) as an experiment to extend the holes for 'championship meetings'. At the same time a Greens' Sub-Committee Report to the Finance Committee Meeting suggested that a programme of reconstructing the first nine greens to USGA standards be embarked upon. A uniform standard of green was needed to match up with the new greens at a cost of £8,000 - £9,000 per green. The matter was left on the table.

Back in March 1996, the Cefnamwlch Agent had already discussed the possibility of sharing the land between the Club and the farm [alongside the New Course 11th Hole] in order to improve practice ground facilities. In February 1999, the Club began serious correspondence with the Cefnamwlch Agent regarding purchasing or renting this land as a Practice Ground. The Agent recommended the Club liaise directly with the Tenant (Robert Williams) regarding renting. The selling of the land was not an option.

...and The New Millennium

By February 2000, negotiations between Club and Tenant re leasing this land [by the 11th Hole] were proving very positive. In April 2000, the Tenant agreed to a 5 year lease at £2,000 per year but 4 months later this was increased by another £2000 per annum because the Club had requested an extra 40 yards width.

In October 2001, a drainage channel was constructed across the 3rd and 7th Holes. At the same time, the notion of microtining or penciltining the greens came into force.

A report from the Course Architect in July 2002 outlined work that he considered necessary. He recommended the Course should have 3 loops of 9; the old front 9 greens should be rebuilt to USGA standard; the new 8 greens should be re-contoured and the Point greens should also be rebuilt to USGA standard. The estimated cost was £450,000 with the architect's fees set at 10%. He also accepted the work could be done in stages!

It was decided to look at the idea of 3 loops of nine in the first instance. By Easter 2003, a draft plan had been drawn up and Members' opinions were sought. No conclusions were drawn and the matter was left on the table.

In 2004, a questionnaire developed by the Strategy and Policy Committee was distributed to Members in an effort to ascertain which way the Club should develop.

In 2005, the Executive, with the Course Architect's approval, agreed to try out a proposed change to the 18 holes' sequence as this plan involved the least expenditure to the Club. The sequence was as follows:

Red Course: Holes 1, 2, 3, 7, 8, 9, 14, 13, 10
Blue Course: Holes 11, 12, 15, 6, 4, 5, 16, 17, 18
Yellow Course: Holes 11-18 (Old Course)
                adding the Old 12th (93 yards)

This plan was intended to be trialled for 6 weeks in February and March but after 3 weeks it was abandoned due to protests from Members largely complaining about the amount of walking between the tees.

November 2004:

Report from Independent Analysis of Questionnaire to Members:

The majority of respondents want a solution that provides a three nines set-up. However, it is apparent that many are not convinced of the need for extensive changes to the course to achieve this goal, even though a good number recommended the re-laying of the old greens to USGA standards. Many would prefer a low cost, low impact solution with the money saved going towards improving the clubhouse and catering.

Recommendations:

Given the members' dual wish to achieve a course of three nines (without wholesale changes) on the one hand, and to have much improved club facilities and catering on the other, the following is recommended based solely on the responses to the questionnaire:

1. Find an economical and low impact solution to create the desired three nines
2. Plough the funds this would free up into improving the clubhouse and catering.

Due to damage to the 4th and 5th Greens as a result of severe storms in the beginning of 2005, it was necessary to returf the 4th green. It was even suggested that the 4th green be moved away from the cliff. At the latter end of 2005, large landslips were reported in the 'Pot' and near the RNLI boathouse in Lifeboat Bay.

In December 2005, new back tees were built for the 2nd, 3rd, 11th, 13th, 14th and 15th Holes. This meant that the Course length off the back (Blue Tees) increased to 6,718 yds with a SSS of 73.

In 2006 'Golf World' magazine ranked Nefyn and District Golf Club the 93rd Best Course in UK and Ireland.

Due to severe problems being encountered on several greens during the summer of 2006, many greens were reconstructed and completely returfed to USGA standards in the autumn. It was apparent that the greens were diseased because Greens' Staff did not have the opportunity to aerate the greens at the appropriate time in the past, due to the prospective loss of green fee revenue. The 2nd, 6th and 11th to 17th Greens were returfed, after creating new contours underneath. The 3rd Green was completely reconstructed. The work was carried out by P McAteer and his groundstaff in a period of 4-6 weeks and they were congratulated on their achievements.

The 13th and 16th Greens on the Point were returfed in February 2007 and the 18th Green (New Course) was returfed after creating new contours underneath in November 2007.

The Ladies' Course was modified in 2006. At the request of the Ladies, the 7th Tee was moved across to the Men's Winter Tee; a new 15th Tee was built reducing the 15th to a Par 4 and a new 17th Tee was built, effecting a shortening of the 17th Hole but still keeping it as a Par 5. The Ladies' Course was re-measured and a new SSS of 74 was brought in. The Ladies' 7th Tee was brought back to its original position (same yardage) when the Tee was reconstructed in 2007.

Currently, a few improvements are being carried out to the Course following the recommendations of David Williams, Golf Design. Three new bunkers have been placed on the left hand side of the dog-leg on the 2nd; the bank in front of the greenside bunkers on the 2nd Hole has been removed and the innermost bunker extended; a protective hump has been created at the rear of the 4th Green; the size of the Ladies' 17th Tee has been doubled because of health and safety concerns on the previous narrow Tee; shrubs and greenery have been planted on many fairways e.g. 1st, 3rd, 13th and 17th and a new bunker has appeared in front of the 7th Green.

Sadly, 'an economical and low impact solution to create the desired three nines' has yet to be found.

The Ground Staff (2008)

THE DEVELOPMENT OF THE COURSE - DATBLYGIAD Y CWRS

The Captains - Y Capteiniaid

THE CAPTAINS
Y CAPTEINIAID

Rhoddwyd y bywgraffiadau byr canlynol gyda'i gilydd o ffeithiau hanesyddol fel yr adroddwyd hwy yng Nghofnodion Pwyllgorau'r Clwb, cyfweliadau gyda chyn-Gapteiniaid, nodiadau bywgraffiadol a ysgrifennwyd gan y Capteiniaid eu hunain a chyfweliadau gyda sawl Aelod o'r Clwb ac aelodau o'r cyhoedd.

The following short biographies have been put together from historical facts as reported in the Club's Committee Minutes, interviews with past Captains, biographical notes written by the Captains themselves and interviews with many Club Members and members of the public.

THE EARLY YEARS
1908 - 1913

JOHN BEAUMONT
1908 & 1915

OUR FIRST OFFICIAL CAPTAIN

John Beaumont was elected Captain at the Club's first AGM (August 3rd, 1908). He was on the initial Steering Committee and from the inauguration of the Club in 1907, he was totally active in all matters that transpired within the Club. However, very little is known about his private life apart from the fact that he was married and was a generous Captain, for reference is constantly made in the Minutes to his providing souvenirs for various competitions e.g. for the Courtenay Lord Cup throughout 1910. In 1923, he was made a Life Member of Nefyn and District Golf Club 'in consideration of valuable services to the Club and as being one of its pioneers' (Minutes AGM 1923). He died two years later, in 1925, and his passing must have left an enormous void within the Club.

B RYMAN-HALL
1909

Very little information is available regarding B R Ryman-Hall. His name is entered in the list of Members for 1908-09 alongside another member of the family, E A Ryman-Hall.

It is also known that B Ryman Hall was the first Secretary at the Club. His term as Secretary seemed to pre-date the first AGM but he was officially elected in August 1908. In August 1909, he resigned as Secretary when he took up the position of Captain.

It was during B Ryman-Hall's Captaincy that the first Clubhouse was burnt down with many Members' personal possessions and clubs being destroyed. The temporary Clubhouse was opened on July 23rd and one week later, Ryman-Hall tendered his resignation as Captain. No reason appears to be given and the Committee accepted his resignation 'with regret'.

Original thatched-roofed Clubhouse erected 1908

H G ROBERTS
1910

Ychydig o wybodaeth sydd ar gael am gefndir Hugh G Roberts ar wahân i'r ffaith ei fod yn berson busnes lleol. Mewn Cyfarfod o Bwyllgor y Clwb ar Orffennaf 30ain 1910, cynigiwyd ac etholwyd H G Roberts yn Gapten tros dro o ganlyniad i ymddiswyddiad y Capten, B Ryman-Hall, ac fe gadarnhawyd ei enwebiad fel Capten yn y Cyfarfod Cyffredinol Blynyddol y mis dilynol.

Ar Ebrill 15fed 1911, yn dilyn ymddiswyddiadau o'r Pwyllgor, penodwyd Hugh Roberts i edrych ar ôl y gwaith ar y cwrs a bu haf 1911 yn un o'r hafau sychaf mewn hanes! Yng

Very little information is to hand about H G Roberts other than he was a local business man. In a Club Committee Meeting dated July 30th 1910, H G Roberts was proposed and elected as acting Captain as a result of the resignation of the Captain, B Ryman-Hall. He was then confirmed as Captain at the Club's AGM the following month.

On April 15th 1911, as a result of several resignations from Committee, Hugh Roberts was elected as Course Supervisor during one of the driest summers ever recorded! At the Club's AGM on August 12th 1911, H G Roberts was asked to continue as Captain, but he refused due to work commitments.

DR R H GRIFFITHS
1911

Nghyfarfod Cyffredinol y Clwb ar Awst 12fed 1911, gofynnwyd iddo barhau fel Capten ond fe wrthododd oherwydd pwysau gwaith.

Adwaenid Dr R H Griffiths gan rai fel 'Doctor Bach' Castellmarch, Llanbedrog. Roedd yn ŵr priod gyda dwy ferch a fu'n byw ym Mhwllheli yn ddiweddarach. Treuliodd gyfnod hirfaeth fel meddyg ardal Nefyn, gan weithio yn y Tŷ Doctor yn Egryn, Nefyn.

Etholwyd ef yn Gapten y Clwb ar Awst 12fed 1911. Cydweithiodd yn galed gyda Mr Bovill, asiant Ystâd Cefnamwlch, i geisio cael ffordd fetel o Groeslon Penrhos (ger hen Westy'r Linksway) i fyny i'r Clwb, ond ni wireddwyd y gobaith yma am sawl blwyddyn. Dr Griffiths fu'n llwyddiannus i gael y Clwb i ymuno ag Undeb Golff Sir Gaernarfon ac ef a lywiodd y Pwyllgor i enwi tyllau'r cwrs am y tro cyntaf, arferiad sydd wedi parhau ar gyfnodau hyd heddiw.

Dr R H Griffiths, the 'Little Doctor' from Castellmarch, Llanbedrog, was a married man with two daughters, who spent an extended period as Doctor at Nefyn, practising in the surgery where Egryn is today (opposite the old Red Garage).

He was elected Captain in August 1911 and worked diligently with George Bovill, the agent at Cefnamwlch, in an attempt to build a metal road from the Penrhos crossroad (by the old Linksway Hotel) up to the Club. Dr Griffiths was successful in getting the Club to join the Caernarvonshire Golfing Union and it was he who steered the Committee to name the holes on the course for the first time, a practice which has continued periodically up to the present day.

ARTHEN OWEN
1912 & 1924

Mae'n amlwg fod Arthen Owen yn un o grŵp o Aelodau Gwreiddiol a sylfaenodd Clwb Golff Nefyn, gan y cofnodir ef yn bresennol yng nghofnodion pwyllgor cyntaf Clwb Golff Nefyn a gynhaliwyd yn Nhafarn Tŷ Coch (Mawrth 14eg 1908). Bu hefyd yn weithgar gyda sefydlu Clwb Golff Pwllheli ar ddechrau'r ganrif a gwasanaethodd fel Ysgrifennydd Anrhydeddus a Thrysorydd yno.

THE CAPTAINS - Y CAPTEINIAID

Yn ôl ei alwedigaeth, cyfreithiwr oedd Arthen Owen, gyda'i swyddfa ym Mhwllheli. Bu'n aelod o Bwyllgor y Clwb o Awst 1908 hyd at Ebrill 1911, pan ymddiswyddodd. Serch hynny, bu'n gweithio'n ddiwyd fel cyfreithiwr ar ran y Clwb. Ar Fawrth 9fed 1912 cwblhawyd y les ar gyfer tir newydd y Clwb gan Arthen Owen. Cytunwyd i'w ethol fel Aelod Oes o'r Clwb, yr anrhydedd uchaf allai'r Clwb ei gyflwyno iddo am ei waith diflino a arbedodd arian mawr i'r Clwb. Ar Awst 10fed yr un flwyddyn, etholwyd Arthen Owen yn Gapten y Clwb, anrhydedd a dderbyniodd eilwaith yn 1924.

Arthen Owen was recorded as being present at the first ever meeting of Nefyn Golf Club, held at the Tŷ Coch Inn, on March 14th 1908, and is recognised as being one of the Founders of the Club. He had also been involved, at the turn of the century, in founding Pwllheli Golf Club where he served as Honorary Secretary and Treasurer.

Arthen Owen was a solicitor, based at Pwllheli. He was a member of Nefyn Golf Club from August 1908 up to April 1911, when he resigned. However, he continued to work diligently and gratuitously as a solicitor on behalf of the Club and was rewarded by being elected a Life Member in March 1912 in recognition of his services to the Club. Five months later, he was elected Captain, an honour which he was to accept again in 1924.

CAPTEN WATKIN WILLIAMS 1913

Adwaenid Capten Williams fel Capten Watkin Williams, Pwll Parc, Edern a Phenarth. Bu'n Gadeirydd Pwyllgor y Golff am sawl blwyddyn ac roedd yn rhan o deulu enwog, sef perchnogion Cwmni Llongau Pwll Parc. Roedd Watkin yn un o dri mab a bu'r teulu'n byw yn Nhyncoed, Edern am gyfnod. Gweithiai Watkin ar longau ei dad a llongau eraill a llwyddodd i gyrraedd y swydd o Is-Gapten.

Yn 1913, pan etholwyd Watkin Williams yn Gapten Clwb Golff Nefyn a'r Cylch, roedd allforiant glo i bedwar ban y byd ar ei anterth a gweithiai Watkin allan o Gaerdydd, prif borthladd allforio glo Prydain. Yn y byd masnach, yng Nghaerdydd, adweinid y Cwmni fel y 'Golden Cross Line'. Gwnaeth ei gartref ym Mhenarth yn ystod y cyfnod yma.

Fel ei frawd hynaf, Owen, prynodd gyfranddaliadau mewn llongau stêm a thros y deng mlynedd ar hugain dilynol buont yn berchnogion ar dros ugain o longau stêm - Llongau Pwllparc. Yn anffortunus, erbyn tridegau'r ganrif ddiwethaf, aeth y cwmni i'r wal gyda dyledion o filoedd o bunnoedd. Fodd bynnag, rhaid oedd edmygu dewrder y ddau frawd yma a bydd pobl Pen Llŷn yn cofio am Longau Pwllparc fel un o benodau mwyaf yn hanes morwrol yr ardal.

Ar Fehefin 6ed 1942, etholwyd Capten Watkin Williams yn Aelod Oes o'r Clwb. Bu farw yn 1944.

Captain Williams was known as Captain Watkin Williams of Edern and Penarth (Cardiff). He chaired the Committee at Nefyn Golf Club for several years.

Captain Watkin Williams was descended from a renowned family of seafarers and ship owners, namely, Pwll Parc (Edern) and Penarth Shipping

Company. Watkin was the youngest of three sons and the family lived at Tyncoed, Edern for a period. Watkin worked on his father's ships and he qualified as a First Mate.

In 1913, when he was elected Captain of Nefyn Golf Club, coal export to all parts of the world was at its peak. Watkin worked out of Cardiff, at that time Britain's main coal exporting port, and his company was known as the 'Golden Cross Line'.

Like his older brother, Owen, Watkin bought shares in steam ships and during the ensuing thirty years they owned over twenty steam ships – referred to as the 'Ships of Pwll Parc'. Unfortunately, by the 1930s, the Company had gone into receivership with debts of thousands of pounds. However, the two brothers' courage had to be admired and the folks of Llŷn remember the 'Ships of Pwll Parc' as a major chapter in the area's seafaring history.

In June 1942, Captain Watkin Williams, Pwll Parc, was elected a life member of Nefyn Golf Club. He was to survive a further two years before his death in 1944.

Winifred Maud Garnett Janion playing the 3rd Hole in April 1913. [Pre-1912, this had been the 1st Hole.]

THE WAR YEARS
1914 - 1918

REV R CYNFELIN JONES
1914

Penodwyd y Parch R Cynfelin Jones yn Berson Plwyf Nefyn yn 1906 a bu'n weithgar wrth sefydlu Clwb Golff Nefyn yn 1907. Fe'i hetholwyd ef yn Gapten y Clwb yng Nghyfarfod Blynyddol y Clwb, Awst 22ain 1914. Yr oedd yn gefnogol iawn wrth ganiatáu i Aelodau o'r Adran Iau chwarae mewn cystadleuthau agored y Clwb ond, fel y disgwylid, gwrthwynebai'r syniad o chwarae golff ar y Sul.

Bu Cynfelin Jones yn Ymddiriedolwr y Clwb am gyfnod ond ymddiswyddodd ar Orffennaf 31ain 1930 oherwydd y posibilrwydd o chwarae golff ar y Sul. Cyflwynwyd Tlws Cynfelin Jones i'r Clwb yn 1987 gan ei deulu.

The Rev R Cynfelin Jones was appointed Vicar of the Nefyn Parish in 1906 and he was instrumental in founding the Golf Club in 1907. He was a Trustee of the Club and was elected Captain at the AGM in August 1914. As a Captain, he was very supportive of Juniors playing in open competitions. He strongly opposed playing golf on Sundays and in fact resigned his Trusteeship in 1930 over this very issue. The Cynfelin Jones Trophy was presented by his family to the Club, in his memory, in 1987.

J T LITTLE
1916 - 1918

J T Little was elected Captain of the Club at the AGM in August 1916. He was engaged as a cable operator in the Telephone Relay Station at the Cecil Hotel. Very few meetings of the Committee were held at this period due to the First World War and the Course was closed from December 1916 to December 1918.

Very little information is available about the Captain during these War Years. However, relatively recently, it was realised that J T Little was the only Captain not to have his photograph in the Clubhouse. By a stroke of luck, on September 18th, 1987, a letter was received from Dr Margaret Little enclosing a photograph of her father, J T Little. This photograph completed the Club's gallery of portraits of Past-Captains.

> **Dec 15th 1916:** Mr Thomas and Sec met Capt W-F and Bovill at Cefnamwlch the net result of which was that Capt W-Finch very generously promised to allow one year's rent if the club decided to go on but if the club would shut down he would forego all rent until the end of the war and allow the club to collect grazing rents etc. He would help to reinstate the Course and extend the lease to cover the blank period. After a long discussion it was resolved to take a plebicite of the members of the club. (sic)
>
> **Dec 29th 1916:** Result of voting re closing of club until end of Nov
> For closing   20
> For keeping open 7
> Not voted   14
> It was resolved as result that links be closed as from Saturday 30th Dec 1916.

POST WAR TO SECOND WORLD WAR 1919 - 1938

R REES THOMAS
1919 & 1920

Ychydig iawn o wybodaeth sydd ar gael am R Rees Thomas. Fe'i penodwyd yn Gapten y Clwb ar Fedi 1af 1919, rhyw ychydig fisoedd ar ôl ail-agor y Clwb. Yn ystod ei gyfnod fel Capten bu cryn drafodaeth rhwng y Clwb ac Ystâd Cefnamwlch ynghylch les y Clwb.

Yn bendant, uchafbwynt cyfnod R Rees Thomas, oedd rhoi gwahoddiad i'r ddau olffar enwog, James Braid a J H Taylor, i Nefyn i chwarae mewn gêm arddangos i'r cyhoedd. Ar wahân i'r pryd mawreddog a drefnwyd yn y Clwb yn dilyn y gêm fawr yma, bu'r Capten, R Rees Thomas, yn gyfrifol am dalu costau pryd arall i'r gwŷr bonheddig yn y Bryn Awel.

R Rees Thomas was elected Captain on September 1st 1919, a few months after the re-opening of the Club. The highlight of his year in office was inviting two famous golfers, James Braid and J H Taylor, to Nefyn for an exhibition match. In addition to the luncheon which was arranged by the Club in the Clubhouse following this match, the Captain entertained the two honoured guests at the Bryn Awel at his own expense.

ERNEST TWEEDALE 1921 & 1922

The Tweedales were prosperous cotton factory and mill owners from Rochdale who frequented Nefyn for many years. Ernest Tweedale's name is synonymous with the Club's 'Blue Ribbon' Competition, the Tweedale Challenge Cup, which he presented to the Club in 1927. This prestigious Cup is played for annually during the Summer Meeting in August.

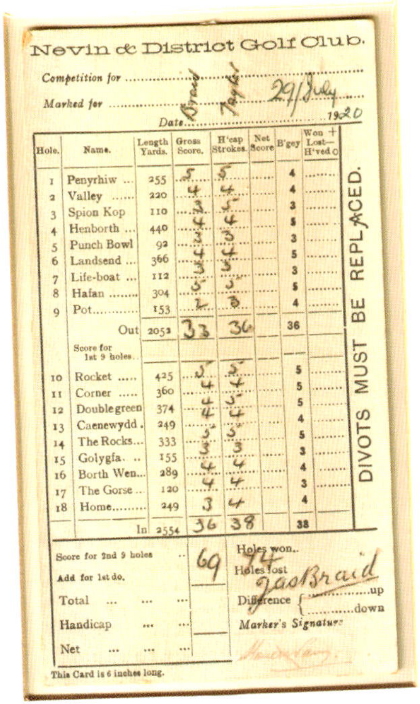

During Ernest Tweedale's Captaincy, the subject of selling intoxicating liquor was regularly debated; reciprocal membership between Nefyn and Pwllheli was instigated and there appeared a first reference to the appointment of a Professional at the Club (July 24th, 1922).

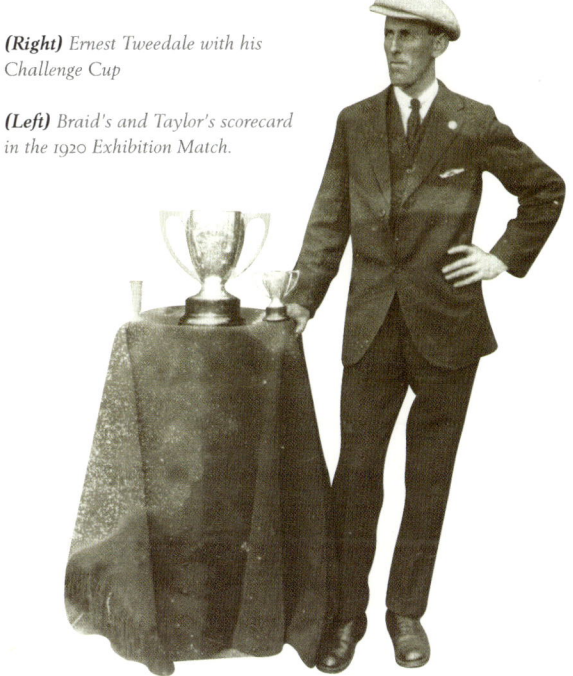

(Right) Ernest Tweedale with his Challenge Cup

(Left) Braid's and Taylor's scorecard in the 1920 Exhibition Match.

O H PARRY 1923

Adwaenid Owen Henry Parry fel Owie ac roedd yn fab i deulu oedd yn berchnogion Gwesty. Priododd Owie gyda Mair Parry (yn perthyn i deulu Ivy Dale) o Forfa Nefyn. Byddai'r genethod yn chwarae golff fel O H Parry ei hun. Credir fod tad O H Parry yn frawd i dad W J Parry - taid Lt Col Robin Parry a Tom Parry.

THE CAPTAINS - Y CAPTEINIAID

Bu Owie a George, ei frawd, yn cadw'r Red Garage yn Nefyn am flynyddoedd ac atgyweiriwyd y mwyafrif helaeth o beiriannau cynnar y Clwb gan Owie a'i frawd. Bu O H Parry yn aelod o Bwyllgor y Clwb am flynyddoedd lawer gan chwarae rhan weithgar iawn dros y Clwb.

Dewiswyd ef ar sawl achlysur i drafod materion y Clwb gyda Mrs Mary Williams, Porthdinllaen. Byddai'n llwyddo i gael ymateb cadarnhaol ganddi, fel y cytundeb i greu maes parcio newydd ger tŷ'r clwb, ychydig o ddyddiau cyn iddo ymddiswyddo fel aelod o Bwyllgor y Clwb!

Owen Henry Parry, known locally as Owie, was the son of a hotel owner. It is believed that his father was a brother of Lt Col Robin Parry's grandfather, W J Parry.

Owie and George, his brother, owned the Red Garage in Nefyn for a number of years. The majority of the Club's early machinery was repaired by Owie and his brother. O H Parry was a regular member of the Nefyn Golf Club Committee for several years, playing a very prominent part in the Club's affairs. He was selected on a number of occasions to discuss Club matters with Mrs Mary Williams, Porthdinllaen. He was successful in getting positive responses from her, such as an agreement to open a new car park near the Clubhouse, and this only a few days before he resigned as a member of the Club Committee!

W GLYNNE JONES
1925

Hanai W Glynne Jones o Sir Fôn. Yn ôl y sôn, roedd yn ŵr o deulu cefnog, teulu yr honnir iddynt adeiladu hanner Lerpwl yn y bedwaredd ganrif ar bymtheg. Yn wir, mae yno sawl stryd wedi ei henwi ar ôl y teulu. Roedd un ferch iddo, Joan, yn feddyg ac roeddynt yn byw yn Edern pan oedd W Glynne Jones yn Gapten Y Clwb.

Roedd Glynne Jones yn ffrindiau mawr â meddyg oedd yn byw yn Edern (Dr Varley, a fu'n Gapten yn 1932). Byddai'r ddau yn chwarae tipyn o golff trwy'r tridegau a byddai'r cadis (gan gynnwys H D Jones) yn awchu am gael cadio iddynt.

It is believed that W Glynne Jones was a descendant of a wealthy Anglesey family who were responsible for building the greater part of Liverpool in the nineteenth century. One of his daughters, Joan, was a doctor, and the family lived in Edern when he was Captain of the Club.

Glynne Jones was a great friend of Dr Varley, who also lived in Edern, and was Captain of the Club in 1932. Both played a great deal of golf through the 30s and the club caddies were very eager to carry their bags! (See H D Jones' reminiscences in the Chapter 'I remember...')

CHARLES WILLIAM RICHARDS
1926

Charles Richards (grand-father of Stanley Richards Cresswell, Captain 1987) was born in 1860. With his brother, Silas, Charles started the firm known later as Charles Richards & Sons, manufacturing nuts, bolts & rivets for industry. Charles soon bought out his brother to become sole owner and was later given the freedom of Darleston, West Midlands as one of the area's major employers.

The Richards family visited Nefyn every summer in the 20s and 30s. Their baggage arrived before them on the Company's blue lorry and when the locals saw the lorry, they knew that summer had arrived!

BRIGADIER SIR WILLIAM WYNNE-FINCH
1927 & 1956

Sir William's mother, Maud Emily Wynne-Finch, was one of the Founder Members of Nefyn & District Golf Club. Sir William attended Eton College and was commissioned into the Scots Guards in 1911. He was awarded an MC in the First World War and in 1919, he was seconded to the Sudan Defence Force. On leaving the SDF, he travelled the world before settling down at Cefnamwlch to run the estate in collaboration with Mr George Bovill. Mr Bovill was a well known land agent who was very much involved with developments at the Golf Club.

Sir William married an American lady, Miss Gladys Waterbury of Convent Station. In 1938, he was recalled to the army and served throughout the Second World War. Following the War, he worked in local government and also became a Knight of St. John. He was Lord Lieutenant of Caernarfonshire from April 1941 until January 1960. In June 1960, he was knighted in the Queen's Birthday Honours.

Brigadier Sir William Wynne-Finch worked unstintingly with Nefyn and District Golf Club and was a wonderful Landlord. He was elected Captain in 1927 and again in 1956. Although he had no golfing prowess, he nevertheless was extremely supportive of the Club and interested in all its developments. As 'Colonel Wynne-Finch, Cefnamwlch, Edern' (sic. Club Minutes), he had succeeded his mother as President of the Club on her death in 1946, a position he held until his own death in December 1961. Lady Gladys Wynne-Finch was then elected Club President at the following AGM, April 1962.

R A PUGH
1928

Rennell A Pugh was elected Captain on August 22nd 1928 at the Club's AGM. In the AGM Minutes, the Chairman, Rennell A Pugh, congratulated the Ladies' Section for formulating a Committee to see to the Ladies' affairs and then went on to appeal 'for a little more unity as a considerable amount of friction had been experienced in the past'. He suggested that 'any comments the Ladies had that would help improve the Course etc. would be treated with greatest consideration and sympathy by the Club Committee!' (sic)

During his year in office, Rennell A Pugh presented a Cup (See History of Cups and Trophies) and in our Centenary Year, the Rennell A Pugh Cup was placed on a new plinth and played for by the Ladies' Section as a 4BBB Competition. This is to become an annual event.

July 1928: It having been brought to the attention of the Hon Sec, that the Edeyrn Flower Show was being held on the same date as the Annual General Meeting, namely the 18th, a special emergency meeting was convened to deal with the matter. Proposed by G S Pittman, seconded by Rev. W. Pierce Owen that the Annual General Meeting be held on the 22nd of August.

July 1929: It was pointed out that the intention to hold the Annual General Meeting on the 17th of August would clash with the Edeyrn Flower Show, and also the Sheep Dog Trials at Nevin. Proposed by G.S.Pittman, seconded O.H.Parry that it be postponed to August 21st.

Aug 28th 1929: In view of the fact that a considerable number of people non members of the Club were utilising the Club's Parking place for their Cars it was decided, to display a Notice board in a prominent place at the foot of the Links stating that the Parking Place was for Golfers only, and that other Cars should be charged at the rate of 2/6 per day. (sic)

F E THOMPSON
1929

H S THOMPSON
1934

The Thompson family used to stay in a hotel in Nefyn every summer. The two brothers were very alike. Locals used to refer to them as Thompson Mawr (Large) and Thompson Bach (Small) even though they were both small in stature! The local caddies used to compete to carry their bags. In those days, players with only half a dozen hickory shafted clubs in their bags were able to hire caddies easily. The Thompson brothers were such golfers!

Frank Thompson's electon as Captain was delayed because of a clash with local functions (see left: July 1929)

The issue of Sunday Golf was considered at the AGM of 1930, when F E Thompson was retiring. The ballot was lost by 42 votes to 26.

H S Thompson (Captain in 1934) was instrumental in securing the services of Mr J H Turner, Golf Course Architect, Abingdon, who was to design new holes on the new ground which had been acquired. Turner described the links thus, 'Your course is situated upon one of the most beautiful sites I have ever seen…' His new design had no blind shots or any crossings.

CAPTAIN O G OWEN
1930

Cafodd Capten O G Owen ei fagu yn Delfryn, Morfa Nefyn ac roedd yn un o nifer o Gapteiniaid llong yn yr ardal. Fel sawl Aelod lleol arall, ni fyddai'n llogi cadi yn y Golff.

Yn ystod ei flwyddyn fel Capten, roedd sawl plentyn yn arfer cadio yn ystod oriau ysgol!

Bu Capten Owen yn gyfrifol am ddarbwyllo Jones y Pro i hepgor yr arferiad yma! Ar ddechrau 1931, derbyniwyd ymddiswyddiad J H Jones, y Pro a phenodwyd Mr Riley. Bu ambell i ffrwgwd rhyngddo ef â Chapten Owen ynglŷn â phwy oedd yn gyfrifol am oruchwylio gwaith ar y cwrs. Cafwyd sawl cwyn yn ystod ei flwyddyn fel Capten am gyflwr y cwrs.

Captain O G Owen was brought up in Delfryn, Morfa Nefyn, and was one of a number of seafaring captains in the area. He followed in the tradition of local Members who did not hire caddies at the Club.

During his Captaincy it was realised that several children were caddying on the course during school time! Captain Owen was responsible for persuading Jones, the Pro, to stop this habit. Jones' successor as Pro, a Mr Riley, and Captain Owen disagreed strongly on several occasions regarding the supervision of the Golf Course, largely on account of numerous complaints about the state of the Course.

REV PREB GOUGH 1931

Yng Nghyfarfod Blynyddol y Clwb ym mis Awst, 1931, penodwyd y Parch Preb A W Gough yn Gapten, ond byr iawn fu ei dymor gan y bu farw ar Hydref 14eg 1931. Yn dilyn ei farwolaeth, penodwyd R Ivor Jones yn Gapten.

At the Club's AGM in August 1931, the Rev. Preb A W Gough was elected Captain but his Captaincy only lasted until his unexpected death on October 14th. A photograph of the Rev Gough is included amongst the Club's long list of Captains. Following his death, R Ivor Jones was elected Captain and Dr S C Varley elected Vice-Captain.

R IVOR JONES 1931

R Ivor Jones oedd Prifathro Ysgol Edern cyn Ellis Tudur Roberts (Capten y Clwb yn 1946). Aeth o Edern i ddysgu i Ysgol Craig y Don, Llandudno. Roedd R Ivor Jones yn un o'r 'hen scŵl' ac arferai reoli gyda grym. Er mai Ysgol Eglwys oedd Ysgol Edern yn wreiddiol, capelwr oedd R Ivor Jones ac roedd yn ffrindiau mawr gyda theulu Hughes Roberts, Glanrhyd. Roedd yn un o bedwar aelod a arferai chwarae'n rheolaidd gyda'i gilydd. Cyfeiriwyd atynt fel y 'Band of Hope' ac ni fyddant yn arfer llogi plant lleol i gadio iddynt.

Un o uchafbwyntiau ei Gapteniaeth oedd prynu tractor cyntaf y Clwb yn dilyn blynyddoedd o weithio gyda cheffyl. Tractor ail-law Beta Magneto (£142) a pheiriant lladd gwair gyda phum torrwr (£180) a brynwyd.

R Ivor Jones was Headmaster at Ysgol Edern before Ellis Tudur Roberts (Club Captain in

1946). He moved from Edern to Ysgol Craig y Don in Llandudno. He was one of the 'old school', governing with a rod of iron! Even though Ysgol Edern was a church school, R Ivor Jones was a chapel goer and was a great friend of the Roberts family at Glanrhyd Farm, Edern.

One of the highlights of his year was the purchase of the Club's first tractor following years of working with a horse. A second hand Beta Magneto tractor was purchased for £142 together with a Quintiple Mower for £180.

DR S C VARLEY 1932

Dr S C Varley was an away Member, referred to in those days as a Visiting Member, who used to spend his holidays in Cil Llidiart, Edern. Cil Llidiart is found down the lane just past Edern School. He was a great friend of W Glynne Jones, Captain in 1925 and the two regularly hired locals to caddie for them.

In August 1939, Dr Varley offered a Cup to be played for annually. The Club accepted the offer but suggested that the Cup should be won outright since the Club had an abundance of cups!

It was during Dr Varley's Captaincy that the contract of Mr Riley, the Pro, was terminated and Dr Varley was Chairman of the sub-committee who selected A D Grace, from 29 applicants, as the Club's Professional.

T JONES 1933

Ychydig o wybodaeth sy'n hysbys am T Jones. Arferai fyw ym Mrynmor, Nefyn. Credir iddo fod yn un o'r Aelodau Cyntaf a sefydlodd y Clwb a threuliodd gyfnod fel Ysgrifennydd (diwedd 1918) a Thrysorydd y Clwb o 1918 i 1932.

Yn ystod Capteiniaeth T Jones, cwblhaodd y Clwb gytundeb gyda Chapten Wynne-Finch i rentu tir ychwanegol (bron i ddeunaw acer). Yn yr un flwyddyn, ac am y tro cyntaf yn hanes y Clwb, cyflogwyd dau fachgen i gadw golwg ar yr unfed twll ar ddeg (deuddegfed ar y Penrhyn erbyn heddiw) i atal anafiadau i gerddwyr oedd yn cerdded i Dafarn Tŷ Coch a Whitehall. Parhaodd yr arferiad yma yn achlysurol tan 1994 pan agorwyd y Cwrs Newydd.

T Jones, as he was always referred to at the Golf Club, resided at Brynmor, Nefyn and it is believed he was a Founder Member of the Club. He held the position of Secretary for the latter half of 1918 and was Treasurer at the Club from 1918 until 1932.

During T Jones' Captaincy, the Club completed an agreement with Captain Wynne-Finch to rent additional land (nearly 18 acres). In the same year, and for the first time in the Club's history, two local lads were employed to keep a look-out on the 11th hole (present 12th on the Point) to prevent injuries to pedestrians walking to Tŷ Coch and Whitehall. One of these lads was the 1989 Captain, H D Jones! This custom remained until 1994 when the New Course was opened.

CAPTAIN W J PARRY
1935

Captain W J Parry was Lt Col R W Parry and Tom Parry's grandfather. He retired from the Merchant Navy having served as Captain for several years, and lived at Waen, Nefyn, which his family had built.

He presided as Chairman of the Executive Committee during his term of office as Captain as well as the greater part of H S Thompson's Captaincy in 1934-35. [H S Thompson was only able to visit the Club for his annual leave in August of each year!]

During Captain Parry's Captaincy, a gate with keys for the residents of Porthdinllaen was installed by the Clubhouse for the first time.

He enjoyed his golf but there is no record of his having any great golfing skills.

C S BUCKLEY
1936

Charles Sidney Buckley spent his working life in the textile industry. He was responsible for establishing the Henry Bannerman Company who traded as Banner Brand. He was brought up in Gatley and moved to Hale in the mid-30s.

He married in 1906 and he and his wife, Winifred, spent their honeymoon at the Nanhoron Arms Hotel, Nefyn, and began an on-going love affair with Nefyn and the Golf Club. This has now passed down through the generations to his great, great grandchildren. Charles and Winifred had two children, Harold (Captain of Nefyn Golf Club in 1958-59) and Kathleen who has reached the youthful age of 93 at the time of writing!

Charles became Captain in 1936 and although he never achieved a low handicap, he did have a reputation as an excellent putter!

June 20th 1936: Agreed to fix Welsh translations of the Notice Boards on the Course as it was stated by members there are still persons in the neighbourhood who are ignorant of the English language.

CAPTAIN W E PRICE
1937

Adweinid Capten W E Price fel Capten Price, Twmpath, Morfa Nefyn. Bu un ferch iddo, sef Mrs Hughes, yn byw yn Nhy'n Pwll a phriododd ei ferch arall Capten Wil Williams, Tir Bedw, Edern.

Bu Capten Price yn Ysgrifennydd y Clwb am gyfnodau byr rhwng ysgrifenyddion eraill. Etholwyd ef yn Aelod Oes o'r Clwb ym mis Awst 1945 a thalwyd teyrnged glodwiw iddo ym Mhwyllgor Cyffredinol y Clwb, 1956, pan gyfeiriwyd at ei ymdrechion diarbed ac egnïol dros y Clwb yn ystod cyfnod y Rhyfel.

in the South Wales Borderers based in Southern England but came out of the Army in 1928.

He was elected Captain of the Club in 1940, at the beginning of the War. During his Captaincy, he spent most of his time in Chester as Manager of Moore and Brock Builders Merchants. In his absence, the Club Meetings were usually chaired by Captain Price or J E Roberts.

Captain W P Parry, in the late 70s, centre of middle row, with Captain Dan W Jones on his right and Dafydd Williams, Porthdinllaen, on his Left. **Back row, Left to Right:** *Twm 'Teacher' John Jones, Rita Nicholson (Stewardess) and Owie J Roberts, Glanrafon.* **Front row Left,** *G I Hughes and* **Right,** *Patrick McAteer.*

Captain Parry's family lived in Chester for many years but he retired to his native Nefyn and played a great deal of golf. In spite of having a wooden leg, he used to play several rounds a week and was reputed to particularly enjoy club outings!

He was re-elected on to the Golf Club Committee at the AGM of 1961.

June 1st 1940: It was agreed for the present to leave the veranda open at night to provide shelter for Home Defence Units on observation duty... ...It was decided to allow members of his Majesty's Forces temporarily stationed within 10 miles of the Club House to become Visiting Members at half the ordinary daily rates charged to the general public and to advise the Officer in Charge at Penrhos to this effect.

July 24th 1940: An application by Capt O'Farrell for permission to use the Locker Room for LDV men to sleep in was granted on the understanding given by Capt. O'Farrell that the men will tidy up the room after use and that he will accept full responsibility for any accidental or other damage done.

On 14th May, 1940, Anthony Eden appealed on radio for men to become Local Defence Volunteers (LDVs). In the broadcast Eden asked that volunteers should be aged between 40 and 65 and should be able to fire a rifle or shotgun. By the end of June nearly one and a half million men had been recruited.

HENRY PARRY
1941

Adwaenid Henry Parry fel Harry Parry. Bu'n ddeintydd ysgolion am flynyddoedd lawer, gyda Mrs Laura Wyn Roberts yn gynorthwyydd abl iddo. Byddent yn teithio o amgylch yr ysgolion, gan weithio o'u deintyddfa mewn carafán. Gyrrai Harry ei hun o gwmpas mewn Morris Oxford mawr du.

Roedd Harry yn ffyddlon iawn i'r Golff ac yn ffyddlon i'r bar. Byddai yn un o'r ychydig rai fyddai'n blasu potel o gwrw o'r enw 'White Label'. Dim ond Harry fyddai'n cael y fraint o dywallt cynnwys y botel i wydr yn araf yn ei ffordd arbennig ef ei hun gan adael rhyw hanner modfedd o waddod yr hopysen ar ôl.

Roedd Harry'n olffiwr cymedrol, ac yn ôl cofnodion y Clwb, bu'n chwarae oddi ar raddnod o 11 am gyfnod.

Symudodd teulu Dilys Morgan, darpar wraig Harry, i fyw i Forfa Nefyn o Ddeiniolen yn 1925. Roedd ei thad yn Weinidog yng Nghapel y Bedyddwyr, gyferbyn â'r Post. Mae Gwyn Morgan, brawd Dilys, pêl-droediwr enwog yn ei ddydd, yn dal i fyw yn Nefyn yn 90 oed.

Henry Parry was known as Harry Parry. He was the local school dentist for many years, with Mrs Laura Wyn Roberts as his able assistant. They travelled around local schools and set up their surgery in a mobile caravan.

Harry was faithful to the Golf Club and to the bar. He was one of a few people who used to drink 'Worthington White Label'. Only Harry was allowed to pour his drink slowly from the bottle into a glass, leaving half an inch of sediment at the bottom!

Harry was a fair golfer, and, according to Club records, he played off 11 at one period. Harry's wife's father was a Minister in the Baptist Chapel opposite the post office in Morfa. Gwyn Morgan, Harry's brother-in-law, a famous footballer in his day, still lives in Nefyn at 90 years of age.

> **Jan 10th 1942:** Resolved: That the resolutions (June 1st 1940) passed by the Committee exempting members of His Majesty's Forces and the Mercantile Marines from paying subscriptions be deleted... it is hoped that as many members as possible will pay the usual fees and charges ...as the remission of so many fees and charges will be a very great financial strain on the Club.

R S BLENCOE
1942

R S Blencoe first joined Nefyn Golf Club in 1909-10 and after a long association with the Club for over 32 years, he was elected Captain in 1942.

He was Headmaster of a Private Residential School at Bodelwyddan. He married the daughter of a Dr Phillips from Morfa Nefyn who lived in Mr and Mrs Gurns' house on the cliff road not far from Pwll William and La Casina.

> **Apr 2nd 1943:** Members of the Forces were to be allowed the facilities of the Course at half the usual fees.

ROBERT THOMAS
1943

Roedd Robert Thomas (Robin Crugan, fel yr adwaenid ef) yn hanu o deulu Iorwerth a Gerallt, Nefyn. Roedd y teulu'n enwog fel adeiladwyr llongau yn yr hen ddyddiau ac felly, roeddynt yn deulu cefnog.

Ail-briododd Robin â Mrs Nefyn Williams, gweddw yr enwog Barchedig Tom Nefyn Williams. Roedd Robin yn olffiwr brwdfrydig gan chwarae i 11 ar un cyfnod. Treuliodd sawl blwyddyn yn Gadeirydd Pwyllgor y Lawntiau.

THE CAPTAINS - Y CAPTEINIAID

Robert Thomas (Robin Crugan, as he was better known) hailed from the families of Gerallt and Iorwerth (opposite the Holborn Estate) in Nefyn. The family was famous for shipbuilding in the olden days and they were, therefore, quite prosperous.

Robin's second marriage was to Mrs Nefyn Williams, widow of the renowned Methodist minister, Tom Nefyn Williams.

He was an enthusiastic golfer, playing off a handicap of 11 at one time, and was Chairman of the Greens' Committee for several years.

MAJOR OWEN ROBERTS 1944

Magwyd Owen Roberts ym mhentref Llanllyfni, ger Penygroes. Teiliwr a chapelwr Batys brwd oedd ei dad. Symudodd Owen i Nefyn yn 1922 ar ei apwyntiad i'w swydd gyntaf fel athro yn Ysgol Gynradd Nefyn, lle treuliodd ei holl yrfa ym maes addysg plant, gan ddyrchafu i swydd Prifathro yn gynnar yn ei yrfa. Bu'n Brifathro ar Ysgol Nefyn tan Haf 1967, pan ymddeolodd.

Cyfarfu ag Elisabeth, ei ddarpar wraig pan oedd yn y coleg. Ymunodd Owen â'r Clwb Golff ynghyd â Mrs Roberts yn niwedd y dauddegau. Yn 1933 roedd graddnod Owen ar lyfrau'r Clwb yn 6.

Ymysg ei gyd chwaraewyr roedd tri o hoelion wyth y Clwb, Harry Parry (Capten 1941), D A Williams (Capten 1957) a John Evan Roberts, Glanrhyd (Capten 1939). Byddai Owen yn hoff iawn o roi rhyw geiniog neu ddwy ar y gêm, ymarfer sydd wedi parhau dros y degawdau!

Etholwyd Owen Roberts yn Gapten Clwb Golff Nefyn yn Awst 1944, a chynigiwyd swydd Ysgrifennydd Anrhydeddus y Clwb iddo ym Mis Hydref, 1947. Yn 1965, etholwyd ef yn Aelod Oes a phan ymddeolodd yng Ngorffennaf 1977, derbyniodd rodd ymddeoliad hael iawn gan y Clwb a'r aelodau. Yn 1984, etholwyd ef yn Llywydd y Clwb, swydd yr ymgymerodd â hi nes ei farwolaeth yn 1995. Cyflwynwyd mainc gan ei ferch, Sian, i'r Clwb er cof am ei thad ym mis Medi 1997.

Defnyddid rhai o adnoddau Ysgol Nefyn i ddyblygu papurau a chofnodion y Clwb ar yr hen seiclo steilyr a byddai Noel a Sian, y plant, yn treulio oriau yn dosbarthu llythyrau a chofnodion y Clwb ar eu beiciau rownd Nefyn, Boduan, Morfa, Edern a Thudweiliog. Mae Miss Annette Jones (Capten y Merched 1978) yn cofio sawl achlysur pan fu'n helpu i ysgrifennu enwau a chyfeiriadau Aelodau'r Golff ar ffurflenni yn amser yr ysgol pan oedd hi'n ddisgybl!

Bu Owen Roberts yn weithgar iawn mewn llawer o feysydd yn y Clwb. Bu'n ymgyrchu i gael caniatâd i chwarae golf ar y Sul ac ar ôl sawl blwyddyn, cafwyd pleidlais ddigonol yng Nghyfarfod Blynyddol y Clwb ar Awst 25ain 1957.

Un maes y treuliodd amser mawr yn ymgyrchu ynddo oedd menter prynu'r Clwb yn y pumdegau pan fu'n gweithio'n ddiwyd i godi grantiau tuag at y fenter. Ei siomiant fwyaf yn ystod ei gyfnod fel Ysgrifennydd oedd methiant y Clwb i brynu Gwesty'r Linksway. Roedd yn ŵr o flaen ei ddyddiau, mae'n amlwg – cymaint o fuddsoddiad fuasai'r pryniant yma wedi bod erbyn heddiw.

Byddai Owen yn croesawu nifer mawr o ymwelwyr ac Aelodau i'r Clwb. Byddai'n gyfeillgar ag Aelodau dros Glawdd Offa, fel teuluoedd Buckley, Murray a Cooper. Yn aml iawn, rhoddai Owen neges i geidwad y ffynnon fod ei 'usual' yn golygu dwbl pan y cai wahoddiad i gael tropyn gydag un neu ragor o'r byddigions!

Roedd gan Owen ymadroddion lu a byddai'n eu harfer yn rheolaidd yn ei sgyrsiau. Dyma rai ohonynt: 'Mi gymith mwy na hyn i'n trechu ni!' 'Cyntaf i'r felin gaiff falu...' 'Os cnau sydd yn y sach, Cnau ddaw allan, bobol bach!' 'Nofiwch am y lan!'

Owen Roberts was raised in the village of Llanllyfni, near Penygroes. His father was a tailor and a staunch Baptist. Owen moved to Nefyn in 1922 on his appointment to his first teaching post at Nefyn Primary School, where he spent his entire teaching profession. He was appointed Headmaster early in his career and retired in 1967.

He met Elizabeth, his wife at teacher training college. They joined the Golf Club in the 1920s and Owen's handicap in 1933 is recorded as being 6. Among his playing partners were three of the Club's stalwarts, Harry Parry (Captain 1941), D A Williams (Captain 1957) and John E Roberts Glanrhyd (Captain 1939). Owen was keen on a little 'flutter' while playing golf, a practice which continues to this day at the Club!

Owen Roberts was elected Captain in 1944 and in October 1947 he became the Club's Honorary Secretary, a position he held for 30 years. In 1965, he was elected a Life Member of the Club and when he retired in July 1977, he received a generous retirement fund from both the Club itself and from the Members. In 1984, he was elected President and he died in office in 1995. His daughter, Sian Roberts presented a bench to the Club, in memory of her father, in September 1997.

Some of the resources from Nefyn School were used to produce papers and minutes on the old duplicators and Noel and Sian, his children, used to spend hours on their bikes distributing letters and Club minutes around Nefyn, Boduan, Morfa Nefyn, Edern and even Tudweiliog. Annette Jones (Lady Captain, 1978) recalls as a child how she helped on many occasions to write the

Owain Roberts as President, enjoying his favourite tipple with friends. **From Left to Right:** *Laura Jane, The Vicar E W Thomas, Fiona Vaughan Thomas, Meirwen Collier and Laura Wyn Roberts with Anne Thomas seated.*

names and addresses of Members on envelopes in school time!

Owen Roberts was active in many aspects of golf club life. He was at the forefront of the campaign to get Sunday golf and after several years a majority vote was reached at the AGM of August 25th 1957. In the fifties he spent a great deal of time on the campaign to purchase the Course from the estate. He worked diligently to raise grants for this purchase. His greatest disappointment was the Club's failure to buy the Linksway Hotel. He was a man ahead of his years – this purchase would have been such a good investment for the Club by today!

Owen used to welcome a great number of visitors to the Club. He befriended several Members from the other side of Offa's Dyke, such as the Buckleys, the Murrays, the Coopers and many more. Very often, Owen would signal to the bar attendant that his 'usual' meant a double when he was invited to have a drink with the honoured company!

Owen had many sayings and idioms in Welsh, English and Latin and he would use them regularly. Some of his famous quotes were: 'Mi gymith mwy na hyn i'n trechu ni!' ('It will take more than this to defeat us!') 'Cyntaf i'r felin gaiff falu…' (First come, first served…) 'CC – Christ and Carrots', 'Swim for the shore!', 'Kangaroo Court!', 'Ipso facto' and 'Tempus fugit.'

> **July 9th 1966:** The committee missed the presence of the Club's efficient Secretary, Owen Roberts, through indisposition and expressed a wish for a speedy recovery to his usual good health. The Captain (Richard Williams) was instructed to deliver in person a large bottle of tonic – not under 70% proof – to be taken under his own discretion as a stimulant during his macho hours of solitude. A chorus of the Committee members expressed 'Iechyd Da!' (sic).

A renowned Welsh harpist from Denbighshire arrived very early for a concert one Saturday. She was royally entertained by Owen Roberts, Secretary, and by the time the concert started, she was rather the worse for wear. Consequently, she was referred to as **'The half-pissed Harpist!'**

WING COMMANDER H SLEIGH
1945

Wing Commander Sleigh had a long career in the RAF and resided at Cliff Castle, Nefyn. He was always referred to as 'Wing Commander'. He married a Mrs Lee, whose niece was Ena Bellhouse (later to become Lady Captain of the Club in 1948, 1957 and 1968).

Miss E Trenholme, our Life Member, recalls the Wing Commander as being a stern man and she and her friends were quite frightened of him! He was very fond of playing golf and was regularly seen on the Course. He was a good golfer, playing off a handicap of 6.

Wing Commander Sleigh was elected Captain of the Club at the AGM of August 1945, three months after VE Day. On the same day, the death of the President, Mrs Maud Wynne-Finch was announced. During his year as Captain, the Wing Commander chaired the Sub-Committee which interviewed a short list for the position of Club Professional. The shortlist comprised J B Robertson, C Rawstrom and A D Grace's re-application. In fact only A D Grace attended and he was appointed after a long protracted interview session.

Interesting Facts at Nefyn Golf Club as reported in 1945:

- *A reconditioned Fordson Tractor was bought by the Club for £165.*
- *Mrs A D Grace was employed to assist in the clubhouse at £1-5-0 per week.*
- *A Local Member was defined as a person living within a six miles radius.*
- *A pint of beer was sold in the clubhouse at 1/4d and all teas were 1/3d.*

OWEN ROBERTS' ERA AS SECRETARY 1946 – 1976

ELLIS TUDUR ROBERTS
1946

Cafodd Ellis Tudur, fel yr adwaenid ef, ei fagu yn Stryd Warden, Llanberis. Treuliodd gyfnod yn y Rhyfel Cyntaf yn darllen mapiau i Swyddogion ac adnabu Hedd Wyn. Ar ôl y Rhyfel aeth i ddysgu ac fe'i penodwyd yn Brifathro Ysgol Edern yn 1936. Ellis Tudur oedd Prifathro cyntaf cydawdur y llyfr hwn ac er ei fod yn fyr o gorff, roedd yn ddisgyblwr llym iawn! Byddai plant Ysgol Edern ei ofn ac ni feiddient symud pan fyddai'r Austin Seven bychan yn dod i fyny Lôn y Rhos am yr Ysgol! Ymddeolodd yn 1955 ond bu farw yn 1957. Yn ei amser hamdden byddai'n mwynhau garddio a mynd i'r 'Bryn' am beint. Cawsai bleser mawr o chwarae golff gan chwarae oddi ar raddnod o ddeunaw.

Bu'n ddiwyd iawn gyda materion y Lawntiau a Chystadleuthau yn y Clwb am flynyddoedd lawer ac fe'i hetholwyd yn Gapten y Clwb yn 1946. Cofia H D Jones, oedd newydd ymuno â'r Clwb, gael sgwrs ag Ellis Tudur un diwrnod: 'Dach chi 'di dod i le da,' meddai Ellis Tudur, 'dwi'n deud wrthoch chi fod pawb o bwys yn yr ardal yma yn perthyn i fan hyn!'

Ym mis Hydref 1996 (hanner can mlynedd ar ôl Capteiniaeth Ellis Tudur) prynwyd cwpan mewn siop hen greiriau yng Nghricieth oedd yn dynodi ei bod wedi ei chyflwyno i aelod o Glwb Nefyn yn 1946 gan y Capten, Ellis Tudur Roberts. Cytunodd Stan Roberts (mab Ellis Tudur) y buasai Adran y Dynion yn cael chwarae am y gwpan yn flynyddol, ond na fuasai'n un o brif gystadleuthau'r Clwb. Ers 1996, chwaraeir am gwpan Tudur Roberts ar ddechrau'r tymor golffio.

Ellis Tudur, as he was known, was brought up in Warden Street, Llanberis. He was called up during the First World War and was employed reading maps for Officers. After the War, he went into teaching and was appointed as Headmaster at Edern School in 1936. Ellis Tudur was the first headmaster of the co-author of this book and is remembered as being very short of stature but a stern disciplinarian! Edern schoolchildren were frightened of him and they would not dare move when his Austin Seven came up Lôn Rhos towards the school! He retired in 1955 but only enjoyed two years of retirement before his death in 1957. In his leisure time, he enjoyed gardening and visiting the Bryncynan Inn. He also enjoyed his golf and played off 18 handicap.

*Ellis Tudur Roberts **(Right)** playing 'ping-pong' with Owen Roberts in the games' room. This was a favourite pastime on rainy days.*

He worked hard on the Greens' and Competition issues in the Club for many years and he was elected Captain in 1946. H D Jones recalls, when he had just joined the club, having a conversation with Ellis. 'You've come to a good place here,' said Ellis, 'I'm telling you that anyone who's anyone in the area is a Member here!'

Fifty years after Ellis Tudur's Captaincy, in October 1996, a cup was discovered in an antiques shop in Criccieth. The inscription showed that it had been presented to a Member of Nefyn Golf Club in 1946 by the then Captain. This would have been Ellis Tudur Roberts. Stan Roberts (Ellis Tudur Roberts' son) agreed that the trophy could be played for annually by the Gent's Section, but that it should not be a major competition. Ever since 1996, the Tudur Roberts Cup has been played for at the beginning of the golfing season.

MAURICE WYNN JONES 1947

Roedd Maurice W Jones yn byw ym Mrynmor, Ffordd y Traeth, Nefyn ac roedd yn perthyn i Dafydd Griffith Williams, tad Dafydd Williams, Porthdinllaen. Byddai Maurice Brynmor, fel yr adwaenid ef, yn cadw siop ddillad ar y Stryd Fawr, gyferbyn â hen Siop R J Jones, y Fferyllydd.

Wrth dderbyn ei Gapteiniaeth yn 1947, soniodd ef am y dyddiau cynnar pan dderbyniwyd rhoddion tuag at sefydlu'r Clwb presennol. Ychwanegodd Maurice, 'Mae'r cynnydd ers y dyddiau cynnar hynny yn berffaith amlwg ac mae llwyddiant y Clwb i'r dyfodol yn ddiogel.'

Maurice W Jones lived at Brynmor, Beach Road, Nefyn and was related to Dafydd Griffith Williams, the father of Dafydd Williams, Porthdinllaen.

Maurice Brynmor, as he was known, was proprietor of a draper's shop in Nefyn High Street, opposite the old R J Jones, Chemist's shop.

On accepting the Captaincy in 1947, Maurice recalled the days when donations were received towards the formation of the present Club. He continued by saying, '...the progress since those days is self evident and the future success of the Club is secure.'

EDWIN JONES
1948

Ychydig iawn o wybodaeth sydd ar gael am Edwin Jones. Deallir ei fod yn hanu o Langefni. Credir ei fod yn ddarlithydd yng Ngholeg Madryn pan oedd yn Goleg Amaethyddol. Symudwyd Coleg Madryn i Blas Glynllifon yn 1952.

Very little information is available about Edwin Jones. It is understood that he hailed from Llangefni. It is believed that he was a lecturer in Madryn College when it was an Agricultural College. Madryn College was moved to Glynllifon College (near Penygroes) in 1952 and today it is part of Coleg Meirion Dwyfor Tertiary College.

Mar 6th 1948: It was resolved to empower the secretary (Owen Roberts) to negotiate for the purchase of Gin from a certain Liverpool firm provided it was of satisfactory quality!

Aug 7th 1948 (AGM): The Captain proposed a hearty vote of congratulation to our Life Member, Mr Wm Johnson, Pwllcrwn, Morfa Nevin on attaining his 94th birthday and the celebration of 63 years of married life. The meeting was then closed in perfect harmony. [often minuted at close of AGM]

Below is seen a list of the categories of membership in Edwin Jones' year as Captain (1948):

Number of Local Gents:	104
Number of Country Gents:	99
Junior Members:	23
Number of Local Ladies:	109
Number of Country Ladies:	57
Total:	392

Twenty four new lockers were built and these were for Local Members only.

ROBERT DAVIS OWEN
1949

WILLIE REES OWEN
1953

Hogiau lleol oedd Robert a Willie, wedi'i magu yn Dolwen, Nefyn. Roeddynt yn gystadleuol mewn pêl-droed a golff, gyda'r ddau wedi chwarae oddi ar 'scratch' ar un cyfnod. Yn ogystal, bu'r ddau yn Gapteiniaid Clwb Golff Nefyn a Chlwb Minchinhampton (Swydd Caerloyw).

The two brothers Robert and Willie were born in Nefyn and both qualified as Dentists from Liverpool University, where they represented the University at golf and football.

Robert represented Wales at amateur level in football and boxing. Both brothers practised in

Robert Davies Owen, with cap and cigarette, standing behind Dai Rees, pointing out the line to Wally Smithers at his side, in the Exhibition Match of 1950.

Stroud, Gloucestershire, returning to Nefyn for holidays and naturally, to play golf.

Robert and Willie were very competitive golfers, both having played to scratch at their peak. They both represented the Caernarfonshire County Team on numerous occasions.

Robert and Willie took part in an exhibition match at Nefyn against Dai Rees and Wally Smithers of Long Ashton GC, Bristol (referred to in Will Parry Williams' reminiscences in the Chapter 'I remember...').

Both brothers became Captains of Nefyn and Minchinhampton, Stroud, their Club in Gloucestershire. Willie Rees Owen became president of Minchinhampton New Course Club in 1976, only retiring in 1982 when he was made an honorary Life Member for his dedication and work for the Club.

During his Captaincy at Nefyn, in October 1949, the Captain, Robert Davies Owen, offered a set of Henry Cotton irons to the best 3 cards from 5 during the Monthly Spoons from November to March. In the event of a tie, there was to be an 18 holes play-off.

It was during Willie Rees' Captaincy in 1953, that the myxomatosis epidemic was at its peak across the country. Rabbits had been pests on the Course for a few years and now, diseased rabbits' carcases were in abundance and had to be removed.

Both Robert and Willie's respective families have many wonderful memories of the two of them enjoying a brotherly competitive match at Nefyn. They never lost their love of the game or of Nefyn Golf Club.

J IDRIS LEWIS
1950

Brodor o'r Gaerwen, Ynys Môn, oedd J Idris Lewis. Ym 1933 symudodd o Langollen (lle bu'n golffio'n frwdfrydig) i weithio ym Manc y Midland, Nefyn. Ymunodd â Chlwb Golff Nefyn, lle bu'n Drysorydd Cynorthwyol i H Llewelyn Roberts am rai blynyddoedd. Enillodd Wobr y Capten (Capten W E Price) - hambwrdd arian hardd - yn 1937. Ym 1941 daeth yn Drysorydd y Clwb, swydd y bu ynddi tan 1952. Ei brif ddiddordeb arall oedd Capel Soar, Nefyn, lle bu'n ben-blaenor.

Ar ôl ei flynyddoedd yn Drysorydd, etholwyd Idris Lewis yn Aelod Oes. Yr oedd mor ddedwydd yn Nefyn nes iddo wrthod, ddwywaith, â chymryd ei symud (a'i ddyrchafu) gan y Banc. Ganwyd dau fab i'r teulu, Robyn a Richard. Mae'r mab hynaf, Dr Robyn Léwis, yn gyn-Archdderwydd Cymru.

Ymddeolodd Idris Lewis yn 1959 a bu farw yn 1971 yn ei gartref yn Nefyn.

J Idris Lewis was brought up in Gaerwen, Anglesey. In 1933, he moved from Llangollen, where he was a very enthusiastic golfer, to work in the Midland Bank at Nefyn. He joined Nefyn Golf Club, where he became assistant Treasurer to H Llewelyn Roberts for several years. He won the Captain's Prize in 1937. In 1941 he became the Club Treasurer, a position he held until 1952. His other main interest was Soar Chapel, Nefyn where he became the leading deacon.

Following his years as Club Treasurer, Idris Lewis was elected a Life Member of the Club. He was so content at Nefyn that, on two occasions, he refused transfer and promotion by the Bank. His two sons, Robyn and Richard, live in Nefyn. The elder, Dr Robyn Léwis, is a past Archdruid of Wales. He retired in 1959 and died at home in Nefyn in 1971.

Nevin and District Golf Club Captain's Prize 1937. Ennillwyd gan J Idris Lewis (sic) Uwch y Don Nefyn

W L DAVIES 1951

Hanai W L Davies o Laniestyn ac roedd ei frawd, Idris Davies, yn Ysgolfeistr yn Nhudweiliog lle'r oedd llawer o'r teulu'n byw. Roedd 'Willie Egg', fel yr adwaenid ef, yn gweithio i'r 'Cooperative' yn hel wyau rownd Pen Llŷn a mynd â nhw i Benrhos. Symudodd i fyw i Afallon, Llanfair PG yn 1957 ac agor busnes wyau yn y Gaerwen.

Cofia H D Jones gêm golff a chwaraeodd yn erbyn W L Davies yn y pumdegau. Ar ôl i W L Davies fethu pyt fer ar un twll, ni ynganodd air gyda H D am weddill y rownd!

Cwblhawyd Siop Newydd y Pro yn ystod Capteiniaeth W L Davies a symudwyd y ffordd i Borthdinllaen trwy gau'r giât ar ben Lôn Penrhyn Bach ac agor ffordd heibio Tŷ'r Clwb at sied Ceidwad y Lawntiau. Roedd y ffordd yn parhau, fel y mae heddiw, o'r sied i Dŷ Coch fel ffordd arw, heb wyneb metel arni.

W L Davies was brought up in Llaniestyn. His brother, Idris Davies, was Headmaster at Tudweiliog, where some of the family lived. 'Willie Egg', as he was known, worked in the Cooperative stores for years and used to travel around Llŷn to collect eggs to take to the packing station at Penrhos. He moved to Llanfair PG on Anglesey in 1957 and started an egg business at Gaerwen. (Miss E Trenholme's mother used to keep hens and she had to wash their eggs before W L Davies would collect them from her once a week!)

H D Jones, our ex-Treasurer, Captain and present Life Member, recalls a golf game he played against him in the 1950s. After W L Davies missed a short putt on a hole, he did not utter a word for the remainder of the round!

The new Pro's Shop was completed during W L Davies' Captaincy and the roadway to Porthdinllaen was moved from Lôn Penrhyn Bach (by the present 10th tee) to a new road surfaced by the Cefnamwlch Estate, from the present Clubhouse down to the Greenkeeper's Shed. This road continued, as it does today, as a non-metalled surface from the Shed onwards to Tŷ Coch.

JACK DARROCK
1952

Jack Darrock was Manager of Carreg Llam Granite Quarry and he stepped into the Captaincy when Ivor Davies withdrew. We know little about Jack other than he was a good golfer, playing off a handicap of 7 at one time.

R GLYN WILLIAMS
1954

Ymunodd R Glyn Williams, (Ardwyn, Morfa Nefyn) â'r Clwb ar ôl yr Ail Ryfel Byd. Roedd wedi bod yn chwarae golff yn Nefyn ers rhai blynyddoedd pan ymunodd Brian Hefin, ei fab hynaf, fel Aelod ifanc deuddeg oed yn 1951.

Partneriaid golff cyson R G Williams ar y pryd oedd tri cyn-gapten sef Ellis Tudur Roberts (Prifathro Ysgol Edern), John Evan Roberts, Glanrhyd a J Idris Lewis (Cyn-Drysorydd). Yn fynych ar brynhawn Sadwrn yn yr haf byddai Brian yn cario bag ei dad am ddeunaw twll, yna te gan Mrs Edge a 9 twll arall ar ôl te, pryd y byddai Brian yn cael chwarae y tu ôl iddynt gyda chlybiau addas iddo fo (wedi'u torri i lawr).

Maintfesurwr oedd R Glyn Williams, yn bartner yng nghwmni L C Wakeman a'i Bartneriaid yng Nghaernarfon, gyda gofalaeth am weithgareddau'r cwmni yng Ngogledd Cymru. Bu Richie Glyn, fel y'i hadwaenid, yn teithio'n ddyddiol yno am bron i 40 mlynedd.

Roedd yn hoff iawn o chwaraeon ac wedi bod yn rhedwr chwim a pheldroediwr medrus pan oedd yn ifanc. Roedd wedi gwirioni gyda golff ac yn hynod o gystadleuol. Enillodd nifer o gystadleuthau dros y blynyddoedd gan gynnwys y Tweedale pan yn Is-Gapten yn 1953. Dywed Brian, 'Er i'n nhad fod yn siomedig i mi golli yn y final y flwyddyn ganlynol, ac yntau erbyn hynny'n Gapten y Clwb, roedd yna hefyd elfen o falchder ei fod yn parhau i fod y golffiwr gorau!' Bu'n chwarae i 8 a 9 am flynyddoedd a daeth i lawr i 7 hefyd am gyfnod.

Bu'n Gynghorydd Sir yr ardal o ganol y pumdegau hyd ei farwolaeth yn 1985. Ef oedd Cadeirydd olaf Cyngor Sir Caernarfon yn 1973 a bu hefyd yn Gadeirydd Cyngor Sir Gwynedd yn ystod y saithdegau. Roedd yn Ynad Heddwch ar y Fainc ym Mhwllheli a bu'n Ddarllenwr Lleyg yn Neoniaeth Llŷn am nifer fawr o flynyddoedd.

Bu ei feibion, Brian Hefin ac Adrian, yn hynod o lwyddiannus mewn cystadleuthau'r Adran Iau a chystadleuthau'r Clwb yn y pumdegau.

From Left to Right: Richie Glyn Williams (Captain 1954) with Willie Rees Owen (Captain 1953), Brian Hefin Williams (son) and Robert Davies Owen (Captain 1949).

R Glyn Williams of Ardwyn, Morfa Nefyn, joined the Club after the Second World War. He had been playing golf at Nefyn for a number of years when his son, Brian Hefin, joined at the age of twelve, in 1951.

His usual golfing partners were three ex-Captains, Ellis Tudur Roberts (Headmaster of Edern School), John Evan Roberts, Glanrhyd and J Idris Lewis (Past-Treasurer) and Brian, his son would often caddy for his father.

R Glyn Williams was a quantity surveyor by profession, a partner with L C Wakeman and Partners at Caernarfon, with responsibility for Company business throughout North Wales. Richie Glyn, as he was called, travelled to Caernarfon daily for nearly forty years.

He was very fond of sports and was a good sprinter and footballer in his youth.

He was infatuated with golf and was very competitive. He played to 8 and 9 for many years and was down to 7 at one stage. He won several competitions over the years, including the Tweedale Challenge Cup when he was Vice-Captain in 1953.

He was the County Councillor for the area from the mid-fifties until his death in 1985. He was the last Chairman of the Caernarfonshire County Council in 1973 and became Chairman of Gwynedd County Council in the same decade. He was a Justice of the Peace and a Lay Preacher in the Llŷn Deanery for several years.

His son, Brian, and his younger brother, Adrian, were very successful in Junior and Club competitions in the fifties.

CAPTAIN HUGH ROBERTS OBE 1955

Magwyd Capten Hugh Roberts yn Edern ac enillodd Ysgoloriaeth i Ysgol Ramadeg Botwnnog yn 1908. Ymunodd â'r Clwb Golff yn niwedd yr 1920au.

Cychwynnodd ei yrfa ar y môr fel stiward yn ystafell fwyta'r llongwyr ar Orffennaf 6ed 1910 gyda Llongau Pwll Parc. Perchennog y Cwmni oedd Capten Watkin Williams, Edern a Phenarth. Enillodd Hugh ei diced fel Capten yn 1922.

Capten Hugh Roberts oedd Capten y Llong, M V Athellaird a suddwyd gan dorpido ar Orffennaf 2ail 1940, 600 milltir i'r De Orllewin o 'Land's End'. Treuliodd saith diwrnod mewn bad achub. Cyhoeddwyd ei enw yn y London Gazette ar Hydref 8fed 1940 lle y cymeradwywyd ef am ymddygiad dewr yn y Llynges Fasnachol. Yn ogystal, ef oedd Capten y Llong M V Athelknight a drawyd gan dorpido ar Mai 26ain 1942 yng

THE CAPTAINS - Y CAPTEINIAID

Nghanol Môr yr Iwerydd. Hwyliodd ei fad achub, gyda phum morwr ar hugain ar y bwrdd, am 1,200 o filltiroedd dros 25 diwrnod nes cyrraedd St Bartholomew yn India'r Gorllewin. Ar Ragfyr 22ain, 1942, 'derbyniodd Capten Hugh Roberts yr OBE am wasanaeth arbennig yn y Llong M V Athelknight pan ymosodwyd ar y llong gan y gelyn.' (Gwelir hanes ei fywyd yn gyflawn ar www.rhiw.com)

Graddnod golff isaf Capten Hugh oedd 12 yng Nghlwb Golff Nefyn. Enillodd Gwpan Her Bwcle yn 1955, ei flwyddyn fel Capten y Clwb.

Hugh Roberts was brought up in Edern and won a scholarship to Botwnnog Grammar School in 1908. He joined the Golf Club in the late 1920s. He began his sea-faring career as a Steward in the Officers' Mess on July 6th 1910 with 'Pwll Parc Ships Company' whose owner was Captain Watkin Williams of Edern and Penarth. He gained his Master's ticket in 1922.

Captain Hugh was Master of two vessels which were torpedoed during the Second World War. He was commended for brave conduct and awarded the OBE in 1942. [See www.rhiw.com]

His son G T Robberts, of Arwel, Edern, was Captain in 1980.

Hugh's lowest handicap at Nefyn Golf Club was 12. He won the Buckley Challenge Cup in his year as Captain in 1955.

DA WILLIAMS 1957

Magwyd David Arwel Williams ym Modarborth, gyferbyn â'r Red Garage yn Nefyn cyn symud i Lwyn. Penodwyd DA yn rheolwr ar Fanc y Midland yn Nefyn ac yn rhinwedd ei swydd, fel oedd yn draddodiad yng Nghlwb Golff Nefyn ar y pryd, bu'n Drysorydd y Clwb o 1952 i 1964. Etholwyd ef fel Trysorydd Undeb Golffio Caernarfon a'r Cylch ym mis Medi 1958.

Priododd merch DA â Willie Rees Owen, (Capten y Clwb yn 1953), ac oherwydd llwyddiant Willie Rees ym myd golff, cymerodd DA lawer mwy o ddiddordeb yn y gêm yn dilyn hyn ac fe'i penodwyd yn Gapten y Clwb yn 1957. Yn yr un cyfarfod, pan yr etholwyd ef yn Gapten, pleidleisiwyd i agor y Clwb ar y Sul.

Roedd DA yn ŵr diymhongar gyda gwên ar ei wyneb yn barhaol. Ymddiswyddodd o'r Clwb yn 1964 ac yn niwedd y chwedegau aeth i fyw i Gaerloyw/Gloucester gyda Robert, ei ŵyr, a'i deulu. Roedd teulu yn bwysig iawn i DA ac ymddiddorai hefyd mewn garddio. Byddai'r cwsberis gorau yn Nefyn ganddo!

David Arwel Williams was brought up at Bodarborth, opposite the Red Garage in Nefyn, before the family moved to Llwyn. DA, as he was referred to, was appointed Manager of the Midland Bank in Nefyn and, as was traditional in those days, part of his duty was taking on the task of Treasurer of Nefyn Golf Club (1952-1964). He was also elected Treasurer of the Caernarfonshire & District Golfing Union in September 1958.

DA and Beatrice Williams had a daughter, named Kathleen, who married Willie Rees Owen, Club Captain in 1953. Due to Willie Rees being a renowned golfer, DA took a great deal more interest in golf following the marriage and he was elected Club Captain in 1957. At the same AGM, the Membership voted in favour of Sunday golf for the first time.

One of DA's clubs, a hickory shafted putter, is still being used today by his grandson, Robert Rees Owen, at Freshwater Bay Golf Club on the Isle of Wight.

DA was a very unassuming man who always greeted people with a ready smile He resigned from Nefyn Golf Club in 1964 and in the late 60s he moved to Gloucester to live with Robert's family.

D A Williams (centre) pictured in 1947 with **Left to Right:** *Harry Parry (Captain 1941), Willie Rees Owen (Captain 1953), Annie Williams Gwynfryn (Lady Captain 1933 and 1953) and J Nevin McCurdy (Secretary 1909 - 1911).*

C H BUCKLEY
1958 & 1959

Charles Harold Buckley (Hal) was brought up in Hale, near Manchester and visited Morfa Nefyn on holiday throughout his life. He was involved in the textile industry with Banner Brand, a company which his father, Charles (Club Captain in 1936) had established. Harold Buckley supplied many sets of flags to the Club for the holes on the Course.

As an enthusiastic and competitive single figure handicapped golfer, Harold was keen to get involved with the Golf Club. He served on the Committee for over 25 years and became Captain in 1958. He was Chairman of the Finance Committee for many years. At that time, the golfing year ended in August, but in 1959 it was changed to start and end on Easter Saturday (AGM). Hal thus remained in office for 18 months and his name appears on two consecutive years on the Captains' Board.

Hal's 70th birthday was a family dinner held at the Linksway Hotel. Some of the participants may have had party hangovers the following day, but not Hal – he went out and played in a competition and reduced his handicap. Sadly, he died very suddenly six months later, in January 1982.

Hal won the Tweedale Challenge Cup, the Club's Blue Ribbon competition, on a number of occasions. On one occasion in the sixties, his handicap was temporarily reduced from 9 to 4 after a very good score in the qualifying round of the Tweedale.

PETER H LANE
1960

Peter came to live to Morfa Nefyn when he was 18 months old, living at Noddfa and then Pen y Bryn until the Linksway Hotel was built by his mother in 1936-37. His father was a tall gentleman who worked in the Telephone Relay Station at the original Cecil Hotel. Peter trained

G I Hughes, when responding to his election as Captain at the 1963 AGM, thanked everyone 'for the help he had to reach the Captain's Chair. He was a builder by trade and could put bricks together in a better way than words for delicate speeches. But by the same token, he warned everyone that he was not deaf and dumb!' (sic)

G I always had a great interest in the Club and spent hours helping with transporting tons of soil and tarmac, without claiming a penny in costs. He was a Trustee of the Club for several years and was elected Captain in 1963.

ALF W WHALLEY 1964

Alf Whalley was Chairman of the Greens for many years in the 70s and was responsible for many reconstruction schemes on the Course. He was responsible for planning the back tee on the 12th hole on the Old Course as well as a few other tees. He was a great supporter of Junior Golf at the Club and presented several prizes to the Section.

Alf had spent some years in Canada before returning to Nefyn. He lived with his wife, Rene, at Perth Celyn, Edern, for many years while he was at Nefyn Golf Club. It is believed that he was employed in domestic planning and while at Perth Celyn, he supervised a large extension being built there.

Mrs Rene Whalley was Lady Secretary for a period and Lady Captain in 1962.

CAPTAIN WILL ROBERTS 1965

Ymunodd Capten Will Roberts o Argraig, Edern, â Chlwb Golff Nefyn yng ngwanwyn 1945.

Yn 1937, aeth, yn 16 oed, fel prentis at danceri 'Athel Lines' a graddiodd fel Capten yn 1947, y flwyddyn y priododd â Nan Roberts, Swyddfa Bost, Edern. Arhosodd gydag Athel Lines gan weithio fel peilot yng Nghamlas Suez. Pan dynnodd y DU allan o Suez yn 1954 cyn Argyfwng 1956, dychwelodd Capten Will, fel y cyfeirid ato, adref. Ymunodd â 'Prince Line' lle bu'n gofalu am longau teithwyr, gwaith a roes bleser mawr iddo.

Yn dilyn ei ymddeoliad o'r môr, bu'n Bostfeistr yn Edern ond ni chymerodd at y swydd.

Cafodd Capten Will sawl llwyddiant ym myd golff, yng Nghlwb Nefyn ac mewn sawl Clwb arall. Roedd ymysg nifer dethol iawn o bobl sydd wedi ergydio o gwmpas cwrs Nefyn mewn llai o ergydion na'i oed! Byddai ei gyflwyniadau unigryw wrth dderbyn gwobrau ac wrth annerch Aelodau fel Ysgrifennydd y Clwb yn llawn hiwmor. Roedd yn uchel iawn ei barch gydag Undeb Golff Cymru (WGU) a byddai'n brysur iawn hefyd ym myd golff yr ifanc yng Nghymru.

Cofia T G Gruffydd iddo chwarae yn erbyn Capten Will yng Nghystadleuaeth Bwrw Allan y Senglau yn y nawdegau. Roedd Capten Will yn rhwbio'i ddwylo yn awchus wrth edrych ymlaen at y gêm yma, a theimlodd ar ben ei ddigon pan drawodd ei ail ergyd ar y twll cyntaf i chwe throedfedd o'r twll ac yntau'n derbyn siot gan TG! Fodd bynnag trawodd TG ei ail ergyd ef i'r twll am ddau a methodd Capten Will gyda'i byt. Os bu ceg gam erioed! Byddai Capten Will yn mwynhau ennill cystadleuthau ond byddai hefyd yn colli gydag urddas. Roedd yr un peth yn wir amdano pan fyddai'n trafod ac yn anghytuno ar bynciau ym mhwyllgorau'r Clwb. Ni fyddai'n dal dig at neb, hyd yn oed ar ddiwedd trafodaeth danbaid!

Ar Hydref 20fed 2000, derbyniwyd newyddion trist am farwolaeth Capten Will. Bu'n weithgar ar bob pwyllgor yn y Clwb gan wasanaethu fel Ysgrifennydd (1976-1980), Capten (1965) ac Ymddiriedolwr. Gwahoddwyd ef i fod yn Llywydd y Clwb ond ni wnaeth dderbyn y swydd.

Captain Will Roberts, of Argraig, Edern, joined the Club in the spring of 1945.

In 1937, as a 16 year old, he began his apprenticeship with Athel Lines' tankers and graduated to the rank of Captain in 1947, the same year as he married Nan Roberts, The Post Office, Edern. He remained with Athel Lines and became a pilot in the Suez Canal. With the withdrawal of the UK from Suez in 1954, prior to the Crisis of 1956, Captain Will, as he was affectionately called, returned home. He joined the Prince Line where he was in charge of passenger ships. This pleased him immensely.

After retiring from the sea, he was Postmaster at Edern for a period, a position with which he was not too enamoured!

(Top Right) Receipt of Captain Will's original Entrance Fee and Subscription 21.04.45

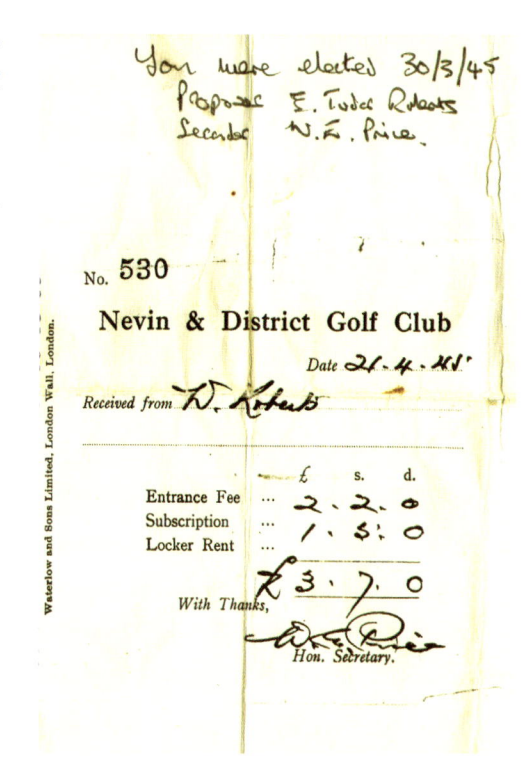

Feb 14th 1985: The Captain (I R Williams) informed the meeting that Capt W Roberts had been elected [as Representative for District 1 – Gwynedd] to the Welsh Golfing Union and all members present tendered their congratulations. [Capt Will continued his representation of Gwynedd for many years.]

THE CAPTAINS - Y CAPTEINIAID

Captain Will was a very successful golfer at Nefyn and several other clubs. He was among a select few at Nefyn who managed to return a score less than their age! His deliveries when receiving prizes were eloquent and humorous, as were his presentations as Secretary. He was highly respected as a Member of the Welsh Golfing Union (now GUW) and was very much involved with Junior Golf in Wales.

Here are some of Capt Will's successes at Nefyn Golf Club: Muriau Cup 1950, Buckley Challenge Cup 1966, Victory Cup 1968 and 1988, Courtenay Lord Cup 1989, Seniors' Trophy 1995, and the ROC Trophy 1998.

T G Gruffydd recalls a match against Capt Will in the Club Singles' Knockout in the 90s. Capt Will was rubbing his hands in anticipation of a good match and when he put his second shot at the first hole six feet away from the pin and being in receipt of a shot, he was ecstatic. However, when TG hit a six iron straight into the hole for a two, Capt Will missed his six footer and was not too pleased! Capt Will enjoyed winning competitions, but in fairness, always lost with good grace. The same was true when he was debating matters and disagreeing in Committee Meetings at the Club. He would never hold a grudge against anyone, even after a very heated exchange!

Captain Will in one of his many roles, this time as Referee for the Tweedale Final in 1980.

On October 20th 2000, the Club was saddened by the announcement of Captain Will's death. He had served on every committee in the Club and held the position of Secretary (1976-1980), Captain and Trustee. He had been invited to be Club President on more than one occasion but for some reason had graciously refused the invitation.

RICHARD WILLIAMS
1966

Magwyd Richard Williams (Dick Porthdinllaen fel ei hadwaenid) yn Fferm Porthdinllaen ac felly bu Richard yn gysylltiedig â'r Clwb o'i blentyndod. Ymunodd â'r Clwb ar ôl y rhyfel yn 1946 a gwasanaethodd ar y Pwyllgor am flynyddoedd fel Cadeirydd y Lawntiau a Chadeirydd y Pwyllgor Gemau a Graddnod.

Bu'n gofalu am Gystadleuthau'r Adran Iau ac ef fyddai'n trefnu Pencampwriaeth Bechgyn Sir Gaernarfon am flynyddoedd maith gyda Dennis Grace, y Pro.

Roedd Dick yn chwaraewr cystadleuol iawn, yn cael mwynhad mawr o chwarae mewn cystadleuaeth ac mewn gemau yn erbyn Aelodau eraill. Ar un achlysur pan oedd Clwb Nefyn yn chwarae yn erbyn Clwb Caernarfon yn y chwedegau, roedd Dick a'i bartner chwe twll i lawr gyda chwech i chwarae ar y Penrhyn.

Yn nodweddiadol iawn o ddygnwch Dick, enillodd ef a'i bartner y chwe twll olaf i wneud y gêm yn gyfartal! Bu'n chwarae oddi ar raddnod o 6 ar un adeg. Mae ei enw ar sawl Bwrdd Anrhydedd yn y Clwb wedi ennill nifer o gwpanau (gweler isod). Yn anffortunus, byddai Dick yn cael cyfnodau o siancio. Ar un achlysur, pan oedd o flaen y grin cyntaf, dechreuodd siancio. Rhyw saith neu wyth ergyd yn ddiweddarach roedd Dick yn yr un lle, yn union wedi taith o amgylch y grin! I oresgyn y diffyg yma, byddai Dick yn tsipio gydag un llaw!

Bu Dick yn gweithio i gwmni Manweb ar hyd ei oes fel trydanwr a byddai'n gwneud gwaith atgyweirio trydanol yn y Clwb yn rheolaidd.

Bu Medi, ei wraig, yn Gapten Adran y Merched yn 1991, tair blynedd cyn marwolaeth Dick yn 1994.

Richard Williams or Dick Porthdinllaen as he was called, was brought up on Porthdinllaen Farm and he was thus involved with the Club from his childhood. He joined the Club in 1946 and served on the Committee for several years as Chairman of Greens and Chairman of Match and Handicap Committees.

He was responsible for the Junior Section's Competitions and he organised the Caernarfonshire Boys' Championship with Dennis Grace, the Pro, for many years.

In 1966, the Club bought the land from the Cefnamwlch Estate and in his acceptance speech on being elected Captain, Dick stated he 'could claim the Captaincy as part of his birthright, having been born and bred on the land in Porthdinllaen.' He then acknowledged that the retiring Captain (Captain Will Roberts), 'being a professional navigator, had sailed the 'Ship of State' successfully round the Porthdinllaen Rocks and we were now embarking on a lifelong cruise as owners of the property, a matter the coming generations should cherish with joy and pride'. Far-reaching words - even to 2007!

Dick was a very competitive golfer and played off a handicap of 6 at one time. He once came back from six down with six to play to level a fourball match against Caernarfon! His name appears several times on the Honours Boards in the Club. His successes include: Muriau Cup 1974, Festival Cup 1954, 1959 and 1961, and the Victory Cup 1955, 1956 and 1958.

Occasionally however, Dick had periods where he had bouts of shanking. On one occasion he began shanking in front of the first green. Seven or eight shots later saw Dick in exactly the same place having completed a full circle of the green! Later he began to chip with one hand only and this seemed to rectify the problem!

An electrician by trade, Dick worked for Manweb all his life and he regularly undertook electrical repairs at the Club. His wife, Medi, was Captain of the Ladies' Section in 1991.

C IAN MURRAY 1967

Charles Ian Murray was the eldest son of Richard Hollins Murray and Elsie Murray. Ian and his wife Molly came to Nefyn in 1948 with Harold and Mary Buckley, originally staying at Sea Breezes on Beach Road before finally joining up at Bwthyn Bridin. When the Buckley household started to enlarge, the Murrays moved to Bro Terfyn.

Ian ran the family Estate Agency practice of 'Stuart Murray & Co' which traded from Bridge Street in Manchester and which migrated to Altrincham during the Second World War. He was joined by his brother Athol and ultimately by his son Stephen. Whilst looking after the interests of clients, the firm also represented the management work of the development/investment companies of the Murray family which are now known as the 'Hollins Murray Group.'

According to his son Stephen, Ian was not a spectacular golfer, although he did play off a single figure handicap. Stephen added he was however excellent at the 19th, an asset which seems to have been passed down in the family. He was a member of the 8 ball which teed off regularly at 9.00am for an uninterrupted round. Among those playing were Hal Buckley, Jack Bingley and Robbie Robinson together with four stout junior caddies.

Ian was Captain at Ringway Golf Club and served the Committee there for many years.

Oct 13th 1967: Notice of Motion: It was resolved to close the Club Parking Ground to others than golfers in the future. (sic)

IVOR E WILLIAMS
1968

Roedd Ivor E Williams, rheolwr banc yn ôl ei alwedigaeth, yn byw yn Henllys, Ffordd yr Ala, Pwllheli, ond preswyliodd am gyfnod ar Lôn Penrhos ym Morfa Nefyn.

Bu Ivor yn cynorthwyo fel Ysgrifennydd yn y Clwb am gyfnod byr ac o dan ei gadeiryddiaeth, dechreuwyd trafodaethau am ymestyniad, gyda tho gwastad arno, i lolfa'r Clwb. Derbyniwyd tendr J Jones, Llanaelhaearn. Ar yr un adeg trefnwyd system wresogi newydd i'r Clwb gyda'r Bwrdd Nwy.

Yng nghyfnod Ivor Williams, chwaraewyd am wobr y Capten yn ystod cyfarfod mis Awst. Dechreuwyd y gystadleuaeth gyda chystadleuaeth fedal i'r dynion gyda'r 8 gorau yn gymwys i chwarae mewn cystadleuaeth bwrw allan.

Pan gyrhaeddodd Ivor Williams y Clwb ar Noson y Cyfarfod Cyffredinol wrth iddo gael ei ethol fel Capten, fe sylweddolodd nad oedd yn gwisgo tei! Felly bu rhaid iddo droi'n ôl o ddrws y Clwb a dychwelyd i Bwllheli i chwilio am dei! Ar ôl y digwyddiad yma, trefnwyd i gael teis sbâr yn y bar ar gyfer Aelodau!

Ivor Williams was a bank manager and lived at Henllys, Ala Road, Pwllheli. He also lived in Lôn Penrhos, Morfa Nefyn, for a while.

He assisted as Club Secretary for a period and under his chairmanship, initial discussions took place regarding a flat roofed extension to the Club Lounge. The tender of J Jones, Llanaelhaearn was accepted for £18,253 in February 1969. At the same time the Captain was able to negotiate a new gas central heating system with the Gas Board.

In Ivor's year, the Captain's Prize Competition was played in his August Meeting. Following a qualifying medal round, the leading eight men would play a match play knockout.

When Ivor arrived at the Club for the Annual General Meeting on the occasion of his being elected as Captain, he realised that he was not wearing a tie and had to return to Pwllheli to fetch one! Since this occurrence, spare ties are always available behind the bar!

CAPTAIN DAN W JONES 1969

The Official Opening of the Clubhouse Lounge Extension in March 1970.
Captain Dan W Jones receiving the Portrait of Brigadier Sir William Wynne-Finch loaned from Captain Charles Wynne-Finch **(second Left)**. Pictured also are Lady Captain, Eve Worrall and Secretary, Owen Roberts. The Portrait was later officially presented to the Club by Captain Charles at the AGM of 1970.

Roedd teulu Capten Dan W Jones yn hanu o ardal Chwilog ond symudodd y teulu i fyw i Dyddyn Llan, Llangybi yn ddiweddarach. Capten Llong oedd Capten Dan, fel yr adwaenid ef, ac uchafbwynt ei yrfa oedd cael ei apwyntio'n harbwrfeisitr ym Mhorthladd Southampton, o ble yr ymddeolodd.

Chwaraewr golff llawchwith oedd Capten Dan. Arferai siglo'r clwb yn hamddenol ac yn bwrpasol iawn yn ôl, cyn dychwelyd y clwb yn nerthol ar gefn y bêl.

Cafodd Capten Dan barch mawr gan yr holl Aelodaeth. Yn rhinwedd ei swydd fel Capten, cafodd y pleser o agor yr estyniad newydd i lolfa'r Clwb ynghyd â'r Llywydd, Capten Charles I E Wynne-Finch yn ystod Dathliad Gŵyl Dewi'r Clwb ar Fawrth 6ed, 1970.

Roedd gwraig Capten Dan yn ferch i Capten Griffith, Glan Beuno, Efailnewydd. Ymfudodd ei ferch i America ac mae un o'i wyresau'n astudio am radd yn Rhydychen ar hyn o bryd.

Roedd Capten Dan yn uchel iawn ei barch yn lleol. Roedd yn un o Sylfaenwyr y Clwb Bach yn Nefyn ynghyd â Chymdeithas Golff Hynafgwyr Llŷn.

Captain Dan W Jones' family were originally from the Chwilog district but later moved to Tyddyn Llan, Llangybi. Dan was a sea-captain and the high point of his career was when he was made Harbour Master of the Port of Southampton, from where he retired.

Captain Dan, as he was called, was a left-handed golfer. He used to have a slow, deliberate backswing, followed by a determined swing and follow-through.

Captain Dan was well respected by all Members. During his Captaincy, he had the pleasure of opening the new extension to the Club Lounge together with the President, Charles I E Wynne-Finch. This Official Opening was during the St David's Dinner on March 6th 1970. The Secretary, Owen Roberts, in describing the preparation for the evening in the Club Minutes, stated, 'The ceremony and Festive Board would be arranged with decorum and propriety!' (sic)

Under his chairmanship, the annual subscriptions were revised, giving consideration to higher joining fees for Away Members.

Thus in 1970:-

Local Joining Fee:
Men: £6	Ladies: £4

Joining Fee (Over 6 miles):
Men: £12	Ladies: £8

Subscription:
Men: £6	Ladies: £4
Juniors: £1	Lockers: 10/-

Captain Dan was held in high esteem in the locality. He was a Founder Member of the Constitutional Club in Nefyn and also of the Llŷn Golf Veterans' Association.

Club Minutes re. Uwch-y-Don (Bottom Car Park)

Mar 14th 1969: The Club delegation had met with the Estate over the Uwch-y-Don Parking Ground and it was agreed to pay £250 p.a. for a lease of 3 yrs subject to the usual conditions...

May 14th 1982: ...the new rent for the Car Park should be £1,000 p.a. over the whole of the next five year period. It was resolved to accept this rent in the final instance but that the secretary (Lt Col R W Parry) should continue his negotiations in the hope that the rent could be reduced to £950 p.a.

Oct 30th 1987: A letter from the Agents of Cefnamwlch Estate suggesting a new rent of £1,250 per annum for the bottom car park [Uwch-y-Don], this rent to be for a further 5 years. It was resolved to accept these terms.

HENRY FITZPATRICK
1970

Henry came to Morfa Nefyn in 1946 with a company from Liverpool who was on contract to J O Jones Builders, the builders of Edern Primary School. It was his employers who introduced Henry to the Golf Club but though he enjoyed his golf, he was more interested in football and captained the Nefyn United Team.

Henry did not play a great deal of golf but was a good Club Member and spent many years on Committee, being Chairman of House for ten years as well as voluntarily providing a great deal of electrical work for the Club. He believed it to be a great honour to be invited to be Captain and he proudly opened the Exhibition Match on Sunday, July 26th, 1970 comprising Dai Rees, Dave Thomas, Bernard Hunt and Peter Alliss. A great deal of money was raised for charity as a result of this Exhibition Match.

HENRY FRAY
1971

Harry, as he was referred to, and his brother Stanley, were brought up in Bolton and moved to Nefyn in 1935 when their father took over the Sportsman Hotel. Having initially been interested in pharmacy, Harry took on an apprenticeship with Manweb. In 1939, he joined the RAF at Preston and progressed to Warrant Officer. At the end of the War in 1945, Harry joined the Navy Fleet Air Arm based in Scotland. Shortly afterwards, he returned to Nefyn and became a salesman with Lever Brothers, finally retiring to Pwllheli.

Harry joined the Club soon after the War, playing golf regularly. He was very competitive, his lowest golf handicap being 8. He has his name on the Club Honours Boards several times. He won the Wynne-Finch Challenge Bowl in 1965, the Muriau Cup and Festival Cup in 1998 and the ROC Trophy during his Captaincy in 1971. He was a valuable member of the House and Competition Committees for a number of years.

On one occasion, having lost his ball over the cliff on the previous hole, Harry took a brand new Dunlop 65 ball out of its black wrapper on the 12th Tee on the Point. Instead of throwing the wrapper into a gorse bush below the tee, Harry inadvertently threw the ball, which was never seen again!

R FRANK EVANS
1972

Frank Evans was brought up in Aigburth, Liverpool. During 1942-43 he was posted to the RAF camp at Penrhos near Pwllheli where he served as a fitter. It was during this wartime service that Frank met his future wife, Enid. At the end of the war and whilst living at Abersoch, he became Post Master at Butlin's Holiday Camp, Penychain, before moving to Nefyn Post Office in 1947.

Very soon after arriving at Nefyn, Frank was proposed as a Member of the Golf Club by D A Williams, (Captain in 1957 and Treasurer of the Club) who was related to Enid. Frank was a social golfer and was very much involved with Clubhouse matters being Chairman of House and Entertainment Officer for many years. He was particularly insistent on a Clubhouse Dress Code.

Frank and Enid were Captain and Lady Captain of the Club in 1972, the first husband and wife to serve together as Captains. Their eldest son, Gwilym, was Captain of Criccieth GC in 1982 and of Porthmadog GC in 1992.

Frank and Enid Evans in 1972 as the Club's first concurrent husband and wife Captains.

WILLIAM R HUGHES
1973

Magwyd Wil (WR fel yr adwaenid ef) yn Edern a dysgodd ei golff cynnar gyda chlybiau pren yn y Gors Wyllt, Edern, ac wrth gadio yn y Golff.

Bu'n gweithio i Gwmni Crosville ar hyd ei oes, fel gyrrwr ac fel peiriannydd. Roedd WR yn gwmni da bob amser a chyfarchai bawb gyda gwên. Priododd ag Anne, athrawes ysgol gynradd a ganwyd mab iddynt o'r enw Gwyn. Bu Gwyn yn chwarae oddi ar 4. Enillodd Bencampwriaeth Bechgyn Gwynedd yn 1964 a bu'n gapten Clwb Golff Baron Hill, Biwmaris. Ef oedd Prifathro Ysgol Pentraeth cyn ei farwolaeth gynnar yn 52 oed yn 1998.

Byddai WR yn achub y blaen ar y golffwyr eraill bob pnawn Sadwrn yng nghwmni Rhys Griffith Garej y Ffôr, John Williams Troed yr Allt ac eraill. Ni fedrai ddioddef chwarae y tu ôl i chwaraewyr eraill, yn enwedig rhai araf! Chwaraewr golff dygn iawn oedd Wil. Roedd ganddo reolaeth arbennig ar ei law dde wrth gadw'r bêl rhag crwydro i'r dde. Byddai bob amser y cyntaf ar y ti i gael gorffen yn fuan ac yn aml iawn byddai'n rhedeg o'r ti gan dynnu ei drol ar ei ôl.

Aelodau eraill a chwaraeai gydag ef oedd H D Jones, Huw Pritchard Tanyfron Edern, ac H T Williams (tad Tecs) Gerddi, Edern oedd yn gweithio ar y cwrs. Yn ddiweddarach byddai'n chwarae gyda Tom Hookes, Bryn Williams (Abersoch) a Tom Griffith, Mairlys, Edern (Tad TG).

Cafodd gryn lwyddiant yn y Clwb gan ennill sawl cwpan. Enillodd Wobr y Capten yn 1963 yn erbyn un o'i ffrindiau pennaf, Tom Griffith, ac eto yn 1966 yn erbyn Evan Hughes. Daeth WR ag anrhydedd i'r Clwb pan enillodd gystadleuaeth Harp - Golffar y Flwyddyn yng Nghlwb St Pierre yn 1970, gan orffen yn ail y flwyddyn ganlynol.

Bu WR yn weithgar ar Bwyllgor y Clwb am flynyddoedd a bu'n mynychu cinio Cyn-Gapteiniaid y Clwb ymhell i'w wythdegau.

WR, as he was referred to, was raised in Edern and worked for the Crosville Bus Company all his life, as a driver and as chief mechanic. He was always good company and greeted people with a beaming smile.

WR would be first off the tee on a Saturday afternoon in the company of Rhys Griffith, John Williams Troed yr Allt and others. He could not tolerate slow players in front of him. He was a very competitive player and regularly put his right hand to good use in averting a slice. Having driven off, he would run off the tee pulling his trolley behind him.

He was very successful, winning several cups at the Club and elsewhere. He won the Captain's Prize in 1963 against one of his best pals from Edern, Tom Griffith (the co-author's father), and again in 1966 against Evan Hughes. WR brought honour to the Club when he won the Harp Golfer of the Year at St Pierre Golf Club, a feat he nearly repeated the following year when he was runner-up.

WR worked tirelessly on the Club Committee for many years and he continued to attend the Past-Captains' Dinner well into his eighties.

CHARLES I E WYNNE-FINCH
1974

Charles Wynne-Finch was brought up on the family's main estate at Voelas, Pentrefoelas. He attended Eton College and served in the Coldstream Guards from 1948-54. On leaving the army, he went to Cirencester Agricultural College and then farmed the estate at Voelas. In 1967, after his marriage to Rosemary Austin, he moved to Cefnamwlch and took responsibility for both family estates. He and Rosemary had three children. The son, David, now farms at both estates following in the family tradition.

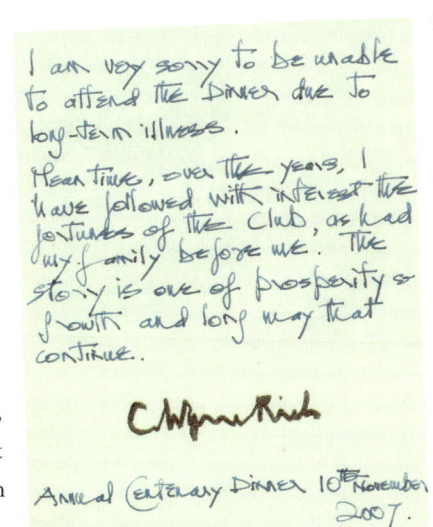

Letter from Captain Charles Wynne-Finch read by the Club Captain, Emyr L Evans at the end of the Centenary Dinner, November 10th 2007.

Captain Charles served on the Agricultural Advisory Committee for Wales and was Chairman of the Gwynedd Division of the Welsh Water Board for ten years. He also served on the Committee for Wales of the National Trust for a considerable number of years.

Charles Wynne-Finch was always interested in developments at the Golf Club. At the AGM of 1966, it was reported that our President, Lady Wynne-Finch was suffering from continued ill-health and the Club was 'fortunate in having the consent of Captain Charles I E Wynne-Finch of Tai'n y Maes, Pentrefoelas, her nephew, to accept Presidency of the Club'.

In 1974, he was elected Captain as well as being Club President, a first for the Club. He went on to hold the Presidency for another ten years before resigning in March 1984 due to pressure of work.

During his Captaincy in 1974, when he chaired all Executive Meetings with purpose, fairness and determination, Captain Charles instigated the possibility of acquiring more land for the Club with the tenant of Porthdinllaen Farm, David Williams. Eventually, in 1975, some 13 acres were released to develop three new holes around Abergeirch.

During the AGM of 1970, Captain Charles Wynne-Finch officially presented the Club with the oil painting of his uncle, the late Brig. Sir William Wynne-Finch. This painting had been kindly loaned by Captain Wynne-Finch for the official opening of the Club in March 1970.

EVAN HUGHES
1975

Ganwyd Evan Hughes yn Nhŷ Clyd, Penrhos, Morfa Nefyn a dechreuodd ei yrfa fel plymar trwy reidio beic i Abersoch yn ddyddiol. Symudodd i Ben Bedw yn ddiweddarach i weithio gyda Chwmni Cammell Laird am ddeng mlynedd. Yno fe gyfarfu â'i wraig. Bu'n chwarae pêl-droed i dîm y Mersey Royals yn Tranmere.

Daeth yn ôl i Ben Llŷn i gyd-weithio â'i frawd G I Hughes (Capten 1963) ar dai'r cyngor am sbel cyn sefydlu ei fusnes plymio ei hun. Bu'n Aelod gweithgar o dîm Sefydliad Brenhinol y Bad Achub ym Mhorthdinllaen am nifer o flynyddoedd.

Ymunodd Evan â Chlwb Golff Nefyn tua 1960, etholwyd ef yn Gapten y Clwb yn 1975, Llywydd o 1996 i 1999 a gwasanaethodd ar y Pwyllgor am flynyddoedd lawer. Yn ystod ei flwyddyn yn Gapten, cwblhawyd pryniant 13 acer o dir ger Abergeirch i greu tri thwll newydd. Cafodd lwyddiant mewn cystadleuaethau yn y Clwb, gan ennill sawl cwpan, fel Cwpan Muriau, Festival, Victory a'r ROC. Cafodd lwyddiant hefyd gydag Enid Evans (Y Post) yng Nghwpan Pedwarawdau Cymysg Wynne-Finch. Bu'n chwarae oddi ar raddnod o 5 ar un cyfnod a'i uchafbwynt oedd cyrraedd Rownd Derfynol Gwobr y Capten yn erbyn W R Hughes yn 1966 pan oedd Richard Williams (Porthdinllaen) yn Gapten. Bu farw Evan Hughes ar ddechrau 2007.

Evan Hughes in the late 70s enjoying a drink with his golfing friend Paddy Mills. Jack Gillow is the Steward in the Bar.

Evan Hughes was born in Tŷ Clyd, Morfa Nefyn and was a plumber by trade. He was employed by Cammell Lairds for ten years and, while in Birkenhead, he played football for the Mersey Royals at Tranmere. He returned to Pen Llŷn to partner his brother G I Hughes (Captain 1963) in building council houses before setting up his own plumbing business. He was a valued working Member of the RNLI Team at Porthdinllaen.

Evan Hughes joined the Golf Club in 1960. He was elected Captain in 1975, President from 1996 to 1999 and served on the Committee for several years.

Evan was a good golfer, playing off a handicap of 5 at one time. He won many cups – the Muriau, the Festival, the Victory and the ROC to mention a few – but he believed the pinnacle of his golfing success was in reaching the Final of the Captain's Prize against WR Hughes in 1966.

RHYS GRIFFITH
1976

Yn dilyn ei briodas gyda Judith Roberts, Argraig, Edern, daeth Rhys yn gyfarwydd â chwarae golff trwy frodyr Judith, Capten Will Roberts a Chapten Hugh Roberts. Ar ôl hyn, byddai Rhys yn gweld 'twll haul' mewn glaw ac eira! Roedd Rhys yn berchen ar swing go anghyffredin, ond serch hyn fe enillodd sawl tlws a chwpan, gan gynnwys Tlws ROC yn 1970 a Thlws Buckley yn 1977. Byddai'n chwarae'n gyson ar brynhawn Sadwrn, fel arfer gyda Chapten Will Roberts, W R Hughes, John Williams neu Tom Griffith.

Treuliodd Rhys nifer o flynyddoedd ar B wyllgor y Clwb ac etholwyd ef yn Gapten yn 1976, pan fu'r haf poethaf ers hydoedd. Cychwynwyd adeiladu tri thwll newydd ger Abergeirch yn ystod y sychder yma.

Following his marriage to Judith Roberts, Argraig, Edern, Rhys was introduced to the game of golf by her brothers, Captain Will and Captain Hugh Roberts. From then on, Rhys was hooked! For him, it never rained on the golf course! He had a very unusual swing but it did not prevent him from winning several competitions, including the ROC Trophy and the Buckley Trophy.

> **Oct 8th 1976:** Regarding the addendum of Senior Members to Rule as remitted from the AGM, Members (Men at 65, Women at 60) of ten years standing and in receipt of the State Retirement Pension may become Senior members of the Club at One-half of the Annual Subscription operative at the time. They shall not be entitled to vote at an Annual General Meeting or an Extraordinary General Meeting. (sic)

Rhys served on the Committee for several years and he was elected Captain in 1976, which was the hottest summer on record! It was during this drought that work began on the three new holes at Abergeirch.

Rhys inherited the Garage at Four Crosses from his father and spent many years running the business before handing over to his son, Gwyn Rhys. He was a valued Justice of the Peace for many years.

From Left to Right: Captain H E Roberts, G T Roberts and Rhys Griffith with daughter Sian in the 1950s.

> **Mar 25th 1978 (AGM):** ...103 Members have taken advantage of this privilege [reduced subscription for senior members - see left]

1977 – 1999

J C KILNER
1977

Cliff Kilner hailed from Lancashire and became a Member the Club in the early 40s. As a small boy he used to holiday in Pwllheli and during his first marriage hired a house for family holidays at Maes-y-Ddôl, which was next to the old bakery in Nefyn. Sadly he became a widower with very small children but then happily met and married Joan, who also had strong Nefyn connections, and following their marriage in 1952, they visited Nefyn frequently.

Whilst living in Bolton, Lancashire he became managing director of his own plant hire firm in Westhoughton. He retired to live in Nefyn permanently in 1981 until his death in 1997 aged 84 years. He had many Welsh friends and acquaintances with whom he met up in the Clubhouse regularly in the early evening for a beer and a chat. The Golf Club was very much a part of his life and he was a keen supporter of the local RNLI.

Cliff was an average golfer and preferred the companionship and the exercise rather than having a strong competitive spirit. He would always leave his golf bag at the top of the hill on the 8th hole with the confidence to take only the putter and an iron down to the 9th tee!

In 2007, Cliff's daughter, Mrs Hilary Keegan, presented a bench in memory of her parents to the Club.

JOHN WILLIAMS
1978

Dechreuodd John Williams, (Joni Troedyrallt, fel ei hadweinid), chwarae golff yn y Gors Wyllt, Edern, fel sawl un arall o'i gyfnod, gyda'i frodyr a'i ffrindiau. Yn nechrau tridegau'r ganrif ddiwethaf byddai'n gadi yn y Golff yn Mhorthdinllaen. Byddai hefyd yn casglu peli mewn mannau fel Ogof Bebyll ac yna'n eu gwerthu'n ôl i'r golffwyr fyddai wedi'u colli!

Ar ôl gadael y fyddin, fe ddaeth yn ôl i Ben Llŷn, yn brifathro i'r Rhiw, ac yn dilyn nifer o brofiadau mewn ysgolion lleol, cafodd ei benodi'n brifathro Ysgol Troedyrallt, Ysgol Cymerau'n ddiweddarach. Fe ymaelododd â Chlwb Golff Nefyn gan chwarae ddwywaith yr wythnos yn yr haf a phob Dydd Sadwrn trwy'r gaeaf. Gostyngwyd ei raddnod o 17 i 13 ar ôl ei sgôr o 80-17-63 (Sgôr Safonol 69) yn Rownd Gyntaf Gwobr y Capten yn 1970. Enillodd Wobr y Capten y flwyddyn honno ac efelychodd ei fab, Geraint, y gamp yn 1976. Yng Nghwpan Buckley yn Awst 1971, gostyngwyd graddnod John ymhellach, o 13 i 9 ar ôl sgôr o 76-13-63.

Bydd ambell i aelod yn cofio Diwrnod Gwobr y Capten yn yr wythdegau, a John erbyn hyn yn ei saithdegau, yn taro 'slice' i ben to'r Clwb ar ei ddreif gyntaf a dal i ddod yn drydydd yn y gystadleuaeth. Bu iddo hefyd dorri llinyn y gar wrth redeg i fyny ochr y deuddegfed twll ar y trwyn. Roedd o'n taeru'r adeg hynny mai Dic Harris oedd wedi ei daro!

John Williams started playing golf, like several others at the time, with his brothers and friends at Gors Wyllt, a marshy area below Ysgol Edern. He frequently caddied at the Golf Club and used to collect golf balls in places like the 'Pot' and then sell them back to their owners!

From Left to Right: John Williams, Captain Will Roberts, Rhys Griffith and W R Hughes at a Past Captains' Dinner at the Golf Club.

On leaving the army, John Williams returned to Llŷn as Headmaster of Ysgol Rhiw and, after a few other headships, was appointed Headmaster of Ysgol Troedyrallt (later Cymerau), in Pwllheli. He joined the Club, playing regularly twice a week and on Saturdays in the winter. His handicap was reduced from 17 to 13 after scoring 80-17-63 (SSS 69) in the Qualifying Round of the Captain's Prize in 1970.

John won the Captain's Prize that year and his son, Geraint repeated the feat in 1976. In the Buckley Trophy in August 1971, John's handicap was further reduced from 13 to 9 after a score of 76-13-63.

Members recall on one Captain's Day, with John by now in his seventies, how he sliced the ball on to the Clubhouse roof with his first shot and still finished third in the Competition. On another occasion, he pulled his hamstring when running up the side of the twelfth hole on the Point and argued vehemently that Richard Harris had hit him with the ball!

ALUN JONES 1979

Ymaelododd Alun Jones â Chlwb Golff Nefyn yn 1972 yn dilyn ei apwyntiad fel Rheolwr Banc y Midland yn Nefyn. Roedd traddodiad yn y cyfnod yma o apwyntio Rheolwr Banc y Midland yn Drysorydd y Clwb. Felly, fe'i hapwyntiwyd yn Drysorydd yn 1972, swydd yr ymgymerodd â hi tan fis Mawrth 1983.

Yn ddiweddarach, symudodd Alun i fod yn rheolwr Banc y Midland ym Mhenygroes ac yn nes ymlaen i swydd rheolwr swyddfa gyda Chwmni Griffith, Williams, Cyfrifwyr Siartredig ym Mhwllheli.

Honnai Alun na fu erioed yn lawer o olffiwr ond byddai'n mwynhau ychydig o dyllau gyda'r nos, o ran adloniant yn fwy na chystadleuaeth!

Etholwyd Alun yn Gapten y Clwb yn 1979, ac yn ei swydd cafodd gryn bleser wrth lywio pwyllgorau a llywyddu cyngherddau yn ei ffordd ddihafal ei hun.

Alun Jones joined Nefyn Golf Club in 1972, following his appointment as Manager of the Midland Bank at Nefyn. The Manager of the Midland Bank was traditionally invited to be Treasurer at the Club and consequently, Alun was appointed Treasurer at the AGM of 1972, a post he held until March 1983.

Later on, he moved to be Manager at the Midland Bank in Penygroes and subsequently as Office Manager at Griffith, Williams & Co, Chartered Accountants, Pwllheli.

Alun claims that he was never much of a golfer, but he did enjoy playing a few holes in the evening for entertainment rather than competition!

He was elected Captain of the Club in 1979, a role from which he derived much pleasure particularly in steering various committees and presiding over Club social functions in his own inimitable way.

G T ROBERTS 1980

Dilynodd Griff Roberts ei dad fel Capten y Clwb ac mae'n gefnder i ddau Gapten enwog arall, sef Capten Will Roberts a Chapten Hugh E Roberts. Daeth Griff Arwel, fel y'i hadwaenid, i gysylltiad â Chlwb Golff Nefyn gyntaf fel cadi yn blentyn tair ar ddeg oed, ychydig ar ôl yr Ail Ryfel Byd. Ymunodd â'r Clwb fel Aelod Iau yn 1947.

Cwblhaodd Griff gwrs fferylliaeth yn 1955 a threuliodd ei yrfa gyfan fel Rheolwr Fferyllfa gyda Boots, y Fferyllwyr. Treuliodd 29 o'r blynyddoedd hyn gyda Boots yng Nghaernarfon.

Bu'n chwarae golff oddi ar raddnod o 5 am gyfnod ond ei raddnod arferol am gyfnod hir oedd 8/9. Mae'n awr yn chwarae oddi ar 18, canlyniad bod mewn damwain car ddifrifol. Bu Griff yn fuddugol yng Nghwpan Victory yn 1951 a Chwpan Her Tweedale yn 1958.

Treuliodd sawl blwyddyn ar bwyllgorau'r Clwb. Etholwyd ef yn Gapten yn 1980 ac ef oedd Llywydd y Clwb yn y cyfnod 1999-2002. Ar hyn o bryd, mae'n un o Ymddiriedolwyr y Clwb.

Griff followed his father, Captain Hugh Roberts (1955), as Captain of Nefyn Golf Club and is a cousin of two other famous Nefyn Club Captains, Captain Will Roberts and Captain Hugh E Roberts.

From Left to Right: Captain Hugh Roberts (Father of G T Roberts), Rhys Griffith, John Williams (Troed yr Allt, Pwllheli) and Captain Jack Roberts, Argraig, (Brother of Captain Hugh Roberts and father of Captain Will Roberts and Captain H E Roberts) at the 1st Tee in the late 50s.

Griff's first association with Nefyn Golf Club was as a thirteen year old caddie just after the Second World War. He joined as a Junior Member in 1947.

He qualified as a pharmacist in 1955 and throughout his career he was employed by Boots, the Chemist. He was Manager of their Caernarfon Branch for 29 years.

His lowest golfing handicap was 5 but his avarage was 8/9. He now plays off 18, having suffered a serious road accident. Griff won the Victory Cup in 1951 and the Tweedale Challenge Cup in 1958.

Griff spent many years on Club committees and was elected Captain in 1980. He was Club President from 1999 - 2002 and is currently one of the Club Trustees.

RICHARD EDGAR JONES
1981

Magwyd Dic Ed, fel yr adwaenid ef, a'i unig chwaer yn Nefyn. Yn dilyn cyfnod yn gwneud ei Wasanaeth Cenedlaethol yng Nghaerloyw, aeth Richard i'r Coleg i hyfforddi fel athro.

Priododd Richard a Helen Edgar yn 1953. Yn yr un flwyddyn fe'i penodwyd yn Bennaeth yr Adran Ffiseg yn Ysgol Ramadeg Pwllheli. Yn nes ymlaen fe'i apwyntiwyd ef yn Ddirprwy Brifathro. Treuliodd ddeng mlynedd ar hugain yn y byd addysg ym Mhwllheli.

Cychwynodd cysylltiad Richard â'r Clwb trwy Owen Roberts oedd yn Brifathro ar Helen, ei wraig, yn Ysgol Nefyn. Ymunodd Richard a Helen â'r Clwb ar Fehefin 6ed 1962.

Roedd Richard yn olffiwr da, ond heb fod yn or-ddisglair, ei raddnod gorau fu 14. Arferai chwarae golff ym mhob tywydd, ac yr oedd ganddo nifer o ffrindiau - Cymry pybyr- yn gwmni iddo. Mae'r 'criw' o Gymry hyn yn dal ati o hyd. Ymdrechodd Richard i Gymreigeiddio'r Clwb - ymdrech galed iawn pan oedd ambell Gymro Cymraeg yn parhau i deimlo mai Saesneg oedd 'iaith iawn i'r Clwb'.

Cafodd Richard a Helen oriau o bleser yn chwarae golff, a byddent yn cefnogi pob prif achlysur yn y Clwb. Bu Helen yn Gapten Adran y Merched yn 1974. Etholwyd Richard yn Gapten y Clwb yn 1981 ac ef oedd Llywydd y Clwb o 2002 hyd ei farwolaeth yn 2004.

Dic Ed, as he was referred to, was brought up in Nefyn. Following a period of national service in Gloucester, Richard undertook a teacher's training course. He was Head of Physics at Pwllheli Grammar School and later promoted to Deputy Head at the School.

Richard's link with Nefyn Golf Club started through Owen Roberts, who was his wife's Headmaster at Ysgol Nefyn. Richard was a respectable golfer, who maintained he did not achieve great heights. His lowest handicap was 14. He would play in all weathers and he had a regular circle of Welsh friends during his entire golfing period – a circle which still exists and regularly faces the elements!

Richard was elected Captain in 1981 and President from 2002 till his death in 2004. He worked hard to have equal rights for the Welsh language at the Club, but came across obstacles when certain fellow countrymen insisted that 'the Club's language should be English'!

Richard and his wife, Helen, had many hours of pleasure playing golf and they always supported every main function at the Club.

Helen Edgar Jones became Lady Captain in 1974.

LAURENCE A BARBET
1982

Laurence Alan Barbet always described himself as a lucky man. Of thirty eight who joined the Royal Marines together, he was one of only three survivors. He was diligent, dedicated and charismatic, a host whose parties were remembered by his guests for decades afterwards.

First ever Pro-Am held at the Club in September 1982, organised by the Captain, Laurence Barbet. Here Laurence is seen with the Club President, Captain Charles Wynne-Finch presenting the Best Gross Prize (69) to T Gareth Gruffydd.

THE CAPTAINS - Y CAPTEINIAID

He was a successful Chester Estate Agent who took up golf in his forties. Although married with nine children and perennial putting problems, he managed to get down to a nine handicap!

He always maintained that he chose to retire to Morfa Nefyn because he had never seen so many octogenarian golfers playing anywhere else and he looked forward to joining them.

Laurence was a popular, larger than life character. His love of the Club, the Course and Llŷn made for a very happy retirement, crowned by being made Captain, one of the proudest events of his life. Many remember the 'Snooker Supremo' for his meticulous organisation of snooker competitions.

Robin picks up some putting tips from a Junior in the mid 90s.

LT COL ROBIN W PARRY
1983

Robin was educated at Towyn School, Merionethshire, and after graduating in Law from Liverpool University and completing his Articles at Chester, he joined the Legal Services of the Army to do his National Service. He was promoted to Lieutenant Colonel and remained in the Army until his retirement to Morfa Nefyn in 1980. He and his wife, Sheila, ran the Cecil Court Hotel for a little while. In Robin's year as Captain, the incumbent stewards (Mr and Mrs Tyrrell) resigned their position and the catering for the North Wales Alliance Meeting at Nefyn was taken on by Robin and Sheila. Therefore, while he was Captain and Secretary, he took on the mantle of Caterer as well!

Robin was appointed Honorary Secretary in March 1980 and remained in position until his retirement in April 1994. He was then made a Life Member of the Club.

In 1983, Robin was elected Captain of the Club following a strong family tradition and being the third generation of his family to captain the Club. (His father, Captain Will Parry had been Captain in 1940 and his grandfather, Captain WJ Parry before him in 1935). So unusual was the fact that three generations had become Captains of the same golf club, that it prompted The Royal and Ancient Golf Club of St Andrews to write personally to Robin to comment on the feat, saying how very rare it was to find such a family tradition within the one club.

Robin played off 5 handicap for a period and continued to play off single figures into his seventies. He was very competitive but, as was his nature, he had a short fuse on occasions, and would often dance and shout after missing a short putt!

In the Club Minutes of April 1997, 'Lt Col R W Parry appealed against a recent reduction in his handicap. It was resolved that there was no right of appeal and that the decision should stand. Lt. Col Parry (who was a Member of the Match & Handicap Committee) stated that he was still unhappy and that he would take the matter up with the R & A!' A month later, 'Lt Col R W Parry informed the meeting that he did not intend to take the matter of his reduction in handicap any further despite still feeling that he had been the victim of an injustice'. [Could this have been the only instance of Robin losing his case?]

When the 'swindle' was introduced to the Gent's Section in the 70s by Peter Littlewood, Robin introduced 'gimmies' which originally were a putter handle length, but soon developed to be a dustbin lid width because of his fear of missing short putts! His putting let him down so much that he eventually decided to putt with the 'broom handle' putter.

However, Robin had a great deal of success at Nefyn and at Vicars Cross, Chester, where he was a former Member. His name appears on the Honours Boards at Nefyn in the following competitions: Festval Cup 1979, Wynne-Finch Challenge Cup 1984, Cynfelin Jones Trophy 1987 and 1988, Muriau Cup 1992 and Winter League 1996.

In April 2004, Robin was elected President of the Club and remained in post until his death in February 2006. The Parry family suffered a further loss when Robin and Sheila's elder daughter, Sian died at 49, in the September of the same year.

Many people will recall an incident or have a tale to tell about their relationship with Robin. He was extremely popular, had a dry sense of humour and was profoundly sincere. He would fight strongly for what he believed and this was shown in the way he dealt with his cruel illness, refusing to give in until the very end.

In the Service of Thanksgiving for his Life held in February, 2006, St David's Church at Nefyn was full to capacity showing the affection people held for Robin. He undoubtedly had been a firm and charismatic pillar of the Golf Club.

Robin lights up for the last time before smoking was banned at Public Meetings in the Clubhouse.

JAMES P BENTLEY
1984

James Pemberton Bentley was brought up in Blackburn and attended Clitheroe Grammar School. Jim left school at 16 years of age and took an apprenticeship with a tool company. He joined the RAF Voluntary Reserve in 1942 and went on to join the Scottish Regiment, the Black Watch, where he served his time as a PT instructor for three years.

Upon demob. Jim took up his trade as a tool maker but found it difficult to settle down to civilian life and eventually joined the family business of running a hotel.

Jim's mother and her sister bought the Nanhoron Arms Hotel around 1950 and Jim came to Nefyn to help them and worked in the 'Nan' for 12 years. It was at this time that he took an interest in the Golf Club. He received lessons from Dennis Grace and Jim attained a single figure golfing

Captain Ian Cooper with President, Jim Bentley at the Annual Prize Presentation Evening, 2006.

handicap, playing off 5 for a while. He won the Wynne-Finch Challenge Cup in 1976 and the Festival Cup in 1996. During Jim's earlier days at the Club, he served on several committees and held the posts of Chairman of Greens and Chairman of House. He was elected Captain of the Club in 1984 and President in 2006.

Jim was also a long serving member of the RNLI Crew at Porthdinllaen. His varied duties were First Aid, Signal Man, Wireless Operator and Radar Operator. While serving in the RAF, Jim had studied navigation and was able to apply this knowledge during his 30 years with the RNLI.

At the tender age of 81, Jim married Rhiannon, (Old Post, Nefyn) in May 2007. Both Jim and Rhiannon had been widowed and everyone was delighted that they found happiness again in each other. The reception in the Woodlands Hall was attended by a great number of people all echoing the very best of wishes to this popular young couple! Jim and Rhiannon have very generously provided a new Presidents' Board to the Club in the Centenary Year.

I R WILLIAMS
1985

Magwyd Ioi ym Motwnnog, yr hynaf o naw o blant ac yn un o efeilliaid. Nid yw Ioi wedi symud llawer o'i filltir sgwâr ar wahân i ymweliadau a Chaerdydd i weld y werin yn chwarae rygbi!

Cychwynnodd Ioi weithio fel clerc a chyfrifydd gyda Billy Vaughan Williams ym Mhwllheli yn 1962 gan symud i Adeiladwyr Gwynedd yn 1966. Arhosodd ym maes cyflenwyr adeiladu gyda Jewson tan ei ymddeoliad.

Club President, Ioi Williams, is congratulated by Gordon Smith, Captain of the Eryri Past Captains' Association, on winning the EPCA Individual Medal at Nefyn in September 2007

Dechreuodd ymddiddori mewn golff yn y chwedegau pan fyddai'n ymweld â'r cwrs ar fore Sul gydag Eric Wilson o Westy'r Penrhyn Arms yn Sarn, gan ymuno a'r Clwb yn 1966-67. Cyfeillgarwch yw'r elfen bwysicaf wrth chwarae'r gêm i Ioi er ei fod wedi ennill ambell i brif dlws yn y Clwb. Bu'n chwarae oddi ar 5 ar un cyfnod, yn dilyn sisyrniad reit dda gan Stan Cresswell, Ysgrifennydd y Gemau.

Ioi oedd yn gyfrifol am gael Adran y Merched a'r Adran Iau i chwarae yn Nhlws Cynfelin Jones am y tro cyntaf. Yn 1985 pan etholwyd ef yn Gapten, penderfynodd Ioi gynnal Diwrnod y Capten am y tro cyntaf. Cyn hyn fe chwaraewyd am Wobr y Capten mewn cystadleuaeth bwrw allan oedd yn parhau am wythnos gyfan. Yn ddiweddar, pan ei etholwyd yn Llywydd, cyflwynodd Ddiwrnod y Llywydd ym mlwyddyn canmlwyddiant y Clwb, arferiad mae Ioi yn hyderu wnaiff barhau yn y dyfodol.

Mae Ioi wedi bod ar Bwyllgor y Clwb ers 1976, ar wahân i gyfnod byr o chwe mis. Yn ystod y cyfnod yma mae wedi cadeirio sawl is-bwyllgor, bu'n Drysorydd o 1984-1987 ac ef a benodwyd yn Llywydd y Clwb ym Mlwyddyn ein Canmlwyddiant.

The eldest of nine children, and one of twins, Ioi was born in Botwnnog and has not wandered far from his native locality – apart from the occasional visit to Cardiff to see Wales playing rugby!

Having started work as a clerk and accountant with Billy Vaughan Williams in Pwllheli, Ioi moved into the building trade and was Manager of Jewsons in Pwllheli up to his retirement. He joined the Club in 1966-67 and although he has won several trophies, he is not that competitive, preferring the companionship and friendship the game offers rather than winning prizes. Even so, he once played off a handicap of 5!

Ioi Williams with Winners Alex Brown (40pts) and Christine Smith (39pts) on his President's Day, September 2007.

With the exception of a mere six months, Ioi has served on the Executive Committee of the Club since 1976 and has chaired many Sub-Committees. He was Treasurer of the Club from 1984 to 1987 and was elected President in our Centenary Year.

It was Ioi's proposal that saw the Cynfelin Jones' Trophy being opened to 'all Adult Members and Special Category Juniors'. Ladies thus were allowed to play for the first time in one of the Club's major trophies! During his year of Captaincy, in 1985, the Captain's Prize was changed to be played in one day – the Captain's Day – and the Competition became a single medal round.

As President of the Club, Ioi introduced the President's Day in September 2007, an event he hopes will continue and become a feature of our golfing year.

GRESHAM T OWEN
1986

Brodor o Nefyn yw Gresh, fel y'i hadwaenir, ac ymunodd â Chlwb Nefyn yn ei ugeiniau cynnar. Cafodd ei addysg yn Ysgol Ramadeg Pwllheli cyn dilyn cwrs yn Lerpwl fel syrfëwr meintiau. Apwyntiwyd ef i weithio gyda Wakeman & Partners yng Nghaernarfon cyn dechrau busnes ei hun fel pensaer a syfëwr meintiau.

Ymunodd Gresh â'r Clwb ar Ionawr 1af 1966 a chydiodd y gêm ynddo'n gyflym iawn. Mae wedi cynorthwyo'r Clwb gyda sawl cynllun adeiladu ac ef a fu'n gyfrifol am gynllunio'r estyniad lle mae'r ystafell snwcer heddiw.

Bu'n Gadeirydd Pwyllgor y Lawntiau am gyfnod oddeutu pymtheng mlynedd yn y saithdegau a'r wythdegau. Yn ystod y cyfnod yma, bu'n weithgar iawn gyda Capten Will Roberts yn trafod pryniant tir gydag Ystâd Cefnamwlch a datblygiad tri thwll newydd ger Abergeirch. Etholwyd ef yn Gapten yn 1986 ac yn dilyn ei flwyddyn fel Is-Lywydd, ymddeolodd Gresh o Bwyllgor y Clwb yn 1988.

Anrhydeddwyd Gresh yn ddiweddar pan gafodd ei enwebu i fod yn Llywydd y Clwb ar ddiwedd blwyddyn ein Canmlwyddiant.

Gresh was brought up in Nefyn and joined the Golf Club in his early twenties. He was educated at Pwllheli Grammar School before following a Course at Liverpool as a Quantity Surveyor. He was appointed to work with Wakeman & Partners at Caernarfon before starting his own business as an Architect and Quantity Surveyor.

He joined the Golf Club on January 1st 1966 and progressed rapidly as a golfer. He has assisted the Club with several building plans and he was responsible for planning the extension which houses the snooker room.

He chaired the Greens' Committee for a period of around fifteen years in the 70s and 80s. During this period, with the assistance of Captain Will Roberts, he was active in discussions with the Estate regarding the purchase of land and the development of three new holes at Abergeirch. He was elected Captain in 1986 and was nominated to be President at the AGM of 2008.

STANLEY R CRESSWELL 1987

Stan was born in Walsall on 24th June 1921. Having been educated at the Queen Mary's Grammar School, Stan enlisted in the Royal Air Force as a Boy Apprentice (one of Trenchard's 'Little Brats'), on the 38th Entry at RAF Halton in Sept 1938. After completing his 2 year training in engines, he saw service in the UK and numerous far flung lands such as Singapore, Java, Australia & Palestine.

March 1952 saw him leave the Royal Air Force and join the family business of Criterion Stampings in Willenhall and within ten years, Stan had become the Managing Director.

He retired in 1982 and took up permanent residence in Morfa Nefyn. Soon after retiring he decided, along with Richard Kim, Ken Fitzpatrick, Gresham T Owen and Brian Owens, to sail the 33 foot yacht Donnabella 3208 miles, over 5 weeks, to the Azores and back again! Some achievement!

Stan's first ties with the Club were through his family's annual holidays, from the age of 3 weeks old! He recalls first swinging a club during the August fortnight's Junior Competitions of 1936 but showed no real interest in the game.

In 1968, however, aged 47, Stan took up golf with his great friend Jim Ashwell at Great Barr GC just outside Walsall and later at Druid's Heath

Golf Club. He joined Nefyn Golf Club the following year. Later, Stan's wife Pam, daughter Hazel and son Paul, joined the Club, Pam being at one time Lady Secretary. Stan and Pam were wonderful hosts for several thirsty and hungry members of the Club on Saturday evenings (and Sunday mornings!) at their 'Hellfire Club'.

Stan was a good golfer, a keen competitor and achieved a 7 handicap. His many successes include the Courtenay Lord Cup in 1981, the Barbet Salver in 1985 and the Seniors' Scratch Trophy in 1987. In 1983, son Paul won the coveted Tweedale Challenge Cup and in his presentation speech mentioned that he thought 'my Dad is past it'! 'Dad' rose to the challenge and the following year, much to his delight, Stan won the Tweedale himself!

Stan's best round of all time was in a friendly fourball one Sunday morning in the 70s when he returned a gross 71 (with a 7 on the 17th) on the Old Course. Although he remembers the score, he cannot remember much about the celebrations that particular Sunday afternoon!

R M WILLIAMS 1988

Magwyd Robin Moi, fel y'i hadwaenid, yn 9 Pistyll Terrace, Pistyll yn un o saith o blant. Erbyn hyn, dim ond tri sy'n dal yn fyw ac mae Robin yn byw yn Abererch ers 53 o flynyddoedd.

Dechreuodd Robin weithio yn bedair ar ddeg oed yng Ngbamp Cefleisiog lle y byddai'n symud polion dur a gosod ynysyddion. Yn nes ymlaen dilynodd brentisiaeth gosod briciau gyda Chwmni John Owen Jones a dechreuodd gwmni adeiladu ei hun yn 1958. Bu'r cwmni'n bodoli hyd 1985 ac ar un adeg roedd 35 o weithwyr ar y llyfrau.

(Right) *Captain Robin Moi presents his Lady Captain, Anne Thomas, with a bouquet of flowers on her Lady Captain's Day.*

Dechreuodd Robin chwarae golff yn y chwedegau a bu'n cyd-chwarae'n rheolaidd gyda G I Jones, Capten 1992 (ei ffrind pennaf), Jim Bentley, Rhys Griffith ac Evan Hughes. Bu'n chwarae oddi ar raddnod o 9 am sbel ond am y mwyafrif o'i amser byddai'n chwarae oddi ar 12 neu 13. Uchafbwynt aelodaeth Robin oedd cael ei ethol yn Gapten y Clwb yn 1988.

Mae Robin yn dal i ymweld â'r Clwb, fel arfer ar brynhawn Mercher pan fydd yn chwarae snwcer gyda Cledwyn Davies.

Robin, one of seven children, was brought up in 9 Pistyll Terrace, Pistyll, but has lived in Abererch for the past 53 years. He began working as a fourteen year old in the Cefleisiog Camp (between the Bryncynan Inn and the village of Dinas) where he assisted with moving steel poles and installing insulators. Later, he completed an apprenticeship as a bricklayer with John Owen Jones, Builders, before setting up his own building business in 1958. His Company existed until 1985, with as many as 35 workers employed at one stage.

Robin started playing golf in the 60s, and he regularly partnered G I Jones, Captain (1992) and his best pal (they lived next door to one another). Among his other playing partners were Jim Bentley, Rhys Griffith and Evan Hughes. He played off 9 at one stage, but for the majority of his golfing career, he played off 12 or 13. The highlight of Robin's association with Nefyn Golf Club was being elected Captain in 1988.

H D JONES
1989

Ganwyd Hugh D Jones (HD fel ei adwaenir) yn un o ddau frawd ym Mhenbedw ond symudodd y teulu yn ôl i Ben Llŷn pan oedd HD yn ifanc iawn. Ysgolfeistr oedd Hugh yn ôl ei alwedigaeth a bu'n dysgu yn Birmingham cyn symud i Llangybi fel Prifathro yn 1958. Bu'n byw yn Nhŷ'r Ysgol yn Llangybi trwy gydol ei gyfnod fel Prifathro tan 1983, pan ymddeolodd a symud yn ôl i'w gartref ym Morfa Nefyn.

Mae Jane, ei wraig, yn hanu o Edern ac mae ganddi gysylltiadau teuluol â Phorthdinllaen, Bryniau a Hirdre Uchaf. Ganwyd dwy ferch i Hugh a Jane, sef, Gwenda ac Eirian. Mae Hugh yn gapelwr selog ac yn Flaenor yng Nghapel Moreia, Morfa Nefyn.

Ymaelododd Hugh â Chlwb Golff Nefyn yn 1948. Nid yw'n proffesu i fod yn fawr o olffiwr ond mae wedi mwynhau'r gwmnïaeth oedd yn gysylltiedig â'r gêm. Apwyntiwyd ef yn Drysorydd y Clwb yn 1987, swydd y gweithiodd yn ddygn arni am bedair blynedd ar bymtheg. Cafodd bleser mawr o gael ei ethol yn Gapten yn 1989, ac yn 2006, pan ymddeolodd o'i swydd fel Trysorydd yn 86 mlwydd oed, etholwyd ef yn Aelod Oes o'r Clwb - anrhydedd oedd yn hollol addas a haeddiannol.

Edrychwch ar y Bennod 'Dwi'n cofio...' am fwy o hanes HD yng Nghlwb Golff Nefyn.

Hugh D Jones, affectionately known as HD, one of two brothers, was born in Birkenhead but his family moved back to Llŷn when he was very young. He was a schoolmaster by profession and taught at Birmingham before moving to Llangybi as Headmaster in 1958. He lived in the School House at Llangybi throughout his tenure as Headmaster until 1983, when he retired and moved back to the family home in Morfa Nefyn.

Jane, HD's wife, hails from Edern and they have two daughters, Gwenda and Eirian. Hugh is a fervent chapel goer at Capel Moriah in Morfa where he is a Deacon.

Hugh became a member of the Golf Club in 1948. He has no claim in the golfing field but always enjoys his golf and the socialising that goes with it. He was appointed Treasurer in April 1987, a position he held for 19 years. He was delighted at being elected Captain in 1989 and in 2006, when he retired, aged 86, from the position of Treasurer, HD was made a Life Member of the Club – an honour which was truly befitting and well deserved.

For further insight into HD's life at the Club, please refer to the Chapter entitled 'I remember...'.

Dyfed Parry Thomas receives the Captain's Prize from HD in the Summer Meeting of 1989.

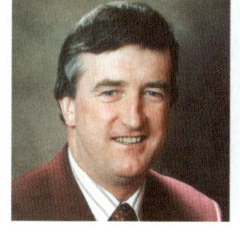

T G GRUFFYDD
1990

Magwyd 'TG' yn Nhan y Fron, Lôn Llan, Edern, ac wedi symud i Mairlys ger y Groesffordd, mynychodd Ysgol Edern pan agorwyd yr Ysgol Newydd yn 1950. Ei Brifathro cyntaf oedd Ellis Tudur Roberts, Capten y Clwb yn 1946. Yn dilyn cyfnod yn Ysgol Botwnnog, treuliodd dair blynedd yn y 'Normal' ym Mangor yn hyfforddi fel athro a bu'n Bennaeth Addysg Gorfforol yn Wallasey a Chaernarfon cyn dychwelyd i'w hen Ysgol ym Motwnnog. Yn ystod ei gyfnod yno, bu'n dilyn cwrs Addysg Arbennig yng Ngholeg Caer, lle y cyfarfu â'i ddarpar wraig, Shan. Priodwyd y ddau yn 1979 gan fyw yn Yr Wyddgrug a bu TG yn gweithio i'r Gwasanaeth Addysg Arbennig yng Nghlwyd tan ei ymddeoliad cynnar yn 1997. Mae eu mab, Dafydd, yn ddylunydd graffeg ac ef sydd wedi bod yn gyfrifol am ddylunio a chynhyrchu'r llyfr yma.

Symudodd Gareth a Shan yn ôl i Ben Llŷn yn Chwefror 2007 ac erbyn hyn maent wedi ymgartrefu yn Wern y Wylan ger y Clwb Golff. Mae Gareth yn parhau i weithio fel cyfieithydd rhan amser tra bo Shan, nid yn unig yn Ysgrifennydd Adran y Merched yn y Clwb ac yn cadw trefn ar Gystadleuthau'r Merched, ond hefyd yn weithgar gyda'i cherddoriaeth.

Ar wahân i chwarae pêl-droed, ei brif ddiddordeb ers dyddiau cynnar oedd chwarae golff a rheilffyrdd (roedd ei dad yn orsaf feistr ar Reilffordd Arfordir y Cambrian). Fel sawl un arall, dechreuodd yn y Golff trwy gadio er mwyn hel arian i brynu clybiau. Bu'n ffortunus iawn o gael cyd-chwarae â charfan gref, gystadleuol yn y Clwb o dan adain Dennis Grace, y Pro yn y pumdegau hwyr a'r chwedegau. Ymysg ei gyd chwaraewyr oedd William Lloyd Griffith, Gwyn Hughes, Gareth Wyn Jones, Eurwyn Evans, Moi Parri, Paul Smart, Merfyn Lloyd, John Roberts Gerallt (Nefyn), Roy Portlock ac yn ddiweddarach, Gresham Owen.

Ymysg ei lwyddiannau fel Aelod Iau: Gostwng ei raddnod o 30 i 9 dros chwe wythnos o wyliau haf yn 1962; ennill Cwpan Courtenay Lord dair blynedd yn olynol; Cydradd gyntaf gyda G Bullen (North Wales) ym Mhencampwriaeth Bechgyn Sir Gaernarfon yn Nefyn yn 1963; Pencampwr Bechgyn Gogledd Cymru (Tlws W E Roberts) yng Nghonwy yn 1963; Cynrychioli Tîm Bechgyn Gogledd Cymru 1962-64.

Ymysg ei lwyddiannau fel aelod llawn yn Nefyn: Ennill nifer o gwpanau a llwyau; Pencampwriaeth y Clwb 17 gwaith rhwng 1969 a 1996; Cwpan Her Tweedale chwe gwaith; Gwobr y Capten ddwywaith; Record y Cwrs deirgwaith; 66 yn 1971 ar y Cwrs Gwreiddiol (Sgôr Safonol - 69); 64 yn 1974 eto ar y cwrs gwreiddiol (Sgôr Safonol - 69) a 67 yn 1977 ar yr Hen Gwrs gan gynnwys tyllau newydd ger Abergeirch (Sgôr Safonol - 71). Bu'n chwarae oddi ar 'Scratch' am gyfnodau rhwng 1976 ac 1981.

Ymysg llwyddiannau TG oddi cartref: Record cwrs Port (67) yn 1977; Prif Fedal Harrison yng Nghlwb Wallasey yn 1972; Pencampwriaeth Clwb Pwllheli yn 1975; Nifer o gwpanau yn Padeswood a Bwcle yn yr wythdegau; Tlws Corson i ardal Gogledd Orllewin Prydain ym Mhrestatyn yn 1976; Tarian Ashburnham (Undeb Golff Cymru) gydag Aled Rees (Cricieth) ym Mhrestatyn; cynrychioli Tim Gogledd Cymru ar sawl achlysur, cynrychioli Tim Sir Gaernarfon a Fflint rhwng 1969 a 1990 gydag un cyfnod o dair blynedd heb golli gêm yn y senglau a Phencampwr Sir y Fflint yng Nghlwb Rhuddlan yn 1982.

Bu'n gwasanaethu ar Bwyllgor y Clwb o 1973 hyd 2007 gydag ychydig o flynyddoedd gwag ar y daith. Bu'n Gadeirydd y Pwyllgor Gemau a Graddnod am ddau gyfnod ac uchafbwynt ei amser yn y Clwb oedd ei benodiad fel Capten yn 1990 a chydweithio gyda Shan, ei wraig, i gwblhau'r hanes yma am Glwb Golff Nefyn.

Ym mlwyddyn ei Gapteiniaeth, cyflwynodd TG a Chapten Adran y Merched, Carys W Jones, gloch y Capteiniaid i'r Clwb. Mae'r gloch yn crogi yn lolfa'r Clwb a chaiff ei defnyddio i ddistewi'r dorf cyn anerchiad y Capteiniaid!

Course Record (Original Course) (64) in 1974 in the Festival Cup and First Round of the Club Championship. TG went on to score 68 in the second round and thereby won the Club Championship with a total score of 132 (6 under Par).

Ers 2002, bu TG yn weithgar yn cyfieithu materion a hysbysebion y Clwb o'r Saesneg i'r Gymraeg er mwyn bodloni polisi dwyieithog y Clwb. Mae'n ymddiddori mewn trenau stêm a bydd yn treulio tipyn o'i amser hamdden yn adeiladu a chynllunio lein fach yn ei gartref. Mae'n gefnogwr pybyr o Glwb Pêl-droed Lerpwl ac ymysg ei ddiddordebau eraill mae reidio beic a mynd â'r cŵn am dro efo Shan.

Ym mlwyddyn ein canmlwyddiant, dechreuodd TG dim snwcer yn y Clwb gan gymryd rhan yn Adran 3 Cynghrair Snwcer Llŷn. Mae'r tîm yn llwyddiannus a hyd at Ionawr 2008, mae nhw'n dal ar frig y Gynghrair. Aelodau cyson y tîm snwcer yw Pat McAteer, Ian Hamilton, Alan Brumby, Bobby Jones, H Eirwyn Jones a TG. 'Roedd y diweddar John Alun Jones yn gyd-sylfaenydd y tîm.

TG was brought up in Lôn Llan, Edern and after moving to Mairlys by the village shop, he attended Ysgol Edern when the new school opened in 1950. His first Headmaster was Ellis Tudur Roberts, Club Captain in 1946. Following his education at Ysgol Botwnnog, he trained as a PE teacher and his first appointment was as Head of Physical Education in Wallasey. Keen to return to Wales, and particularly to Llŷn, Gareth was then appointed Head of PE in Caernarfon before returning to his old school at Botwnnog. During his period at Botwnnog, he followed an Advanced Diploma course in Special Education at University College Chester, where he met his wife to be, Shan. They were married in 1979 and lived at Mold while TG worked for the Special Needs Support Service in Clwyd, until his early retirement in 1997. Their son, Dafydd now works as a graphic designer and has been responsible for designing and producing this book.

TG and Shan moved back to Llŷn in February 2007 and have made their home at Wern y Wylan near the Golf Club. TG continues to work as a part time translator, while Shan is currently Secretary and Handicap Secretary of the Ladies' Section at the Golf Club.

Apart from playing football, TG's main interests from an early age were golf and railways. His father was a Station Master on the Cambrian Coast Railway. Like many others of his time, Gareth started by caddying in order to collect enough money to buy clubs. He was very fortunate to be able to play with a keen, competitive group of friends under the guidance of Dennis Grace, the Pro, in the late 50s and early 60s. Amongst his co-golfers were William Lloyd Griffith, Gwyn Hughes, Gareth Wyn Jones, Eurwyn Evans, Moi Parri, Paul Smart, Merfyn Lloyd, John Roberts Gerallt (Nefyn), Roy Portlock and later on, Gresham Owen.

TG joined the Club as a Junior in 1958, aged 11. Amongst his successes as a Junior Member were: Reducing his handicap from 30 to 9 over the six weeks summer holidays in 1962; Winning the Courtenay Lord Cup for three years in succession; Joint Winner of the Caernarfonshire Boys Championship with G Bullen (North Wales) in 1963; Winner of the North Wales Junior Championship at Conwy in 1963 and representing North Wales Junior Teams from 1962 to 1964.

Amongst his successes as a Full Member at Nefyn are: Winning several cups and Monthly Spoons; the Club Championship on 17 occasions from 1969 to 1996; the Tweedale Challenge Cup 6 times; the Captain's Prize twice; the Course Record three times; 66 in 1971 - post 1933 course (SSS 69), 64 in 1974 - again on the original course (SSS 69), and 67 in 1977 - on the Old Course which included the new loop around Abergeirch (SSS 71). He played off scratch for periods between 1976 and 1981.

Amongst his successes away from Nefyn were: Course Record at Porthmadog in 1977 (67); the Harrison Medal at Wallasey GC in 1972; Pwllheli Club Championship in 1975; several trophies at Padeswood and Buckley CG in the 1980s; the Corson Trophy (for invitees from North Wales and North West England) at Prestatyn in 1976; the Ashburnham Shield (WGU) with Aled Rees (Criccieth) at Prestatyn; playing for the North Wales Team; representing Caernarfonshire and Flintshire County Teams 1969-1990, with one period of three years when he was unbeaten in singles matches, and Flintshire Champion at Rhuddlan GC in 1982.

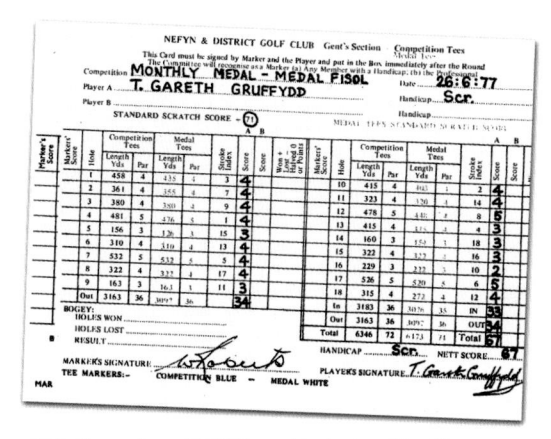

TG's Course Record (Old Course) in the June Monthly Medal, 1977, playing off scratch, recording 13 pars and 5 birdies!

TG served on the Golf Club Committee from 1973 until 2007 with one short gap of three years in the middle. Certainly, the highlights of his Membership were his election to Captaincy in 1990 and, more recently, being asked to compile the History of the Club with Shan.

In his Captaincy Year, TG, together with the Ladies' Captain, Carys W Jones, presented the Captain's Bell to the Club. This hangs in the Lounge and is used to call all Members to order!

Since 2002, TG has been busy translating reports and Club notices from English into Welsh in keeping with the Club's bilingual policy. He is very interested in steam trains and spends some of his spare time designing and building a model railway at home. He is a staunch Liverpool supporter and his other interests include riding his mountain bike and taking their dogs for a walk with Shan.

In the Centenary Year, TG started a Club Snooker Team, which played in the 3rd Division of the Llŷn Snooker League. The Team is successful and to date, February 2008, they are at the top of the League Table. Regular members of the Team are Pat McAteer, Ian Hamilton, Alan Brumby, Bobby Jones, H Eirwyn Jones and TG. The late John Alun Jones was a Founder Member of the Team. (See the Team Photo in the Chapter on Teams and Groups).

DAVID E G COOPER
1991

David's grandmother first came to Nefyn in 1895, arriving in a pony and trap. Both his grandparents and father were Members at Nefyn Golf Club, so David was introduced to the game at an early age. He became a Full Member of the Club in 1957, having previously been a Junior Member for many years. When he married Claire Buckley in 1967, this brought together two families who had been holidaying and golfing at Nefyn for over 50 years.

David was born in Hale and has lived there ever since. David and Claire and their family frequently visit Morfa Nefyn and have a most enviable abode at the bottom of Lôn Bridin, at the entrance to Morfa Nefyn Beach.

After leaving Radley College, near Oxford, David spent his two years of National Service in the army (1953-55) before going to work for one of the family's businesses. This was a small up-market chocolate company, Coq d'Or, based in Manchester. The mid-60s saw a change of career, when David became a stock broker and he remained a Member of the Stock Exchange for nearly forty years until his retirement in 2002.

David has been a Member of the Golf Club for over 60 years and was elected Captain in 1991. He served on the Committee for over ten years and, as a Trustee, is still involved in the running of the Club.

T Gareth Gruffydd receiving the Seniors' Scratch Trophy at the Centenary Presenation of Prizes, September 2007.

G I JONES
1992

Magwyd Ivor Burgess, fel y'i hadwaenid, ym Mwthyn Bach, Minffordd ar Ystâd Portmeirion, yn un o bump o blant.

Dechreuodd weithio fel peiriannydd morol yn y Ffowndri ym Mhorthmadog ac yn dilyn hyn bu yn Singapore tan 1946. Wedi dychwelyd i'w famwlad, bu'n gweithio am ddeng mlynedd gyda Chwmni Alpha Laval yn ardal Caerfyrddin yn cynhyrchu peiriannau godro - roedd galw mawr amdanyn nhw yn dilyn y rhyfel. Yn nes ymlaen symudodd Ivor i Ynys Môn, lle y cafodd swydd fel cynrychiolydd gwerthiant gyda chwmni Burgess. Yn ddiweddarach, symudodd i Bwllheli gyda'r Cwmni.

Dechreuodd Ivor chwarae golff gyda Robin Moi Williams (ei ffrind pennaf), Ellis Roberts (Ellis Berch) a Gwyndaf Hughes, yn y chwedegau yn Nefyn ar ôl eu cyflwyno i'r Clwb trwy Owen Roberts, yr Ysgrifennydd. Ni fu Ivor yn rhagori ar y maes golff ond bu'n chwarae oddi ar raddnod o 18 am gyfnod. Roedd yn aelod bodlon iawn, yn mwynhau ei getyn a chafwyd amser braf yn ei gwmni.

Mae mab Ivor, Richard, yn ddirprwy i Patrick ar Dîm y Lawntiau a buasai Ivor yn dotio at ei wyres fach, Lois, mae'n siŵr.

Bu Ivor farw yn 1996.

Ivor Burgess, as he was known, was brought up in Bwthyn Bach, Minffordd on the Portmeirion Estate and was one of five children.

He started working as a marine engineer at the Porthmadog Foundry and later moved abroad to work in Singapore until 1946. Having returned to his homeland, he worked for ten years with the Alpha Laval Company in Carmarthen, producing milking machinery which was in great demand following the war. He moved to Anglesey, where he was appointed as a Sales Representative with the Burgess Company. Later on, he moved to Pwllheli with the Company.

Ivor started playing golf in the 60s with his closest friend Robin Moi Williams, Ellis Roberts (Ellis Berch) and Gwyndaf Hughes, having been introduced to the Club through Owen Roberts, the Secretary. Ivor did not excel at golf but did play off a handicap of 18 at one period. He was popular and a very contented Member, always seen enjoying his pipe.

Ivor's son, Richard, is Patrick McAteer's Deputy on the Greens' staff.

IEUAN M ELLIS
1993

Hyfforddwyd Ieuan fel athro yn y Coleg Normal, Bangor, ac yn dilyn cyfnod yn dysgu yn Ysgol Ffordd y Dyffryn, Llandudno, symudodd i fyw i Ben Llŷn yn Ionawr 1960, fel Prifathro Ysgol Pont-y-Gof, Botwnnog.

Ni wyddai Ieuan nemor ddim am golff. Doedd golff ddim yn gêm i werin Llanbabo! Gwyddai am Dai Rees a'i lwyddiant oherwydd mai

Cymro oedd, ond ar wahân i hynny, gêm hollol ddieithr iddo oedd golff. Perswadiwyd ef i drio'r gêm gan griw o gyfeillion da ac ymaelododd ym Mhorthdinllaen yn 1964. Diolch iddyn nhw, syrthiodd mewn cariad â'r gêm. Cofiwch, bu sawl cyfnod du - methu'n lân a llwyddo!

Ni ddychmygodd Ieuan yn ôl yn 1964 y byddai ryw ddiwrnod yn Gapten y Clwb (1993). Bu'n flwyddyn hynod o brysur, ond un a roddodd bleser di-ben-draw iddo.

Bu hefyd, am gyfnod, yn Ysgrifennydd Anrhydeddus ac yna am beth amser yn Ysgrifennydd Graddnodau. Nawr mae ef yn un o'r Ymddiriedolwyr. Dywed Ieuan mai un o'r pethau gorau ddigwyddodd iddo wedi symud i Lŷn oedd dod yn Aelod ym Mhorthdinllaen. Dros y blynyddoedd mae wedi cael pleser a mwynhad yn golffio ac wedi cael cyfle i ddod i adnabod llawer a gwneud llu o gyfeillion da.

Yng Nghwpan Victory ar Orffennaf 4ydd 1970, sgoriodd I M Ellis 82-18-64. Ar y diwrnod, doedd hyn ddim digon da i ennill! Ar y pryd, roedd Ieuan yn chwarae oddi ar 24 a chafodd sisyrniad reit dda o 24 i 16! Yn nes ymlaen, fel Ysgrifennydd y Graddnodau, gallai Ieuan hogi ei siswrn ei hun!

Atgoffir rhai ohonom o stori amdano yn chwarae yn ei gystadleuaeth gyntaf yn y Clwb. Aeth i Siop y Pro ac yno roedd Marian Grace i'w helpu. Gofynnodd Ieuan am gerdyn a gofynnodd Marian am ei enw, 'I M Ellis' meddai. 'Na, dwi eisiau eich enw llawn,' atebodd Marian. 'I M Ellis,' meddai Ieuan eto. Meddyliai Marian ei fod yn dweud 'I am Ellis!'

Ieuan trained as a teacher in the Normal College, Bangor, and following a period teaching at Dyffryn Road School in Llandudno, he moved to Llŷn in January 1960 when he was appointed Headmaster of Ysgol Pont-y-Gof, Botwnnog.

Prior to moving, Ieuan knew very little about golf. Golf was not a pastime for the folk of Llanbabo (Deiniolen, near Llanberis)! He had heard of Dai Rees and his successes as a Welsh golfer, but apart from that, golf was a completely unknown experience for him. He was persuaded to try the game by a group of good friends and he joined the Club in 1964. Thanks to them, he fell in love with golf although there were many periods where success was very limited!

Little did he think at the time that one day he would be Captain of Nefyn Golf Club. His year in office was extremely busy and one that he thoroughly enjoyed.

For a short period of time, he acted as Honorary Secretary and was Chairman of the Match and Handicap Committee for many years. At present, Ieuan is one of the Club's Trustees. He always believed joining Nefyn Golf Club was one of the best things he ever did after moving to Llŷn. Over the years, he has had great pleasure in golfing and has had the opportunity to get to know and befriend many members.

In the Victory Cup in 1970, Ieuan, whose handicap was 24, had to play off 18. He achieved an excellent score, 82-18-64, which sadly, was not good enough to win! However, he was immediately reduced to 16! Such a severe reduction was allowed in those days and later on, as Match and Handicap Secretary himself, Ieuan was able to sharpen his own handicap scissors with vigour!

One is reminded of a story when Ieuan was playing in his first ever competition at Nefyn.

He entered the Pro's Shop and there was Marian Grace waiting to serve him. Ieuan asked for a card and Marian asked him for his name. 'I M Ellis' said Ieuan, 'No' said Marian, 'I want your full name.' 'I M Ellis' said Ieuan again. 'Your full name!' Marian insisted. 'I M Ellis!' Marian was getting angry and obviously thought Ieuan was saying 'I am Ellis!'

JOHN C BLORE
1994

John's mother hailed from Wrexham and he was very proud of this Welsh link when he visited and later on lived in Morfa Nefyn. John graduated in Civil Engineering at Liverpool University and worked as a Chief Engineer for Ford in Spain, the United States and Germany as well as at Halewood. John's wife, Eileen, was brought up at Ivydale in Morfa and it was she who introduced John to the haven that is Porthdinllaen.

John was an extremely keen golfer and was absolutely thrilled, despite his nervousness in medal competitions, when he won his first major trophy, the Festival Cup, in 1988. He was out of luck however, when it came to the Presentation Evening as, in error, his trophy was presented to another Member!

John enjoyed raising money for charities, such as the Alder Hey Hospital in Liverpool, Guide Dogs for the Blind and the RNLI. He took part in sponsored walks and once walked from Liverpool to London.

He worked diligently on committees at Nefyn Golf Club and with his engineering background, he was a real asset to the House Committee and general house matters. John was elected Captain in 1994, but very sadly, died in Office.

REV E WHELDON THOMAS
1995

Daeth cyswllt cyntaf y Parch Eirwyn Wheldon Thomas (Wyn) â'r Clwb yn 1975 pan benodwyd ef yn Ficer ar Blwyfi Grŵp Nefyn. Fodd bynnag, roedd Wyn yn adnabod llawer o'r Aelodau gan ei fod wedi'i fagu'n lleol yn Llaniestyn.

Gwahoddwyd ef i ymuno â'r Clwb lle y derbyniodd groeso cynnes. Roedd tad Marian Grace, sef Dennis Grace, newydd ymddeol fel y Pro a derbyniodd y Ficer ei wersi cyntaf gan John Pilkington. Ei raddnod cyntaf oedd 24, ond erbyn yr amser yr ymddeolodd yn 2001, roedd ei raddnod i lawr i 11.

Derbyniodd Wyn wahoddiad i fod yn Gapten y Clwb yn 1995, profiad ac anrhydedd a werthfawrogodd yn fawr. Yn ystod y cyfnod yma, roedd llawer o newidiadau ar droed yn y Clwb, yn adeiladol oddi mewn i'r Clwb ac ar y cwrs, pryd yr ymestynnwyd o 18 i 27 twll.

Ers 1997, mae Wyn wedi'i ddyrchafu i Canon E W Thomas. Mae ef a'i wraig, Ann (Capten Adran y Merched yn 1988), yn hynod o falch mai eu merch, Fiona, yw Capten Adran y Merched ym Mlwyddyn Canmlwyddiant y Clwb yn 2007.

Canon and Mrs Thomas are pictured attending the Centenary Ball, August 2007, with daughter Fiona (Ladies' Captain) and son, Stephen.

The Rev Eirwyn Thomas' first link with the Club was in 1975 when he became the Rector of the grouped Parishes of Nefyn. However, he was already acquainted with several Members as he had been brought up locally in Llaniestyn.

Eirwyn or Wyn as he was called, was invited to join the Club where he received a great welcome. Marian Grace's father, Dennis Grace, had retired by this time and Wyn received lessons from John Pilkington. His first handicap was 24, but by the time he retired, in 2001, his handicap was 11.

He accepted an invitation to be Club Captain in 1995, an honour which he really appreciated.

At this time, the Club experienced great practical changes - substantial restoration of the Clubhouse and the extending of the Course from 18 to 27 holes.

The Rev Thomas was made a Canon of Bangor Cathedral in 1997.

The Canon and his wife, Anne, herself a Past Lady Captain (1988), are extremely delighted and proud that their daughter, Fiona, was chosen to be Ladies' Captain for the Centenary Year, 2007.

DEREK CLULOW
1996

Derek joined the Merchant Navy in 1944 and left in 1954 to join the Manchester Ship Canal Pilot Service, having obtained his Master's Certificate. He served in the MSC Pilot Service for 34 years, retiring in 1988 and wrote several books on seafaring. He and his wife, Jean, always enjoyed their holidays in Pen Llŷn, Derek being

Derek Clulow as Captain, presents the Victory Cup to Canon E Wheldon Thomas (second Left). Also pictured Left is John Richardson with the Tweedale Challenge Trophy and Right, Pete D'Aoust with the Muriau Cup.

a keen golfer. Ian, their son, visits Nefyn to play golf annually and daughter, Wendy, lives in Canada.

Derek's first visit to Nefyn Golf Club was in 1958, whilst holidaying at Tudweiliog. He became a Member of the Club in 1962. For a period of 12 months he recalled his handicap reaching 'the dizzy heights of 9' but generally he used to play to a steady 12. However, according to Derek, as age crept up on him, his handicap increased steadily over the years.

Derek was a very humorous character and regularly kept his audience entertained with remarks and jokes. Many Members, young and old, will remember him as the charismatic organiser of the Charity 'Snakes Competition' in the Summer Meetings of the 90s. His whistle and call for order - 'PEOPLE!' - could be heard down on the beach... and brought instant order!

'Game for a laugh' ...Derek dons his swimming trunks to attend to the pin in the snow on the 18th green (Old Course).

Derek was a fervent Everton supporter and he took the ribbing as much as he gave!

When visiting Llangollen Golf Club a few years ago, he was very fortunate not to kill himself. He had inadvertently put his buggy into reverse in the car park and drove over a steep embankment only to be saved by a tree trunk! ...and without a drop having passed his lips! He emerged from the buggy and as expected, made a joke of the affair.

In recent years Derek suffered ill health but he and Jean still visited the Club regularly although his golfing days were over. Derek sadly passed away in March 2008.

CAPT HUGH E ROBERTS 1997

Ganwyd Hugh yn Argraig, Edern i deulu morwrol gyda diddordeb mewn golff. Ymunodd Hugh â'r Clwb drigain mlynedd yn ôl fel Aelod Iau a threuliodd ei holl wyliau ysgol yn chwarae a chadio.

Ar ôl cael llwyddiant gyda'i arholiadau Lefel O, gadawodd Hugh yr Ysgol Ramadeg gan ymuno â'r Llynges Fasnachol. Pan fyddai adref ar wyliau, treuliai Hugh ei holl amser yn y Golff yn chwarae gyda'i ddiweddar dad, Capten John Roberts a'i ewythr Capten Hugh Roberts (a fu'n Gapten y Clwb yn 1955). Tra roedd Hugh adref ar ei wyliau, cyfarfu â'i ddarpar wraig, Laura Wyn, yn y Clwb. Priodwyd y ddau yn 1964 ac mae ganddynt ddau o blant, Linda ac Alwyn. Etholwyd Laura yn Gapten Adran y Merched yn 1992.

Mae sawl aelod o'i deulu wedi bod yn Gapteiniaid yn y Clwb. Roedd ei ddiweddar frawd Will (Capten Will) yn Aelod Blaenllaw.

Pan ymddeolodd Hugh o'i yrfa ar y cefnforoedd yn 1992, etholwyd ef yn Aelod o Bwyllgor Gwaith y Clwb a bu'n Gadeirydd Pwyllgor y tŷ am ddeng mlynedd. Etholwyd ef yn Gapten yn 1997 ac yn ystod Gŵyl yr Haf y flwyddyn honno, cyflawnodd Hugh ei binacl golff trwy ennill Cwpan Her Tweedale am y tro cyntaf.

Yn 2004, gwahoddwyd Hugh i fod yn Gapten Cymdeithas Cyn Gapteiniaid Eryri.

Hugh was born in Argraig, Edern, to a nautical family who were very interested in golf. Hugh joined the Club sixty years ago as a Junior Member and he used to spend his entire holidays golfing and caddying.

After being successful in his O level examinations, Hugh left the Grammar School and joined the Merchant Navy. When he came home on leave, he would spend a great deal of time at the Golf Club, playing with his late father, Capt John Roberts and his uncle, Capt Hugh Roberts (Captain in 1955). It was while on leave that he met his future wife, Laura Wyn, at the Golf Club. They married in 1964 and have two children, Linda and Alwyn. Laura became Lady Captain of the Club in 1992 and Ladies' County Captain in 2007.

> **Nov 7th 1997:** ...a Health and Safety inspection had been carried out by the local authority recently and that we had received a 'clean' report... The Secretary stated that he wished to record his appreciation for the work carried out by the Head Greenkeeper (Patrick McAteer) and his staff to ensure that we were, in the words of the inspector, 'far superior to any other club in the area'...

Several members of Hugh's family have been Captains at the Club. His late brother, Will (Capt Will), was a Past Captain, Secretary and Trustee of the Club.

When Hugh retired from his duties as sea captain in 1992, he was elected on to the Executive Committee and served as Chairman of the House Committee for ten years. He was elected Captain in 1997 and during the Summer Meeting of that year, Hugh achieved his golfing pinnacle by winning the Tweedale Challenge Cup. In 2004, Hugh was elected Captain of the Eryri Past Captain's Association.

(Left) *Captain H E Roberts with the Tweedale Challenge Cup, the only Club Captain to win the Cup during his year of office.*

NEVILLE INGMAN
1998

Mae Neville yn hanu o gefndir ffermio yn ardal Wrecsam. Milfeddyg oedd Neville yn ôl ei alwedigaeth. Graddiodd ym Mhrifysgol Lerpwl yn 1958 ac yn 1962 symudodd i Chwilog i fod yn bartner yn y Filfeddygfa. Yn 1985, fe'i hapwyntiwyd yn Swyddog Milfeddygol gyda'r Weinyddiaeth Amaethyddiaeth yng Nghaernarfon, gan barhau i fyw yn Chwilog. Ymddeolodd o'i waith yn 2004.

Ei glwb golff cyntaf oedd Cricieth, lle y bu'n chwarae'n rheolaidd cyn ymuno â Nefyn yn 1976. Ei brif resymau dros ymuno â Nefyn oedd cael gwersi gan John Pilkington y Pro, ei awydd i chwarae cwrs gwell a chael graddnod priodol.

Bu'n chwarae oddi ar raddnod o 10 ar un cyfnod, ond erbyn hyn mae'n honni ei fod yn brwydro i chwarae oddi ar 14. Cred ei fod yn frwdfrydig, yn hytrach na llwyddiannus. Mae'n aelod selog o dim yr Hynafgwyr.

Etholwyd Neville yn Gapten y Clwb yn 1998 ac mae wedi treulio nifer o flynyddoedd ar y Pwyllgor, yn bennaf fel Cadeirydd Pwyllgor y Tŷ.

Yn 1983, priododd Neville â Rhiannon, ac etholwyd hi yn Gapten y Merched ar ddiwedd 1997. Felly, am yr ail waith yn hanes y Clwb, gwasanaethodd gŵr a gwraig fel Capteiniaid y Clwb ar yr un cyfnod.

Neville came from a farming family in Wrexham. He qualified as a Veterinary Surgeon at Liverpool University in 1958 and in 1962, he moved to Chwilog to become a partner in a private veterinary practice. In 1985, he was appointed a Veterinary Officer for the Ministry of Agriculture, based at Caernarfon, but continued to live at Chwilog. He retired in 2004.

Neville's first golf club was Criccieth, where he played regularly before he joined Nefyn in 1976. His main reasons for joining Nefyn were to receive tuition from John Pilkington, the Professional, to play a better course and to obtain an appropriate handicap.

His lowest handicap was 10. Now he claims it is a struggling 14 and he believes he is more enthusiastic than successful. He is a regular and faithful recruit for the Seniors on match days.

Neville was elected Captain in 1998 and has been a Member of the Executive Committee including being Chairman of House for a number of years. In 1983, he married Rhiannon and she was elected Lady Captain at the end of 1997. Thus, for only the second time in the Club's history, husband and wife served together as Captains of the Club.

STEPHEN B MURRAY
1999

Stephen (Butch) Murray is the son of Charles Ian and Molly Murray. His father, Ian, was Captain in 1967.

Stephen is a Chartered Surveyor and started work a fortnight after leaving school with 'articles' in Manchester. In 1964 he joined Stuart Murray & Co. becoming a partner in 1968. The Firm was eventually sold to Heywoods in 2002, but Stephen remained a Consultant for a year before finally retiring in 2005. Additionally in 1968, he became a Director of the Murray family firm (Hollins Murray Group) and remains there as a non-executive Director.

Stephen first visited Nefyn in 1948 and he quickly came under the tutelage of Dennis Grace. In his school days, team games took preference to golf, but when rugby started to hurt, golf became the number one. Having had an initial handicap of 12, it was eventually reduced to 8, where it remained for 12 years. Latterly it has crept back to 12 again.

In 1981, Stephen successfully won the Buckley Trophy on the Friday, the Captain's Prize on the Saturday (old format – medal round and three knockout rounds) and qualified for the Tweedale knockout on the Monday - quite a weekend! He takes great pride in having won the Captain's Prize three times – so far unsurpassed!

To acknowledge the long family association with the Club, Stephen presented the Club with the Captain's and Lady Captain's Chairs. Following the presentation, Stephen produced one of his usual pearls when he stated, 'woe betide any strange posteriors who deign to perch themselves thereon!'

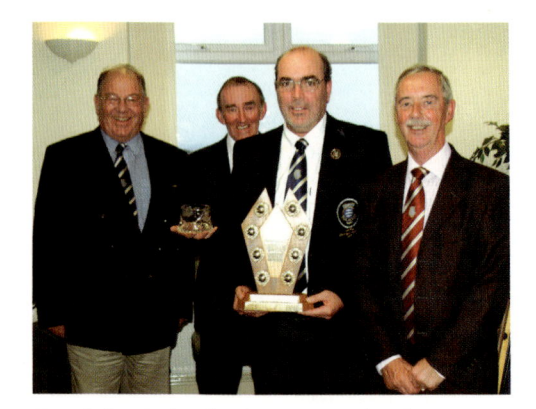

From Left to Right: The Winning Team of Stephen Murray, Club Captain Emyr L Evans and Club President, Ioi Williams, in the Eryri Past Captains' Association's Competition at Nefyn in 2007. Pictured at the back is Gordon Smith, Captain of the EPCA and Vice-Captain of the Club.

In 1988, Stephen had the honour of following his parents in being elected Captain at Ringway Golf Club. In 1999, he was elected our Club Captain.

THE NEW MILLENNIUM 2000-2008

WILL LLOYD JONES 2000

Brodor o Lannor yw Will, a chafodd ei addysg yn Ysgol Ramadeg Pwllheli. Graddiodd mewn fferylliaeth ac adeiladodd fusnes yn cynnwys nifer o siopau fferyllydd yn Llŷn ac Eifionydd. Yn y nawdegau, gwerthodd y siopau ac yn awr mae Will yn brysur gyda'i safleoedd carafannau.

Ymaelododd Will â Chlwb Golff Nefyn yn wreiddiol fel Aelod o'r Adran Iau yn y chwedegau pan fyddai'n chwarae efo'i dad, John Gwilym Jones. Ar ddechrau'r wythdegau, pan deimlodd fod ei yrfa pêl-droed yn dirwyn i ben, ailymunodd Will fel aelod llawn. Nid yw wedi bod yn gystadleuydd cyson, ond mae wedi chwarae oddi ar 12 dros y blynyddoedd diweddar. Bu'n fuddugol ddwywaith yn 1991 pan enillodd Gwpan Festival a Thlws Cynfelin Jones.

Bu Will yn weithgar ar Bwyllgor y Clwb yn y nawdegau ac fe'i hanrhydeddwyd pan etholwyd ef yn Gapten y Clwb dros flwyddyn y Mileniwm. Yn sgil ei weithgarwch, fe'i hetholwyd yn Gadeirydd cyntaf Clwb Golff Nefyn yn 2001, swydd yr ymgymerodd â hi gyda brwdfrydedd a dyfalbarhad. Ymysg y meysydd y bu Will yn eu hyrwyddo yn ystod ei Gadeiryddiaeth oedd sefydlu Pwyllgor Strategaeth a Pholisi, trafod posibilrwydd cael gostyngiad mewn trethi busnes (Clwb Chwaraeon Amatur Cymunedol - CASC) a Strwythur Rheolaeth y Clwb.

Oherwydd anhwylder iechyd a thriniaethau arfaethedig, ymddiswyddodd Will o'r Gadeiryddiaeth yng Nghyfarfod Cyffredinol Blynyddol 2007. Fodd bynnag, mae'n bleser cael adrodd wrth gyhoeddi'r hanes yma fod ei driniaethau wedi bod yn llwyddiannus ac mae'n prysur wella.

Will is originally from Llannor and was educated at Pwllheli Grammar School. He graduated in pharmacy and over the years he built a business comprising several pharmacies in Llŷn and Eifionydd. In the 90s, he sold the shops and re-directed his successful business acumen to caravan sites.

Will joined Nefyn Golf Club in the early 80s when he felt that his footballing career was drawing to a close. He has not been a regular competitor but he has played off a handicap of 12 over the last few years. He completed a double in 1991 when he won the Festival Cup and the Cynfelin Jones Trophy.

Will Ll Jones, as Captain of the Club, congratulating Alwyn Thomas (Nefyn), the Gwynedd Boys' Champion in 2000. Pictured also is Gareth Williams, Gelli Wen, the Club's Junior Captain.

Will worked diligently on the Club Committee during the 90s and he was honoured when elected Club Captain for the Millennium. As a result of his commitment to the Club, he was elected the first ever Chairman of the Club in 2001, a post he undertook with enthusiasm and perseverance. Will was instrumental in setting up the Strategy and Policy Committee and in leading discussions on topics such as the Community Amateur Sports Club (CASC), business rates reduction for the Club and the Club's management structure.

As a result of a health setback and impending treatments, Will was forced to resign from the Chairmanship in the AGM of 2007. We are delighted to report at the time of writing, that the treatments have been successful and he has made an excellent recovery.

R J TAYLOR
2001

Spud, as he is known, was born in Falkirk, Scotland in 1941 but soon his family moved south to England. He first visited the Llŷn Peninsula in 1961 to be the best man at a friend's wedding in Llanaelhaearn. The following year he met Hilary, whose father, Norman Ashworth, introduced him to Nefyn and District Golf Club. Since then he has visited Nefyn many times each year, even when he lived in the USA.

Having read Physics at university, he spent his first 23 years in the very early computer industry. Bad fortune came his way and Spud lost his savings in the fibre-optics and film industries. After this, he actually set up a financial advising business!

He claims his golfing prowess and achievements are negligible - he does have a very unique golf swing! Spud's lowest handicap was 9.6 and he is now back to 16. His only entry on the Club walls, prior to 2007, came from the great honour of Captaincy in 2001.

Spud is renowned for his generosity. In 1986, he presented the Club with the Tatws Trophy (see Chapter on Cups and Competitions) and continued providing additional prizes and a meal for all 'Tatws' Competitors until the end of his Captaincy Year. During his year in office as Captain, he donated a shed to the Club to be placed by the 10th green as a 'half way house' and also a bell for the tenth fairway. He also arranged a 10 hole mixed foursomes competition on New Year's Day followed by cocktails at the Club.

In our Centenary Year, Spud is delighted to win the Tatws Team Trophy.

At the AGM of 2002 Spud was successful in putting forward a motion to introduce a new category of membership - Overseas Members.

Spud is also a member at Royal Lytham & St. Anne's Golf Club.

DR PRYS E OWEN 2002

Magwyd Prys yng Ngarn Fadryn, ond symudodd i fyw i Loegr yn chwech oed.

Dechreuodd chwarae golff yn Otley pan oedd yn darlithio ym Mhrifysgol Leeds ac ymgartrefodd yn Wharfedale, oedd yn nefoedd i ffwrdd o lygredd mwrllwch Leeds.

Yn ddiweddarach yng Nghymru, fel Arolygydd ei Mawrhydi, byddai ei waith yn ei arwain mewn cylch gwrthglocwedd o amgylch y wlad, o Gaerfyrddin i Gaerdydd, Rhuthun a Biwmares. Treuliodd gyfnod byr yn ôl yng Nghaerfyrddin fel Deon Astudiaethau yng Ngholeg y Drindod cyn symud i Forfa Nefyn. Yn ddiweddarach, symudodd i'r Ficerdy ym Mhenrhyndeudraeth, lle mae'n byw gyda'i wraig Susan, Ficer y Plwyf.

Cyflwynwyd ef i Glwb Golff Nefyn gan ei gefnder, Ieuan Ellis, yn dilyn ei ymddeoliad. Nid yw Prys yn honni ei fod yn olffiwr o safon - dywed mai safon ail dim yw ei lefel mewn golff, criced a rygbi! Fodd bynnag, unwaith fe drawodd y bêl fach o amgylch Clwb Harlech mewn 78 ar ddau ddiwrnod yn olynol - camp glodwiw iawn! Rhag ofn nad yw Prys yn cofio, fe enillodd Gwpan Courtenay Lord yn 1992, ac yn 1993 fe gafodd lwyddiant triphlyg wrth ennill Tlws ROC, Pytiwr y Llywydd a Thlws Cynfelin Jones!

Prys was brought up in Garn Fadryn, but moved to England at six years of age.

He started playing golf in Otley while lecturing at Leeds University and made his home in Wharfedale, one of the Yorkshire Dales' longest and most beautiful valleys and a haven away from the smog pollution of Leeds.

Back in Wales as an H M Inspector, his work took him in an anticlockwise circle around the country, from Carmarthen to Cardiff, to Ruthin and Beaumaris. There was a brief spell back in Carmarthen as Dean of Studies at Trinity College. He then settled in Morfa Nefyn before moving finally to the Vicarage in Penrhyndeudraeth, where he lives with his wife Susan, the Vicar of the Parish.

Prys was first introduced to the Club, after his retirement, by his cousin, Ieuan Ellis.

He does not claim any golfing prowess - believing himself to be second team level only in golf, cricket and rugby! However, he did once score two gross 78s in consecutive days' competitions at Royal St David's, Harlech. No mean feat! In case Prys has forgotten, he won the Courtenay Lord Cup in 1992, and in 1993 he had a triple success in claiming the ROC Trophy, the President's Putter and the Cynfelin Jones Trophy!

JOHN DAVISON 2003

Nefyn's visit to Wilpshire Golf Club, near Blackburn, arranged by their Centenary Captain, John Davison.

John's first link with the Club was in the mid-60s, playing high handicap golf, while enjoying the wonders of Nefyn on holiday. He recalls memories of 'eight guys trying to muster eight jackets and eight ties so that they could have a drink on a Sunday night under the watchful eye of Owen Roberts – Bless him!'

John's professional career was involved in management and marketing in the textile clothing business.

Like all golfers, his game had highs and lows. He managed a single figure handicap for a number of years but was much more relaxed playing in the lower teens, winning the odd sovereign! He accompanied the Club Members on a golfing week to Malaga in Spain in the November of his Captaincy year. The week was good humoured – none more so than when John was slapped in the face with a custard pie by the waitresses on the last night! Who arranged that?

John is also a Member at Wilpshire Golf Club near Blackburn. He was very honoured to be elected their Centenary Captain in 1990 and invited Nefyn to play there (see photo above).

For many years John has been involved in organising Wilpshire's local golf association events - Amateur, Pro-Ams and Leagues. In 2007, he supported his wife, Penny, in her Lady Captaincy year at Wilpshire.

As a family, the Davisons believe they have been very fortunate to have been able to become regular Members of the Club over the last thirty five years. They continue to enjoy the camaraderie and value the friendships they have made over these years. They also delight in the whole district surrounding Morfa Nefyn.

H E JONES
2004

Magwyd Eirwyn yn Nhŷ'r Weirglodd, Pistyll, a threuliodd ei blentyndod ym Mhistyll ac yn Ysgol Nefyn.

Dechreuodd weithio i'r Fonesig Niwbwrch yn ei chanolfan garddio yn Nhŷ Crwn, Boduan cyn symud i Fotacho Wyn ger y Bryncynan. Yn dilyn hyn, treuliodd gyfnod ym mecws Llithfaen cyn symud i Hufenfa De Arfon am gyfnod byr. Yna dechreuodd fusnes ei hun yn paentio ac addurno ar ddechrau'r chwedegau cyn symud ymlaen i adeiladwaith. Mae wedi treulio cryn amser ar bwyllgorau'r Clwb, yn enwedig y Pwyllgor Tŷ ac ef a gwblhaodd yr estyniad trawiadol diweddaraf i'r Clwb - yr Ystafell Fwyta yn 2006, ynghyd â newidiadau i'r gegin ar ddechrau 2008.

Bu Eirwyn yn chwarae ambell i gêm ar Gwrs Golff Nefyn cyn ymaelodi'n llawn yn 1976. Mae wedi mwynhau'r elfen gystadleuol a bydd yn edrych ymlaen at Deithiau i Glybiau eraill a'r gystadleuaeth 10 twll ar nos Fercher pan fydd rhyw buntan neu ddwy yn cyfnewid dwylo! Ei raddnod isaf fu 12 a bu'n fuddugol yn y gystadleuaeth Parau'r Haf yn ddiweddar. Mae'n edrych ymlaen at gael ei enw ar un o fyrddau enillwyr y prif gystadleuthau.

Mae Eirwyn yn briod â Carys ac mae ganddynt ddau o blant, Sian a John. Bu Carys yn Gapten y Merched (1990) ac yn 2007-2008, hi yw Llywydd Merched y Clwb. Yn 1999, cyflwynodd Eirwyn a Carys dlws o'r enw 'Tlws Môr a Mynydd' i Adran y Merched. Chwaraeir am y tlws hon yn flynyddol yn ystod Gŵyl yr Haf.

Eirwyn was brought up in Pistyll and spent his early years in the village and at Ysgol Nefyn. He started working for Lady Newborough in her Gardening Centre at Tŷ Crwn, Bodfean, before moving to Botacho Wyn near the Bryncynan pub. Following this he was employed in a bakery at Llithfaen before moving to South Caernarfonshire Creameries at Y Ffôr for a short period. He then began his own painting and decorating business in the early sixties before moving on to construction. He has spent a number of years on Club Committees, especially the House Committee and it was Eirwyn who built the latest extension to the Club – the impressive new Dining Room in 2006, as well as the kitchen renovations and extension at the beginning of 2008.

Eirwyn played a few games of golf at Nefyn before joining as a full Member in 1976. He has enjoyed the competitive side of golf and always looks forward to Club Outings and the Wednesday night competitions when a couple of pounds are exchanged! His lowest handicap was 12 and he won the Summer Fourball Knockout Competition in 2006. He looks forward to getting his name on one of the major competition honours boards.

Eirwyn is married to Carys and they have two children, Siân and John. Carys herself was elected

Lady Captain (1990) and in 2007-2008, is Ladies' President of the Club. In 1999, Carys and Eirwyn presented a trophy to the Ladies' Section. This was 'Tlws Môr a Mynydd' and it is played for annually in the Summer Meeting.

Captain H E Jones, with grandson Huw, presents a cheque for £6000 to Child Development Wales (Now Specialist Children Services) of Pwllheli. **Pictured also, Left to Right,** *are daughter Siân Teleri Hughes, Zoe Woods, Senior Community Paediatric Physiotherapist, Nurse Helen Jones, son-in-law John Hughes and wife Carys.*

RICHARD L E RIMMINGTON
2005

Richard, a chartered accountant, has lived in Stockport during most of his working life. He first played at Nefyn in the mid 60s, when he started visiting the Llŷn Peninsula with friends, including John Davison. He recalls them both becoming Green Fee Members in 1970. After working for accountants Coopers & Lybrand in California in 1973-1974, Richard became a Full Member on his return in 1975. For many years he and his wife Angela, who joined the Club in 1990, stayed in a caravan at Tudweiliog, until they bought a cottage, Pentrellech [Slate Village] in Edern in 1985, where they now spend most of their time.

Captain Richard Rimmington and Lady Captain Dorothy Humpherson with Guest Speaker Andrew Murray, Ex-professional Golfer and BBC Five Live & Sky Sports Commentator, at the 2005 Annual Dinner at the Club.

They are both Members of Heaton Moor Golf Club, where Richard was Captain in 1982 and President in 1996. He also served as Honorary Treasurer in 1977-1978 and again from 1992 to 1994. Angela was Captain in 2000. From the mid-70s to the mid-90s Richard had a single figure handicap, mainly 8 and 9. His best golfing year was at Heaton Moor in 1985, when he won the Captain's Prize, the Singles and, with Angela, the Mixed Knockout. He was also delighted to win Steven Murray's Captain's Prize at Nefyn in 1999. In addition, Richard won the Wynne-Finch Cup in 2004 and the Tudur Roberts Cup in the early part of the Centenary year.

Since retiring as Captain at Easter 2006, Richard has been Honorary Treasurer and Angela has done the double by becoming Ladies' Treasurer in 2007. Richard is still closely involved with his old school, Stockport Grammar School, where he became a Governor in 1992, taking over as Chairman in 2002. With a handicap hovering between 12 and 13, he believes his best golfing days are over, but he still loves playing at Nefyn with his Welsh and English friends in competitions, in friendlies and with the Seniors in their matches both home and away.

IAN COOPER
2006

Ian's parents first joined the club around 1961 and moved to Morfa permanently in 1970. His father, Bob, was an extremely likeable character who enjoyed socialising at the Club. Ian joined as a Junior for a couple of years as a 15 year old but resigned when his band, in which he was the drummer, turned professional. He re-joined in his early twenties. Married to Jean in the mid-70s, they have two children, Zoe and Sian.

From 1964 to 1968, Ian was a professional drummer with Wynder K Frog and had a hit record in 1966 with Green Door. Between 1969 and 1983 he trained and became a fabrication engineer and in 1983 he became Managing Director of his own engineering company. This he sold in 2000 and moved to Nefyn to retire.

In the couple of years leading to the Club Centenary, Ian was instrumental in organising the Centenary Ball and formed a club band. This was aptly called 'The Tailor Maid Band' and they performed on his Captain's Day in 2006 and in the Centenary Ball on August 11th 2007.

Ian, with Jean's assistance, has been very supportive of golf and social events at Nefyn over the years. He was instrumental in organising numerous social functions, including the Centenary Ball, Rag Dances and concerts of all descriptions. Ian's lowest golf handicap was 11 and the highlight of his recent performances at Nefyn was winning the Buckley Challenge Trophy in 2000.

Captain Ian Cooper keeps the beat for his Tailor Maid Band on his Captain's Night in August 2006.
(Photo; Dewi Wyn, Pwllheli)

THE CENTENARY CAPTAIN CAPTEN Y CANMLWYDDIANT

EMYR L EVANS
2007-2008

Ganwyd Emyr yn ail o dri brawd a magwyd hwy ym Mhencaenewydd. Cafodd ei addysg gynradd yn Y Ffôr (Fourcrosses bryd hynny) ac addysg uwchradd yn ysgol Penrallt a Glan y Môr, Pwllheli, cyn treulio tair blynedd yng Ngholeg Amaethyddol Cymru yn Aberystwyth. Ar ôl gadael y Coleg treuliodd gyfnod byr yn gweithio gydag Amaethwyr Eifionydd cyn treulio 6 mlynedd gyda'r Weinyddiaeth Amaeth yn gyfrifol am redeg y Bwrdd Hyfforddi Amaethyddol yng Ngwynedd. Yna, yng nghanol yr wythdegau, newidiodd ei gôt a mynd i fyd masnach, gan weithio i gwmni gwrtaith rhyngwladol Kemira. Bu'n un o dim o bump yn gyfrifol am redeg y cwmni yma yn y DU a Gweriniaeth Iwerddon.

Mae Emyr yn briod â Marian, athrawes ysgol, ac mae ganddynt dri o blant, Rhys, Tudur a Ffion. Maent wedi ymgartrefu yn Nhŷ'n Giât, Llanystumdwy. Er gwaetha'r ffaith fod ei swydd a'i gyfrifoldebau wedi mynd ag Emyr i bellafoedd Ewrop a rhannau eraill o'r byd tros yr ugain mlynedd ddiwethaf, penderfynodd ef a Marian barhau i fyw yn eu cartref. Gwnaethant hyn er mwyn i'r plant gael y cyfle i adnabod eu teidiau a'i neiniau, cael tyfu i fyny i fod yn rhan o'r gymdeithas Gymraeg a chael gwreiddiau i fod yn falch ohonynt... ac wrth gwrs, i gael dal i chwarae golff yn Nefyn!

Ers yn ifanc iawn, dangosai Emyr, a'i ddau frawd, ddiddordeb mewn chwarae golff. Roedd eu tad, Dyfed, yn chwarae golff ac arferai'r tri brawd gadio iddo ef a'i gyfeillion ymysg eraill. Ymddengys enw Dyfed ar Fyrddau'r Enillwyr yn y Clwb, ond nid mor rheolaidd ag enw ei fab, Emyr... a gall y patrwm yma barhau wrth i Tudur ymgiprys â'r her deuluol.

Ymunodd Emyr â'r Clwb fel Aelod o'r Adran Iau pan oedd yn ddeng mlwydd oed yn 1967. Fodd bynnag, ni chymrodd y gêm o ddifrif nes iddo adael y coleg. Erbyn yr wythdegau hwyr, roedd ei raddnod i lawr i rif sengl ac ar hyn o bryd, mae'n chwarae oddi ar 5. Enillodd Emyr Dlws ROC yn 1990 ac 1995, Cwpan Courtenay Lord yn 1991 ac 1993, Cwpan Victory yn 1992, Cwpan Muriau yn 1995 a Chwpan O H Parry yn 2006.

Mae Tudur, ei fab, yn dilyn ôl ei draed ac er bod Emyr yn dotio at ei lwyddiant, a chan gofio fod Tudur yn dal yn y brifysgol, mae yna rywfaint o gystadleuaeth rhwng y ddau! Bu Tudur yn fuddugol yn Nhlws Buckley yn 2001 ac mae wedi ennill Pencampwriaeth y Clwb ddwy flynedd yn olynol yn 2006 a 2007. Yn Nhlws ROC yn 2006, cipiodd Tudur y Tlws, un ergyd yn well na'i dad, ond yng Nghwpan O H Parry, yn hwyrach yn y flwyddyn, Emyr a orfu. Ym Mlwyddyn y Canmlwyddiant enillodd Tudur eto yn Senglau'r Haf yn erbyn ei dad. Mae cystadleuaeth ffyrnig rhwng y tad a'r mab!

Mae Emyr wedi cynrychioli'r Clwb ar sawl achlysur ynghyd â chael ei ddewis yn Gapten i'r Tim 'Scratch'.

Anrhydedd mawr oedd gael ei ethol yn Gapten ym Mlwyddyn y Canmlwyddiant. (Gweler atgofion Emyr yn y bennod 'Dwi'n cofio...')

Emyr, one of three sons, was born and bred in Pencaenewydd. He received his primary education at Y Ffôr (Fourcrosses) and his secondary education at Ysgol Penrallt and Glan y Môr, Pwllheli, before spending three years at the Welsh Agricultural College in Aberystwyth. On leaving College, he spent a brief time with Eifionydd Farmers, and subsequently, six years with the Ministry of Agriculture, responsible for running the Agricultural Training Board in Gwynedd. In the mid-80s, he moved to work in commerce with a Company called Kemira, an international fertilizer company. He became one of a team of five responsible for running the company in the UK and the Republic of Ireland.

Emyr is married to school teacher Marian. They have three children, Rhys, Tudur and Ffion and they live in Ty'n Giât, Llanystumdwy. Even though his work responsibilities took him across Europe and other parts, he and Marian decided to stay in Llŷn and Eifionydd. Emyr comments this was 'so their children could have the opportunity to get to know their grandparents, to be raised in a Welsh environment and to have roots to be proud of ...and of course, to continue to play golf at Nefyn!'

From an early age, Emyr and his two brothers showed interest in golf. Their father, Dyfed, played golf and the three brothers used to caddy for him and his friends among others. Dyfed's name appears on the Honours Boards in the Club but not quite as frequently as his son's, and this trend may continue as young Tudur is already taking up the family challenge!

Emyr had joined the Club as a Junior when he was about ten years old, in 1967, but it was not until he left College, however, that he took up the game more seriously. By the late 80s, he was down to a single figure handicap and he currently plays off 5. He won the ROC Trophy in 1990 and 1995; the Courtenay Lord Cup in 1991 and 1993; the Victory Cup in 1992; the Muriau Cup in 1995 and the O H Parry Cup in 2006!

Emyr's son, Tudur, is fast following in his father's footsteps and although Emyr is very proud of his son's achievements, bearing in mind he is still at University, there is fierce competition between them! Tudur won the Buckley Trophy in 2001, and has been Club Champion for the last two years. In the ROC Trophy in 2006 Tudur beat his father by one shot. His father then went on to beat Tudur by a greater margin when he won the OH Parry Cup in the same year. This Centenary Year saw son Tudur beat his father in the final of the Singles' Knockout! Never has there been such competition between father and son!

Emyr has represented the Club on many occasions and has captained the Scratch Team. He was highly delighted to be elected Captain for the Centenary Year and felt greatly honoured.

(Please see Emyr's reminiscences in the Chapter entitled 'I remember...')

Emyr enjoys a celebratory drink with his wife Marian and son Tudur at the end of the 2006 Presentation Evening.

Past Captain's Dinner February 2008
Standing from Left to Right: *Dr Prys Owen, Canon E Wheldon Thomas, R J (Spud) Taylor, Gresham T Owen, T Gareth Gruffydd, Captain Hugh E Roberts, H D Jones, Neville Ingman, Jim P Bentley and H Eirwyn Jones.* **Seated:** *Mrs Dilys Ll Owen, Richard L E Rimmington, Captain Emyr L Evans, Ladies' Captain Fiona V Thomas, Griff T Roberts and Ieuan M Ellis.*

PAST CAPTAINS AND COMMITTEES
CYN GAPTEINIAID A PHWYLLGORAU

Past Captains and Committee Members 1954 /55
Standing Left to Right: *W L Davies, Unknown, Alec Smart, H M Jones, John Evan Roberts, Unknown, Richard Jones, Unknown and Harry Parry*
Seated: *D A Williams, Owen Roberts, Richie Glyn Williams, Captain Hugh Roberts and Ellis Tudur Roberts*

Past Captains, 1956
Standing Left to Right: *John Evan Roberts, Maurice W Jones, Robert Thomas, Captain Hugh Roberts, J Idris Lewis, and Richard Glyn Williams*
Seated: *Henry Parry, Brig. William Wynne-Finch and Owen Roberts*

Past Captains and Committee Members 1996
Standing Left to Right: *Barry Owens, Huw G Williams, Ioi Williams, Lt Col Robin W Parry, Derek Clulow, Gresham T Owen, Stan Cresswell, Jim Bentley, Dennis Humpherson, Hugh D Jones, T Gareth Gruffydd, Capt Hugh E Roberts, David E G Cooper, Will Ll Jones and Ieuan M Ellis*
Seated: *Laurence Barbet, Richard Edgar Jones, Evan Hughes, Will Hughes, Captain Will Roberts, Rhys Griffith, John Williams and Griff T Roberts*

The Ladies' Committee 2007
Standing Left to Right: *Gwyneth Smith, Sylvia Dennett, Treasurer Angela Rimmington, Enid Bloxham, Ladies' Secretary and Handicap Secretary Shan E Gruffydd, Barbara Parsons and Ex-Officio Megan Roberts*
Seated: *Ladies' Vice-Captain, Janet Brown, Ladies' Captain Fiona V Thomas and Ladies' President Carys W Jones*

THE CAPTAINS - Y CAPTEINIAID

THE LADY CAPTAINS - CAPTEINIAID Y MERCHED

THE LADY CAPTAINS AND DEVELOPMENTS WITHIN THE LADIES' SECTION
CAPTEINIAID Y MERCHED A DATBLYGIADAU YN ADRAN Y MERCHED

Fel ag yn y Bennod ar Gapteiniaid y Dynion, casglwyd y wybodaeth o nifer o ffynonellau.

As in the Chapter on the Captains of the Club, the information in this Chapter has been gleaned from a variety of sources.

Many Lady Captains are referred to by their Christian names. However, some Ladies in the past were always addressed by their full title and surname and we have respectfully continued this tradition for these particular Ladies when discussing them.

It will be evident also that Lady Captains' names appear on the Ladies' Captain's Board according to the trend of the time, the married ladies taking their husbands' names e.g. Mrs Frank Evans rather than Mrs Enid Evans. From 1980 onwards, this practice was discontinued.

Cychwyn Adran y Merched
Ychydig o wybodaeth sydd ar gael am ddyddiau cyntaf Adran y Merched. Rhestrir 19 o Ferched ymysg Aelodau Cychwynnol y Clwb yn 1907, ac o'r rhain, roedd pymtheg ohonynt yn wragedd i ddynion oedd yn Aelodau. Ychydig iawn a chwaraeai mewn cystadleuthau yn y dyddiau cynnar a byddai'r nifer o gystadleuwyr bron bob tro o dan ddeg. Roedd y sgorio'n uchel ar y cychwyn - 107 net yn ennill cystadleuaeth! Yn raddol, gwelwyd gwelliant yn ansawdd y golff ynghyd â chynnydd yn nifer Aelodau Adran y Merched.

Yn ystod y deng mlynedd ddilynol hyd at 1917, ymunodd 19 o ferched ychwanegol â'r Clwb a rhwng diwedd y Rhyfel Cyntaf ac 1927, ymunodd 71 o ferched eraill. Roedd yn anodd dehongli'r nifer union gan fod nifer o'r merched yn Aelodau oedd yn ymweld, a rhai eraill yn ymddiswyddo ac ail-ymaelodi'n gyson. Yn ogystal, roedd hi'n anodd dehongli a oedd 'Miss' yn Aelod llawn ynteu yn eneth ifanc. Mae'r cofnodion cyntaf sydd ar gael o Bwyllgor y Merched yn dyddio o Fehefin 3ydd 1933. Fodd bynnag, mae'n amlwg y cedwid cofnodion cyn hyn ond credwn i'r rhain gael eu colli pan losgwyd Tŷ'r Clwb yn 1928.

The Ladies' Section is born.
Little is known about the early days of the Ladies' Section. There were 19 Ladies listed as Inaugural Members of the Club in 1907 and of these, 15 of them were wives of Gentlemen Members. Very few played in competitions and the number of entries in the early days was virtually all in single figures. The early scoring was often high. A 90 nett and 107 nett won two competitions in 1910.

> **May 1908:** Ladies Challenge Cup – 18 holes match play against bogey.
>
> Won by Miss Roberts – 8 down

Gradually, the golf improved and the number of Lady Members increased. During the next ten years, up to 1917, another 19 Ladies joined the Club and between the end of the war and June

1927, another 71 Ladies had joined. The exact number on roll is hard to decipher as so many were visiting Members who often resigned and rejoined and it was sometimes impossible to decipher whether a 'Miss' were a Full member or a 'Juvenile'.

The first surviving Minutes of the Ladies' Committee are dated June 3rd 1933. It is evident that previous Minutes did exist because they are referred to in later documentation. We surmise many of these were destroyed in the Clubhouse fire of 1928. However, the Minutes between 1928 and 1933 are also missing.

Earliest Committees

It is reported in the Minutes of the Standing Committee, [Executive Committee], that the Lady Members of the Club had formed a small Committee as early as 1913 to look after their interests and to arrange matches.

In 1921, there is a reference to the Lady Secretary and in 1928 'Miss A B Jones (Lady Secretary) was sanctioned 12/6 for postal expenses'.

> **July 1913:** Resolved that the Ladies be empowered to arrange matches and competitions and that any suggestions their committee may make with regard to any improvement or alteration shall receive the careful attention of the Golf Committee.

At the AGM of August 1928, a question was asked by the Vicar, Rev H Williams regarding the status of Lady Members of the Club and why were they not represented on the Executive Committee! A reply by a Dr Miller was that in his varied experience, this project had been tried in many clubs but never successfully! The Secretary, Mr Pittman, informed the Meeting that 'any suggestions the Ladies cared to lay before the Executive Committee were invariably treated with the greatest consideration and sympathy'.

> **July 1928:** It was decided to provide something in the nature of a small box in the Ladies Dressing Room, as many of the Ladies complained that they were too short to take their clubs from the lockers!

> **September 1928:**
> Captain: Miss Bellhouse
> Vice-Captain: Mrs J J Thomas
> Hon Secretary: Mrs Pittman
> Committee:
> Mrs Williams   The Vicarage, Nevin
> Miss K O Jones   Rhos, Morfa Nevin
> Miss S Phillips Bwlchglas, Morfa Nevin
> Miss A B Jones   Preswylfa, Nevin

This may very well be the first formalised Committee of the Ladies' Section.

The First Recorded Ladies' Committee

On Saturday, September 29th 1928, a Ladies' Meeting was held at the Clubhouse, chaired by Captain O G Owen, a Member of the Executive Committee. This meeting is recorded in the Club's Minutes but it is not stated who was in attendance. It does appear to be a formal occasion with officers duly proposed and seconded.

In April 1931, a letter was read from the Ladies' Secretary to the Executive Committee. She said that the Ladies wished to appoint local Lady Captains in the future but many Ladies were debarred from this position 'on account of the fact that they were expected to find so many prizes'. She asked the Executive whether they would provide 'one prize for the Summer Meeting that would compensate the Ladies'. This was agreed.

The Earliest Lady Captains

The earliest known Lady Captains were Miss M G Bellhouse in 1928 and Mrs J J Thomas in 1929. Nothing is known about Mrs Thomas other than she later became Vice-Captain during the war years. Miss Bellhouse, however, became a pillar of the Golf Club and was Lady Captain on another three occasions, 1948, 1957 and 1968.

Miss Bellhouse first joined the Club in August 1924. Nothing is known about her or her Captaincy at this stage other than to report that by 1927, 114 ladies had registered as Members (Club's Minutes). As implied earlier, caution must be applied when looking at all membership figures. Many Members appear to re-join occasionally, but not always, with a different address or a different name, but with no mention of their possible resignation beforehand. The figures do not always tally!

THE LADIES' SECTION 1933 - 1945

MISS A WILLIAMS
1933 & 1953

Ganwyd Annie Williams yn Gwynfryn, Nefyn. Capten llong oedd ei thad a byddai ei mam yn cadw llety lle y bu Annie'n gweithio cyn rhedeg y busnes ei hun, yn dilyn marwolaeth ei mam. Bu'n llwyddiannus gyda'r un ymwelwyr yn dychwelyd flwyddyn ar ôl blwyddyn. Meddai ar gymeriad cryf, ond roedd yn berson hael a charedig. Yn ystod y Rhyfel cadwai faciwîs a gweithiai dros y Groes Goch. Roedd hi'n hoff iawn o blant a byddent hwythau yn ei haddoli hi. Roedd yn arddwraig frwdfrydig ac yn aml fe'i gwelid yn yr ardd am chwech yn y bore!

Ymunodd Annie Gwynfryn, fel y cyfeirid ati, â Chlwb Golff Nefyn yn 1927 gyda'i ffrindiau Buddug a Kaleen Owen (Dolwen), chwiorydd y brodyr Robert Davies Owen (Capten y Clwb yn 1949) a Willie Rees Owen (Capten yn 1953).

Bu'n berson blaenllaw ar Buyllgor y Merched am gyfnod hir. Etholwyd hi'n Gapten y Merched yn 1933, ac eto yn 1953. Bu'n Ysgrifennydd Adran y Merched am ddwy flynedd yng nghanol y pumdegau ac etholwyd hi'n Is-Lywydd y Merched yn 1982. Yn yr un flwyddyn, fe'i hetholwyd yn Aelod Anrhydeddus o'r Clwb.

Roedd Annie'n olffwraig frwd ac enillodd sawl gwobr gan gynnwys prif dlysau. Enillodd lwyau a medalau arian dirifedi. Enillodd Ddysgl Rhosyn Dr Griffiths ar chwe achlysur rhwng 1931 a 1963, ac enillodd Cwpan Cefnamwlch bedair o weithiau. Enillodd Wobr Capten y Merched (Mrs Fenwick) yn 1970.

Yn ôl Cofnodion Cyntaf Adran y Merched sy'n dyddio o Fehefin 3ydd 1933, cyhoeddodd y Capten, Miss Annie Williams, ei bwriad i enwi tim o Adran y Merched i herio Tim Adran y Dynion. Yn ystod ei Chapteiniaeth roedd Gŵyl yr Haf yn rhedeg o Ddydd Llun, Awst 14eg, i Ddydd Gwener, Awst 18fed a bu'n llwyddiant mawr gyda nifer mawr yn cymryd rhan. Yn ystod ei blwyddyn, cynhaliwyd gyrfa 'bridge', gyrfa chwist, cystadleuaeth ping-pong a dawns ffurfiol. Yng Nghyfarfod Cyffredinol Cyntaf Adran y Merched a gofnodwyd yn Awst

At the AGM of 1990, Marian Grace, the Secretary, reported she 'had the Minutes of the previous 50 years to hand and our success was due to specifically named ladies - here today - Miss Annie Williams, Miss Mary Roberts, Mrs Dilys Parry and the late Miss Bellhouse'. (sic)

Annie's 'Gully'.

Annie will be forever remembered for 'Annie's Gully'. She was determined that Ladies who had a good drive from the Old 17th Tee should not be penalised as their ball rolled down the slope towards the cliff edge and she campaigned loud and clear for many years.

As early as January 1938, there had been a request to the Men's Committee that the out of bounds penalty be taken away from the 17th (when specifically driving from the Ladies' Tee). There was no reply forthcoming from the Executive. This request continued for years. [There was a constant change in terminology when the Ladies referred to the Club's Main Committee. It was often called 'The Men's Committee' but also referred to as the Executive, or Executive Committee and sometimes simply 'The Men'.]

> **July 1950:** *The 17th Fairway came under discussion. A good drive from the Tee is apt to have a very unfortunate finish, trickling as it often does into the rough. The Secretary was asked to contact the Men's Secretary to see if it were possible to make this particular stretch of land GUR, or have a trench dug, out of which a ball may be picked without penalty. It must be quite understood that this must be a ball off the Tee.*

Members remember a mound being built and there is no doubt that a trench was also dug out in front of the mound. The Ladies again wrote for clarification but received no reply.

> **June 1962:** *The bank on the 17th came under fire again. For a long time this has been a serious thorn in Miss Williams' flesh... The Ladies were informed by the Professional [Dennis Grace] that all matters such as this must be settled by the Men's Committee and, as they are expected to have a meeting at the week-end, we must possess our souls in patience until we know their verdict.*

And so they did, for again no decision was forthcoming.

In the late 70s there was much discussion once more and when Bethan (Ogwen) Rees-Jones, was elected Captain in 1981, she asked for a definitive ruling from the Pro, John Pilkington. Shortly afterwards, a notice appeared in the Locker Room explaining the free drop, without penalty but nothing is minuted in Club records. Ironically though, research shows that the Male Members of the Club have always, within living memory, had a Local Rule allowing a free drop at this point, without penalty for any shot!

With the redesigning of the Centenary Score Card, 'Annie's Gully' appears for the first time as a Local Rule. It is now formally identified as an immovable obstruction under Rule 24/2. Annie's ghost is thus laid to rest!

Extract Form Score Card 2007

Local Rules:
Immovable Obstructions – Rule 24-2(m).
The trench named Annie's Gully on the right hand side half way along the 17th hole (Old Course)

> *N.B. Extracts highlighted on a blue background throughout the book are from the Ladies' Committee's Minutes.*

MRS S J SLEIGH
1934

Mrs Lee, of Cliff Castle, married Wing Commander Sleigh after the death of her first husband and they both lived at Cliff Castle. She originally hailed from Lytham St Anne's and was a nurse by profession. Wing Commander Sleigh was later to become the Captain of the Club in 1945.

Mrs Sleigh was elected Captain at the AGM of August 1933, when there were only 6 Members present! During her Captaincy, the Ladies' Competitions were as follows:

Medal Round   First Saturday in the month
Bogey Competition   Second Wednesday
Extra Day Score   Third Wednesday

By the end of the year the Monthly Medal had been changed to the 1st Wednesday of the month because so many men were playing on Saturdays! Ironically, at the same time, the Ladies' Committee had asked the Club's Committee to reduce the minimum number from 6 to 4 players for the medal to be valid, as so few Ladies were actually playing!

Prizes were given for players up to 29 handicap and then for players 30-36 handicap together with non-handicapped players. It was decided when there was a tie for a competition, a decision should be made on the result of the last 9 in an 18 hole competition and the second 18 for a 36 hole competition as stipulated in the LGU rules. Team matches included matches against Pwllheli, Bangor and Abersoch and a Team was selected to play in the Caernarvonshire Union for the first time.

Mrs Sleigh was a very generous Captain and presented many prizes and spoons. A Captain v Secretary's match was arranged which had a high number of entries (22) and both teams were entertained to tea by Mrs Sleigh.

MRS WILLIAMSON
1935

Little is known about Mrs W Williamson other than she served on the Committee for many years. Her husband A C Williamson served on the Executive Committee throughout the 1930s. In the very first recorded entry of competition results in the Ladies' Minutes, Mrs Williamson is reported as having won an Open Stroke Play Competition on 19 July 1933 with a score of 102-28-74.

The Minutes of 1935 show that there was an increased interest in team matches and Porthmadog Club asked to be included. There is a mention of Extra Day Cards for the first time and 'a Running Competition was planned for each Wednesday and Saturday through the winter months!' This, one assumes, was an eclectic competition! It is also minuted that the Ladies were upset when the ping-pong table disappeared and the Men were requested to return it immediately! A Competition was held so that the money raised could go to buy ping-pong balls! Ping-pong was obviously a very popular pastime in those days.

MISS JOHNSON
1936

Miss M M Johnson and her mother had joined the Club in May 1919. A Mr W Johnson was a member of the Club's Executive Committee for many years around the same time and was made a Life Member in 1930. It is believed he may have been her father. Miss Johnson was a good badminton player and must have played golf quite regularly as her name appears in the Minutes winning various competitions.

Some Members recall her buying a small house opposite the Linksway called Penrhos Cottage and changing the name to 'Tŷ Bach' which literally translated means 'Small House'. However, the locals quickly pointed out that 'Tŷ Bach' in Welsh actually referred to the toilet at the bottom of the garden! She quickly changed the name again, this time to 'Tŷ Clyd' (Cosy House)!

At the AGM of 1936, it was proposed that 'the Ladies' Committee should comprise 8 Members: The Lady Captain, the Lady Vice-Captain, the Secretary and 5 elected Members. A 'Visiting' Member, representing the Summer Visitors should be included for holidays and summer months'. Interestingly, in those days the nomination for Lady Vice-Captain was open to all Lady Members. Anyone could forward a nomination to the Committee for discussion. During 1936, Ladies' Foursomes were introduced for the first time and played on the 4th Wednesday of the month.

MISS D R McCURDY
1937

Rosaline McCurdy lived in Morfa Nefyn and was a sister of Nevin McCurdy who had been Club Secretary for two years (1909-1911). She served on the Ladies' Committee for many years and won many golfing competitions at the Club. Miss McCurdy joined the Club in August 1916 and very much later married Ralph, who was Ena Bellhouse's brother. There was sometimes confusion in the Club between the Miss and the Mrs Bellhouse!

There were only two Ladies' Committee Meetings held in her year of office. In the Club's Executive Minutes however, it reports competitions were to be held on Coronation Day, May 12th. The proceeds were to be put towards King George's Playing Fields, organised by the Nefyn Branch of the British Legion. Mr C S Buckley and Miss McCurdy, the Captains at the time, promised to present prizes for this purpose and the Committee passed a vote of thanks to them. Miss Nellie Trenholme remembers the occasion and recalls receiving a Spoon from Miss McCurdy on this day.

MRS D ANDREWS
1938

Little is known about Mrs Andrews other than she won quite a few competitions including the Dr Griffiths' Rose Bowl in 1939. She also captained the Nefyn Team in inter-club matches.

During her year of office, the LGU was asked to 'allow 2 x 9 holes for Bogey 74 for handicap'. This year also saw the start of debates regarding Annie's Gully (see above under Miss A Williams, 1933).

MISS M ROBERTS
1939, 1949 & 1966

Miss Mary Roberts lived at Rhyllech Mansion, Efailnewydd with her brother, Bill, and was a charming lady of the manor. She was extremely popular, enjoyed her golf and Members recall enjoying playing with her.

Miss Roberts Rhyllech, as she was called, joined the Club in September 1932 with her brother, William Armitage Roberts. She was a good golfer and won many competitions including the Dr Griffiths' Rose Bowl in 1945 and 1948 and the

Cefnamwlch Cup in 1948, 1964 and 1971. She won the Lady Captain's Prize in 1946 with an 88 gross! She was very supportive of new members in the Club and was held in high esteem by all.

Miss Roberts served on the Ladies' Committee for many years and was Acting Lady Secretary for a while. In 1984, she was elected Lady Vice-President.

During this year of her Captaincy, the issue of Ladies' tees not being placed on LGU Tees raised its head for the first time. This complaint against the Greens' Staff was to continue for a long time and over the years many letters were sent to the Club Secretary regarding the issue.

MRS J COWBURN
1940

Mrs Ethel Cowburn joined the Club with her husband in 1921. Her husband served on the Club's Executive Committee for many years and frequently chaired meetings in the absence of the Club Captain. They lived in Bryn Beuno, Tŷ'n Pwll, Nefyn.

Recorded in the Ladies' AGM Minutes of April 1940:
There was a formal proposal and ....all agreed that 'we should ask the men's committee to allow us slab cake for tea'.

Mrs Cowburn was elected Lady Captain in 1940 and at the AGM of 1941 it was agreed that 'the Present Captain, Mrs Cowburn, Vice-Captain, Mrs J J Thomas and Committee continue throughout the war'. (Mrs Jannette J Thomas had been Lady Captain in 1929.) There were only 4 members present at this AGM – the two officials with Miss Mary Roberts, Acting Secretary and Miss Annie Williams. Mary Roberts then resigned and Mrs Mervyn Jones continued as Secretary throughout the war.

The Course was closed during these war years and there are no records of any Committee Meetings of the Ladies' Section, although the main Executive Committee met occasionally.

THE NEXT TWENTY YEARS 1946 - 1965

MRS E MERVYN JONES
1946 & 1954

After the war, at the Ladies' AGM of 1945, a completely new Committee was set up and Mrs Mervyn Jones, Penman, was asked to serve as Captain for 1946. She was also thanked for her 12 years' service as Secretary of the Ladies' Section.

Local Members will remember Mrs Mervyn Jones as Mrs Hughes, La Casina, before she married Mr Mervyn Jones. She won quite a few competitions but her only Major was the Dr Griffiths' Rose Bowl in 1950.

> **July 1946:** A request from the Ladies Committee for cooperation with the House Committee was discussed. The Secretary was asked to convey verbally to the Ladies Secretary, that their cooperation and assistance would be sought if and when there were matters affecting our mutual interests.(sic)

During this year of her Captaincy, the Ladies were consulted regarding the refurbishment of the Clubhouse. The ping-pong table was eventually found and returned to the Ladies' Section and the Club Committee agreed that the upstairs room be used for games. On one golf match occasion, when rain stopped play, the teams played ping-pong instead.

Mrs Mervyn Jones was a very generous lady and gave many prizes to the Ladies' Section. She also gave many gifts for the Clubhouse e.g. curtains, pictures and ashtrays!

MRS HENRY PARRY
1947 & 1955

Magwyd Dilys Parry yn Neiniolen yn ferch i weinidog. Symudodd y teulu i fyw i Nefyn yn 1925. Roedd ei brawd, Gwyn, yn bêl-droediwr medrus a chafodd dreialon gyda Chlwb Arsenal. Mae Gwyn wedi ymddeol ac yn byw gyda'i wraig ym Mro Gwylwyr, Nefyn.

Priododd Dilys â Harry Parry oedd yn ddeintydd ysgolion. Trwy Harry, fe'i cyflwynwyd i'r Clwb Golff a bu'r ddau'n Aelodau selog am flynyddoedd. Gwasanaethodd Dilys ar y Pwyllgor am sawl blwyddyn a bu'n Ysgrifennydd Adran y Merched am bron i bum mlynedd. Etholwyd hi'n Is-Lywydd y Merched yn 1985.

Bu Dilys yn chwarae golff yn rheolaidd ac enillodd nifer o gystadleuthau. Ei phrif fuddugoliaeth, un a'i gwefreiddiodd, oedd ennill Cwpan Cefnamwlch yn 1967.

Mrs Dilys Parry was a minister's daughter and came to Nefyn from Deiniolen in 1925. Her brother, Gwyn Morgan, was a local footballing hero who had trials with Arsenal. Gwyn has retired and he and his wife now live at Bro Gwylwyr, Nefyn.

Dilys married Harry Parry, who was a school dentist and through Harry, she was introduced to the Golf Club. They both became dedicated Members. Dilys served on the Ladies' Committee for many years and was Secretary for close on five years. She was elected Ladies' Vice-President in 1985.

She played golf quite regularly and won a few competitions. She was particularly thrilled to win her only Major, the Cefnamwlch Cup, in 1967.

During her year of Captaincy, improvements to the Clubhouse were on going and the Club Committee were taking heed of the Ladies' suggestions! The Dr Griffiths' Rose Bowl was altered to a medal round with the leading four nett scores then qualifying for match play.

MISS M G BELLHOUSE
1948, (1928) 1957 & 1968

Ena Bellhouse was a niece of Mrs Sleigh, Cliff Castle (Lady Captain 1934), and she came from the North of England to live with Wing Commander and Mrs Sleigh at Cliff Castle. She was very close to the Sleighs and was almost like an adopted daughter.

Miss Bellhouse was a keen and successful golfer. She played for the Nefyn Team on many occasions, playing for the First Team when two teams attended County Meetings. She won the Dr Griffiths' Rose Bowl in 1936 and 1954 and the Cefnamwlch Cup in 1965.

Miss Bellhouse was a dynamic and hard-working Captain. During this year of office, many inter-club matches were played, with Maesdu now joining the group. The Summer Meeting saw the Ladies buying their own prizes instead of being given vouchers by the Club.

The highlight of this golfing year was playing for a new Cup which was presented by Mrs Wynne-Finch, the wife of the Club President. This Cup was not named in the Minutes but from the description it must have been the Cefnamwlch Cup. In this, its first year, it was won by Mrs Seth.

At the AGM of 1948, the Secretary, Mrs Birnage, reported that there had been many improvements to the Club. 'Electric light, curtains and easy chairs have made the Clubhouse a very much nicer and more comfortable place to come to and have been praised by visitors in the summer'. (sic)

> **November 1947:** Mr Robert Jones reported that the wiring of the premises was well in hand.
>
> **December 1947:** Mr Robert Jones was empowered to buy a Lighting Plant suitable for the needs of the Club.

MISS M ROBERTS
1949, (1939) & 1966

(See 1939 for biographical details)

During this year of Miss Roberts' Captaincy, there was concern that only a few ladies were playing in competitions.

It was decided that the Cefnamwlch Final was to be a really big occasion with tea and cakes served afterwards.

> **October 1949:** The Men's Committee had suggested that the Ladies gave up their room for the men. 'This is a matter on which our ladies felt very strongly... and it was agreed that the Ladies Room be retained for our own use.'

This was the year the Winter Eclectic Competition began. Ladies could take out many cards as they wanted at 3d a card. Prizes were still being donated from Members e.g. Miss Bellhouse' prize was played for on 23rd February and won by Miss Annie Williams – a beautiful pair of nylon stockings!

Rhosneigr asked to be involved in inter-club matches.

Two Honours Boards were finally ready for display and an emergency meeting was held to discuss from what dates these Boards should run. One was the Lady Captain's Board and the other, the Cefnamwlch Cup. Some Ladies felt the Captain's Board should date from the opening of the present Clubhouse but as the Secretary pointed out, the records for the early 30s were not intact and it was finally agreed that the Lady Captain's Board should start at 1945 and the Cefnamwlch at 1948.

enillodd wobrau ac yn ystod ei Chapteiniaeth yn 1952, enillodd Ddysgl Rhosyn Dr Griffiths.

Gwasanaethodd Gwen ar y Pwyllgor am nifer o flynyddoedd a chafodd ei phlesio'n fawr pan ei gwahoddwyd i fod yn Gapten Adran y Merched.

Gwen and her twin sister Mary were born and brought up in White Hall, Porthdinllaen with brother Dafydd and older sister Jennie. After leaving Botwnnog Grammar School, Gwen went to Liverpool and qualified as a dispensing chemist. She regularly assisted as a locum in R J Jones' Chemist Shop in Nefyn but her first post after qualifying was with a group practice of doctors in Leek, Staffordshire. The distance did not deter her young boy-friend, Tomi Pen Bont, from visiting her and she frequently returned home for holidays. They soon married and settled in Llŷn. Tomi and Gwen took over running the Pen Bont Hotel in Sarn from Tomi's parents but as Tomi was involved in farming and running a haulage business, the responsibility of running the hotel fell firmly on Gwen's shoulders.

Gwen Roberts, as she was before she married, joined the Golf Club in May 1921. Hers was the era of Annie Gwynfryn, Dilys Parry, Eileen Seth, Win Ogwen Jones, Mary Roberts (Rhyllech), Mary Davies and Mary Roberts, the vet's wife from Pwllheli. These ladies thoroughly enjoyed their golf and the social side that arose from their friendship on the Course. Mary Bernard, Gwen's daughter, recalls the ladies frequenting the old Bay Tree Restaurant in Morfa Nefyn on their way down from the Golf Club and spending many an evening putting the world to right over countless cups of coffee.

Club Captain W L Davies with Lady Captain Gwen Toleman Jones on his right, at a Christmas Function in the Clubhouse, 1951.

The Ladies enjoyed their team matches both at home and away. It was during Gwen's Captaincy that they stayed overnight for the first time while playing in the Caernarfonshire Union Meeting. This was held at Conwy and the Minutes report the meticulous planning that went into the booking of 7 single rooms at the Castle Hotel in Deganwy! This practice was to continue for many years and several Captains recall the fun and enjoyment of these overnight stays. In recent years this practice has been resurrected and in 2007, our Ladies stayed in Llandudno and Holyhead.

Gwen was a fairly good golfer. Her long game was particularly good and she was noted for her driving with a 2 iron. Her putting tended to let her down and although she could have progressed considerably with practice, she preferred to spend the time with her family at home. Practising putting appeared an unexciting alternative! Nevertheless, Gwen did win prizes and won the Dr Griffiths' Rose Bowl in her Captaincy Year, in 1951.

Gwen served on the Ladies' Committee for many years and was delighted to be elected Lady Captain.

During her year of office, Caernarfon Golf Club became involved in interclub matches for the first time. It was agreed to have a Winter

Competition over 9 holes on a weekly basis and the prize? - a golf ball! This in fact, continued right up to 2007 when the prize was changed to a choice of a bottle of wine or 3 golf balls!

> *September 1951:*
> The Recreation Room should be made available for the entertainment for the Children's party.
>
> *October 1951:*
> The Club would support the Ladies in running the Christmas Party......the House Committee being given full powers to act in conjunction with the Ladies' Committee.

During this year also, the Lady Captain and Lady Secretary were invited to sit on the House Committee. In Sept 1951, it is minuted that Mrs T M Jones proposed 'the Children's Party be held on Dec 22nd'. This is the first mention in any Minutes of what became, and still is, a highly popular annual event. In December, Mrs T M Jones and the Lady Secretary were asked to go and buy the presents that would be given out by Father Christmas. For many years, these presents had to be bought in Morfa Nefyn one year and in Nefyn the next, so that the local shop keepers were kept happy!

MRS W P Y SETH
1952

Mr and Mrs William Pratt Ywel Seth came to Nefyn from Scotland at the end of the war. They lived in Penogfa on Nefyn Beach. Mr Seth had been injured by a canon backfiring during the war when he served in the forces as an engineer. They had 2 children, Duncan and Jean, who were looked after by Mrs Cath Rees of Nefyn. Duncan was a prominent Junior in the Club in the 50s when Juniors used to win Major Prizes regularly. It is believed he qualified as a Professional Golfer and went abroad to work. Jean qualified as a teacher and went to teach in the Midlands.

According to Mrs Rees and others, Mrs Eileen Seth was very much a 'Lady'. She was gentle, easy going and very kind, a very good badminton player and an expert cook! Mrs Rees recalls her cooking traditional Scottish recipes. Her homemade ox-tail soup had quite a reputation and in Eileen Seth's words was 'something to stick to your ribs'!

Mr and Mrs Seth joined the Club in March 1946. They both enjoyed their golf and Eileen's world revolved around the Club. The Seths were great friends with Owen Roberts (Club Secretary) and his wife Bet (Lady Captain 1950) and Eileen played a lot of golf with Bet. The four used to play cards regularly of an evening in each others' houses.

Eileen Seth served on the Ladies' Committee for many years and was Secretary of the Ladies' Section for over three years. She was a keen golfer and won many competitions including the Dr Griffiths' Rose Bowl on three occasions and the Cefnamwlch Cup also on three occasions.

During her Captaincy, money was raised through bridge drives, whist drives and various competitions e.g. putting competitions, and the money so raised went to the Ladies' Fund or the Children's fund. It was agreed to have an Honours Board for the Dr Griffiths' Rose Bowl and the Winners' Names were agreed to run from 1945. There was concern over the 15th Tee in the winter and the Greens' Committee was asked to improve and level the Tee.

The Ladies' Committee in the early 50s
Outside the Clubhouse, where the snooker room now stands.
Back Row: Left to Right: Bet Roberts (Captain 1950), Eva Birnage (Captain 1961), E Mervyn Jones (Captain 1954).
Front Row: Annie Williams (Captain 1933 and 1953), Eileen Seth (Captain 1952), Gwen Toleman Jones (Captain 1951) and Dilys Parry (Captain 1955)

MISS A WILLIAMS
1953 (& 1933)

(See 1933 for biographical details)

During Miss Williams' second term of office, Harlech and Criccieth joined the interclub match events. There was a special Coronation Competition and the 'Men's Section' were thanked for their cheque. The Executive had specifically requested the cheque be split into three prizes – 1st £2-15-0, 2nd £1-10-0 and 3rd £1-0-0. Agreed 1st Prize should be bought 'off Mr Grace'.

Christmas 1952 saw the Ladies asking the House Committee for a Christmas Tree for the children's party and it was decided to bring the age limit down to 15.

The County Meeting was held in Nefyn in September, 1953.

The Ladies' Committee in 1953
Back Row: Left to Right: Bet Roberts (Captain 1950), Eileen Seth (Immediate Past Captain), E Mervyn Jones, (later in the year to become Vice-Captain on resignation of Rene Whalley)
Front Row: Mary Roberts (Captain 1939 & 1949), Rene Whalley (Vice-Captain), Annie Williams (Captain), Dilys M Parry (Secretary: Captain 1947 and later in 1955)

MRS E MERVYN JONES
1954 (& 1946)

(See 1946 for biographical details)

During Mrs Mervyn Jones' second year of office, it was agreed that the SS should be 71 from Jan 1954.

The Club Championship was to be 'over 27 holes – 18 + the Back 9, as the Ladies felt 36 holes around the hilly conditions was too taxing'.(sic) This was the first mention of a Club Championship *per se*.

It was agreed that all semi-finals and finals for all the Cups and the Captain's Prize should have markers in their match play!

County Championship was fixed for April 29th-30th at Nefyn. Lunch would be served in Clubhouse during the Championship at 3/- per person...and Mrs Pauline Lane undertook to buy and cook the joint - a 20lb sirloin of beef!

MRS HENRY PARRY
1955 (& 1947)

(See 1947 for biographical details)

At the AGM of 1954, the incoming Captain, Dilys Parry, presented Mrs Edge with a silver cigarette case and lighter for her 25 years of faithful service to the Club as Stewardess.

In 1955, the Lady Captain's Prize was moved out of the Summer Meeting to June. Permission was then sought from the Men's Committee for a Bogey Competition be held in the Summer Meeting instead of the Lady Captain's Prize. The handicap limit for Bogey and Stableford was to be 30 but it is unclear whether this was only for the Summer Meeting.

In April 1955, the Captain, Mrs Parry, offered a prize for a 9 Hole One Club Competition. In subsequent years, a putter was added to make a Two Club Competition.

MRS J OGWEN JONES
1956

Roedd Mrs Win Ogwen Jones yn enedigol o bentref y Rhiw. Byddai yn gwneud llawer o waith cymdeithasol ac yn dda am wneud pethau gyda'i dwylo – fferins a gwniadwaith. Bu'n arddangos ei gwaith mewn arddangosfa yn Llundain unwaith.

Yn yr Adran Efydd fu Mrs Ogwen Jones am ei gyrfa golff a byddai'n chwarae'n rheolaidd bob pnawn Dydd Mercher. Yng Nghyfarfod Cyffredinol Adran y Merched ar ddiwedd ei chyfnod fel Capten, cyflwynodd nifer o wobrau i'r merched oedd wedi sgorio'n dda yn rheolaidd yn ystod y flwyddyn.

Yn 1981, cyflwynodd Mrs Ogwen Jones Dlws ar Ddiwrnod Capten ei merch, Mrs Bethan Rees-Jones. Dyma oedd cychwyniad Pencampwriaeth y Merched, ac yn ddiweddarach adwaenid y gystadleuaeth fel 'Tlws Ogwen Jones'. Byddai'r bedair merch gyda'r 4 sgôr gros gorau, yn chwarae am y Bencampwriaeth mewn cystadleuaeth bwrw allan. Mae Bethan Rees-Jones yn parhau i gyflwyno gwobrau er cof am ei mam i'r gystadleuaeth yma. Etholwyd Mrs Ogwen Jones yn Is-Lywydd y Clwb yn 1988, y wraig gyntaf i gael ei hethol yn dilyn y teulu Wynne-Finch. Bu'n Llywydd y Merched o 1994-96. Gwnaethpwyd hi'n Aelod Oes (y wraig gyntaf yng Nghlwb Nefyn) yn 1994, a phedair blynedd yn ddiweddarach, dathlodd ei phen-blwydd yn 90 oed yn y Clwb gyda'i ffrindiau lu.

Mrs Win Ogwen Jones, brought up in the village of Rhiw, was very much involved in social work. She also enjoyed practical activities, from making sweets to needlework and once had her work exhibited in London.

Mrs Ogwen Jones joined the Club in February 1936. She was a regular player on a Wednesday and played all her golf in the Bronze Section. In her Captain's retiring speech at the AGM of 1956, she gave a prize to a lady Member, Mrs R Whalley, for the greatest reduction in handicap during the year. She also gave prizes for the best six cards returned in the year: The Silver Division Prize being won by Miss E Bellhouse and the Bronze Division by Mrs D Parry.

In 1981, Mrs Ogwen Jones volunteered to buy a crystal bowl to be played for in her daughter, Bethan Rees-Jones' Captain's Day. This was for the best Gross Score on the Day and was the birth of the Club Championship as we know it. It was won by Dr E Buchanan. Having discussed this further with daughter Bethan however, Mrs Ogwen Jones wanted a more permanent annual competition to be played and proposed a change of format for what became the 'Ogwen Jones Club Championship Competition'. The Committee approved and the Competition became a medal round with the best 4 gross scorers then playing a Knockout. Mrs Ogwen Jones bought prizes annually for the Competition and the Ladies' Section bought a shield to be engraved as a memento. Two shields are in existence and they were finally replaced with a cut glass trophy in 2007. The Competition is in the same format today and Mrs Bethan Rees-Jones presents prizes in memory of her mother. (See Chapter on Trophies and Competitions)

Mrs Ogwen Jones was elected a Lady Vice-President in 1988, and later, following on from the Wynne-Finch family, she was the first lady Member to be elected Ladies' President (1994-1996). She was elected a Life Member of the Club in 1997 and was the first lady to receive this honour from the Club. Soon after, she celebrated her 90th birthday with all her friends at the Golf Club.

MISS M G BELLHOUSE
1957 (& 1948)

(See 1948 for biographical details)

This was the year the Club celebrated its Golden Jubilee although there is no mention anywhere in the Ladies' Minutes of any kind of celebration during the year. However in the Executive Minutes, it was reported that Two Jubilee Competitions were played in September comprising an 18 Hole Medal and a Fourball Best Ball Bogey.

It was during the AGM of this year that the Male Membership voted in favour of Sunday Golf and from March 1958, the Clubhouse and Bar opened on Sundays for the first time.

> *May 1957:* The Secretary was asked to write to the Men's Committee to ask for an increase in the amount of food in the 2/- tea!

> *June 1957:* It was decided to ask for more bread and butter for tea – and if charged more, then the Secretary should have an interview with the Men's Secretary and the Chairman of House Committee.

MRS V S EDWARDS
1958

Mrs V S (Di) Edwards lived in Chester but had a holiday home in Morfa Nefyn. From the Minutes it appears she played for the Nefyn Team and during her Captaincy Year, playing off 30 handicap, hers was one of the 4 best nett scores to qualify for the Cefnamwlch Cup Knockout.

Mrs Di Edwards played golf with Nellie Trenholme and Gladys Roberts. Nellie recalls she was quite a seamstress and made her own clothes. When Mrs Edwards and her husband retired to Morfa Nefyn, they bought a house called 'Triarddeg' (Thirteen) near Evan Pritchard's Garage.

It was during her Captaincy year that the Committee agreed to set up 9 hole competitions or putting competitions for those who could not manage to play 18 holes. It was also the year that Dorothy Wood gave her medal prize in the Summer Meeting for the first time.

> June 1958: Letter from Owen Roberts stating the Ladies' Room was being given to the new Steward and Stewardess... The Lady Secretary was asked to reply conveying the very strong feeling of all the Ladies on the Committee and all the Lady Members of the Club!

MRS P H LANE
1959

Pauline came to Morfa Nefyn in 1947 and was appointed receptionist at the Linksway Hotel where she replaced Betty, Peter Lane's sister.

She married Peter Lane in 1949, joined the Golf Club and started playing golf. She claims not to have reached a great height in her golf but nevertheless, she won several prizes. Her lowest handicap was 27 and she remembers ruining many medal cards with a 10 here or a high score there. However, she excelled in match play as is testament in her winning the Captain's Prize in 1978, the Dr Griffiths' Rose Bowl in 1977 and the Cefnamwlch Cup three times, 1968, 1976 and 1980.

Pauline was Handicap Secretary for two years in the late 70s and Secretary in 1982. She thoroughly enjoyed her year as Lady Captain in 1959 and her period as Lady President, from Nov 1996 extending through to Easter 1999 because of the re-positioning of the date of the Ladies' AGM.

The Lady President's Brooch, bought for £135, was presented for the first time at the AGM of 1997 as Pauline was beginning her second year as Lady President.

Pauline feels very honoured at having been made a Life Member at Nefyn Golf Club, for, she says, 'Nefyn Members mean the world to me'. She feels sorry to have had to leave the district but she felt that the time was right for her to be near her family in Lancashire.

Peter, Pauline's husband, was Captain of the Club in 1960, following on from Pauline's Year. Peter particularly supported the Juniors at the Club and after his untimely death in 1981, Pauline offered a trophy, in May 1982, to be named 'The Lane Trophy'. This was to be played by Juniors annually in the August meeting in Peter's memory. The annual replicas are provided by the Lane Family. In February 1988, it was resolved to have an Honours Board for the Lane Trophy. The Club was delighted that in our Centenary Year, Pauline travelled from Garstang to present the trophy to the winning Junior, Matthew Astbury.

MISS E TRENHOLME
1960

Ganwyd Ellen Trenholme (Nellie) ym Manceinion yn 1917 ynghyd â'i brawd, Jim. Roedd ei thad yn beiriannydd gyda'r GEC a'i hewythr, Tom, ddechreuodd gwmni 'Nefyn Blue Buses'. Symudodd Nellie i fyw i Nefyn gyda'i Nain a'i Thaid pan oedd hi'n dair oed.

1960 was the year the Ladies wrote to the Men's Committee to ask if they could have their own bank account. The men refused... 'because they never refused them anything they wanted... and it is advisable to carry on as they were!' (sic). This was so frustrating for the Ladies as they had to formally ask the Men for everything – from paper towels to sanitary bins!

A letter was written to Lady Gladys Wynne-Finch in January 1960, inviting her to become the first Lady President of the Club, an honour she happily and very willingly accepted. She subsequently was elected Club President following the death of her husband, at the Club's AGM of 1962.

MRS E BIRNAGE
1961

Mr and Mrs Birnage came here from the Manchester area where Mr Birnage was an insurance broker. They lived in a large house, Westerley, on the way down to the beach in Morfa Nefyn. At first they came only for summer holidays, with their housekeeper in tow. Mrs Birnage joined the Club in December, 1938 and they eventually moved here permanently.

Their house had wonderful golden plums and pears and a particular young lady, who subsequently became a Lady Captain and Lady President of our Club, in her youth, would go with her male partner in crime and steal these pears, plums and apples when the Birnages were away! They were never caught and she lives to tell the tale!

The Birnages had a daughter Claire who married Trefor Taylor from Pwllheli. Claire played golf in Nefyn and Pwllheli and was a good friend of Annette Jones. Later the Birnages moved to Pwllheli where their daughter Claire, now lives.

Mrs Birnage was Ladies' Secretary from 1947 to 1951 and again for one year in 1961-1962. She was also Secretary of the Caernarfonshire Ladies' Golfing Union for a period. She had some wonderful phrases in her reporting of the Minutes. In June 1962, while awaiting a response from the Men's Committee regarding a decision on 'Annie's Gully' (17th Fairway) she was the one who stated, 'we must possess our souls in patience until we know their verdict'.

It was during Mrs Birnage's Captaincy that the Ladies held their first ever Extraordinary General Meeting, on March 1st 1961. This was called because the Committee could not agree with a motion that had been passed at the previous AGM regarding the selection and nomination of a new Vice-Captain.

After much discussion it was finally agreed that, 'Any member could suggest a name for Vice-Captain and put it to the Committee. The final word to come from the Committee before the lady concerned is contacted and the name then put on the AGM notice board'. (sic)

It was also agreed 'that no member shall serve on the committee for more than two years and thereafter shall not be eligible for re-election for one year'.

MRS A W WHALLEY
1962

Rene Whalley came to Llŷn with her husband from Canada where he had been working and they lived at Perth Celyn, Edern. He was an architect and was responsible for many reconstructions on the Course. They had two children – the son went into farming in North Wales and the daughter emigrated to Canada, where Rene went when her husband died.

Rene joined the Club with her husband in June 1947 and her address is given as 'Tan y Dderwen, Nevin'. Rene was a good golfer although her name only appears on the actual Honours Boards once – the Dr Griffiths' Rose Bowl in 1961. She nevertheless won many other competitions. She tended to be quite an independent lady and kept herself very much to herself.

During her Captaincy, meetings were held at houses of the officials while extensions to the Clubhouse were completed. During her year of office, after much discussion it was decided to have referees for the Dr Griffiths' Rose Bowl and Cefnamwlch Cup Finals and also for the Lady Captain's Prize, which took a similar format in those days.

Rene Walley was Ladies' Secretary from 1967 to 1970.

MRS A E SMART
1963

Pip Smart is one of our senior Lady Members at Nefyn Golf Club. On her first visit to Nefyn, she stayed at one of the coastguard houses by the Club with her two young children. During the August Bank Holiday of 1950, while attending a local riding school, she met Alec, had a whirlwind romance and they got married in the November.

Pip joined the Club in August 1934 and she has been a Member of the Club ever since. She was the very first Handicap Secretary, holding the position for five years and Secretary of the Ladies' Section for three years. Following her Captaincy in 1963, she was elected County Captain for the period 1969-72 and was also County President. She was a Welsh Ladies' Selector for over six years and her lowest Club handicap was 7.

Pip won the Dorothy Wood Trophy on numerous occasions as well as other Ladies' Section's trophies. She adored Team Games and was instrumental in starting the Ladies' Leagues, i.e. Shield Matches.

Pip, Owen Roberts and Dennis Grace ran the August Meeting Competitions for many years. In fact, she recalls her buying Owen Roberts the odd drink or two but Owen always seemed to have left his change at home when it came to his round!

In January 1963, it was agreed that the Ladies should fix a game to play with Juniors and the Juniors should have a hot-pot supper afterwards. This Match against Juniors actually went ahead in September and both the Match and hot pot supper paid for by Ladies were a great success. Consequently another match was arranged, this time Ladies and Juniors v the Men!

MRS G ROBERTS
1964

Mrs Gladys Roberts was originally from the Bolton area and came to Nefyn as a young girl to work as Nanny and Companion to Miss Nellie Trenholme's Auntie Margaret. Gladys met and married Ben, who was a Member of the Golf Club and a bus driver for the Nefyn Blue Buses.

Gladys showed no interest in golf for some time. She had one daughter, Brenda, who married Michael Martin, another golfer and Member at Nefyn.

Nellie Trenholme invited Gladys to the Club and she became a Member. It is unclear exactly when she joined but she certainly played golf during the war years (See Nellie's recollections in the Chapter 'I remember…') At this time, she and Ben were living in Gwynle, Nefyn, close to Nellie and the two became very great friends. Gladys took to the game like a duck to water and soon reduced her handicap and played in the Silver Division. She was very competitive and was an excellent match-player. She won numerous competitions and her name appears frequently on the Honours Boards in the Club. She won the Dr Griffiths' Rose Bowl on five occasions, 1966, 1969, 1979, 1980 and 1982 and the Cefnamwlch Cup on four occasions, 1972, 1973, 1977 and 1981. She won the Lady Captain's Prize in 1980. Members recall her game. She was not a particularly long hitter but was accurate and lethal round the greens. Pauline Lane recollects her putting. 'She would close one eye, look at the hole, line her putter, open the other eye and put the ball straight into the hole!' Perhaps we should try it?

In 1992, Gladys was elected Ladies' Vice President of the Club. She was Handicap Secretary of the Ladies' Section for nearly eight years. Gladys died, aged 92, during our Centenary Year.

> **Oct 1964:** In the preparations for the AGM, a notice was to be put up stating 'All members attending the meeting will be cordially invited to tea by the Lady Captain'. This had been agreed because it was felt that in the past this invitation to tea had been abused by certain members who didn't or couldn't attend the AGM but still came to tea! (sic)

MRS M LEIGH MORGAN
1965

Mrs Margaret Leigh Morgan with her husband, Val, ran the Vic in Llithfaen before they retired to Edern. They owned a famous parrot that not only talked but imitated Margaret in many ways, for example, in her blowing her nose! Margaret is remembered for having her hair immaculately twisted like 'ear-phones' over her ears! Margaret and Val both played golf and she served on the Ladies' Committee for many years. She was Lady Secretary in 1962 and again in 1966.

Margaret was responsible for swelling the ranks on Wednesday afternoons. When she was Captain, she made a concerted effort to try and find more local ladies to join the Club and play golf during the week. In the Annual Dinner, she named Annette Jones and Marian Grace amongst others, as examples of ladies who had just taken up the game and were playing regularly on Wednesdays and thoroughly enjoying themselves. She encouraged Members to invite others to join and a new influx of ladies then did join – Members like Mrs Enid Evans – and the numbers on Wednesdays began to increase.

A new system of handicapping was announced on Feb 1st 1965 and each Club was directed to appoint a Handicap Secretary to deal with these new Regulations. Pip Smart was appointed the Club's first Handicap Secretary.

> **Dec 1965:** *It was proposed ...and agreed that towels be placed in the wash room for the convenience of golfers wishing to clean balls after play. Also nailbrushes were necessary.*

'EVERYTHING TOOK OFF'
(AGM 1966)
1966 - 1978

MISS M ROBERTS
1966 (& 1949)

(See 1949 for biographical details)

Lady Captain's Day, 1966.
Pictured in the evening are the Ladies who took part in Miss Mary Roberts' Lady Captain's Day. **Front Row, second from Right leaning forward,** *is Mignon Fenwick, the winner. On her right is the Lady Captain, and on her right, front row is Pip Smart, Runner-up. Harry Parry managed to get into the photo!*

It was at the AGM of 1965 that an Invitation Day was first proposed. It was the new Lady Captain, Miss Roberts that proposed 'we have an Invitation Day Foursomes at Nefyn, when we could invite friends to enjoy the beauty of our course'. It was felt that the Ladies Fund should cover the cost of the prizes and also make some contribution towards tea. It was left to the Committee to decide on the date and it actually took place in April 1966.

In June, there was a change of format for Lady Captain's Day. From being a knockout, it was now to be an 18 hole medal, one division only, with a nett first and second prize.

It was in 1966 that the Winter Eclectic Competition was resurrected. Mrs Mair Griffith presented 2 prizes for the two divisions (Scratch to 23 and 24 – 36) . Each player had to buy 12 cards at 3/- and the Competition was played 'on the last 9 holes if playable!' This Winter Eclectic proved to be very popular and kept the interest in golf alive during the winter months.

At the AGM of 1966, the Secretary said that 1966 was 'when everything took off... There were 4 inter-club matches and 30 competitions played during the year. 28 Ladies competed in Invitation Day and 20 Ladies went on the first Outing to Conway'. At the meeting, the retiring Lady Captain was particularly thanked for being so supportive of beginners.

MRS L G EVANS
1967

Mr and Mrs Lloyd George Evans were Members of the Golf Club for many years but little is known about her, other than she joined the Club in January 1960. Mr Lloyd George Evans served on the Executive Committee for some years but resigned when they both moved away to Oxford to live. They lived in Gorphwysfa, Mynydd Nefyn, for a while before moving down to Nefyn, behind Cliff Castle.

Annual Club Dinner in 1967
Pictured Left to Right: Lloyd George Evans, and his wife Lady Captain Clara Evans, Mrs Tom Poole, Stewardess, and her daughter Jane Poole, Stella Fitzpatrick (Lady Captain 1999) and husband Henry Fitzpatrick (Chairman of House Committee 1967, Captain 1970) with Tom Poole, Steward.

During Mrs Clara Evans' Captaincy, Lady Wynne-Finch resigned and Mrs Rosemary Wynne-Finch consented to be our Lady President.

It was also during 1967 that a new Competition, namely the RNLI Spoon Competition, was played and this continues annually to the present day. The money raised was given to the Men's Section who then presented a £5 donation to the RNLI.

Annie Williams introduced another new Competition during this year. This was an 'All Win a Prize Competition' and was held in March. She felt strongly that some Members never really had any chance of winning a prize and this was her way of ensuring everyone won something! This has since become a tradition on our Autumn and Spring Outings together with our Christmas Cheer Competition!

July 1967: Mrs Murray (Visitor Representative on the Committee and married to the Club Captain) asked the Lady Captain and the Committee 'if there was anything the Men's Captain could do for us then let her know. This was much appreciated'! (sic)

MISS M G BELLHOUSE
1968 (1928, 1948, 1957)

(See 1948 for biographical details)

At the 1967 AGM when she came into office, Miss Bellhouse said she felt like the 'proverbial bad penny turning up again'. This was her fourth term of office as Lady Captain of the Club!

Miss Bellhouse served on the Ladies' Committee for a considerable number of years and was very knowledgeable about golf rules and etiquette. She was Secretary of the Ladies' Section for five years in the 70s and was elected Ladies' Vice-President in 1982.

Annette Jones (Lady Captain, 1978) remembers learning a lot about the game of golf from her. When they first started playing golf in the early 60s, she and Marian Grace were quite in awe of playing with her, and at times quite terrified! 'Never ground your club in the bunker' she would say in a tone of voice that made them shudder and guaranteed they would remember that voice every time they stepped into a bunker!

At the AGM of 1968, it was confirmed that Rule 36 in the Golf Book of Rules laid the responsibility for organising competitions in the hands of the Committee and was nothing to do with an AGM!

During 1968, the Australian Spoon Competition was played for the first time and Nefyn contemplated sending a team to play in the Welsh Team Championship held in October at Nefyn, also for the first time. However, the Minutes show no evidence of a team being selected nor the Championship taking place at Nefyn!

MRS S WORRALL
1969

Eve's first contact with Nefyn Golf Club came through Alec and Pip Smart, some fifty years ago. Eve, and Sam her husband, became best of friends with Alec and Pip (Captain 1962 and Lady Captain 1963). They were all good golfers and enjoyed many happy games together. They regularly supported Club functions, thoroughly enjoying each occasion.

Eve was very involved with golf from an early age. She was Captain of her own Club, Oxley Park, in Wolverhampton, more than once and progressed into the Staffordshire Ladies' Team. She became County Captain, then a Member of the English Ladies' Golf Association (ELGA) Committee and finally President of Staffordshire Ladies' Golf. Staffordshire became County Champions on two occasions during her Captaincy. Her lowest handicap was 8.

At the AGM of November 1968, a proposal was passed that the Ladies' AGM should move to Easter to coincide with the Men's AGM. This was so that the Captains' years of office could run concurrently and Eve agreed to serve as Lady Captain for sixteen months. During her Captaincy, Eve offered to present a new Honours Board to the Club, namely the Lady Captain's Prize Board and her husband, Sam donated a beautiful shield to record the winners of the Lady Captain's Prize. Twenty years later, daughter, Miss Worrall, bought a new Lady Captain's Prize Shield.

During Eve's Captaincy, a Grandmothers v The Rest Match was held. A Rule was passed that 'if a stone was within 6 inches of a ball in a bunker it may be removed, the playing marker having being first informed'.

The new Club House Extension was officially opened at the St David's Day Dinner, March 1970. (See Captains' Chapter, 1969, Captain Dan W Jones.)

Nefyn Golf Club, Owen Roberts and many others, played a big and happy part in Eve's life. Di Carroll, her daughter, maintains her mother was at her happiest in Nefyn. Her mother's influence has passed down though the generations and her family continue to be Members of the Golf Club. However, according to Di, they are not such accomplished golfers as her mother but they do play regularly and happily support the Club.

July 1969: Lady Captain said that she had been informed by the Capt and Men's Sec (Captain Dan Jones and Owen Roberts) that they reserved the right to arrange Mixed Foursomes, entertainment etc without consulting the Ladies' Committee and would put a notice on the board.

MRS H G FENWICK
1970

Mignon Fenwick was born and lived in Oldham, Lancashire where her mother owned a sweet shop and her father played in the Hallé Orchestra. After leaving school, she started work as a 'carpet sewer' at Buckley-Proctors in Oldham. There she met Elizabeth Walton, the Head Buyer, who decided to set up her own business and asked Mignon to work for her. This she did and worked in the business after Elizabeth Walton died.

Mignon married Geoff Fenwick who used to come down to Nefyn for holidays. He brought her with him on one occasion and when she saw the Drapery Shop, London House, in the village, she made up her mind to buy it one day and retire to Nefyn. This she actually did in 1962 and named it 'Elizabeth Walton'. She was an astute business woman and had an appealing way with her customers, many of whom came many miles to buy her clothes.

In June 1963, she joined the Golf Club and became Lady Captain in 1970. She was Lady Secretary 1971-1973 and again 1977-1981. She retired in 1979 owing to ill health and died in December 1983.

During 1970, there was a plea from Mrs Pip Smart, the County Captain, that the Ladies should promote Junior Golf and take advantage of the excellent training facilities on offer by the County. Indeed, Miss Bellhouse provided a prize for a Junior Competition in August and it was intended to be an annual event. A County Match for Girls and Boys was held at Nefyn in the summer, with the Nefyn Ladies providing all the prizes.

On July 29th 1970, there was a hugely successful Exhibition Match at the Club involving Dai Rees, Peter Alliss, Dave Thomas and Bernard Hunt. The total takings were £673, £458 of which was given to the charity, 'Lord Roberts' Homes'.

September 1970: The Ladies had written to the Hon Secretary asking that the spring on the locker room door be mended. The Hon Sec 'told the ladies to bring it up again when things were a bit quieter'. [A new spring was fitted in the following January!]

MRS E TOLEMAN-JONES
1971

Roedd Elsie Toleman-Jones yn briod i un o bartneriad Pierce Jones and Sons, Pwllheli ac roedd hi ei hun yn hannu o Bwllheli. Byddai ei thad yn gwerthu burum mewn siop yn Mitre Terrace yn y dre.

Arferai Elsie ddod yn selog i'r golff bob dydd Mercher ac roedd hi'n boblogaidd iawn. Roedd pawb yn mwynhau chwarae efo hi gan ei bod yn gwmni mor dda. Bu'n gwasanaethu ar Bwyllgor y Merched am nifer o flynyddoedd a chafodd ei hethol yn Is-Lywydd y Merched yn 1989. Yn 1956 enillodd Gwpan Cefnamwlch a Dysgl Rhosyn Dr Griffiths.

Elsie Toleman-Jones was from Pwllheli and married into the Pierce Jones and Sons Partnership there. Her father sold yeast in a shop in Mitre Terrace in the town.

Elsie was a Member at both Pwllheli and Nefyn Golf Clubs and had been Lady Captain at Pwllheli in 1959. She came regularly to play golf in Nefyn every Wednesday and was very popular. Current local Members recall that Ladies were eager to play with her because she was such good company!

Elsie served on the Committee for some years and was made Lady Vice-President in 1989. She won many prizes but her peak performance came in 1956 when she won both the Cefnamwlch and the Dr Griffiths' Rose Bowl.

During Elsie's year of office, Mrs Lane offered a prize and proposed a Winter Competition which was extremely successful in keeping interest during the winter months. Ladies received 1 point for entering, 2 points for being runner-up and 3 points for winning, on a weekly basis.

MRS FRANK EVANS
1972

Magwyd Enid yn y White Horse yn Llanengan ac yn nes ymlaen yn Tegfan, Abersoch. Yn dilyn ei dyddiau ysgol, ymunodd â'r WRAF yng nghyffiniau Rhydychen cyn dychwelyd i Benrhos, lle cyfarfu â'i darpar ŵr, Frank. Ar un cyfnod, bu'n cynorthwyo ei thaid i edrych ar ôl siop Glandulyn, Abersoch.

Merched y Glannau at the Official Opening of the Extension to the Club, March 1970.
From Left to Right: Front Row: Rhiannon Jones, Buddug Williams, Gwen Hughes, Gwen Thomas, Mair Pritchard Ellis, Madge Parry and Marian Grace.
Back Row: Helen Mai Roberts, Margaret Williams, Laura Wyn Roberts, Enid Evans, Nellie Trenholme, Vivian Rees Jones, Wenna Davies Hughes and Annette Jones.
(Apart from Margaret Willams and Madge Parry, they were all Members of the Golf Club.)

Ar ôl priodi, symudodd y teulu i fyw i Swyddfa Bost Nefyn yn 1947 ac yno y magwyd pump o blant. Cymerai Enid ddiddordeb mawr mewn cerddoriaeth ers y dyddiau cynnar pan fu'n cystadlu yng nghôr ei thaid. Roedd yn gyfeilydd heb ei hail ac yn dalentog iawn am chwarae heb gopi. Yn aml, byddai Enid yn cyfeilio i nifer o Aelodau a fyddai'n canu o gwmpas y piano. Byddai Sam Worrall yn cyd-gyfeilio gyda hi ar adegau ac yn aml iawn byddai'r adloniant yn ymestyn ymhell i'r nos!

Bu'n arwain ac yn cyfeilio sawl côr a bu ei chôr, Merched y Glannau, yn difyrru sawl cynulleidfa yng Nghlwb Golff Nefyn. Ar y cychwyn, roedd Enid wedi ffurfio grŵp sgiffl i gystadlu yn Eisteddfod flynyddol Sefydliad y Merched yn Edern yn y chwedegau. Yn sgil eu llwyddiant, penderfynodd ddatblygu'r grŵp yn gôr ffurfiol a ganwyd 'Merched y Glannau'. Trefnwyd agoriad ffurfiol i estyniad Lolfa'r Clwb ar Ddathliad Dydd Gŵyl Dewi, Mawrth 6ed 1970 a gwelir Merched y Glannau, a fu'n difyrru ar y noson yn y llun ar y chwith.

Ymunodd Enid a Frank â'r Clwb Golff yn 1948 a buan iawn y daeth elfen gystadleuol Enid i'r brig ar y Cwrs Golff, lle bu hi'n llwyddiannus wrth ennill sawl cwpan. Fodd bynnag, ond un prif gystadleuaeth a enillodd Enid, sef Dysgl Rhosyn Dr Griffiths ym mlwyddyn ei Chapteiniaeth. Byddai'n cael pleser mawr o chwarae mewn cystadleuthau pedwarawdau cymysg ac ar un achlysur rhoddodd gerydd i Shan, yn dilyn ei phriodas â Gareth Gruffydd, am ddwyn ei phartner oddi arni!

Yn dilyn cyfnod hir ar bwyllgorau Adran y Merched, etholwyd Enid yn Gapten Adran y Merched yn 1972, yr un flwyddyn â'i gŵr, Frank. Dyma'r tro cyntaf yn hanes y Clwb i ŵr a gwraig fod yn Gapteiniaid ar yr un pryd.

Ym mis Mai 1992 ymddiswyddodd Enid o'i swydd fel Ysgrifennydd Teithiau'r Merched, tasg roedd wedi ymgymryd â hi ers 1972. Cyflwynwyd iddi lun mewn ffrâm o Dŷ'r Clwb mewn cydnabyddiaeth o'i gwaith caled. Yn 1999 etholwyd hi'n Llywydd y Merched am ddwy flynedd.

Enid was brought up in the White Horse Inn, Llanengan and later at Tegfan, Abersoch. Following her school days, she joined the WRAF in the Oxford area before returning to Penrhos, where she met her husband to be, Frank. At one stage, she helped her grandfather to look after the Glandulyn Stores at Abersoch.

Following their marriage, Frank and Enid moved in 1947 to the Post Office at Nefyn, where they brought up five children. Enid had shown a great deal of interest in music from a very early age when she used to compete with her grandfather's choir. Music was in her blood.

She was a wonderful pianist and very talented in the art of playing by ear. Following many annual general meetings and Club dinners, Enid would accompany Members singing around the piano. Sam Worrall occasionally joined her on the piano and there was often a good 'knees up' after the official business.

A typical sing-a-long with Enid at the ivories.

Enid conducted and accompanied several choirs and her choir, 'Merched y Glannau' [Ladies of the Shores] entertained many audiences at Nefyn Golf Club, especially at St David's Day Dinners.

Originally, Enid had formed a 'skiffle group' to compete at the annual WI Eisteddfod held in

> **March 1969:** It was resolved to thank Mrs Enid Evans and her troupe of talented players for such an excellent programme. [St David's Day Dinner entertainment]

Edern in the 60s. Such had been their success that she decided to develop this group into a formal choir and 'Merched y Glannau' was born. The Official Opening Ceremony of the Extension to the Clubhouse took place at the St David's Day Dinner (1970) when the Choir sang and pictured earlier above are those who actually performed on that evening.

Enid and Frank had joined the Club in 1948 and her competitive spirit soon came to the fore on the Golf Course. She was very successful and won several prizes although her only Major in the Ladies' Section was the Dr Griffiths' Rose Bowl in her Lady Captain's Year.

Enid particularly enjoyed playing in mixed foursomes competitions and on one occasion she chided Shan, following her marriage to Gareth Gruffydd, for taking her regular mixed foursomes partner away from her!

Megan M Williams is congratulated by Enid Evans for being the first ever winner of the Seniors' Silver Salver in 1988.

In September 1987, Enid Evans presented a Silver Salver to the Ladies' section for the Best Aggregate Score for LGU Medals from April to October. Originally, the eligibility for entry was confined to Local Ladies aged 55 and over.

Enid served on the Ladies' Committee for many years and in 1972 she was elected Lady Captain. Husband Frank was elected Club Captain at the AGM of 1972 and they became the first husband and wife to be Captains of the Club in the same year!

July 1972: The first ever Ladies' Outing to Holyhead [May 1972 - organised by Lady Captain Enid Evans] had cost 75p Green Fee and 70p for coffee on arrival, light lunch and tea.

In May 1992, Enid resigned as Outing Secretary, a task she had diligently undertaken since 1972. The Members presented her with a framed picture of the Clubhouse in recognition of all her hard work. In 1999, she was elected Lady President, an office she held for two years. This was the second time she had been elected the Lady President of a Club as the honour had been bestowed on her in 1991 by Abersoch Golf Club.

MRS P F MITCHELL
1973

Betty Mitchell (Peter Lane's sister) was born in Morfa Nefyn and lived in the village until 1948 when she married Peter Mitchell. They moved to Birmingham, where she still resides.

Her first memory of Nefyn Golf Club is when she entered the children's putting competition at the tender age of five. This was an annual event in August. Betty became a Junior, then a Full Member and eventually became Lady Captain in 1973. Sadly she is not able to play golf any more and consequently she has recently resigned from the Club.

There had been a decision at the AGM of 1971 that the AGM of 1973 should be moved back to November, allowing for easier account keeping. It would also mean the Ladies would be more in line with the LGU Year. It was decided to have 2 AGMs that year. A 'Visiting Member' was elected Captain at the April AGM for 7 months only and a local Captain then elected at the November AGM for the following year! This Visiting Member Captain was Betty Mitchell.

Ten years later, in 1983, Betty became Lady Captain at Edgbaston Golf Club.

MRS R EDGAR JONES
1974

Roedd Helen Edgar yn briod â Richard Edgar Jones, (Capten 1981). Cyfarfu'r ddau tra 'roeddynt yn yr ysgol ym Mhwllheli gan symud i Fangor,

THE LADY CAPTAINS - CAPTEINIAID Y MERCHED

Richard i astudio Ffiseg yn y Brifysgol a Helen i hyfforddi i fod yn athrawes ysgol gynradd yn y Coleg Normal. Dychwelodd y ddau i Ben Llŷn i briodi. Apwyntiwyd Richard yn Bennaeth Ffiseg ym Mhwllheli ac ymunodd Helen â staff Owen Roberts yn Ysgol Gynradd Nefyn.

Rhoddodd Helen y gorau i ddysgu pan anwyd eu mab, Iwan. Ni ddychwelodd i'r ystafell ddosbarth a bu'n edrych ar ôl siop ddillad merched ym Mhwllheli am gyfnod o ryw ugain mlynedd. Roedd teulu Helen wedi bod yn berchen ar y siop ers 1896 a gofalwyd amdani gan ddwy fodryb iddi. Ymfalchïai Helen yn ei hymddangosiad gan wisgo'n drwsiadus bob amser.

Ymunodd Helen a Richard â Chlwb Golff Nefyn yn 1962 a buan iawn y datblygodd Helen i fod yn gystadleuol. Bu'n chwarae oddi ar 24 ar un cyfnod ac er iddi ennill nifer o wobrau bychain, daeth ei 'hawr fawr' pan enillodd Gwpan Cefnamwlch ym mlwyddyn ei Chapteiniaeth a chael ei henw ar y Byrddau Anrhydedd.

Yn 1974, pan oedd Helen yn Gapten, rhaid oedd dileu nifer fawr o gystadleuthau oherwydd tywydd gwael. Cafwyd cynigiad gan Marian Grace a gadarnhawyd gan Bwyllgor y Merched, y dyliai'r penderfyniad i ddileu cystadleuaeth fod yn nwylo Capten y Merched, yr Is-Gapten ac Ysgrifennydd y Merched. Pe na byddant hwy ar gael, yna dylai tair Aelod arall o Bwyllgor y Merched wneud y penderfyniad.

Ym Mehefin 1975, gwahoddwyd deg o Aelodau Adran y Merched, yn cynnwys Helen Edgar, gan Gapten Dan W Jones i chwarae gyda'i wahoddedigion - y 'Master Mariners' o Southampton. (Gweler llun y grŵp isod.)

Helen Edgar oedd y gyntaf o Gapteiniaid y Merched i arwyddo Cofnodion Pwyllgor y Merched yn y Gymraeg. Byddai'n mynnu llenwi ei cherdyn sgorio yn y Gymraeg ac yng Nghyfarfod Cyffredinol Blynyddol 1974, traddodwyd y diolchiadau i Helen yn y Gymraeg gan Annette Jones. Dyma'r tro cyntaf y cyfeiriwyd at yr Iaith Gymraeg yng nghofnodion Pwyllgorau Adran y Merched.

Etholwyd Helen Edgar yn Gapten Adran y Merched yng Nghlwb Golff Pwllheli yn 1992.

Helen Edgar, as she was called, was married to the late Richard Edgar Jones, (Captain, 1981). They met while at school in Pwllheli and went to Bangor together, he to the University to read Physics while she went to the Normal College to train as a primary school teacher. They returned to this area and married. Dic Edgar was appointed Head of Physics in Pwllheli while Helen was appointed a teacher at Nefyn School, under the Headship of Owen Roberts.

Helen gave up teaching when their son, Iwan, was born. She never returned to the classroom but took over a ladies' clothes shop in Pwllheli for a period of at least 20 years. This shop had been in the family since 1896 and had been run by two aunts. Helen herself had great pride in her appearance and was always smartly dressed.

Helen and Dic joined the Club in 1962 and she became extremely competitive. Her lowest handicap was 24 and although she won many smaller prizes, her 'moment of glory', as she called it, was when she won the Cefnamwlch Cup in same year as her Captaincy. She had finally got her name up on the Honours Boards!

During 1974, many competitions had to be cancelled on account of bad weather. It was proposed by Marian Grace and passed by the Committee that the Lady Captain, Lady Vice-Captain and Lady Secretary should make the decision regarding any cancellation. If they were not available, any other 3 members of Committee were to act on their behalf.

In June 1975, Capt Dan W Jones asked the Ladies' Section for 10 Ladies to play golf with his Master Mariner Guests from Southampton.

This was the year that Dennis Grace, the Pro, retired and the Ladies' Committee bought a table cigarette lighter for him. Mrs Wynne-Finch presented this gift on behalf of the Ladies and it was stipulated that the Committee minutes had to record that 'everyone had a most enjoyable and successful evening'!

Helen Edgar was the first Lady Captain to ever sign the Ladies' Committee Minutes in Welsh. She always insisted on completing her scorecard in Welsh and at the 1974 AGM, it is recorded that Annette Jones gave her vote of thanks to Helen through the medium of Welsh. This is the first ever reference to the Welsh Language in the Ladies' Committee Minutes.

Helen Edgar became Lady Captain of Pwllheli Golf Club in 1992.

MRS J F TRENHOLME
1975

Muriel was born in Shropshire, one of ten children. Her father was a farmer and the family moved to farm in Derbyshire, where Muriel became a Nanny to a little boy whose family used to come down to Nefyn on holiday. It was during a summer evening's cliff walk in Nefyn that she met her future husband Jimmy (Nellie Trenholme's brother). Although they were apart while she worked in Buxton and he was at sea, the romance flourished and they married in Capel Soar in Nefyn, in June 1943.

Muriel joined the Club in May 1959 and enjoyed her golf immensely. Her lowest handicap was 24 and she won many spoons and prizes.

The Master Mariners...with Captain Dan extreme right back row.
Pictured, Left to Right: *Annette Jones, Lady Captain Helen Edgar Jones, Mignon Fenwick, Enid Evans, Pip Smart, Mary Davies, Gladys Roberts, Mary Roberts, Pauline Lane and Connie Butterworth.*

THE LADY CAPTAINS - CAPTEINIAID Y MERCHED

She recalls winning a Prize in Bethan Rees-Jones' Lady Captain's Day, 1981 and was thrilled to win beautiful cut-glass wine glasses. During her year of office, Muriel remembers the Ladies staying overnight when they played in a two-day event and the fun and enjoyment they had on that occasion. It is good to note that these occasions still occur today with equal enjoyment and often great hilarity in abundance! In 1976, she followed in Annette Jones' footsteps in winning the Buckley Challenge Trophy. She played off a 30 handicap and was 'delighted to beat all the men'!

At the AGM of 1976, Miss Annie Williams gave a vote of thanks to Muriel and spoke in glowing terms. She said that 'Mrs Trenholme had been an admirable Captain, so very charming, tactful and always with a smile on her face. She had seen numerous captains come and go but she felt that Mrs Trenholme could not be equalled'. (sic)

MISS N HUGHES
1976

Ganwyd Nell ym Morfa Nefyn ynghyd â'i chwaer, Kathleen, a briododd Jim Bentley. Hyfforddodd fel nyrs a datblygodd i fod yn Sister yn Ysbyty Abergele. Bu'n chwarae llawer o golff yng Nghlwb Abergele a bu'n Gapten Adran y Merched yno yn 1958.

Mrs Billie Needham oedd Uwcharolygydd y Nos yn Ysbyty Abergele pan apwyntiwyd Nell yno fel Sister o Mansfield yn 1953/54. Datblygodd cyfeillgarwch clòs rhwng y ddwy, gan rannu eu hoffter o golff. Wrth inni ysgrifennu'r llyfr yma, cofia Billie, sy'n 92 oed, rai o'r pranciau fyddai'r ddwy yn eu chwarae! Fodd bynnag, roedd Nell yn weithwraig gydwybodol iawn, un brysur, llawn egni ond hefyd yn llym ei disgyblaeth, fel yr oedd sister yn y dyddiau hynny. Byddai'n gweithio yn y Clinig Diciâu (TB) bob Dydd Gwener ac yn nes ymlaen hi oedd y 'Sister Cartref' yn gofalu am Gartref Preswyl y Nyrsys. Roedd Nell yn llawn cymeriad ac yn boblogaidd iawn.

Yn dilyn ei hymddeoliad, symudodd Nell yn ôl i Lŷn ac ymgartrefodd yn Dolydd, Stryd y Plas, Nefyn, lle bu'n edrych ar ôl ei mam am nifer o flynyddoedd. Etholwyd hi'n Gapten Adran y Merched yn 1976 ac yn 1980, fe'i hanrhydeddwyd ymhellach pan ei hetholwyd yn Gapten Cymdeithas Merched Hŷn Siroedd Gogledd Cymru.

Yn 1993, fe'i hetholwyd yn Is-Lywydd Merched Clwb Golff Nefyn.

Roedd Nell yn dipyn o gymeriad. Cawsai bleser mawr yn chwarae golff a hefyd yn chwarae'r 'bandit' yn y Clwb! Byddai'n mwynhau mordeithiau a chlywyd sawl stori ganddi am garwriaethau gwahanol! Fodd bynnag, roedd yn well ganddi fod yn sengl.

Byddai Nell yn hymian yr un gân yn gyson wrth gerdded o amgylch y cwrs. Roedd yn olffwraig frwdfrydig ac yn un daer ar y rheolau! Ni thrawai'r bêl yn bell ond roedd yn syth fel pin lawr canol y llain deg. Rhagorai ar bytio ac enillodd sawl cwpan a llwy a gyflwynid yn y cyfnod hwnnw yn Abergele a Nefyn. Cafodd ei phlesio'n fawr wrth ennill Cwpan Cefnamwlch yn 1982.

Nell was born in Morfa Nefyn and her sister Kathleen married Jim Bentley. She trained as a nurse and was employed at Abergele Hospital. She played a lot of golf at Abergele and became their Lady Captain in 1958.

Mrs Billie Needham, an Honorary Member of Abergele Golf Club, was the Night Superintendent at the Hospital when Nell arrived as a Sister from Mansfield in 1953/54. The two of them became firm friends and shared their love of golf. At the time of writing, Billie is aged 92 and still plays golf regularly. She recalls vividly some of the escapades the two of them got up to! However, Nell was conscientious in her work, busy, bustling and quite strict, as sisters tended to be in those days. She worked in the TB Clinic every Friday and became the Home Sister, in charge of the Residential Nurses' Home. Nell was a loyal and true friend, full of character and very popular.

Nell Hughes, facing camera, at a Dinner Dance at Abergele Golf Club in 1955 with her good friend, Billie Needham on her left.

After she retired, Nell moved back to this area and settled in Dolydd, Palace Street, Nefyn where she looked after her mother for many years. She was elected Lady Captain in 1976 and in 1980 she was further honoured by being elected Captain of the Northern Counties Ladies Veterans' Association. In 1993, Nell was elected Lady Vice-President of our Golf Club.

Those who remember Nell say she was a real 'character'. She loved her golf and also loved the fruit machine in the Club's lounge! She enjoyed cruising and she related many tales regarding her various romances! However she maintained she preferred to stay happily single, often remarking with a smile 'I'm an unwanted treasure!'

Nell always hummed the same tune as she walked on the Course. She was a keen golfer and very strict on the rules! She never hit the ball very far but she was accurate and often down the very middle of the fairway. She excelled at putting and won many cups and silver spoons that were presented in those days, both at Abergele and Nefyn. At Nefyn, she was very proud to see her name up on the Board for winning the Cefnamwlch Cup in 1982.

Nell Hughes, (Right), receives the Putting Prize from Carys Wyn Jones on her Lady Captain's Day, 1990.

MRS F W SMITH
1977

Mrs F W Smith, Hilda, was married to Fred and they ran a factory making children's clothes in the Midlands before they retired to Erwenni, Pwllheli. Hilda was a petite lady, always immaculately turned out and her hair put up in a French roll with never one strand out of place. She was a steady golfer and the Ladies enjoyed playing with her. She and Fred had three children, and their son ran the House of Silver in Pwllheli, across the road from Brian Williams' jeweller's shop.

She and Fred were always ready to help out with any Club function and when Hilda was Lady Captain they were renowned for the numerous parties they gave! In those days, it was traditional for the Lady Captain and Lady Vice-Captain to invite people to their homes for 'get-togethers' – often a cocktail party on a Sunday morning!

Fred provided the music for the famous cabarets performed by Miss Marian Grace and Miss Annette Jones. (Please see Annette Jones' reminiscences in the Chapter entitled 'I remember...')

Hilda was very encouraging to beginners and she arranged competitions for non-handicapped players, including one on her Captain's Day. It was during her Captaincy that it was resolved to buy the retiring Captain a Past Captain's Brooch but unfortunately, this was not available in time to be pinned on Hilda at the 1977 AGM. Mrs Fenwick, the Secretary, was asked to contact all Past Captains to see if they would like to buy the brooch when available at a cost of £4-10-0. This she did and this they did!

MISS A JONES
1978

Ganwyd a magwyd Annette yn Tŷ Cerrig, Stryd y Ffynnon, Nefyn, lle'r oedd yr Hen Westy Nanhoron cyn ei droi yn ddau dŷ, a dyna ble y mae hi'n byw ers Hydref 20fed 1933. Un o Edern oedd ei thad (Swyddog ar y môr) a magwyd ei mam yn Bwlch, Morfa Nefyn. Bu ei mam yn gweithio yng Ngwesty'r Heliwr yn Nefyn. Chwaer ei mam oedd Jane Jones, Stiwardes gyntaf Clwb Golff Nefyn.

Mynychodd Annette Ysgol Nefyn pan oedd Owen Roberts yn Brifathro.

Oherwydd salwch plentyn pan yn ddeg ac eto yn bedair ar ddeg oed, ni fedrodd Annette wireddu ei dymuniad o hyfforddi fel nyrs, a rhaid oedd bodloni ar waith yn Siop Pollecoffs ym Mhwllheli. Gadawodd y swydd yma yn 1962 a mynd i weithio at Mrs Fenwick oedd newydd brynu siop Elizabeth Walton (yr hen London House) yn Nefyn. Ar ôl cyfnod o 17 mlynedd, ymddeolodd Mrs Fenwick a phrynodd Annette y busnes a'i redeg am ugain mlynedd tan ei hymddeoliad ei hun.

Ymunodd Annette â'r Clwb yn Chwefror 1961 a dechreuodd chwarae o ddifrif yn yr haf. Enillodd sawl gwobr ond pinacl y gwobrau oedd ennill Tlws Buckley yn 1975 efo sgôr o 65. Un mlynedd ar ddeg yn ddiweddarach yn 1986, enillodd Ddysgl Rhosyn Dr Griffiths i gael ei henw ymysg y mawrion ar y mur unwaith eto.

Etholwyd Annette yn Gapten y Merched yn 1978 ac yn ystod ei blwyddyn, gofynnodd Adran y Merched i Bwyllgor y Clwb am ganiatâd i osod llun Capten y Merched ochr yn ochr â llun y Capten yn y lolfa. Gwrthodwyd eu cais! Fodd bynnag, y flwyddyn ddilynol cafwyd caniatâd - ond roedd hi'n rhy hwyr i gael llun Annette ar y mur! O'r herwydd, trefnodd Annette i dynnu'r llun isod o'r Cyn-Gapteiniaid yn 1980 a bu yn hongian i fyny ar y ffordd i doiled y merched am flynyddoedd. Dyna barch! Erbyn hyn, mae wedi cael ei osod mewn lle mwy derbyniol.

Ym Mehefin 1978, penderfynwyd cynnal Cinio Capten y Merched a Chyn-Gapteiniaid y Merched. Cynhaliwyd y cinio yng Ngwesty'r Linksway ar Awst 11eg ac Annette oedd y Cadeirydd cyntaf. Trafodwyd ychydig o faterion busnes ond yn y dyddiau hynny, Pwyllgor y

Merched fyddai'n enwebu'r Is-Gapten yn hytrach na'r Cyn Gaptainiaid.

Yng Nghyfarfod Blynyddol Adran y Merched 1978, diolchodd Mrs Pauline Lane i Annette am fod yn Gapten rhagorol, un oedd wedi 'mynd allan o'i ffordd i helpu pawb'. Roeddynt wedi mwynhau cyfarfodydd hapus ac adeiladol o dan lywyddiaeth fedrus Annette, ac ychwanegodd Pauline, '..os ydym am barhau i ethol Capteiniaid fel y chi, gall Clwb Golff Nefyn edrych ymlaen at ddyfodol hapus a llwyddiannus!' Wrth ymateb, siaradodd Annette yn y Gymraeg gan ddweud, a dyfynnir o'r Cofnodion am y tro cyntaf yn y Gymraeg, 'Ni fyddai'r noson yn gyflawn heb ddweud gair yn Gymraeg. Carwn ddiolch i chi i gyd am wneud eich rhan i wneud fy mlwyddyn yn un mor hapus'. Am y tro cyntaf, yn lle cyflwyno blodau fel roedd yr arferiad, cyflwynodd Pwyllgor y Merched fathodyn Cyn-Gapten i'r Capten oedd yn ymddeol.

Pan ymddeolodd Annette fel Llywydd y Merched yng Nghyfarfod Cyffredinol Blynyddol 2007, datgelodd ei dymuniad i gyflwyno tlws newydd, Tlws y Penwaig, i Adran y Merched. Fe'i cyflwynwyd am y tri sgôr gorau yn y Prif Gystadleuthau. Ym Mlwyddyn ein Canmlwyddiant, blwyddyn gyntaf un y Tlws, fe'i henillwyd gan Gapten y Merched, Fiona Vaughan Thomas, gyda sgoriau o 71, 72 a 74 yn erbyn Sgôr Safonol y cwrs o 74.

Etholwyd Annette i Bwyllgor Gwaith y Clwb ar Ebrill 12fed 2001. Yn 2005 cafodd ei anrhydeddu ymhellach trwy gael ei hethol yn Llywydd y Merched am ddwy flynedd. Yn 2006 etholwyd hi yn Gapten Cymdeithas Cyn-Gapteiniaid Merched Eryri.

Annette was born and brought up in Tŷ Cerrig, Nefyn, where the old Nanhoron Hotel was situated before it was converted into two houses and she still lives there to this day. Her father hailed from Edern and was a seaman (1st Officer). Her mother was a cook in the Sportsman's Hotel, Nefyn and had been brought up in Bwlch, Morfa Nefyn. Her mother's sister was Jane Jones, the first Stewardess of the Golf Club. Annette attended Nefyn School when Owen Roberts, the Club's Secretary, was Headmaster.

A childhood illness at the age of 10 and again at 14, prevented Annette following her dream career of nursing and she had to be content with finding work in Pollecoffs, Pwllheli. She left in 1962, and went to work for Mrs Fenwick who had just bought the Elizabeth Walton Shop (London House), Nefyn. Finally, after 17 years, Mrs Fenwick retired and Annette bought the business, which she ran until her own retirement 20 years later.

Annette joined the Club in February 1961 and started playing golf seriously the following summer. Over the years, she won many prizes but her proudest moment was when she won her first major, the Buckley Challenge Trophy, in 1975, with a superb score of 65 nett. Eleven years later, Annette's name appeared once again on the Honours Boards, when she won the Dr Griffiths' Rose Bowl, in 1986.

Annette was elected Lady Captain in 1978 and during her year of office, the Ladies' Committee requested permission to display the Lady Captain's photo alongside the Captain's in the lounge. The Men's Committee refused permission! The following year however, they changed their minds – but sadly this was too late for Annette's photo to be displayed!

Past Lady Captains 1980, *taken in the Grounds of Erw Goch, before the Annual Captain and Past Captains' Dinner at the Hotel. (The Erw Goch Hotel at the time was run by Shirley Roulston and her father.)*
Left to Right: *Pip Smart (1963), Annie Williams (1933,1953), Gladys Roberts (1964), Ellen Trenholme (1960), Elsie Toleman Jones (1971), Eve Worrall (1969), Muriel Trenholme (1975), Dilys Parry (1947,1955), Ena Bellhouse (1928, 1948, 1957, 1968), Nell Hughes (1976), Pauline Lane (1959) Enid Evans (1972), and Annette Jones (1978).*

In June 1978, it was decided to have a 'Captain's and Past Captains' Dinner', chaired by the Lady Captain. This took place at the Linksway Hotel on August 11th and Annette was the first Chairman. There was always some business to discuss but in those days, the Past Captains did not nominate a Vice-Captain - that was always undertaken by the Ladies' Committee.

Annette arranged for the photo (above) to be taken in order that the Club had some photographic evidence of the Past Lady Captains. Until recently, this photo was given a place of honour - in the passageway to the Ladies' toilet! Thankfully, it now has a more respectful position!

At the AGM of 1978, Mrs Pauline Lane thanked Annette for being a super Captain, one who 'had bent over backwards to try and help everybody'. She said they had enjoyed happy and constructive meetings under her capable guidance and 'should we continue to elect Captains such as yourself, Nefyn Golf Club can look forward to a happy and successful future!' In replying, Annette spoke in both Welsh and English and this is quoted verbatim in the Minute Book – the first and last time the Welsh language was ever recorded! 'Ni fyddai'r noson yn gyflawn heb ddweud gair yn Gymraeg. Carwn ddiolch i chi i gyd am wneud eich rhan i wneud fy mlwyddyn yn un mor hapus. The evening would not be complete without a word in Welsh. I would like to thank everyone for their part in making my year such a happy one.' It was at this AGM that the Committee presented the Retiring Captain with a Past Captain's Badge for the first time and Annette was thus the first recipient.

Annette was elected on to the Executive Committee at the April AGM of 2001. In 2005, she was delighted and very honoured to be elected our Lady President (right),

THE LADY CAPTAINS - CAPTEINIAID Y MERCHED

an office she held until 2007. In 2006, Annette was elected Captain of the Eryri Ladies' Past Captains' Association.

When she retired as Ladies' President at the AGM of 2007, Annette announced her intention to donate a new Trophy to the Ladies' Section. This was to be called 'Tlws y Penwaig' (literally 'The Herrings Trophy') for the best 3 aggregate scores in the Major Trophies. In our Centenary Year, it was won by the Ladies' Captain, Fiona Vaughan Thomas with scores of 71, 72 and 74 (CSS 74).

Annette presents Tlws y Penwaig to Ladies' Captain, Fiona Vaughan Thomas in September 2007.

THE PHOTO GALLERY 1979 - 1999

MISS M GRACE
1979

Ganwyd Marian yn ail blentyn i Dennis ac Annie Grace ym Morfa Nefyn yn 1940. Bu ei brawd, Albert, farw cyn ei ben blwydd yn ddwy oed. Mynychodd Marian Ysgol Morfa ac Ysgol Ramadeg Pwllheli.

Bu'n cadw ei siop groser ei hun am nifer o flynyddoedd yn Pantlon, Morfa Nefyn, cyn cychwyn gweithio yn siop y Pro gyda'i thad, Dennis Grace. Yn dilyn hyn, cafodd gyfnod yn gweithio yn Siop Spar yn Nefyn. Ar ei diwrnod cyntaf yn siop ei thad, roedd Marian yn rhannu cardiau cystadleuaeth allan i'r dynion. Daeth I M Ellis, aelod newydd ar y pryd, i'r siop a gofyn am gerdyn i chwarae yn ei gystadleuaeth gyntaf erioed. Gofynnodd Marian iddo am ei enw. 'I M Ellis,' atebodd yntau. Heb oedi, dywedodd Marian, 'A Marian ydwyf i, ond dwi isio'ch enw llawn!' ac âi'n ddicach ac yn ddicach bob tro roedd Ieuan yn ailadrodd mai dyma oedd ei enw!

Ymunodd Marian â'r Clwb fel Aelod Iau ym mis Mai 1953, ond ni ddechreuodd chwarae golff o ddifrif nes iddi ddechrau gweithio yn siop ei thad. Daeth yn Aelod llawn ym mis Rhagfyr 1959 gan ddechrau chwarae yn y chwedegau. Datblygodd ei gêm ac enillodd sawl cystadleuaeth gan gynnwys Gwobr Capten y Merched yn 1974 a Dysgl Rhosyn Dr Griffiths yn 1978. Yn y dyddiau cynnar, chwaraeai yn rheolaidd gydag Annette Jones ac yn ddiweddarach gydag Elsie Hughes.

Bu Marian yn Ysgrifennydd Graddnodau Adran y Merched o 1980 i 1985. Yng Nghyfarfod Cyffredinol Blynyddol 1985, diolchodd Carys Wyn Jones i Marian am yr holl flynyddoedd o waith caled a dreuliodd fel Ysgrifennydd y Graddnodau gan ychwanegu fod ei hanogaeth gyson wedi bod yn hwb i bawb. Pan fyddai'r merched wedi chwarae'n dda gan ennill cystadleuaeth a gostwng eu graddnod, byddai Marian wrth ei bodd.

THE LADY CAPTAINS - CAPTEINIAID Y MERCHED

Roedd ei chyfraniadau a'i gwybodaeth yn amhrisiadwy a chyfannwyd ei safonau uchel gyda'i ffraethineb naturiol wrth ymgymryd â'i dyletswyddau. Cymeriad ar y naw oedd Marian. Hi oedd Ysgrifennydd carismataidd Adran y Merched o 1987 hyd at 1998 a byddai pob Aelod yn edrych ymlaen at ei chyflwyniadau lliwgar a digrif tu hwnt.

Go brin y byddai'r Aelodau a wrandawodd ar ei chellwair gyda Robin Parry yn y cyfarfodydd yma yn anghofio ei ffraethineb parod a'i thafod miniog! Un haf, ymddangosodd gwraig ifanc yn y lolfa oedd yn gwisgo'r nesaf beth i ddim. Deliwyd a'r mater yma'n briodol gan y Pwyllgor, ond yn y Cyfarfod Cyflwyno Gwobrau ychydig o ddyddiau'n ddiweddarach, cawsom ein hatgoffa o'r digwyddiad yma gan Marian. Dywedodd ei bod wedi gwisgo'n briodol y noswaith yma, ac i brofi hynny, cododd ei sgert i ddangos pais goch ymledol drwchus.

Roedd ganddi ei ffordd hollol unigryw o gyhoeddi canlyniadau. Ar y naill law byddai'n annog ac yn clodfori yn hollol ddiffuant ond, ar y llaw arall, gallai fod yn finiog ei thafod a gwawdlyd. Wrth gyhoeddi canlyniadau Taith y Merched un flwyddyn, daeth at y sgôr olaf oedd yn eithriadol o wael mae'n rhaid cyfaddef, a dywedodd nad oedd yn deall o gwbl pam aeth y person yma ar y daith os dyma oedd ei safon!

Roedd Marian yn gydwybodol iawn. Mae ei ffrind, Elsie Hughes yn cofio Diwrnod Gwahoddiad y Merched a Marian yn nesáu at lawnt y twll cyntaf. Baglodd Marian ac er ei bod wedi anafu ei braich, aeth yn ei blaen ac i fyny'r ail dwll nes fedrai hi ddim mynd ymhellach. Dychwelodd i'r Clwb ac arhosodd i bawb orffen ei gêm. Cyhoeddodd y canlyniadau ac aros ymlaen tipyn cyn cyfaddef ei bod mewn poen difrifol ac angen mynd i'r ysbyty. Erbyn hyn, yn ôl Elsie, roedd hi'n naw o'r gloch ac i ffwrdd â hwy i Fangor. Oedd, roedd Marian wedi torri ei braich, ond ni fuasai ar unrhyw gyfrif wedi gadael y Clwb hyd nes fod popeth wedi'i gwblhau.

Yn flynyddol, byddai'r merched yn edrych ymlaen yn awchus am ei Hadroddiad fel Ysgrifennydd yng Nghyfarfod Cyffredinol Blynyddol y Merched. Yn ei hadroddiad cyntaf yn 1988 aeth Marian ati i longyfarch y chwaraewyr yn yr Adran Arian am eu gorchestion yn ystod y flwyddyn a chyfeiriodd atynt fel y Pump Enwog (Famous Five), sef Elsie Hughes, Åse Richardson, Jacqui Wilcox (fel y'i gelwid ar y pryd), Shirley Roulston a'r Aelod ifanc o'r Adran Iau, Fiona Vaughan Thomas. Dros y blynyddoedd cynyddodd eu nifer rywfaint, ond yn 1993 adroddodd Marian fod 'y nifer yn ôl i bump yn yr Adran Arian erbyn hyn, a gyda hyd ymestynnol rhai o'r tyllau newydd [Agorwyd y cwrs newydd yn swyddogol yn 1994] mae'n bosib y bydd llai'r flwyddyn nesaf!'

Roedd Marian yn effeithlon iawn ac ymddangosai ei bod wedi'i thrwytho mewn gwybodaeth o Reolau ers pan oedd yn ifanc iawn. Gweithiai yn ddiflino dros y Clwb ac, yn aml, ni fyddai'r Aelodaeth yn sylweddoli'r ymdrech a roddai i gael pethau i redeg yn esmwyth. Wrth ddiolch iddi yng Nghyfarfod Cyffredinol Blynyddol 1992, dywedodd Annette Jones fod gan Marian amynedd Job ynghyd â doethineb Solomon! Cyfeiriai at Marian fel y wraig gyda'r llaw haearn mewn maneg felfed a lywiai'r Merched i'r cyfeiriad cywir.

Byddai Marian wrth ei bodd yn rhoi perfformiadau cân a dawns gydag Annette Jones ac eraill mewn cyngherddau. Roedd hi'n dalentog ac yn aml iawn byddai'n adlibio oddi ar y sgript, ac o ganlyniad, byddai'n anodd dyfalu beth oedd am ddigwydd nesaf. (Gweler y Bennod 'Dwi'n cofio' lle mae Annette Jones yn trafod perfformiadau Marian ar y llwyfan.)

Uchafbwynt Marian yn y Clwb oedd cael ei hethol yn Gapten Adran y Merched yn 1979. [Cyfeirir eto at gofnod Annette yn y Bennod 'Dwi'n Cofio' yn y Saesneg, i gael golwg ar sut wnaeth Marian sicrhau breintiau i Ddarpar-Gapteiniaid y Merched.]

Roedd Marian yn gefnogwr brwd iawn o'r Adran Iau a byddai'n ceisio cynyddu eu nifer yn rheolaidd. Yn ystod ei Chapteiniaeth, yn bennaf oherwydd llwyddiant Fiona Vaughan Thomas yn yr Adran Iau, penderfynwyd caniatáu i Aelodau o'r Adran Iau chwarae yng nghystadleuthau Medalau Undeb Golffio'r Merched. Fodd bynnag, ni chaniatawyd iddynt chwarae yn y prif gystadleuthau nes eu bod yn ddeunaw oed.

Dywedodd Mary Roberts, wrth ddiolch i Marian am fod yn Gapten rhagorol, fod ganddi ddywediadau bachog a pharod ac ymadroddion i ymdopi gydag unrhyw sefyllfa. Roedd hyn yn hollol wir am Marian. Serch hyn, mae Aelodau yn ei chael yn anodd i gofio'r dywediau hyn gan ei bod yn arfer ymateb mor sydyn. Pan oedd Laura Wyn Roberts am agor ei siop chwaraeon ym Morfa Nefyn, roedd y diweddar Wmffri, Siop Spar Nefyn, yn ofni cystadleuaeth. Gofynnodd i Marian pa fath o siop oedd Laura am agor. Fel mellten, atebodd Marian, 'Siop rhyw; peidiwch â phoeni, Wmffri.' Ar achlysur arall, tra'n chwarae gyda Mary Davies, a arferai brysuro ymlaen, gwaeddodd Marian, 'Mary, dach chi'n chwarae efo mi neu gyda'r rhai o'n blaen ni?'

Daeth y newyddion trist am farwolaeth ddisymwth Marian ym mis Mai 2002 fel sioc i'r Aelodaeth. Mae'r gadair gofeb iddi yn eistedd yn urddasol ar di'r deunawfed twll, llecyn priodol iawn lle y gellir gweld yr Hen Gwrs a'r Cwrs Newydd a phopeth sy'n digwydd! Pan fydd yr adar yn lliwio'r gadair, bydd Aneuryn Thomas, un o hogia Patrick, yn ymweld gyda'i bwced o ddŵr sebon gan ddweud, 'Mae'n adeg i Marian gael rhyw wash bach!'

Marian was born the second child of Dennis and Annie Grace at Morfa Nefyn in 1940. Her brother Albert, tragically died before his second birthday. Marian attended Morfa Nefyn School and Pwllheli Grammar School.

Marian, 2nd from left at a Presentation Evening. Also pictured are Lady President, Mrs R Wynne-Finch, Lady Captain, Jacqui Wilcox and Elsie Hughes with the Club Championship Trophy.

Marian kept her own shop selling groceries for a number of years in Pantlon, Morfa Nefyn, before assisting her father in his Pro's shop at the Club. Following this, she spent a period working in the Spar Shop at Nefyn. On her first Sunday in her father's shop, Marian was responsible for giving out the cards. I M Ellis, relatively new to the Golf Club, entered the shop for his first ever competition. Marian asked him his full name. 'I M Ellis' he replied. Very quickly she answered 'And I am Marian but I want your full name!' and she got progressively crosser as he continued to insist that *was* his full name!

Marian joined the Club as a Junior in May 1953 but it was not until she began working for her father that she became really interested in golf. She became a Full Member in December 1959 and began playing seriously in the early 60s. She progressed to winning several competitions including the Lady Captain's Prize in 1974 and the Dr Griffiths' Rose Bowl in 1978. In the early days she played regularly with Annette Jones and in the latter part of her life with Elsie Hughes.

Marian was Handicap Secretary from 1980 to 1985. Carys Wyn Jones at the Ladies' AGM of 1985, thanked Marian for all her years of hard work as Handicap Secretary and said her encouragement had always been a boost. When the Ladies had played well, winning competitions and reducing their handicaps, Marian had always been delighted. Furthermore, her contributions and knowledge had been invaluable and her high standards, while undertaking her duties, had been complemented by her manner and sense of humour!

Marian was a legend! She was the charismatic Secretary of the Ladies' Section from 1987 to 1998 and all the Members looked forward to her colourful and often hilarious presentations during prize giving ceremonies. No-one who ever experienced her bantering with Robin Parry at those ceremonies will ever forget her quick wit and often quite sharp tongue! One summer, a lady had appeared at the bar attired very skimpily in a white see-through dress and obviously wearing no underwear. This had been dealt with appropriately by the Committee! At the Prize Giving, a few days later, Marian reminded us all of the occasion. She said she had therefore dressed most appropriately that evening – and to prove it, she flipped up her skirt to show an amazingly full red petticoat!

She had her own wholly unique way of announcing the results. She encouraged and praised quite genuinely on the one hand but could be quite humorously scathing and sarcastic on the other. An example was when announcing the results of a Ladies' Outing one particular year. On reaching the last score, which granted was pretty poor, she announced she could not understand why this person had bothered to come along if she could only play that badly!

Marian was truly conscientious. Close friend Elsie Hughes remembers one Invitation Day when Marian tripped while approaching the 1st Green and although she had hurt her arm, she continued up the 2nd fairway until she could go no further because of the pain. She returned to the Clubhouse and waited for everyone to finish the competiton. She announced the results and saw the evening out before admitting she was in excruciating pain and needed to go to hospital. 'By this time', Elsie recalls, 'it was 9pm, and off we set for Bangor. Yes, she had broken her arm but there was no way she was going to leave until the evening had been successfully concluded!'

Members looked forward every year to her annual Secretary's Report at the Ladies' AGM. In her first Report in 1988, she congratulated the Silver Division players for their golfing feats during the year and called them the 'Famous Five'! These were Elsie Hughes, Åse Richardson, Jackie Wilcox (as she was then), Shirley Roulston and the young Junior, Fiona Vaughan Thomas. Over the years, the number increased marginally but by 1993 Marian reported that 'they were now back to only 5 members in the Silver Division, and with the lengthening of some of the new holes [New Course officially opened in 1994] there might very well be even fewer next year'!

Marian was undoubtedly extremely efficient and her knowledge of Rules and Regulations had been instilled in her from a very early age! She worked tirelessly for the Golf Club and Members often did not realise the amount of effort she put in to make matters run smoothly. Annette Jones, in thanking her at the AGM of 1992, referred to Marian as having the Patience of Job combined with the Wisdom of Solomon! She viewed Marian as the 'Lady with the iron hand in the velvet glove' who steered the Ladies gently in the right direction.

Marian used to love performing song and dance routines with Annette Jones and others in Club concerts. She was extremely talented and frequently ad-libbed away from the script with the result that no-one ever knew quite what she would do or say next. [See Chapter 'I remember' where Annette Jones recalls some stage and other occasions with Marian.]

The highlight of Marian's period at the Club was her election as Lady Captain in 1979. [See Annette Jones' reference above to learn how Marian, as Lady Captain, secured privileges for future Lady Captains.]

Marian was very supportive of Juniors and frequently attempted to increase the numbers in the Junior Section. It was during her Captaincy, largely as a result of Fiona Vaughan Thomas' success as a Junior, that it was passed by the Ladies' Committee that Juniors should be allowed to play in LGU Medals. However, they were not allowed to play in the Cefnamwlch Cup, the Dr Griffiths' Rose Bowl nor the Lady Captain's Prize until they reached the age of 18.

Miss Mary Roberts, in thanking Marian for being an admirable Captain, commented that she 'possessed a turn of phrase which enabled her to cope with any situation'. This was so true of Marian. In writing about her, several members were asked to quote some of her 'one-liners' but very few people can actually remember exactly what she said. It was that quickness of response, that appropriateness of the perfect gem that we remember. When Laura Wyn Roberts was about to open her sports shop in Morfa, the late Wmffri, from the Spar in Nefyn, fearing competition, asked Marian what sort of shop Laura was about to open. As quick as lightning, Marian replied, 'Don't you worry Wmffri, she's opening a Sex Shop!' On another occasion, while playing with Mary Davies, who had a habit of walking on ahead, she retorted 'Mary, are you playing with me or with the ones in front?'

Tragically, Marian died suddenly in May 2002, only 62 years of age. The seat in her memory sits on the 18th Tee – a most appropriate place, where one can survey at a glance the majority of both the Old and New Courses and all that's going on! This panoramic view may be seen on the previous pages.

Marian Grace in 2002

MRS D HOLTON
1980

Ganwyd Dilys yn Llangian a phriododd â Bob Holton yn 1956 gan symud i fyw i Nefyn. Tad Bob, A J Holton, oedd gyda'r cyswllt cyntaf â'r Clwb. Ef oedd y Pro yng Nghlwb Moor Hall ger Sutton Coldfield ond symudodd i Nefyn i redeg Bwyty'r Cliff Castle ar ôl Wing Commander Sleigh. Yn dilyn adneuyddiadau i'r bwyty, agorwyd Cliff Castle fel gwesty. Cyfetholwyd A J Holton ar Is-bwyllgor y Lawntiau yn y pumdegau oherwydd ei gefndir proffesiynol, ac yn ddiweddarach gwasanaethodd am sawl blwyddyn ar y Pwyllgor Gwaith.

Byddai Bob yn rhedeg busnes adeiladu cychod yn Nefyn cyn rhedeg siop nwyddau metel Tŷ Newydd ar y Stryd Fawr gyda Dilys o 1983 tan eu hymddeoliad yn 2005. Roedd Bob wedi ymuno â'r Clwb Golff yn y chwedegau, ond nid cyn iddo berswadio Dilys i ymuno yn 1977 y dechreuodd y ddau chwarae golff. Roedd Dilys yn dipyn o chwaraewraig, gan chwarae badminton yn rheolaidd yn y Ganolfan gyda Nellie Trenholme, Pip Smart, Shirley Roulston ac Ena Bellhouse. Byddai hefyd yn mwynhau cerdded eu dau gi ffyddlon.

Bu Dilys ar Bwyllgor y Merched am flynyddoedd a bu'n Is-Ysgrifennydd am gyfnod hefyd. Ar ôl blwyddyn yn unig ar y Puyllgor fe'i henwebwyd yn Gapten y Merched. Roedd yn nerfus a theimlai nad oedd yn haeddu'r anrhydedd. Fodd bynnag, cafodd lawer o fwynhad yn ystod y flwyddyn ac roedd yn werthfawrogol iawn o'r holl gymorth a gafodd, yn enwedig gan Capten Will Roberts, yr Ysgrifennydd ar y pryd. Er gwaethaf ei phryderon, aeth ei blwyddyn heibio'n ddi-stŵr.

Cofia Dilys yr achlysur y cafwyd dau ginio blynyddol yn 1980, yn ei blwyddyn hi fel Capten. Y cinio cyntaf oedd yr un arferol ym mis Chwefror a'r ail ym mis Tachwedd 1980. Efallai yr ystyrid fod y cinio cyntaf yn rhy agos i'r Cinio Gŵyl Dewi ac y buasai cinio ym mis Tachwedd hefyd yn dathlu diwedd blwyddyn Capten y Merched cyn Cyfarfod Cyffredinol Blynyddol y Merched. Felly yn 1980, cafwyd dau ginio.

Bu Dilys yn aelod o Gyn Capteiniaid Merched Eryri ac yn gynrychiolydd Nefyn ar Undeb y Sir yn y nawdegau. Honnai Dilys na chyflawnodd wyrthiau wrth chwarae golff erioed, ond ei bod wedi cael oriau o bleser a hwyl gyda'r merched, pleser mae yn ei golli yn fawr iawn heddiw. Ymddiswyddodd o'r Clwb yn 1997, ac nid ydyw Dilys na'i gŵr, Bob, wedi mwynhau iechyd da yn ystod y ddegawd olaf.

Dilys was born in Llangian. She married Bob Holton in 1956 and they moved to Nefyn to live in 1960. It was Bob's father, A J Holton, who had the first link with the Club. He had been a Professional Golfer at Moor Hall Golf Club in Sutton Coldfield and he moved to Nefyn taking over the Cliff Castle Restaurant from Wing Commander Sleigh. He subsequently closed the restaurant and after renovations, opened a hotel. He was co-opted on to the Greens' Committee in the 50s because of his professional background and then served on the Executive Committee for some years.

Bob ran a boat building business in Nefyn before he and Dilys ran the hardware shop at Tŷ Newydd, High Street, Nefyn from 1983 until their retirement in 2005. Bob had actually joined the Golf Club in the early 60s but it was not until 1977, when he persuaded Dilys to join, that they both took up the game. Dilys had been quite a sportswoman and had played badminton regularly at the Badminton Club in Y Ganolfan at Nefyn. She recalls many happy times there playing with Nellie Trenholme, Pip Smart, Shirley Roulston and Miss Bellhouse! Her other favourite pastime was walking in the area with her two beloved dogs.

Dilys served on the Committee for many years and was Assistant Secretary for a time. She was shocked to be invited to be Lady Captain and was really quite nervous. She had only served on the Committee for one year and truly felt she was not worthy of such an honour. However, she thoroughly enjoyed her year and was extremely grateful for all the support she got from everyone. She particularly recalls Captain Will, the Club Secretary, who was incredibly helpful and supportive. In spite of her fears, her year flew by smoothly!

Dilys recalls she was probably the only Lady Captain to have two Annual Dinners - although she hastens to add she did pay for the second one! The first was the usual February Dinner in 1980 and the second was in the following November. It has remained in November to the present day. It is not minuted anywhere as to the reason for the change. It may be that the February date was considered to be too close to the St David's Day Dinner or, as some long-standing Members believe, it was so that the Lady Captain could attend the (November) Dinner in her Farewell Role before then standing down at the Ladies' AGM later in the month.

September 1980: The Chairman... mentioned that the Annual Dinner would be held at the Woodlands on 1st November and that we had selected Cod Mornay and Roast Duckling from the menu.

It was in 1980 that the Club decided that all main cups and trophies should be left permanently at the Club. The Ladies requested and were granted replicas to award to the winners in the Annual Prize Giving Ceremony.

It was also during Dilys' year that the Ladies wrote to the Men's Committee asking whether two ladies could be co-opted on to the House Committee, where their views could be helpful on such matters as social and fundraising efforts and they might possibly be able to give some suggestions regarding catering! The Men's Committee did not reply to the letter but see below.

April 1980: Ladies Section requested representation ...on Sub Committees which dealt with 'domestic matters'. The (Executive) Committee's response was, 'Chairmen of various Sub-Committees should consult the Ladies Section on matters with which it was felt they could be of assistance and guidance'.

The Men's Committee however did reply to a complaint from the Ladies' Section, in October 1980, about the repulsive and disgusting smell of drains outside the Ladies' Locker Room! [Many current Members will react with a wry smile at this one!] The reply was that the Greens' Staff had been instructed to keep the drains clear and this should solve the problem!

At the AGM of 1980, two proposals were passed. It was agreed that in future, 'the Lady Captain would only pay for tea for the players and her own invited guests on Lady Captain's Day.' The second proposal was to pave the way forward towards the Ladies having their own banking independence and is discussed fully in Bethan Rees-Jones' Captaincy.

Dilys Holton receives a Prize from Annette Jones on her Lady Captain's Day, 1979.

Dilys was a member of the Eryri Past Ladies' Captains and also represented Nefyn on the County Union for a couple of years in the 90s. She claims that she did not perform any miracles while playing golf, but she had hours of pleasure and fun with the Ladies, a pleasure she now misses. She resigned from the Club in 1997 and neither she nor Bob have enjoyed the best of health over the last few years.

AGM November 1980:
Proposed and agreed that the position of Vice-Captain be discussed by the Captain and Past Captains at their Annual Dinner and a sub-committee be formed if necessary to put forward nomination to the [ladies'] Executive Committee.

MRS B REES-JONES
1981

Dechreuodd Bethan chwarae golff pan oedd yn naw oed o dan lygad craff Dennis Grace. Bu'n chwarae i Sir Gaernarfon yn 1963. Ei graddnod isaf oedd 12.

Ymunodd â'r Clwb yn 1952 ac etholwyd hi yn Gapten Adran y Merched yn 1981. Mae Bethan yn Aelod hefyd yng Nghlwb Golff Porthmadog ac etholwyd hi'n Gapten y Merched yno yn 1973.

Bu wrthi'n brysur yn edrych ar Gyfansoddiad Adran y Merched. Casglodd ynghyd y rheolau oedd wedi cael eu derbyn ym Mhwyllgorau Gwaith y Clwb a Phwyllgorau Adran y Merched ers 1966. Ym mis Tachwedd 1982 trefnwyd Cyfarfod Arbennig i drafod a derbyn y rheolau yma. Yn dilyn hyn, cyflwynwyd y Rheolau mewn llyfryn bychan i Gyfarfod Cyffredinol y Clwb, fe'i derbyniwyd a dosbarthwyd copi i bob Aelod o Adran y Merched.

Ym mis Mawrth 1981, pan oedd Pwyllgor y Merched yn trafod Noson Goffi i hel arian i Gronfa Adran y Merched, gwahoddwyd Cadeirydd y Tŷ ac Ysgrifennydd y Clwb i'r cyfarfod. Croesawodd Bethan y ddau ŵr yn gynnes gan ddweud fod hyn yn gam yn y cyfeiriad cywir tuag at gydgysylltiad rhwng y ddwy Adran a hyderai y buasai hyn yn arwain at gydweithrediad pellach.

Bu'r Merched yn gwneud cais am gael eu cyfrif banc eu hunain ers y chwedegau, ond heb lwyddiant. Yn dilyn sawl cais dros y blynyddoedd, gwnaeth Bethan (Is-Gapten) y cynigiad canlynol yng Nghyfarfod Cyffredinol y Merched yn 1981: 'Bydd y Merched yn gyfrifol am eu tâl cystadlu eu hunain, gan gynnwys prynu llwyau misol o'u

THE LADY CAPTAINS - CAPTEINIAID Y MERCHED

cyfrif banc eu hunain'. Derbyniwyd y cynigiad yn unfrydol. Agorwyd y cyfrif ym Manc Barclays y mis canlynol gyda Bethan a Mrs Fenwick, yr Ysgrifenyddes, yn llofnodwyr. O'r diwedd, roedd Adran y Merched yn gallu rhedeg eu busnes yn annibynnol.

Bu ei thad, John Ogwen Jones (1960), a'i mam, Mrs Win Ogwen Jones (1956), yn Gapteiniaid y Clwb o flaen Bethan. Cafodd wefr o gael ei gwahodd i fod yn Gapten Adran y Merched ond roedd yn anesmwyth am y dasg oedd o'i blaen oherwydd cysylltiad hir ei theulu â'r Clwb. Yn ogystal, roedd ganddi deulu ifanc i'w magu a phryderai am sut y gallai gwblhau'r ddwy swydd. Doedd dim angen iddi boeni, cafodd flwyddyn lwyddiannus tu hwnt.

Tlws Ogwen Jones yw Tlws Pencampwriaeth y Clwb ac fe'i cyflwynwyd i'r Clwb gan Mrs Win Ogwen Jones. I gychwyn, chwaraeir rownd fedal a bydd y pedair merch orau yn chwarae am y Tlws mewn cystadleuaeth bwrw allan. Mae Bethan yn cyflwyno'r gwobrau yn flynyddol er cof am ei mam.

Bethan started playing golf when she was nine years old under the watchful eye of Dennis Grace. She played for Caernarfonshire in 1963 and her lowest handicap was 12.

Having joined the Club in July 1952, Bethan was elected Lady Captain in 1981. In addition she chaired the AGM in 1982, as Immediate Past Lady Captain, because the Lady Captain, Mrs Peggy Whitfield, had died in office. Bethan also played golf at Porthmadog Golf Club where she was elected Lady Captain in 1973.

She was very much involved with the Constitution of the Ladies' Section. She compiled a set of rules and resolutions that had been passed at various Executive and Ladies' Committee Meetings since 1966. In November 1982, an Extraordinary Meeting was held where these Rules were read and approved. Following this, the Rules were presented in a small booklet which was submitted and approved at the AGM before being given to each Lady Member.

In March 1981, when the Ladies' Committee were discussing a Coffee Evening to raise funds for the Club, the Chairman of House and the Men's Secretary were invited to the meeting. Bethan warmly welcomed them saying she felt it was a step in the right direction towards further liaison between the two sections and she hoped it would lead to further co-operation!

As early as 1960, the Ladies had asked for their own Bank Account but had met with little success. After many other requests over the years, it was Bethan, as Vice–Captain who finalised a proposal to be put before the Ladies' 1981 AGM. The proposal read 'That the Ladies be accountable for their own entry fees, including monthly spoons, to be purchased from their own banking account' (sic) and was passed unanimously. The following month, the Account was opened at Barclays and the Captain, Bethan, and Secretary, Mrs Fenwick, were the two named signatories on the cheque book. At last it meant that the Ladies' Section could run their own business independently.

Both her father, John Ogwen Jones (1960) and her mother, Mrs Win Ogwen Jones (1956) were Club Captains before Bethan. She herself was thrilled to be invited to serve as Captain although she was filled with trepidation at the task ahead of her due to her family's long association with the Club. She also had a young family to bring up and was anxious as to how she could juggle family commitments and golf. Her fears were unfounded and she had a truly smooth and successful year.

The Ogwen Jones Trophy is the Ladies' Club Championship Trophy and was presented to the Ladies by Mrs Win Ogwen Jones. This is a Medal qualifying round and the Ladies recording the best four gross scores then go forward to the knockout stage. Bethan generously presents the prizes every year in memory of her mother, not only for the Winner and Runner-up, but also for the other two Qualifiers.

MISS M E WHITFIELD 1982

Ganwyd a magwyd Peggy Whitfield ym Morfa Nefyn. Arferai ei mam gadw siop groser Cae Ifan ym Morfa, adeilad o wneuthuriad pren

April 1981: Agreed Men are asked to look out for Ladies on blind holes

wedi'i baentio'n wyrdd, drws nesaf i Erw Goch ar Lôn Isaf. Cyflogwyd ei thad, oedd yn gweithio yn y Parciau Cyhoeddus yn Lerpwl cyn symud i Lŷn, ar y Cwrs am sbel. Byddai Peggy yn hoff iawn o arddio, cerdded a dringo, ac yn dilyn ei hymddeoliad i Forfa Nefyn, byddai'n gwahodd ei ffrindiau i wleddoedd blasus.

Athrawes Gwyddor Tŷ oedd Peggy yn ôl ei galwedigaeth a bu ar staff Ysgol Eifionydd ym Mhorthmadog am nifer o flynyddoedd cyn cael dyrchafiad i swydd Uwch Athrawes. Arferai chwarae golff ym Morfa Bychan yn y cyfnod yma a byddai'n aros mewn llety yn y dref. Etholwyd hi yn Gapten ar Glwb Golff Porthmadog yn 1956. Er ei bod yn Aelod yng Nghlwb Nefyn ers 1934, ni wnaeth ddechrau chwarae'n rheolaidd yma tan ei hymddeoliad yn y chwedegau.

Roedd Peggy'n wraig hyfryd dros ben, yn llawn bywyd ac yn boblogaidd iawn ymysg ei disgyblion a'i chyd-aelodau. Fel sawl athrawes arall yn ei chyfnod, roedd yn dueddol i fod yn arglwyddiaethol ei ffordd. Edrychai 'mlaen

i'w hymddeoliad a chafodd wefr fawr o gael ei hethol yn Gapten y Merched yn Nefyn. Fodd bynnag, syfrdanwyd y Clwb gyda'i marwolaeth ddisymwth yn ystod ei Chapteiniaeth yn 1982.

Cofia Cyn-Lywydd Plaid Cymru, Dafydd Wigley, ei 'Anti Peggy' yn serchog. Roedd ei fam a mam Peggy yn ffrindiau pennaf ers eu dyddiau ysgol cynnar ym Mhwllheli. Ystyrid 'Anti Peggy' fel un o'r teulu a chofia Dafydd hi fel person bywiog a charedig dros ben. Byddai Peggy yn meddwl y byd o Dafydd, yn enwedig gan ei bod hithau yn Bleidydd cadarn. Byddai'n cynnig gwydriad o sieri i'w ffrindiau adeg y Nadolig o botel a dderbyniai'n flynyddol gan Dafydd gyda label Senedd Llundain arni!

Ym mis Rhagfyr 1983, derbyniodd Adran y Merched hambwrdd arian gan ei chyfnither, er cof am Peggy – y 'Whitfield Salver.' Yn wreiddiol, chwaraeid am yr hambwrdd fel cystadleuaeth Bwrw Allan y Gaeaf.

Peggy Whitfield was born and bred in Morfa Nefyn. Her mother ran a grocer's shop, 'Cae Ifan', a small green wooden building next door to Erw Goch. Her father, an Englishman who had worked in Public Parks in Liverpool, was employed on the Golf Course for a period. Peggy herself loved gardening, obviously influenced by her father! She also enjoyed walking and climbing and after retiring to Morfa Nefyn, she enjoyed entertaining her friends with delicious suppers!

Peggy qualified as a Domestic Science teacher and taught for a number of years at Ysgol Eifionydd in Porthmadog, where she was promoted to Senior Mistress. She played golf at Porthmadog Golf Club while teaching and lodging in the town and was elected Lady Captain there in 1956. Although she had joined our Club as early as 1934, she did not play golf frequently here until the 1960s, when she retired.

Peggy was a delightful person, full of life and was extremely popular. She was another of the 'old school' and like so many school teachers, tended to be quite dominant in some ways. She looked so forward to her retirement and was thrilled and proud to be invited to be Lady Captain at Nefyn. In June 1982, Peggy died very suddenly, while in office, and it was a very sad period for the Club.

Past Plaid President Dafydd Wigley remembers 'Auntie Peggy' with great affection. Her mother and his mother were the closest of friends, and had been so since their school days together in Pwllheli. To all intents and purposes, 'Auntie Peggy' was treated as one of their family and he remembers her as a vivacious person, full of life and very kind. Her friends recall she, in turn, held him in the highest regard and proudly offered sherry at Christmas from his annual Christmas bottle with the Houses of Parliament on the label!

> *April 1982:* Miss Annie Williams and Miss M G Bellhouse were elected honorary members following the deaths of A D Grace Esq and J E Roberts MBE

In December 1983, it was agreed by the Ladies' Committee that they should graciously accept the offer of The Whitfield Silver Salver which had been offered to the Ladies by Peggy's family. It was decided this should be a Competition open to all Members and originally was to be a Winter Knockout.

MRS L REICH
1983

Lily was brought up in Lancashire. During the War she was conscripted to the Metro Vickers Aircraft factory where they built Lancaster bombers.

She first came to Nefyn around 1955 and was a good friend of Stanley and Joyce Parsonage, the local coastguard and his wife. Lily joined Nefyn Golf Club in 1962, the year after her husband Ronnie joined, paying a subscription of two guineas (£2-2-0) with a joining fee of three guineas (£3-3-0).

Lily retired to Llŷn in 1980 and now resides at Tŷ'r Ysgol, by Edern Church.

In 1982, during Lily's year as Vice-Captain, the Lady Captain, Peggy Whitfield, died in office and Lily gallantly stepped in, chaired all Committee Meetings and guided the Section forward. It was no easy task and she met the challenge with great courage and efficiency. It was also Lily who had the enterprising idea of planting beautiful shrubs outside the Ladies' Locker Room and around the Putting Green, giving much pleasure to Members and visitors alike.

Under the tutelage of Dennis Grace, Lily won the Captain's Prize in Enid Evans' Captaincy Year in 1972. She maintains however, that her only real golfing claim to fame was winning the first prize with Jim Axon at a Pro-Am Tournament in Pwllheli in 1983.

MRS L FRAY
1984

Leah was brought up in Venice and was the oldest of ten children. She met her future husband, Stan, in the Army Station Office in Venice, where he was an engineer. She returned to Wales with him, they married and had two children. The family lived in Nefyn for years before moving to Y Ddôl in Edern to retire. Stan was a gifted golfer, playing off 3 at one time.

Leah joined the Club on April 21st 1965, the exact same day as her Lady Vice-Captain, Joan Kilner. She enjoyed her golf but rarely socialised in the Club, preferring to be at home looking after her family.

Leah attained a handicap of 21 and won the Dr Griffiths' Rose Bowl in 1989 and the AD Grace Trophy in 1993. The real highlight of her golfing achievements however, was winning the final of the Dorothy Wood Memorial Trophy in 1984, against Anne Thomas, on the 19th hole with a chip-in!

January 1984: Agreed a Member could play a Competition on the alternate day, Saturday, because she was working on Wednesdays. It was not agreed that another member could do so as she worked nights, because she was obviously free during the day to play golf!

October 1984: Ladies allowed in Men's Bar due to curtailing of heat in Clubhouse.

The 10th Anniversary of the Eryri Ladies' Past Captains' Association
Left to Right: *Nellie Trenholme, Muriel Trenholme, Enid Evans, Pauline Lane, Marian Grace, Gladys Roberts and Lady Captain, Leah Fray.*

It was during Leah's Captaincy that the AD Grace Trophy was presented to the Club by Dennis Grace's daughter, Marian, for the outright winner of a new winter eclectic competition.

MRS J KILNER
1985

Joan originally came from Bolton. Her parents had retired to Nefyn from London when she was a young adult and so she had been coming frequently to see them during holiday periods.

THE LADY CAPTAINS - CAPTEINIAID Y MERCHED

She trained as a nurse at Manchester Royal Infirmary where she became Nurse of the Year and later became a district nurse and a midwife.

She met and married Clifford Kilner in 1952. Cliff had been widowed and was bringing up very young children on his own. Soon afterwards they bought the house that her parents had previously been renting at Glan-y-Llyn, Lôn Pwll William, Morfa Nefyn and retired there permanently in 1981.

Joan took up golf in the mid-60s and was a Member in both Bolton and Nefyn. She seemed to quickly get the hang of the game and came to love it, sometimes going up to the Club in the very early morning to practise. Her daughter recalls she would often take her son-in-law, Brian, for 18 holes leaving her daughter to care for their three very young children! She regularly won prizes, her major being the Lady Captain's Prize in 1983. She won the A D Grace Trophy in 1989 and 1991. We are told some of the crockery and glasses she won are still in use in the house in Lôn Pwll William which continues to be a home for her daughter's family.

Initially reluctant to leave Bolton, Joan soon immersed herself in local life and did try to learn Welsh although she found it very difficult. Joan had many, many friends in Nefyn and was very popular. She was elected Lady Captain in 1985 and was a very diplomatic leader, an exceptional host and always took great pride in her appearance.

Meirwen Collier (Left) and her sister Laura Jane Williams seated, pictured with Joan Kilner after an outing.

During Joan's Year, the Ladies' Locker Room was re-vamped and Joan played a large part in securing the new Powder Room for the Ladies, after the demise of the old dining-room. Also during her year, the Birdie Tree and Paperback Library were begun.

Sadly Joan developed a brain tumour in 1997 and died very quickly, aged 74, just two weeks after husband Clifford, who had been Club Captain in 1977.

MRS D ROBERTS 1986

Roedd mam Dorothy yn hanu o Morfa Nefyn, ond ganwyd Dorothy yn Lerpwl. Penderfynodd ei theulu ymfudo i America, ond ar y funud olaf tynnodd ei mam yn ôl a symudodd i Nefyn gyda Dorothy yn blentyn ifanc iawn. Dychwelodd ei thad o America ac ymgartrefodd y teulu yn Lôn Bodlondeb, Morfa Nefyn, gyda'i thad yn rhedeg y siop sglodion leol. Bu ei thad farw pan oedd Dorothy yn ei harddegau a bu ei brawd farw'n druenus o ifanc pan yn ddeuddeg oed gyda'r frech goch.

Cyfarfu Dorothy â Dick, ei darpar-ŵr, pan oedd hi'n gweithio ym Mhwllheli, gan briodi yn 1939 pan oedd hi'n ddeunaw oed. Treuliodd Dick gyfnod i ffwrdd yn ystod y rhyfel a phan ddychwelodd yn 1947, cyflogwyd ef gan yr YMCA fel rheolwr hostelau i bobl oedd wedi eu dadleoli. Dros gyfnod o bymtheng mlynedd bu Dick a Dorothy'n teithio ar draws Cymru a Lloegr tra roedd Dick yn ysgwyddo un cyfrifoldeb rheoli hostelau ar ôl y llall. Yn y cyfamser, bu Dorothy mewn swyddi gwahanol, e.e. Rheolwr Stôr Lawley a swydd gyda'r Bwrdd Trydan. Ganwyd un mab iddynt, Glyn, a hyfforddodd i fod yn gogydd uchel ei barch.

Gwireddwyd eu breuddwyd o ddychwelyd i Lŷn pan lwyddodd y ddau i brynu Gwesty'r Goedlan yn Edern yn 1962. Dros y tair blynedd ar ddeg ddilynol, cyfnewidiwyd a datblygwyd y 'Woodlands' yn westy a bwyty llwyddiannus. Ymunodd Glyn, eu mab, â hwy fel cogydd yn ddiweddarach cyn iddo yntau a Mary, ei wraig, brynu a rhedeg tafarn enwog y 'Cliffs' ym Morfa Nefyn.

Daeth Dorothy yn aelod o'r Clwb Golff yn 1964 ond ychydig o golff a chwaraeai oherwydd ei hymrwymiad â'r Gwesty. Pan ymddeolodd Dick a hithau, perswadiwyd hi gan Enid Evans i ddechrau chwarae. Ei graddnod isaf oedd 28. Byddai'n mwynhau ei golff a bu hefyd yn Aelod yng Nghlwb Abersoch. Ni enillodd brif gwpanau'r Clwb ond llwyddodd i sgorio dau 'Dwll ar Un'. Bu'r 'twll ar un' cyntaf ar y pedwerydd twll ar ddeg yn Abersoch (135 llath) a'r ail ar y chweched twll ym Mhorthmadog (119 llath). Bu'n llwyddiannus yng nghyfarfodydd y Sir ac yn Adran yr Aelodau Hŷn. Mae'n ymddangos y byddai Dorothy'n chwarae'n well i ffwrdd o Nefyn!

Cafodd Dorothy ei synnu'n fawr o gael ei henwebu yn Gapten Adran y Merched yn 1986. Perswadiwyd hi gan Dick i dderbyn yr enwebiad rhag ofn y buasai Dorothy'n rhy hen pan ddeuai cynigiad arall!

Plesiwyd Dorothy'n fawr pan gafodd ei hethol yn Llywydd y Merched am y cyfnod 2003-2005.

Dorothy was born in Liverpool, her mother hailing from Nefyn. The family decided to emigrate, but, at the very last minute her mother decided not to follow her father out to America and both mother and very young Dorothy returned to Nefyn. Before long, her father returned from America and they settled in Lôn Bodlondeb, in Morfa Nefyn, her father running the local Chip Shop. Her father died when Dorothy was in her teens and tragically, her younger brother died from measles when he was only 12 yrs old.

Dorothy met Dick, her husband, when she was working in Pwllheli and married him, aged 18, in 1939. Dick was then away in the army during the war and when he returned in 1947, he became employed by the YMCA as a manager of hostels for displaced persons. Over the following fifteen years, Dorothy and Dick travelled Wales and England as Dick took one managerial responsibility after another – by this time being warden in charge of student hostels. Dorothy meanwhile, was employed in various positions e.g. a cashier with Eastern Electricity Board and a Manager of a Lawleys Store. They had one son, Glyn, who trained and qualified to become a highly respected chef.

The pull back to Llŷn proved too strong however and in January 1962, Dick and Dorothy bought the 'Woodlands' in Edern and over the following 13 years, they transformed and developed this into the highly successful 'Woodlands Hotel'. Glyn, their son, joined them as the chef in the latter years before he and Mary, his wife, bought and ran the famous 'Cliffs Inn' in Morfa Nefyn.

Dorothy had actually joined the Golf Club in April 1964 but had little time for golf due to her commitments at the Hotel. When she and Dick retired, she was persuaded by Enid Evans to take up golf. Her lowest handicap was 28 and she thoroughly enjoyed her golf. She became a Member of Abersoch as well as Nefyn. She never won any actual major trophies but did score two 'Holes-in-One'. The first was at Abersoch on the 135 yds 14th hole and the second was at the 119 yds 6th hole at Porthmadog. Dorothy was often successful in County Meetings especially in the Vets section.

Lady Captain Dorothy Roberts presents the Dr Griffiths' Rose Bowl to Annette Jones in 1986.

Newly elected Lady President, Dorothy Roberts, is congratulated by the retiring Lady President Nellie Trenholme.

Dorothy was quite surprised to be invited to be Lady Captain in 1986. Dick persuaded her to accept as she might be too old the next time the offer came her way! It was during her year of office, 1986 that Enid Evans instigated the August Bank Holiday Charity Mixed Foursomes which still runs very successfully today.

Dorothy was delighted to be elected Lady President of the Club from 2003 to 2005.

It was reported in the Ladies' Committee Minutes of October 1986, that there had been a letter of complaint from visitors from the Glenbervie Club in Scotland who had got lost around the Club House! They stated there were no notices around to help people find the way to the Pro's Shop for tickets, or to the Ladies' Locker Room, the Main Entrance or the Men Only areas! The then Secretary had upset them when he told them 'to get out at once' when they inadvertently walked into his office – and then they had not been allowed to retrace their steps through the Men's Bar because an irate Lady Member told them they could not go back that way! The Ladies decided to leave the reply to the Men's Committee!

MRS M CHAFE
1987

Margaret Chafe came originally from Eccles, Manchester. She was a secretary when she married John, a qualified chemist who became

Managing Director of Edward Gorton, Ltd, a Glue and Gelatine Works. They lived in Stockton Heath and Appleton before retiring to Nefyn c.1985.

Margaret and John had three children, Carolyn, Erica and Andrew and as a family, they visited Nefyn on annual holidays from 1947 onwards. Margaret loved walking and rock climbing especially around Penmaenmawr. She and John had played tennis in their younger days and Carolyn, her daughter, recalls how the family would tow their little sailing dinghy down to Nefyn. They all became Members of the Nefyn Sailing Club. Although the rest of the family loved sailing, Margaret herself, however, was not that keen!

She turned to golf late in life, in the 60s and Carolyn recalls her mother 'manoeuvring' her father also towards golf as she saw retirement looming ahead, with their intention to retire to Morfa Nefyn. Margaret won many prizes and her lowest handicap was 20. She reached the Finals of the Australian Spoons with Laura Wyn Roberts one year and went to play at Borth and Ynys Las, near Aberystwyth.

November 1987: It was proposed by Mrs J Wilcox and seconded by Mrs C W Jones that the Sec write to the men's section to ask for permission to use crockery etc in the lounge during the weekend and other days in addition to Weds!

Left to Right: Mrs Joan Kilner, Mrs Muriel Trenholme, Mrs Ogwen Jones and Mrs Margaret Chafe after an outing.

Margaret thoroughly enjoyed her year as Captain. Carolyn recalls her mother 'absolutely loved every minute of her year'. Members recall her tremendous sense of humour and her prowess at the bridge table. She was a quiet person, a truly gentle, 'lovely' lady and 'of the old school' where etiquette and manners were all important. She was a perfectionist and friends also commented on her loyalty and how they valued her friendship.

MRS A V THOMAS 1988

Ganwyd Anne yn Ysbyty Dewi Sant ym Mangor ac fe'i magwyd yng Nghaernarfon. Cyfarfu ag Eirwyn, ei darpar-ŵr, pan oedd hi'n nyrsio yn yr Uned Babanod yn yr un Ysbyty, tra roedd ef yn Gurad ym Mangor. Tyfodd eu perthynas a phriodwyd y ddau yn 1967 gan symud i fyw i Llanddeusant ym Môn, lle y ganwyd Stephen a Fiona.

Ychydig ar ôl penodiad ei gŵr, E Wheldon Thomas, yn Ficer Plwyf Nefyn, ymunodd Anne â'r Clwb Golff a chafodd groeso cynnes. Yn dilyn gwersi gan John Pilkington, cafodd raddnod cychwynnol o 36* a ostyngwyd i 26 ar ôl chwarae mewn nifer o gystadleuthau.

Yn 1988, etholwyd Anne yn Gapten y Merched, cyfnod mae'n dal i'w drysori heddiw. Wrth gael ei phenodi dywedodd Anne fod angen tri pheth i ymdopi â'r swydd, sef croen fel rhinoseros, amynedd fel Job a doethineb Solomon! Yn 1999 etholwyd Anne i wasanaethu ar Bwyllgor Gwaith y Clwb am dair blynedd.

Bu ei phrofiad fel Capten y Merched a'i chyfnod ar Bwyllgor Adran y Merched a Phwyllgor Gwaith y Clwb yn gaffaeliad da iddi yn ddiweddarach pan, ar ôl symud i fyw i Abergele, yr etholwyd hi'n Gapten Adran y Merched yng Nghlwb Golff y Rhyl yn 2005. Dilynwyd Anne, yn Gapten Adran y Merched yn Nefyn, gan ei merch Fiona, ym Mlwyddyn ein Canmlwyddiant.

Pan oedd Anne yn cwblhau ei Chapteiniaeth yng Nghyfarfod Cyffredinol Blynyddol 1989, diolchodd Mrs Win Ogwen Jones (Llywydd y Merched) iddi am 'ein harwain trwy'r flwyddyn yn swynol ac yn atyniadol ac am ei ffordd ddymunol a theilwng o ddelio gyda sefyllfaoedd'.

Anne was born in St David's Hospital, Bangor and was brought up in Caernarfon. She met Eirwyn, her future husband, while she was nursing in the Premature Baby Unit at the same hospital, while he was a Curate at Bangor. Their relationship blossomed over the incubators as he came to the hospital to baptise the little ones. They married in 1967 and moved to Llanddeusant to live where both their children, Stephen and Fiona, were born.

Anne's first link with Nefyn Golf Club was when Eirwyn became the Rector of the grouped Parishes of Nefyn in 1975. After two years, Anne received an invitation to join the Club (January 1977) and she recalls how grateful they were, as a family, for the warm welcome they were given at the Club.

Anne received lessons from John Pilkington and was awarded a first handicap of 36*. After playing in numerous competitions, her handicap was reduced to 26.

In 1988, Anne was invited to become Lady Captain, a period she will always treasure. On her election as Captain, Anne said she believed three things were necessary for the Office and she hoped she had all three – the skin of a rhinoceros, the Patience of Job and the Wisdom of Solomon. In 1999, Anne was elected to serve for three years on the Club's Executive Committee.

Her experience as Lady Captain and her period on both the Ladies' and the Club's Executive Committees all stood Anne in good stead when she was invited to be Lady Captain of Rhyl Golf Club in 2005. This was after she and Eirwyn had left Morfa Nefyn and retired to Abergele in December 2001.

In 2007, Anne's experience must have been of great help to her daughter, Fiona, and contributed to her success as our Centenary Ladies' Captain.

Anne Thomas receives a prize from daughter Fiona in the Ladies' Centenary Open Competition Presentation

THE LADY CAPTAINS - CAPTEINIAID Y MERCHED

When Anne stood down as Captain in the AGM of 1988, Mrs Win Ogwen Jones thanked her 'for guiding us through the year in a charming and prepossessing manner and for her pleasant and exemplary approach to all situations!' At that same AGM, Marian praised Anne's daughter, Fiona. She then listed all Fiona's successes during the year which were all the more remarkable as she was still only 17 years of age.

Another golfer made the headlines during 1988. Mrs Elisabeth Wilson returned two cards for a Course Record during the August Meeting. Both these showed a gross score of 71 and it was agreed both cards should be framed and placed in a suitable position in the Ladies' Lounge or Powder Room.

MISS S ROULSTON 1989

Shirley, one of three children, was born in Liverpool but moved to the Llangollen area at a very young age. In 1966, her father, Peter, bought the Erw Goch Hotel and they moved to Morfa Nefyn to live. Over the years, he and Shirley extended the Hotel and ran a very successful business until Peter's retirement due to ill health in 1982. Shirley recalls her father developing his culinary skills while she specialised in making the puddings and concentrated on running the bar, general cleaning and making the clientele comfortable.

Shirley joined the Golf Club in 1976 largely at the instigation of John Pilkington, the Professional. She started the same time as Anne Thomas and Edwina Littlewood and recalls playing with Edwina for three years before they even put in their cards for handicap! Her first handicap was 36 and she reduced to an impressive 12.

Over the years, she was awarded many prizes and trophies and won the A D Grace Trophy on 5 occasions. Her name appears frequently on the Honours Boards for she won the Cefnamwlch Cup three times and the Dr Griffiths' Rose Bowl twice. Her truly coveted prize, however, was the Lady Captain's Prize in 1996, when Elsie Hughes was Lady Captain. Shirley herself had given a beautiful carriage clock as her own Captain's Prize and was delighted to receive an equally beautiful carriage clock from Elsie seven years later!

Shirley worked hard for the Golf Club. She served on the Committee for a total of 11 years, as Assistant Secretary, Secretary and Handicap Secretary - the latter position she held for a continuous 7 years. In that time, the handicap system was computerised and Shirley is congratulated in the Minutes of January 1999, for 'her quick familiarisation of the system and the informative letter she sent to Club Members explaining it all'. Between 1998 and 2000, Shirley organised the Mail on Sunday Competition.

In 1999, Shirley presented a cut glass Rose Bowl for a Knockout Competition for the Bronze Division players. This prize is competed for annually to this day and Shirley continues to donate the replica prizes.

> *July 1989:* Letter from Men's Sec regarding the dress of the lady members during the hot weather. The [Lady] Sec was asked to enquire what they meant by 'proper dress' and then put a notice on the board.

MRS C W JONES
1990

Magwyd Carys a'i brawd ym Mangor a dechreuodd weithio mewn swyddfa cyfreithiwr. Yn dilyn hyn, fe'i hapwyntiwyd yn glerc yn y Swyddfa Bost ym Mangor. Cofiai'r cloeau diogelwch a roddwyd ar ddrysau'r Swyddfa rhag Byddin Gweriniaeth Iwerddon.

Symudodd i fyw i Ben Llŷn yn 1972 yn dilyn ei phriodas ag Eirwyn a chyrhaeddodd Pistyll ar gefn ei fotor beic enwog i fyw yng nghartref ei fam. Buont yn byw yn Rhosfawr am gyfnod cyn symud i Glanrhyd, Mynydd Nefyn, lle y gweithiodd Eirwyn yn galed dros y blynyddoedd yn atgyweirio a gwella eu cartref. Bu Carys yn gweithio yn Ysgol Glan-y-Môr am gyfnod cyn gadael i gychwyn teulu. Mae gan Eirwyn a Carys ddau o blant, Siân a John, un ŵyr ac un wyres.

Ymunodd â Chlwb Golff Nefyn yn 1977 gyda'r bwriad o gyfarfod pobl a gwneud ffrindiau. Ar un adeg byddai Dennis Grace, cyn-Bro y Clwb, yn ymweld â hwy yn Glanrhyd i roddi cyngor iddynt ar chwarae'r gêm. Ar y cychwyn, byddai'n chwarae gydag Anne Thomas, Edwina Littlewood, Marian Grace ac Annette Jones. Yr adeg honno, meddai Carys, '...byddai rhaid cael gwahoddiad i chwarae gan y merched eraill. Fuasech chi byth yn meiddio gofyn i rywun chwarae gyda chi; felly byddem yn chwarae efo'n gilydd'. Diolch i'r drefn, mae pethau wedi newid!

Roedd Carys yn chwaraewraig frwdfrydig yn yr ysgol, a chymerodd at golff gan ennill nifer o gwpanau yn Adran y Merched gan gynnwys Tlws A D Grace yn 1995 a Chwpan Cefnamwlch yn 2000. Ei graddnod isaf oedd 19 ac uchafbwynt ei llwyddiannau oedd ennill Cwpan Her Buckley yn erbyn holl Aelodaeth y Clwb yn 1983 gyda sgôr anfarwol o 90-27-63. Daeth y siswrn allan a thociwyd ei graddnod i 20 mewn amrantiad! Mewn gwirionedd, daeth ei graddnod i lawr o 33 i 20 y flwyddyn honno a chafodd lawer o ganmoliaeth am y gamp.

Mae Carys wedi cynrychioli Aelodaeth y Merched ar Bwyllgor y Merched am flynyddoedd, ynghyd â chadeirio yr Is-Bwyllgor Graddnodau. Mae hi wedi bod yn Drysorydd Adran y Merched, Capten yn 1990, Ysgrifennydd Adran y Merched o 2003-07 ac ym Mlwyddyn ein Canmlwyddiant mae'n gwisgo mantell Llywydd y Merched.

Byddai Carys yn gweithio'n ddiflino ac yn ddirwgnach ym mhob swydd yr ymgymerai â hi yn y Clwb. Mae'n uchel iawn ei pharch gan yr Aelodau a chwaraewyr, yn ddynion ac yn ferched. Mae'n berson hapus ac anaml y caiff ei chynhyrfu.

Wrth gyflwyno'i hadroddiad terfynol fel ysgrifennydd yng Nghyfarfod Cyffredinol y Merched, 2007, cymharodd Carys Adran y Merched â llong deithio fawr foethus yn galw mewn porthladdoedd gwahanol trwy'r flwyddyn. Roedd 'Porthladd y Cyfarfod Cyffredinol' yn gweld newid criw a rhestrodd Swyddogion Adran y Merched gyda Swyddogion y Llong o'r Llyngesydd i lawr i'r Peiriannydd! Aeth ymlaen i roddi crynodeb o daith y Llong trwy gydol y flwyddyn cyn cyflwyno Mordaith Arbennig y Canmlwyddiant oedd ar fin cychwyn unwaith y buasai'r Llong wedi cael ei sbriwsio a'r Criw newydd yn eu lle.

Ym mlwyddyn ei Chapteiniaeth, gyda Chapten y Clwb, T Gareth Gruffydd, cyflwynodd Carys Gloch y Capteiniaid i'r Clwb. Mae'r Gloch a ddefnyddir i dynnu sylw'r Aelodau i'w gweld yn y lolfa. Yn 1999 cyflwynodd Carys ac Eirwyn dlws i Adran y Merched, sef Tlws Môr a Mynydd. Chwaraeir am y tlws yma gan y Merched yng Ngŵyl yr Haf.

Carys and her brother were brought up in Bangor and it was there that she started working in a solicitor's office. She then was appointed as a clerk in the Post Office and remembers the security locks which were placed on the Post Office doors for protection against the IRA.

Carys met Eirwyn in Bangor and they married in 1972, the famous motor-bike bringing her to live to Pistyll with Eirwyn's mother. They then moved to Rhosfawr and finally to Glanrhyd which they completely transformed and has been the family home ever since. For a while, Carys worked in Ysgol Glan-y-Môr but left to start a family. Eirwyn and Carys have two children, Siân and John, both keen on sport, and two grandchildren.

Carys joined the Golf Club in 1977, initially to meet people and make friends. Eirwyn had joined in 1976 and Carys recalls the retired Dennis Grace going up to Glanrhyd and giving them both some tips on the game! Her early playing partners were Anne Thomas, Edwina Littlewood, Marian Grace, and Annette Jones. She did not put in her 4 cards for handicap however until 1979. 'In those days', recalls Carys, 'you had to wait to be invited to play by the other Ladies. You would never dare ask someone to play with you so we just played together!' Thankfully, times have changed!

Carys, a keen sportswoman at school, soon took to the game and won several cups in the Ladies' Section including the A D Grace Trophy in 1995 and the Cefnamwlch Cup in 2000. The highlight of her successes was winning the Buckley Challenge Trophy against both men and ladies in the August meeting of 1983. Her wonderful score was 90-27-63. The scissors appeared immediately and her handicap was reduced to 20. In fact, that same year Carys was nominated the most improved player of the year for reducing her handicap from 33-20 within the one season. Her lowest ever handicap was 19.

Carys has represented the Membership on the Ladies' Committee for 17 years and has held positions for 13 of those years! She was Handicap Secretary for 4 years in the late 80s, Treasurer for 3 years in the early 90s and Ladies Secretary for 4 years from 2003-2007. She was also Outing Secretary for 2 years. She was honoured to be chosen as Lady Captain in 1990 and was delighted to be Centenary Ladies' President.

Carys gave tirelessly of herself in all the positions she held and in all she undertook for the Club. She is held in high esteem by the Members, players and non-players, ladies and gentlemen. She has the happiest of dispositions and so very rarely is ruffled.

When Carys gave her retiring Secretary's report at the AGM of 2007, she likened the Ladies' Section to a large and luxurious cruise liner, calling in various ports throughout the year. Port AGM was seeing a change of crew and she listed all our Officers in relation to the Ship's Officers from the Admiral down to the Engineer! She then went on to give an amusing résumé of the Ship's voyage throughout the year before introducing the new special

THE LADY CAPTAINS - CAPTEINIAID Y MERCHED

Centenary Cruise that was about to take place once the ship had been spruced up and the new Crew appointed.

In her Captaincy Year, Carys, together with the Captain, T Gareth Gruffydd, presented the Captains' Bell to the Club. This hangs in the Lounge and is used to call all Members to order! In 1999, Carys and Eirwyn presented a trophy to the Ladies' Section. This was 'Tlws Môr a Mynydd' and it is played during the Summer Meeting each year.

Carys Wyn Jones on her Lady Captain's Day with Mary Davies (Ladies' Vice-President) on her right and Win Ogwen Jones on her left.

MRS M WILLIAMS 1991

Ganwyd a magwyd Medi ym Mhwllheli ac yn dilyn ei phriodas â Richard Williams (Capten 1966) symudodd i Dolawel ym Morfa Nefyn. Magodd dri o blant. Mae Elizabeth yn byw i ffwrdd ac mae Dafydd ac Alwyn, y ddau fab, yn golffio'n rheolaidd yn y Clwb.

Ymunodd Medi â Chlwb Golff Nefyn yn 1963 ar ôl i Dick ei gŵr, ei chymell. Fodd bynnag, ni wnaeth ddechrau chwarae o ddifrif tan y saithdegau pan fu'n derbyn gwersi gan John Pilkington, y Pro, ynghyd â nifer o ferched eraill.

Cofia Medi y tro cyntaf y chwaraeodd mewn Cystadleuaeth yn 1977. Roedd hi wedi cael chwe gwers cyn y diwrnod a chwaraeodd gyda Dorothy Wales mewn Cystadleuaeth 9 Twll i Ddechreuwyr a drefnwyd gan Hilda Smith, Capten y Merched. Cawsant bleser mawr o chwarae ar y diwrnod ond buont wrthi am oriau ac ni chawn gyhoeddi eu sgôr yma! Roedd Mel (Spar) a Gareth (Yr Hen Bost) wrth eu digon yn casglu'r cardiau ar ddiwedd y gystadleuaeth ac yn eu dyblau yn chwerthin ac yn holi sut oedd modd cael cymaint o sgôr ar dyllau!

Bu Medi'n weithgar ar Bwyllgor Adran y Merched am flynyddoedd ac fe'i hetholwyd yn Gapten yn 1991, pan roedd hi'n chwarae oddi ar raddnod o 28. Mae hi wedi chwarae golff yn rheolaidd, yn enwedig ar Ddydd Mercher a phrynhawn Sul gyda'i chyfeillion Megan M Williams, Joyce Williams a Dilys Llewelyn Owen.

Medi was brought up in Pwllheli and following her marriage in 1949 to Richard (Dick) Williams, Porthdinllaen, they moved to Dolawel, Morfa Nefyn. They brought up three children and the two sons, Dafydd and Alwyn are regular golfers at the Club. Throughout the years, Medi has faithfully supported all functions in the Club, from golf competitions to cabarets, from carol singing to whist drives!

Medi joined the Club at Dick's instigation in January 1963 but actually did not begin to take golf seriously until the mid 70s when she and five others had six lessons from John Pilkington, the Professional.

Medi recalls the first time she ever went out to play in a competition. She had already been for the group lessons and she and Dorothy Wales entered a '9 Hole Competition for Beginners' organised by the then Lady Captain, Hilda Smith. They thoroughly enjoyed themselves but took hours to play and their score is not allowed to go into print. Suffice it to say that the young lads, Mel (Spar) and Gareth (Nefyn Post Office) who were in charge of the cards, hooted with laughter and questioned how they could score so high on each hole!

Medi was active on the Ladies' Section Committee for several years and was elected Lady Captain in 1991. Her handicap came down to 28 the year before she was elected Captain but after that, she says, it was downhill all the way! She still plays golf regularly with the Ladies on Wednesdays and on Sunday afternoons with her friends Megan M Williams, Joyce Williams and Dilys Llewelyn Owen.

Nellie Trenholme was noted for writing poems thanking the Captains for their year of office and these were occasionally read out at the AGMs. Of Medi, she wrote

I have nothing but praise,
As I look in your face.
Your elegance on all occasions,
Poise, tact and commiserations – when necessary–
Praise when it is deserved,
Modest to a degree,
Never a wrong word.
This is Medi – believe me.

MRS L W ROBERTS
1992

Magwyd Laura ar fferm ym Mhenrhyn Llŷn ac yn y cyfnod hwnnw doedd ganddi ddim diddordeb o gwbl mewn golff. Yn dilyn llwyddiant yn ei harholiadau Lefel O yn Ysgol Botwnnog, ymadawodd â'r ysgol yn 1956 a symudodd y teulu i Forfa Nefyn i fyw. Y flwyddyn ddilynol, apwyntiwyd Laura yn gynorthwyydd deintyddol i'r Deintydd Ysgol, Harry Parry o Nefyn, ac arhosodd yn y swydd hon tan ymddeoliad Harry yn 1959 oherwydd ei iechyd. Byddai Harry yn trafod Clwb Golff Nefyn yn gyson gyda Laura - roedd ef yn Aelod blaenllaw ac wedi bod yn Gapten y Clwb yn 1941.

Ymunodd Laura â'r Clwb yn 1961 gyda'i diweddar ffrind pennaf, Wenna Davies Hughes, am y ffi flynyddol o ddwy gini. Cyfarfu Laura â'i gŵr, Hugh, yn y Golff ychydig o amser ar ôl ymuno pan oedd ef adref ar wyliau o'r Llynges Fasnach. Priodwyd hwy yn 1964 a ganwyd dau o blant iddynt, Linda ac Alwyn. Erbyn hyn mae ganddynt un ŵyr, Liam, ac un wyres, Cara.

Dechreuodd Laura chwarae golff o ddifrif yn dilyn ei phriodas a bu'r ddau yn chwarae'n rheolaidd. Cafodd gyfres o wersi gan Dennis Grace gan ddangos cynnydd sylweddol. Ar ôl toriad i fagu'r plant, dychwelodd i chwarae yng nghanol y saithdegau pan gafodd raddnod o 36.

Dros y blynyddoedd, mae wedi ennill llawer o wobrau a thlysau ac ymddengys ei henw yn rheolaidd ar y Byrddau Anrhydedd yn y Clwb.

Enillodd Ddysgl Rhosyn Dr Griffiths yn 1975 ac 1987, Pencampwriaeth y Clwb yn 1982, Gwobr Capten y Merched yn 1989 a 2004, a Chwpan Coffa Dorothy Wood yn 1999. Ei champ orau oedd ennill Tlws Buckley yn 1989 gyda sgôr net o 60. Torrwyd ei graddnod o 19 i lawr i 14. Yn ogystal, mae hi wedi cynrychioli'r Clwb ym Mhencampwriaeth Timau Cymru.

Mae Laura wedi gwasanaethu ar bwyllgorau Adran y Merched am flynyddoedd lawer ac am y cyfnod 2005-2007 bu'n Drysorydd Adran y Merched. Etholwyd hi'n Gapten yn 1992. Ar yr un adeg roedd Mrs Lilian Shaw, a oedd yn aelod yn Nefyn, yn Gapten Adran y Merched yng Nghlwb Macclesfield, a phenderfynwyd trefnu gemau cartref ac oddi cartref. Cafwyd gemau pleserus iawn am ddeng mlynedd.

Mae Laura wedi bod yn gynrychiolydd Nefyn ar Gymdeithas Golff Merched Siroedd Caernarfon a Môn am sawl blwyddyn yn ogystal â gwasanaethu ar eu Pwyllgor Cyllid. Yn 2003 cafodd wahoddiad gan y pwyllgor yma i fod yn Gapten Siroedd Gogleddol Cymru sy'n ymestyn ar draws y Gogledd cyn belled â Phenarlâg yn Sir Fflint. Ar yr un cyfnod, etholwyd Miss Fiona Vaughan Thomas yn Gapten Cymdeithas Golff Siroedd Caernarfon a Môn; roedd hwn yn gyfnod hanesyddol gyda dwy o Aelodau Clwb Nefyn mewn uchel swyddi ar yr un adeg. Dyma'r sefyllfa eto ym Mlwyddyn ein Canmlwyddiant gyda Fiona yn Gapten Adran y Merched yn Nefyn a Laura yn Gapten y Sir am y ddwy flynedd, 2007 a 2008.

Yn 2000 cyflwynodd Hugh a Laura 'Cwpan Bryn 'Raur' i'r Clwb. Chwaraeir am y Gwpan gan yr Adran Hŷn yng Ngŵyl yr Haf.

Seated Left to Right:
Marian Grace, Carys Wyn Jones and Edwina Littlewood have liquid refreshment half-way round from Lady Captain, Laura Wyn Roberts, on her Lady Captain's Day, 1992.

Laura was brought up on a farm in Llŷn and attended Botwnnog Grammar School. After successful O levels, she left school and the family moved to Morfa Nefyn in 1956. The following year, Laura was appointed Dental Assistant to the School Dentist, Harry Parry from Nefyn, and she remained in this position until he retired in 1959. Harry used to discuss golf matters with Laura quite regularly. He was a prominent Member of the Golf Club and had been Captain in 1941 and his wife, Dilys, the Lady Captain, in 1947.

Laura joined the Club in May 1961, the same time as her great friend, the late Wenna Davies Hughes. The annual fee was 2 guineas (£2-2-0). Laura met her future husband Hugh, at the Golf Club shortly after she joined. He was home on leave from the Merchant Navy at the time. They married in 1964 and have two children, Alwyn and Linda, and two grandchildren, Liam and Cara.

Laura began to take her golf more seriously after her marriage and she and Hugh regularly played together. She had lessons from Dennis Grace and made good progress. She took a break from golf, when the children were born and did not return to playing regularly until the mid-70s, when she was given a handicap of 36.

Over the years, Laura went on to win many prizes and trophies and her name appears frequently on the Honours Boards. She won the Dr Griffiths' Rose Bowl in 1975 and 1987; the Club Championship in 1982; the Lady Captain's Prize in 1989 and in 2004; and the Dorothy Wood Memorial Cup in 1999. She has also represented the Club in the Welsh Team Championship.

Her greatest achievement she recalls, was when she won the coveted Buckley Trophy in 1989. The very few Ladies who have won this prestigious trophy have always been highly delighted to have beaten the men! Her nett score on that day was 60 and her handicap was cut from 19 to 14! This was her lowest handicap.

Laura served on the Ladies' Committee for several years and was Lady Treasurer from 2004-2007. She was elected Lady Captain in 1992. At the same time, Mrs Lillian Shaw, who was a Member at Nefyn, was Lady Captain at Macclesfield Golf Club and it was suggested that the Ladies from both Clubs should play Home and Away Matches. This they did and had so much fun and pleasure that the practice continued for 10 years!

Ladies of Nefyn at Macclesfield with the Ladies of Macclesfield on their first ever Exchange Match in 1992. Pictured centre, in white, Lady Captain of Nefyn, Laura Wyn Roberts and on her left, in red, Lillian Shaw, Lady Captain of Macclesfield.

Laura represented Nefyn as a Delegate on the Caernarfonshire and Anglesey Ladies' County Golf Association for many years as well as serving on their Finance Committee. In 2003, she was elected Captain of the Welsh Northern Counties Ladies' Golf Association. In that same year, Fiona Vaughan Thomas was elected Captain of the Caernarfonshire and Anglesey Ladies' County Golf Association. This was an historic occasion for our Club, having two Members elected to such high office in the Area at the same time.

Pictured Left to Right in 2003: Fiona Vaughan Thomas, County Captain, Dilys Ll Owen, Club Lady Captain and Laura Wyn Roberts, WNCLGA Captain.

Pictured Left to Right, summer 2007: Fiona Vaughan Thomas, Club Ladies' Captain, Laura Wyn Roberts, Ladies' County Captain and Carys Wyn Jones, Club Ladies' President.

In this our Centenary Year, Laura Wyn Roberts has brought yet another honour to the Club by being elected County Captain for two years while Fiona has the honour of being our Centenary Captain.

In 2000, Laura and Hugh presented the 'Bryn 'Raur Cup' for the Veterans Competition held annually in the August meeting.

MRS J WILCOX
1993

Jacqui's parents moved to Wales in 1952 from Cheshire as her father wanted to own his own farm. She was educated at Rhydyclafdy Primary School and Pwllheli Grammar School. She trained at Manchester Royal Infirmary from 1967-70 and qualified as an SRN nurse. She married in 1970 and then worked in Essex as a staff nurse. Her son, Mark, was born in 1974.

Jacqui returned to Wales in 1980 to live in Nefyn and started playing golf. From 1980 onwards, she held various jobs including private nursing in Abersoch and Bodawen Nursing Home in Tremadog. She became a House Matron at Shrewsbury School in 1991 and stayed until 2003 when she retired. Jacqui remarried in 1994 but sadly her husband, Les Gill, died very shortly afterwards. Thankfully, she found happiness again and married Richard Pittaway in 2003. She now lives in Anglesey but travels regularly to play golf with us at the Club.

As far as golfing prowess is concerned, Jacqui's lowest handicap was 13. She won the Lady Captain's Prize in 1976 and 2005. She won the A D Grace Trophy in 1984, the Dr Griffiths' Rose Bowl in 1987, the Club Championship in 1990, and the Cefnamwlch Cup in 2004.

In 1986, Jacqui became the first ever appointed Treasurer of the Ladies' Section, a position she held for two years. She was also Assistant Secretary at one time and was appointed Junior Organiser in 1986. In 1987-88, the Clubhouse was refurbished and Jacqui, together with Joan Kilner, was responsible for making the curtains in the new Ladies' Powder Room. Jacqui took great pride in the general appearance of the Clubhouse. She regularly arranged the flower displays, tidied the garden and planted spring bulbs around the Clubhouse.

When she was elected Captain at the AGM of November 1992, Jacqui apologised in advance for not being able to be as visible as she would like due to her work commitments away from Nefyn. At the end of her year, Members were extremely complimentary of the way she had so successfully combined her work with her Captaincy at Nefyn and it was obvious that her fears had been wholly unfounded.

MRS S IVES
1994

Shirley is originally from Folkestone in Kent. She married Doug, a Major in the Army and spent the following three years with him in Ghana. While out there, they made friends with a couple who had been holidaying in Nefyn and when they returned to this country in 1955, these friends invited them to join them in Nefyn for a week's holiday. They stayed at Caeau Capel Hotel, which was then run by Sam and Clare Sycamore.

They both fell in love with the area and when Doug was stationed at Rhyl, they continued to visit regularly. They bought Sam and Clare's cottage in Ceidio in 1961, visiting almost every weekend and they moved there permanently in 1967. Shirley ran the Nefyn Brownies for twenty years and the Guides for three years.

She joined Nefyn Golf Club on January 1st 1976 and she reached, as she claims, 'the dizzy heights' of a 21 handicap at one stage and winning the A D Grace Trophy twice, in 1987 and 1988. She was disappointed that she never won a Major Trophy although she was runner-up in one of them.

Shirley was delighted to be elected Captain in 1994. She was known for her smile and her gentle sense of humour. She was very caring and visited the sick and those confined to home.

Shirley and Doug between them have 5 children, 10 grandchildren and 6 great grandchildren! They now live in Cadnant, Lôn y Castell, Nefyn.

July 1994: The format of the Invitation Day Tea was changed... Agreed the Meal was £4.80, £5.00 with Coffee. This was a choice of three meals – ham salad, plaice and chips or home-made steak and kidney pie and chips and choice of sweet.

The Prizes were Handbags, Evening Bags, Scarves and Purses at a cost of £100.95p. 12 Balls were bought for 2s and card draw.

MRS S ASHWORTH
1995

Sue was born and brought up in Birmingham and was always very involved in sport, specialising in netball and tennis whilst at school. She in fact played tennis to a high standard until she retired from the game when she moved to Edern in 1962. She had two children, Simon (our current Secretary/Manager) and Sally and both of them joined the Golf Club at the age of 10. They took advantage of the free golf lessons given originally by Dennis Grace on a Saturday morning. Sue herself joined the Club in 1977, having had a Christmas present of 6 golf lessons from her two children! (See Chapter 'I remember…' where Sue recalls her golf lessons with John Pilkington and her early ventures on to the course.)

She won many competitions and trophies and her name appears many times on the Honours Boards. As Sue Dennis, she appears winning the Cefnamwlch Cup, the Dorothy Wood Memorial Cup, the Lady Captain's Prize and the Dr Griffiths' Bowl twice. She married Geoff Ashworth in the early 90s and won the Dorothy Wood again in 1995, when she was Lady Captain.

Lady Captain Sue Ashworth with the Club Captain, Rev. Eirwyn W Thomas

THE LADY CAPTAINS - CAPTEINIAID Y MERCHED

Sue felt extremely honoured to be invited to be Lady Captain and had a very happy year. During her Captaincy, Sue and Geoff presented the Ashworth Cup for a new 18 hole Mixed Foursomes Knockout, with a draw for partners. At first this was a very popular Competition but it became increasingly difficult to organise, often with four different families trying to organise a date, and the Cup was finally withdrawn, much to Sue's disappointment.

Sue now lives in Cyprus but continues to be interested in developments at the Club.

During her Captaincy, she produced a Newsletter to inform Members, especially Away Members, of the year's programme. In 1995, the Whitfield Salver was changed to a Singles Knockout. It was agreed that a Decanter should be presented for the Final of all Monthly Goblet (LGU Medal) Winners and the Senior Ladies' Trophy should be played by all Ladies over 55 not just Nefyn (Local) Ladies. Lis Wilson, a Member and Cheshire Standard Scratch Assessor, recommended an SSI of 74 and this was accepted by Committee. [Confirmation from WLGU arrived December 1995.]

MISS E HUGHES 1996

Magwyd Elsie yn un o ddeuddeg o blant yn Edern. Aeth i Ysgol Gynradd Edern lle yr addysgwyd nifer o aelodau brwd Clwb Golff Nefyn! Cwblhaodd ei haddysg yn Ysgol Botwnnog. Mae ganddi un mab ac un ŵyr. Bu Elsie'n gweithio mewn siop ffrwythau cyn cychwyn ar yrfa fel Gweithiwr Cymunedol.

Dechreuodd chwarae golff yn 1982 ac o 1984 ymlaen dechreuodd ar gyfnod ymestynnol o fuddugoliaethau mewn prif gystadleuthau. Atgoffir Elsie o'e gorfoledd pan enillodd ei phrif gystadleuaeth gyntaf, gwobr Capten y Merched yn 1984. Yn yr un flwyddyn enillodd Bencampwriaeth y Clwb, cyflawniad aruthrol i rywun na wnaeth erioed feddwl y buasai yn ennill dim byd mwy na chystadleuaeth wythnosol ar Ddydd Mercher.

Enillodd Elsie Bencampwriaeth y Clwb ddeuddeg o weithiau rhwng 1984 a 2002; Gwobr Capten y Merched o 1984 i 1986; Tlws A D Grace yn 1985 ac 1986; Dysgl Rhosyn Dr Griffiths yn 1992, 1999 a 2001 a Chwpan Cefnamwlch yn 1993 ac 1998! Chwaraeai ar raddnod o 7 ar ei gorau. Yn ei medal gyntaf erioed, gostyngodd ei graddnod i 30!

Dywed Elsie ei bod yn ddyledus i'w ffrind agos, Marian Grace, am ei chyfeillgarwch clós. Cafodd Elsie groeso mawr gan Marian pan ymunodd gyntaf â'r Clwb a byddai Marian bob amser yn ei hannog i chwarae golff. Byddai merched hŷn y Clwb yn gefnogol iawn iddi hefyd. Cofia Elsie Aelodau fel Annie Williams, Mary Davies, Mary Roberts ac Elsie Toleman-Jones yn ei gwylio'n chwarae trwy ffenestr Tŷ'r Clwb ar brynhawn Dydd Mercher. Petai hi neu ei chyd-chwaraewyr yn methu pyt fer ar y lawnt olaf, yna byddai ymchwiliad a dweud y drefn pan fyddent yn dychwelyd i'r lolfa… ac o ganlyniad gwnaed ymdrech fawr i chwarae'r twll olaf yn dda o hynny 'mlaen!

Bu Elsie'n Ysgrifennydd y Graddnodau am chwe mlynedd rhwng 1989 a 1995. Y flwyddyn ddilynol, fe'i hanrhydeddwyd pan etholwyd hi yn Gapten y Merched. Bu'n gwasanaethu ar Bwyllgor y Merched am gyfnod o un mlynedd ar ddeg.

Dewiswyd Elsie i gynrychioli'r Clwb chwe gwaith ym Mhencampwriaethau Timau Cymru, ond yn anffortunus fe anafodd ei chefn yn 2004 ac nid yw wedi chwarae fawr o golff ers hynny. Ymddiswyddodd dros dro o'r Clwb, ond mae'n bleser cael cyhoeddi ei bod wedi ailymuno a hyderwn y byddwn yn ei gweld yn chwarae golff safonol unwaith eto.

The Ladies' NWLGSA (North Wales Ladies' Golf Shield Association) Shield Team winners of Division 4 (of 8) in 1996, with promotion looming to Division 3!
Front Row: Left to Right: *Carys Wyn Jones, Janet Brown, June Simpson, and Ase Richardson.*
Back Row: *Shirley Roulston, Rhiannon Ingman, Lady Captain Elsie Hughes, Laura Wyn Roberts and Liz Mangham*

Elsie, one of twelve children was raised in Edern. She attended Ysgol Edern and continued her education at Ysgol Botwnnog. She has one son and one grandson.

Elsie worked in a fruit shop before starting her career as a Community Worker.

She started playing golf in 1982 and from 1984 she began an impressive winning streak in the Ladies' Section. She remembers the complete elation she felt when she won her first major competition, the Lady Captain's Prize in 1984, against some of the more experienced golfers of the time. This was the same year as she won the Club Championship and it was a huge achievement for someone who never thought she might win even a weekly competition when she first started playing golf!

Elsie won the Ladies' Club Championship on a remarkable twelve occasions between 1984 and 2002; The Lady Captain's Prize 1984, 1985 and 1986; the A D Grace Trophy in 1985 and 1986; the Dr Griffiths' Rose Bowl 1992, 1999 and 2001 and the Cefnamwlch Cup in 1993 and 1998. Her lowest playing handicap was 7. In her very first medal she reduced her handicap to 30!

Elsie is greatly indebted to Marian Grace and they became firm and very close friends. Marian was extremely welcoming to her when she first appeared at the Golf Club and encouraged her in her golf.

Elsie Hughes and Marian Grace receiving prizes.

Elsie also speaks highly of the older Lady Members who encouraged her and were delighted with her successes. Elsie, like many other beginners at the time, recalls ladies like Annie Williams, Mary Davies, Mary Roberts and Elsie Toleman-

THE LADY CAPTAINS - CAPTEINIAID Y MERCHED

Jones always at the window on a Wednesday afternoon peering out at them playing the 18th Hole. If one of them missed a putt, then there would be an inquisition and a telling off when they got back in…and consequently they always endeavoured to play the 18th better than any other hole on the day!

Pictured Left to Right: Gladys Roberts, Mary Roberts Rhyllech, Mary Davies and Elsie Toleman-Jones

Elsie was Handicap Secretary for six years between 1989 and 1995. The following year, she was honoured by being elected Lady Captain. Altogether, she served on the Ladies' Committee for 11 years.

She was selected to represent the Club on six occasions in the Welsh Team Championship but sadly, in September 2004, she hurt her back and has played very little golf since. She resigned temporarily from the Club but we are delighted she has rejoined and we all hope to see her back playing high standard golf again in the near future.

MRS H GRIFFITH 1997

Magwyd Helen yn Tyddyn Gwyn, Llangian ac mae wedi byw yno, yn yr un cartref, ar hyd ei hoes. Cafodd ei pherswadio i chwarae golff gan ei chwaer oedd eisoes yn Aelod ym Mhwllheli ac Abersoch. Yn fuan iawn roedd golff yn bleser pur iddi ac yn rhywbeth y gallai ei wneud ei hun ar wahân i waith yn y cartref ac ar y fferm.

Cyswllt cyntaf Helen â Chlwb Golff Nefyn oedd pan gafodd wahoddiad gan Dorothy Roberts i ddiwrnod y Merched. Yn ddiweddarach, ymunodd â'r Clwb yn 1983. Cafodd Helen groeso gan y Merched a gwnaeth lawer o ffrindiau. Bydd yn teithio yn ddeddfol bron bob Dydd Mercher o Langian, ym mhob tywydd, ac mae wedi mwynhau pob munud.

Mae ei graddnod rywbeth yn debyg heddiw i beth oedd o ugain mlynedd yn ôl, ond nid yw'n fodlon ei ddadlennu! Yn 1991 cyflawnodd Helen dwll ar un ar gwrs Nefyn. Dyma'r un flwyddyn ag yr etholwyd hi'n Gapten y Merched yng Nghlwb Golff Abersoch.

Pan fu hi'n Gapten Adran y Merched yn Nefyn yn 1997 cafodd lawer o gefnogaeth gan yr Aelodau a bu Marian Grace yn gefn mawr iddi ac yn ffrind cywir. Bu'r diweddar Derek Clulow a Hugh Roberts, Capteiniaid y Clwb yn ystod ei blwyddyn hi, yn gefnogol, yn frwdfrydig a chyfeillgar iawn. Pauline Lane oedd Llywydd y Merched yn ystod ei Chapteiniaeth; roedd Pauline bob amser yn hawddgar ac yn esiampl i'r Aelodau oll.

Helen was brought up at Tyddyn Gwyn, Llangian, where she has lived all her life. She was persuaded to start playing golf by her sister who was a Member at both Pwllheli and Abersoch Golf Clubs. In no time at all, Helen found that golf was a total pleasure, something for herself in contrast to house and farm work.

Helen's first link with Nefyn Golf Club was by invitation from Dorothy Roberts on a Wednesday. She joined in 1983 and was warmly welcomed by the Nefyn Ladies and made many friends. She still travels from Llangian nearly every Wednesday in all weathers and enjoys every visit.

Helen's handicap today is similar to her handicap some twenty years ago, but she does not reveal what it is! In 1991, she had a Hole-in-One at Nefyn. This was the same year as she was elected Lady Captain at Abersoch Golf Club.

When she was elected Lady Captain at our Club in 1997, she had tremendous support across the Club's Membership. Derek Clulow and Hugh Roberts, Club Captains in her Captaincy, were very supportive as also was Marian Grace who she remembers as a very true friend. Pauline Lane was the Ladies' President at the time and Helen had tremendous respect for her, who she felt was an example to all Members. Helen was very well respected herself.

In December 1996, shortly after she became Captain, the Ladies' Committee bought a Lady President's Brooch at a cost of £135 (see Photo under Pauline Lane's Captaincy, 1959).

In February 1997, at a special meeting convened to discuss handicapping, a handicap limit of 36 was set for all major trophies and knockouts (Ladies and Mixed) and a handicap limit of 40 was set for all Stableford Qualifying Rounds.

> *September 1997:* The Committee agreed to finance the Coach for the Ladies' Outing, the Past Captain's Dinner, and any balance [shortfall] for the Lady Captain's Day's Entertainment.

In the Autumn Outing to Holywell, OG, our regular coach driver, presented the O G Evans Autumn Outing Shield for the Ladies. This was well received and is as treasured almost as much as some of our majors!

> *November 1997:* Senior Ladies over 65 or those with disabilities be allowed to play 10 holes comps only. Members to state at the beginning of the golfing year to which category they belonged.

MRS R INGMAN
1998

Ganwyd a magwyd Rhiannon yn Chwilog. Cwblhaodd ei chwrs nyrsio SRN yn Ysbyty'r Royal Infirmary, Lerpwl, ac mae'n dal i weithio yn y byd meddygol yn Ysbyty Bryn Beryl.

Cychwynnodd gyrfa golff Rhiannon yng Nghlwb Pwllheli gyda graddnod o 36. Yn dilyn Aelodaeth am gyfnod byr yn Abersoch, ymunodd â Nefyn yn 1983 pan briododd â Neville.*

Ei graddnod isaf oedd 13. Enillodd Gwpan Cefnamwlch yn 1991 ac 1997, Pencampwriaeth y Clwb yn 1997 a 2003 a Dysgl Rhosyn Dr Griffiths yn 1998 pan oedd yn Gapten y Merched. Mae Rhiannon wedi gwasanaethu ar Bwyllgor y Merched am dros ddeng mlynedd a bu'n Ysgrifennydd y Graddnodau am dair blynedd. Tra roedd hi yn y swydd yma yn 2005 gwahoddwyd hi a Carys Wyn Jones, Ysgrifennydd Adran y Merched, i'r Is-Bwyllgor Gemau a

THE LADY CAPTAINS - CAPTEINIAID Y MERCHED

Graddnod y Clwb. Dyma'r tro cyntaf i'r Merched gael eu gwahodd i'r Is-Bwyllgor yma.

Ar ddiwedd 1997 fe'i hetholwyd yn Gapten Adran y Merched, gan wasanaethu am 18 mis am fod Cyfarfod Cyffredinol y Merched wedi'i symud o fis Tachwedd i'r Pasg. Gwasanaethodd am flwyddyn yn y cyfnod yma gyda'i gŵr, Neville, yr ail ŵr a gwraig yn hanes y Clwb i wasanaethu fel Capteiniaid yr un pryd. Yn 2005 apwyntiwyd Rhiannon ar Bwyllgor Gwaith y Clwb am gyfnod o dair blynedd.

Yn ystod ei Chapteiniaeth, perswadiodd Rhiannon Bwyllgor y Merched i enwebu Tim i chwarae ym Mhencampwriaeth Timau Cymru am y tro cyntaf erioed yn Wrecsam yn 1998. Ers hynny, mae'r Merched wedi chwarae yn y Gystadleuaeth yma bron bob blwyddyn, gan chwarae yn y Gogledd a'r De bob yn ail. Bydd Clwb Golff Nefyn yn cynnal y Bencampwriaeth yma yn 2008.

Cyflwynodd Rhiannon a Neville liain glas melfed ar gyfer y Bwrdd Gwobrwyo, gyda brêd aur a logo'r Clwb arno, yn ystod eu Blwyddyn fel Capteiniaid. Defnyddiwyd y lliain hwn i holl Gyfarfodydd Gwobrwyo'r Clwb nes y prynwyd lliain newydd ar gyfer y Canmlwyddiant.

Born and bred in Chwilog, Rhiannon qualified as an SRN at the Royal Infirmary, Liverpool. She returned to her home area and became a nurse at Bryn Beryl Hospital where she still works as a Staff Nurse.

Initially, Rhiannon was a Member of Pwllheli Golf Club with a handicap of 36*. Following a short period as a Member of Abersoch Golf Club, she joined Nefyn in 1983 when she married Neville.

Her lowest handicap was 13. Rhiannon won the Cefnamwlch Cup in 1991 and 1997, the Club Championship in 1997 and 2003 and the Dr Griffiths' Rose Bowl in 1998. She has served on the Ladies' Committee for 10 years and was Handicap Secretary for 3 years. While she was Handicap Secretary, in 2005, T Gareth Gruffydd, Match and Handicap Chairman, invited her and Carys Wyn Jones, the Lady Secretary, to sit on the Match and Handicap Committee. This was the first time ladies had been invited to this Committee and proved to be wholly beneficial to both the Men's and Ladies' Sections.

Rhiannon was elected Lady Captain at the end of 1997 and served for 18 months until Easter 1999 when the Ladies' AGM moved yet again to Easter to be in line with the Club's AGM. As a consequence, Rhiannon served a full year with Neville, who came in to office as Captain in 1998. They are the second husband and wife in the Club's History to hold office concurrently. In 2005, Rhiannon was elected on to the Executive Committee of the Club for a three year period.

During her Captaincy, Rhiannon persuaded the Ladies' Committee to enter the Welsh Team Championship at Wrexham in 1998. The Ladies have entered this Competition regularly ever since, venues alternating between North and South Wales. Nefyn Golf Club is due to host this prestigious event in June 2008.

Rhiannon and Neville, as Captains, presented the Club with the blue velvet Presentation Table Cloth, complete with gold braid and Club Logo during their year of Office. This cloth continued to be used for all Club Presentations until the Centenary Year when the new Logo necessitated buying another one.

MRS S FITZPATRICK
1999

Stella hailed from Liverpool. After four years in the army, she went to work for the Ministry of Food. She met Henry Fitzpatrick, an electrical engineer, in Liverpool and they married in 1947. Shortly after their marriage, they moved to Jones' Terrace, in Morfa Nefyn.

Stella and Henry raised three children. Kenneth is currently a Maritime Officer for Gwynedd, with responsibility for Barmouth, Aberdyfi & Towyn, Porthmadog and Pwllheli. David is an Ambulance Technician and Suzanne and her husband own 'Llŷn Furnishers' in Pwllheli. Stella has seven grandchildren and two great-grandchildren.

Stella joined the Golf Club as a full Member for 10/6d in February 1952 and she and Henry supported all social occasions – Stella having an uncanny gift for winning at the raffle draws!

Due to family commitments, she did not play golf until the very late 70s. She maintains she soon improved, and began to enter competitions – even occasionally winning!

It was a great honour for Stella to be asked to be Lady Captain. She thoroughly enjoyed her year and especially her Lady Captain's Day in the July when she welcomed her family and friends. Other occasions she recalls that were special were the two Ladies' Outings arranged by Dorothy Humpherson and the presentation she made of nearly £3000 to her chosen charity, the Physiotherapy Department at Pwllheli.

During her Captaincy, the Lady Captain's Chair was donated by the Captain, Mr S B Murray; four new Ladies' Honours Boards were put up; team sweaters were bought for any Ladies' Team representing the Club and Friday Mixed Foursomes were played regularly and proved to be very popular. Fiona Vaughan Thomas captained the successful Welsh Girls' Team, bringing acclaim to Nefyn Golf Club and it was decided a coloured photo of her as the Captain of The Welsh Girls' Team with the Team be framed and put up in Ladies' Lounge. The Executive Committee agreed the Ladies' Captains' photos should be mounted and displayed the same as those of the Club Captains.

Stella is still very active and, as she has done over the years, she still does her best to support the Club. In spite of failing eyesight, she produces mince pies at Christmas, cakes for the coffee mornings and regularly supports all social occasions. Stella had worked in the kitchen at the Linksway with Peter and Pauline Lane for 27 years and this obviously accounts for her culinary skills. When asked how she still managed to produce such delights, she said cooking was second nature to her and she could cook with her eyes closed if necessary!

The sun sets on the 20th Century

THE NEW MILLENNIUM 2000 - 2007

MRS D BARTON
2000

Dorothy started playing golf at the age of eight at Fairfield Golf Club in Lancashire where her parents were Members. Her father was a very good golfer, playing off a handicap of 1 and her mother played off 16. With such a low handicap, it was not surprising that her father spent a great deal of time on the golf course.

Her parents spent many happy holidays in the Nefyn area and thoroughly enjoyed playing their golf at the Club. They stayed at the Nanhoron Arms Hotel, Nefyn, the Cecil Court in Morfa Nefyn and the Woodlands Hall Hotel in Edern.

After leaving Fairfield High School, Dorothy worked in the District Bank. She married at 21 and after her daughters were born, golf took second place. In 1961, she won the Captain's Prize at Fairfield Golf Club having won a play off against her mother! Winning the Captain's Prize at Nefyn in 2006 was both a privilege and a pleasant surprise. It brought back memories of 1961!

An overwhelmed Dorothy accepts the Ladies' Captains' Prize from Megan Roberts in September 2006.

Dorothy and her husband, Fred, moved permanently to Wales in 1991 when they both joined Nefyn Golf Club. Since then, Dorothy has been on the Ladies' Committee for several years and served as Lady Treasurer for four years.

Dorothy was greatly honoured to be elected Lady Captain for the Millennium and her whole Captaincy Year is something she will never forget. In that year, the Executive agreed to waive the green fees for the Charity Mixed Open Foursomes in August, providing all profits went to the named charity; the new Ashworth Trophy, which was the Summer Mixed Knockout competition continued, and the Men's Handicap Committee announced that when gents and ladies played in the same competition, the ladies would receive courtesy shots to take into account the difference in SSS.

Friends dine with the Lady Captain, Dorothy Barton (rear Right) and her husband, Fred (rear centre) at the Millennium Ball, held in August. The Marquee was positioned in front of the Clubhouse with a covered access across the present patio.

MRS Å RICHARDSON
2001

Åse was born in Stavanger, Norway, and moved to England after marrying John Richardson, who was the local Professional in her home town. They have two children, Ian and Ellen, and five grandchildren.

Åse's first link with Nefyn was through the family's friendship with Lt Col Robin Parry and his family. The Richardsons first visited Nefyn in 1962 and then joined the Club in 1972 when they bought the cottage at which they now reside on Lôn Uchaf, Morfa Nefyn.

Åse works as Office Manager in Porthmadog Golf Club and has been there for 10 years. Before she and John came to live in Nefyn in 1986, they were licensees working for Greenall Whitley.

Åse started playing golf in Norway in the early 1960s. Her lowest handicap was 13 and she has won many prizes over the years. She won the Dorothy Wood Memorial Trophy in 1983 and the Cefnamwlch Cup three times, 1987, 1990 and 1995. In her year as Captain, Åse was selected to represent the Club in the Welsh Team Championship in Pennard. At Nefyn Golf Club, she served on several committees and has also been the Club's County representative.

Lady Captain Åse Richardson, immediate Left, leads the fun at the evening meal after the Teams' efforts at the Welsh Team Championship in Pennard, S Wales in 2001.

On Åse's Captain's Day, the weather was horrendous. Many Members recall trying to play against the extreme North West gales. So strong was the wind that some Members' shots were ending up behind them having been caught by the wind! Marian Grace, for one, could not get past the second marker post on the 1st fairway and the Competition had to be abandoned. It was rescheduled for the August Meeting and thankfully the weather was kinder! This was the first time the Lady Captain's Day was held in the Summer Meeting. In our Centenary Year, Fiona Vaughan Thomas also chose to have her Ladies' Captain's Day in the Summer Meeting and it was held on the first Wednesday of the fortnight.

In November 2001, a special meeting was held between the Officials of the Executive and Officials of the Ladies' Committee. Largely as a result of this meeting, the précised Minutes of Executive meetings were to appear on the Main Club Notice Board and the seed was firmly sown to abandon the 'Men's' Bar!

The Victorious NWLCSA 'A' Shield Team
Having been newly promoted from Division 2 at the beginning of the Season, the A Team then went on to win the 1st Division in 2001.

Front Row: Left to Right: Janet Brown, Lady Captain Åse Richardson, Rhiannon Ingman **Back Row:** Elsie Hughes, Janet Ellwood, Sylvia Dennett and Suzanne Hemphill.

MRS D LL OWEN
2002

Ganwyd Dilys yn Llangwnadl yn 1936 a bu hi'n byw yno nes mynd i'r Coleg ym Mangor yn 1954. Cafodd ei haddysg gynnar yn ysgol y pentref ac yna ymlaen i Ysgol Uwchradd Botwnnog.

Bu Dilys yn dilyn cwrs dwy flynedd yng Ngholeg y Santes Fair, Bangor cyn derbyn ei swydd gyntaf fel athrawes yn Lerpwl. Dychwelodd i Ben Llŷn yn 1959 i ddysgu yn Nefyn. Priododd â Gwilym Owen yn 1960 a symud yn ôl i Lerpwl i Gwilym gael dilyn ei yrfa forwrol a hithau i ddysgu yn Ysgol Springwood yn Allerton.

Ar ôl saith mlynedd, diflasodd ar fywyd dinas a symudodd y teulu yn ôl i'w chynefin hi yn Llŷn lle ganwyd eu mab, William, yn 1969. Cafodd Dilys swydd yn Ysgol Llidiardau, Rhoshirwaun, ac yno y bu hi'n dysgu nes ei hymddeoliad fel Prifathrawes yn 1992.

Mae Dilys wedi bod yn Aelod o Glwb Golff Nefyn ers dros ddeng mlynedd ar hugain ac wedi ennill amryw o gystadleuthau, gan gynnwys Cwpan y Canmlwyddiant (Adran y Merched). Cafodd y fraint o fod yn Gapten Adran y Merched yn 2002 pryd y cafodd flwyddyn hapus iawn. Bu'n Aelod o'r Pwyllgor Gwaith am dair blynedd ac ar hyn o bryd mae Dilys yn un o Ymddiriedolwyr y Clwb.

Erbyn hyn, mae Dilys yn mwynhau hamddena, crwydro, chwarae golff a threulio amser yng nghwmni ei dwy wyres, Alaw a Lea. Mae'n dymuno pob llwyddiant i'r Clwb a'r Aelodau yn y dyfodol.

Dilys was born in Llangwnadl in 1936 and she lived there until 1954 when she went to college in Bangor. Her early education was in the village school and later at Ysgol Botwnnog.

Dilys followed a two year teacher training course at St. Mary's College, Bangor before being appointed to her first teaching position in Liverpool. She returned to Llŷn in 1959, to a teaching position at Nefyn. She married Gwilym Owen in 1960 and moved back to Liverpool so that Gwilym could follow his nautical career and she taught at Springwood School, Allerton.

After seven years, she had experienced enough of city life and she and Gwilym moved back to Llŷn, where their son, William, was born in 1969. Dilys was appointed to Ysgol Llidiardau, Rhoshirwaun where she taught until her retirement as Headmistress in 1992.

Dilys Llewelyn Owen receiving the Centenary Cup, 5th, May 2007

The Ladies' Past Captains' Dinner at the Golf Club in 2002.
Front Row: Left to Right: *Pauline Lane, Helen Griffith, Stella Fitzpatrick, Marian Grace, Dorothy Roberts, Carys Wyn Jones, Lady Captain Dilys Ll Owen, Åse Richardson, Gladys Roberts, Nellie Trenholme, Annette Jones and Anne Thomas.*
Back Row: Left to Right: *Elsie Hughes, Medi Bezemer, Shirley Ives, Jacqui Gill, Rhiannon Ingman, Laura Wyn Roberts and Leah Fray.*

MRS M J WILLIAMS
2003

Dilys has been a Member of Nefyn Golf Club for over thirty years and has won several prizes. She won the Dr Griffiths' Rose Bowl in 1996, the A D Grace Trophy in 1997 and has been extremely successful in the Mixed Competitions with her partner, H M Williams. The highlight of all her successes came in the Centenary Year when she won the Centenary Cup, presented by the Ladies' Captain with a score of 102-28-74.

Dilys was elected Lady Captain in 2002 and she enjoyed a very happy year. She was a Member of the Executive Committee for three years and is currently one of the Club's Trustees.

Dilys enjoys relaxing, walking, playing golf and spending time with her two granddaughters, Alaw and Lea. She wishes the Club and all its Members the very best of success in the future.

Mary was born and bred in Malta. She met Edric when she was teaching there and he was on National Service with the RAF. They were married in Wales and settled in Tudweiliog in 1973. Having always been interested in cookery, Mary took over the 'Dive Inn' which she then ran for 20 years. They have 3 children and 9 grandchildren. Son Stephen and daughter Marisa trained at Catering College. Stephen now runs his own fish shop in Pwllheli and Marisa runs the 'Twnti Seafood Restaurant' at Rhydyclafdy. Second daughter, Mandy, follows in her father's footsteps and is a chartered accountant.

Apart from golf, Mary enjoys swimming, reading and travelling. She frequently returns to Malta as many of her immediate family still live there.

Mary joined the Golf Club in the late 80s. Before then, she justly maintains she had no time for golf with running a business and raising a family. Her lowest handicap was 28 and she has won various prizes over the years. Among her successes she lists winning the AD Grace Trophy twice, the Seniors' Silver Salver and an Outing Shield at Porthmadog. She and Edric have won the Charity Mixed Foursomes and in this, our Centenary Year, Mary together with Gwyneth Smith, won the Ladies' Centenary Open 4BBB Stableford with a score of 43 points.

Mary J Williams (Right) with partner, Gwyneth Smith, receiving the Winners' Prize with 43 points in the first ever Ladies' 4BBB Open in July 2007

Mary is also a Member at Abersoch Golf Club and plays in both Clubs on a regular basis. At Abersoch, she has won the President's Cup and the Betty Clarke Trophy.

In November 2003, the new CONGU handicapping system was explained to the Ladies. A new computer terminal was to be set up in the Lounge and the PSI system was to become operational. The very thought of this Player Score Input (PSI) filled some of the Ladies with trepidation but training was promised. By the following AGM, 2004, through no fault of the Club, the system was still not up and running and neither had there been any training as promised from Club System 2000, who were responsible for the programme.

In March 2004, it was finally agreed that the Ladies' Captains' Photos were to be hung in the main lounge or foyer. Also, initial discussions began with regard to enlarging the Locker Room by incorporating the Visitors' Locker Room, as the latter was so rarely used.

MRS J ELLWOOD 2004

Janet was born in Brooklands, Cheshire. The family moved to Bramhall when she was ten years of age and Janet went to boarding school at the Calder Girls' School, in Seascale, Cumberland. She went to Secretarial College and was appointed a school secretary at Manchester Grammar School. She later became the Chairman of Governors at Beech Hall School in Macclesfield.

Janet married Roger, a low handicapped golfer and they lived in Bramhall before settling in Prestbury. Janet became Company Director of the family business, Ellwood's Fabrics Ltd. Following Roger's retirement in 1995, they moved to live permanently in Morfa Nefyn.

Janet's first memory of Nefyn Golf Club was sitting outside the Clubhouse on the veranda in 1949, having a drink of lemonade after her parents had played golf. Since the war years, she had regularly visited Morfa Nefyn for annual family holidays. It was in the Riding School in Morfa Nefyn, opposite the back of Pritchard's garage, where Janet learned to ride and then continued to do so at home, eventually owning her own horse.

Janet recalls receiving a lovely set of golf clubs for her 21st birthday and it was from then on that she really began to play more frequently and tried to reduce her handicap. Her lowest ever handicap was 13. She joined Nefyn Golf Club in the mid 70s having been a Member of Bramhall, Cavendish and Prestbury Golf Clubs and she has represented all four Clubs in team events. In Nefyn, Janet has regularly been a Member of the team competing in the Welsh Team Championship.

Janet has won several prizes and trophies. She won the A D Grace Trophy three times, the Dorothy Wood Memorial Cup three times, and in 2003 won both the Cefnamwlch Cup and the Dr Griffiths' Rose Bowl. Janet has been Match Secretary and worked alongside John Froom in the Pro's shop for three years.

Janet Ellwood, Lady Captain 2004, presents a cheque of £5002 from her Charity Collection to a representative of Air Ambulance Wales.

She was very proud and delighted to be invited to be Lady Captain. During her Captaincy it was decided all Summer Meeting Competitions and the Texas Scramble should be played off 30 handicap. The Executive decided that The Cynfelin Jones Cup Competition was to be played 'by adult Members of the Club and Special Category Juniors', thus allowing Ladies to play for the very first time in what had always been one of the Men's Major Cups. In 2004, three loops of 9 holes were tried but the experiment was unsuccessful. The Locker Room was re-designed and social events became popular in the Club, with bridge meetings, quizzes and many 10 hole friendly competitions.

Janet and Roger have been married for 45 years and Roger has greatly helped and supported Janet's golf. They have two sons, Patrick and Rupert, both keen golfers and past Members of Nefyn, and two grandchildren.

MRS D HUMPHERSON 2005

Dorothy and her husband, Dennis, first visited the area in the late fifties. Dorothy played with their children on the beach while Dennis played golf! Over the years this appears to have been a regular pattern for many 'golf widows' with young children!

Dorothy was an SRN Registered Health Visitor Tutor in the Midlands. In 1987, she retired and moved to Nefyn to live. Between 1990 and 1996, she came out of retirement and worked part-time as a Health Visitor in Llŷn.

Dorothy joined the Golf Club in 1987 and was elected Lady Captain in 2005. She acknowledges her successes at golf have been a little limited. However she is very competitive and claims she occasionally sinks a long putt! She does have extenuating circumstances because she started playing golf late in life and has undergone three major joint replacements recently!

Dorothy Humpherson presents the Woodlands Cup to John Thomas and his mother-in-law Jean Cooper at the Charity Mixed Foursomes Presentation, August 2005. John and Jean went on to win the Cup again in 2007.

Dorothy is very interested in junior golf and would like to contribute more to promote Junior Golf at Nefyn. She assists in the Junior Coaching Sessions on a Saturday morning and has been part of the Tri-Golf Scheme visiting the local schools and coaching Junior Children.

In 2007, The Bannau Trophy was presented for the first time by Dorothy and her husband, Dennis, for the most improved Junior Golfer who has yet to be awarded a CONGU handicap. The winner was John Westley.

MRS M ROBERTS 2006

Ganwyd Megan yn Fron Olau, Mynydd Nefyn yn un o dri o blant. Symudodd y teulu i lawr i Glandŵr, Nefyn, pan oedd hi'n dair oed. Mynychodd Ysgol Gynradd Nefyn ac Ysgol Frondeg, Pwllheli. Yn bymtheng mlwydd oed, gadawodd yr ysgol ac aeth i weithio i Siop Glynllifon (lle mae Siop Spar heddiw) gan symud i siop lysiau ei mam yn Nefyn yn ddiweddarach.

Cafodd Megan bleser mawr o chwarae rownderi a chynrychiolodd y tîm yn y ddwy ysgol. Yn ferch ifanc, byddai'n mwynhau'r sîn gymdeithasol a dyma sut y dechreuodd ei hoffter o ddawnsio. Cofia, pan oedd yn ei harddegau, fynychu'r 'Hop Swllt' a drefnid gan y Ficer ac yna mynd i'r gwersi dawnsio 'ballroom' yn Neuadd yr Eglwys. Gall unrhyw un sydd wedi mynychu noson gymdeithasol yn y Clwb Golff weld nad yw Megan wedi colli dim ar ei sgiliau dawnsio neilltuol. Etholwyd hi yn Frenhines y Carnifal pan oedd yn 13 oed, anrhydedd fawr yn y dyddiau hynny.

Cyfarfu Megan â'i darpar ŵr, Twm, yng Nghapel Isaf Nefyn. Roedd Twm yn gofalu am faes carafanau Y Ddolwen, ar ei fferm, Y Wern. Priodwyd Megan a Twm yn 1970 a ganwyd dau blentyn iddynt, Ian a Nia. Mae Ian yn olffiwr da a bu'n Gapten Adran Iau y Clwb yn 1986. Bu bron iddo a throi yn olffiwr proffesiynol wrth ddilyn gyrfa fel 'Assistant Pro' yng Nghlwb Hawkestone Park, Swydd Amwythig. Bu hefyd yn 'Assistant' ym Mhorthmadog a Chlwb yn Llundain cyn dychwelyd i Ben Llŷn. Bu Nia, ei chwaer, yn gweithio y tu ôl i'r bar yn y Golff am gyfnod.

Dechreuodd Megan gymryd diddordeb yng Nghlwb Golff Nefyn trwy gysylltiad Ian â'r

Clwb. Ymunodd yn 1994 ac yn fuan iawn cafodd wahoddiad gan Anne Thomas i gyfarfod â'r Merched ar brynhawn Mercher. Yn dilyn hyn, ni fedrai Megan gadw draw. Roedd hi wedi gwirioni efo'r gêm o'r cychwyn, er iddi gael cyfnodau anodd fel pawb arall. Cofia chwarae fel partneres i'r Ficer Eirwyn Thomas un tro mewn cystadleuaeth gymysg dros ddeg twll yn fuan ar ôl iddi gychwyn chwarae. Cawsant sgôr ddifrifol o wael ac roedd y Ficer wedi rhoi Megan mewn sawl byncr! Pan ddaethant i'r nawfed twll a Megan mewn byncr unwaith eto, roedd hi'n benderfynol o ddod allan y tro yma. Trawodd gyda'i holl nerth a sglefriodd y bêl ar draws y lawnt ac i'r cwt sinc ar waelod Lôn Penrhyn Bach gyda chlonc atseiniol!

Pan wahoddwyd Megan i fod yn Gapten Adran y Merched, teimlai fod hynny'n anrhydedd fawr ond bu'n petruso'n hir cyn derbyn. Rhoddwyd perswâd arni gan ei ffrindiau a Twm, a chafodd flwyddyn fythgofiadwy. Fodd bynnag, ychydig cyn ei hetholiad i'r swydd, bu rhaid iddi gael llawdriniaeth am gancr. Daeth allan o'r ysbyty ddiwrnod cyn y Cyfarfod Cyffredinol Blynyddol, mynychodd y Cyfarfod a'r diwrnod canlynol cymrodd ran yn ei seremoni Dreifio'i Fewn fel Capten y Merched gyda Chapten y Dynion, Ian Cooper. Roedd hyn yn gyflawniad rhyfeddol gan Megan, sy'n dangos ei phenderfyniad a'i chymeriad. Ei hunig siomiant oedd methu chwarae'r rownd gyfan ar y diwrnod ac roedd yn ddiolchgar i Laura Wyn Roberts am chwarae yn ei lle.

Roedd ei Diwrnod Capten yn un fydd yn aros yn ei chof am byth a hi oedd y Capten cyntaf i gael Noswaith Ffarwelio. Cynhaliwyd sesiwn Dawnsio Gwerin llwyddiannus ar y noswaith yma.

Uchafbwynt arall ei blwyddyn fel Capten oedd Cystadleuaeth Cylchdaith Her Ewrop a chwaraewyd yn Nefyn ar ddiwedd Gorffennaf 2006, cystadleuaeth a fwynhaodd yn fawr. Ar ddiwrnod olaf y Gystadleuaeth yma cynhaliwyd cyfarfod gwobrwyo'r cystadleuwyr ynghyd â Chyflwyniad i Glwb i Barry Owens oedd yn ymddeol ar ôl un mlynedd ar ddeg fel Ysgrifennydd Rheolwr y Clwb. Roedd Megan yn hapus iawn o gael cynrychioli'r Merched fel eu Capten yn yr achlysur yma.

Roedd hi yn ddiolchgar iawn i Ian Cooper am ei gefnogaeth ddi-feth trwy gydol ei Chapteiniaeth. Yn ogystal, gwerthfawrogai gefnogaeth ei theulu a'i ffrindiau agos a'r holl gymorth a dderbyniodd gan y Swyddogion, y Pwyllgor ac Aelodau o Adran y Merched.

Ladies' Captain Megan Roberts, presents the Best Gross Prize at her Ladies' Captains' Day, September 2006, to Sylvia Dennett.

Megan was born in Fron Olau, Mynydd Nefyn, one of three children and the family moved down to Glandŵr, Nefyn when she was three years old. She went to Ysgol Nefyn and then Ysgol Frondeg in Pwllheli. At fifteen, she left school and went to work in a Grocer's Shop, Glynllifon, [where the Spar is today], and later worked for her mother's newly opened Greengrocers' shop, also in Nefyn.

Megan enjoyed rounders and played for the team in both schools. As a teenager, she enjoyed the social scene and there began her fondness of dancing. She recalls frequenting the 'Shilling Hop' arranged by the local Vicar in her early teens, and then going to the ballroom dancing sessions held in the Church Hall. As anyone who has attended social occasions in the Golf Club can testify, Megan is still quite a dancer! She was elected Carnival Queen in Nefyn when she was 13 years old, an enormous honour in those days.

Megan met husband Twm through Capel Isaf in Nefyn where they both still attend regularly. Twm ran the Caravan Site at Y Wern, then called Y Ddolwen. They married in 1970 and had two children, Ian and Nia. Ian was Junior Captain at the Club in 1986 and was a very good golfer. He very nearly turned Professional and in fact did begin a career as Assistant Pro at Hawkstone Park, at Porthmadog and at a municipal course in London before he was drawn back to Llŷn.

It was through Ian that Megan first visited the Club and became interested in golf. Megan joined the Club in 1994 and recalls being invited by Anne Thomas to meet the Ladies on a Wednesday early in the season. 'That was it,' she says, 'from then on there was no keeping me away from the Golf!' Megan loved the game from the start although she has many embarrassing stories of when she struggled with her game. She recalls once partnering the Rev Eirwyn Thomas, in a 10 hole mixed friendly, when she had just started playing. Their score was horrendous and he had put her in several bunkers! When they got to the 9th and she was in yet another bunker, and this time determined to get out first time, she hammered the ball – straight out across the green and into the zinc shed on the pathway behind with an enormous clunk!

When Megan was invited to be Captain, she was highly honoured but, with little real confidence in herself, she was also absolutely terrified. Twm and her friends persuaded her to accept the invitation and she had a wonderful year. A few weeks before her election to office at the Club's AGM, Megan was diagnosed with cancer and underwent major surgery. She came out of hospital the day before the AGM, attended the Meeting and the next day took her 'Drive-in' with Ian Cooper, her Captain for the year. It was an amazing feat and showed Megan's determination and character. Her biggest disappointment was that she could not physically play the full round on that Easter Sunday. She nevertheless was grateful to Laura Wyn Roberts for playing on her behalf.

Captains' Drive-In Easter Sunday 2006.
Pictured centre are the Captain, Ian Cooper and the Ladies' Captain, Megan Roberts together with the Vice-Captains, Fiona Vaughan Thomas and Emyr L Evans.

Her Ladies' Captain's Day is one she will remember for ever and she was the first to have a Ladies' Captain's Evening Farewell Function. This was in the form of a barn-dance and a wonderful evening was had by all.

Another highlight of her year was the European Challenge Tour which came to Nefyn at the end of July 2006 and Megan thoroughly enjoyed that event. On the same afternoon as the Challenge Tour Presentation, there was a Club Retirement Presentation to Barry Owens, who was retiring after 11 years as the Club's Secretary/Manager. Megan was delighted she was able to represent the Ladies as their Ladies' Captain on that memorable occasion.

Megan said she was very indebted to Ian Cooper for his unfailing support throughout her year. She was also extremely grateful for the support of her family and close friends and all the help she had received from the Officials, the Committee and Members of the Ladies' Section.

Ladies' AGM 2007: All reference to Lady Captain, Lady Vice-Captain, Lady President etc. will hereinafter be changed to Ladies' Captain, Ladies' Vice-Captain and Ladies' President etc. in accordance with the 2006 Club's AGM.

THE CENTENARY LADIES' CAPTAIN 2007 - 2008

MISS F VAUGHAN THOMAS 2007

Ganwyd Fiona Vaughan Thomas yn Llanddeusant yn 1971 a symudodd i'r Rheithordy ym Morfa Nefyn pan oedd hi'n ddwy a hanner. Yn yr ysgol, chwaraeai hoci a rownderi. Byddai'n canu yng Nghôr yr Ysgol a dysgodd chwarae'r clarinét a'r piano. Ymunodd â'r 'Brownies' am gyfnod ond dechreuodd chwarae golff cyn trosglwyddo i'r 'Guides'. Graddiodd gyda BAdd mewn Dyniaethau yng Ngholeg St Paul's a St Mary's, Cheltenham ac ym mis Medi 1994 apwyntiwyd hi ar staff Ysgol Uwchradd Sale yn Sir Caer. Mae Fiona yn dal yn yr un ysgol heddiw lle mae'n dysgu Addysg Gorfforol a Hanes ynghyd â bod yn Gydgysylltydd Chwaraeon Ysgolion Cynradd y dalgylch a Chydgysylltydd Cam Allweddol 3.

Mae llwyddiannau golffio Fiona yn nodedig ac mae'n bleser cael eu rhestru yma achos, heb unrhyw amheuaeth, Fiona a roes Adran y Merched ac, yn wir, Clwb Golff Nefyn ar y map ym myd golff amatur merched Cymru. Yn ei blwyddyn olaf yn yr Adran Iau, enillodd Bencampwriaethau Genethod Siroedd Gogleddol Cymru (SGC) a Gwynedd, Tlws y Llywydd ym Mhencampwriaeth Genethod Cymru, etholwyd hi'n Gapten Tîm Genethod SGC, bu'n cymryd rhan ym Mhencampwriaeth Genethod Prydain yn Carlisle a bu'n chwarae dros y Sir, Gogledd Cymru ac mewn Gemau Rhyngwladol.

Parhaodd ei llwyddiant tu hwnt i'w chyfnod yn yr Adran Iau. Bu'n chwarae i'r Sir, enillodd Bencampwriaeth Genethod Sir Gaernarfon a Môn a derbyniodd Liwiau'r Sir. Dewiswyd hi i chwarae i Dîm Merched Dan 21 Cymru, enillodd Dlws Lambert yn Formby a daeth yn ail yng Nghystadleuaeth Pencampwr y Pencampwyr yng Nghlwb De Morgannwg.

Graddnod cyntaf Fiona oedd 32 pan oedd hi'n 11 oed ac erbyn ei bod yn 17 oed, roedd yn chwarae oddi ar 4. Erbyn hyn, mae'n chwarae oddi ar raddnod o 1 a hi sy'n dal Record y Merched ar

Gwrs Newydd Nefyn (Haf 2007). Ym mlwyddyn ein Canmlwyddiant, daeth ei thalent i'r wyneb. Yn ychwanegol i dorri record y cwrs, enillodd Fiona 8 o gystadleuthau gan gynnwys Pencampwriaeth y Clwb a 5 Prif Gystadleuaeth.

Crynhoir y gweddill o'i llwyddiannau eraill yng Nghlwb Nefyn a thu hwnt yn yr adroddiad Saesneg isod.

Yn rhinwedd ei swydd fel Capten y Merched, ac yn enwedig fel Capten y Merched am flwyddyn y Canmlwyddiant, mae Fiona wedi gorfod ymgymryd â theithiau hir i fynychu cyfarfodydd, nosweithiau cymdeithasol, cystadleuthau golff a chyflwyniadau. Mae hi wedi cyflawni ei rôl yn hollol gydwybodol a chyda llwyr ymroddiad.

Fiona Vaughan Thomas was born in Llanddeusant, Anglesey, in 1971 and moved to the Rectory in Morfa Nefyn when she was about two and a half years of age. At school, she played hockey and rounders. She sang in the choir and learned to play the clarinet and piano. She was in the Brownies for a while although golf took over before she progressed into the Guides! She qualified with a BEd Degree in Humanities at St Paul's and St Mary's College, Cheltenham and in September 1994 she began teaching in Sale High School, Cheshire where she still teaches today. In addition to teaching PE and History, Fiona is currently the School's Sports Co-ordinator with Primary Schools. She is also the Key Stage 3 Co-ordinator.

Fiona's golfing successes are quite remarkable and we make no apology for listing them here for she undoubtedly put Nefyn Ladies' Section and indeed, Nefyn Golf Club, firmly on the Welsh amateur map. In her last year as a Junior she won both the WNC Girls' and Gwynedd Championships, won the President's Trophy in the Welsh Girls' Championship, was selected Captain of the WNC Girls' Team, qualified for the British Girls' Championship at Carlisle and played for County, North Wales and International Matches.

In her first year out of the Junior Section, the successes continued. She played for the County, won the C and A Girls' Championship and was awarded County Colours. She was selected to play for the Welsh Ladies Under 21 Team, won the Lambert Trophy at Formby and was Runner-up in the Champion of Champions at South Glamorgan.

Fiona's first handicap was 32 when she was 11 years old and by 17 she was playing off 4. She now plays off 1 and holds the New Course Record here at Nefyn (Summer 2007). In our Centenary Year, her golfing talent showed no limits. In addition to breaking the Course Record, she won no fewer than 8 trophies, including the Club Championship and 5 Majors.

At Nefyn, Fiona was Junior Captain in 1987 and won the Lane Trophy in the same year. She was Club Champion 1987 and 1988, won the Cefnamwlch Cup 1988 & 1989 and the Dr Griffiths' Rose Bowl in 1990.

At County Level, Fiona played for the Girls' Team for 5 years (1985-1990). She won the Gwyneth Rowlands Cup at the C & A Girls' Championship in 1986 and was C & A County Girls' Captain from 1987 to 1989. She played for the WNC (Welsh Northern Counties) Girls' Team from 1985 to 1990 and Captained the Team from 1988 to 1990.

Fiona has played for the C & A Ladies' County Golf Team from 1988 to the present day. She has been C and A County Champion on four occasions (1997-98 and 2003-04) and was honoured by being elected Ladies' County Captain for 2003 & 2004. She has played regularly for the WNC Senior Team since 1990.

Fiona Vaughan Thomas wins the County Championship as a Junior at Porthmadog in 1998.

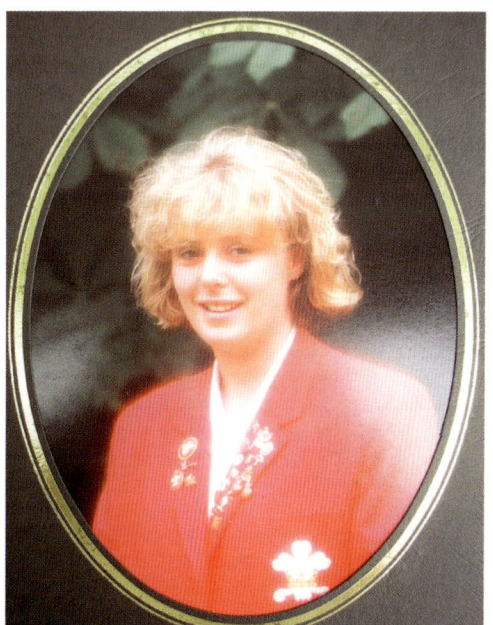

The photo displayed in the Club's Lounge in 1991 of Fiona, 'Welsh School's Internationalist 1987-1989 and Welsh Under 21 Internationalist'.

Fiona, non-playing Captain, with the victorious Welsh U18 Team at the Home International Championship, 1999. Pictured two away to Fiona's Right is Becky Brewerton of Abergele.

Fiona proudly displays the Stroyan Cup back at Nefyn.

She entered her first Welsh Girls' Championship at Trearddur Bay in 1986 and was then selected for Welsh training at Royal Liverpool with John Haggarty (1986-88). Welsh Schools' International Honours followed (1987-1989) and Welsh European U21 International Honours in 1990.

In 1999 and 2000, Fiona was selected as non-playing Captain of the U18 Home International Team. In 1999, she Captained the Wales Under 18 to their first ever Home International win at High Post G C, winning the Stroyan Cup and the Triple Crown. This was a wonderful achievement and for Fiona, it was probably the pinnacle of an amazing golfing career to date.

As Ladies' Captain, Fiona coped with extensive travelling to attend meetings, social functions, golf competitions and presentations. She was undoubtedly the correct choice for the Captaincy in our Centenary Year, fulfilling her role with the utmost dedication and conscientiousness.

THE LADY CAPTAINS - CAPTEINIAID Y MERCHED

THE JUNIOR SECTION
YR ADRAN IAU

Golff yr Adran Iau yw enaid a ffynhonnell pob clwb golff ac nid yw Clwb Golff Nefyn a'r Cylch yn wahanol. Anogid golff yr Aelodau Iau o'r dyddiau cynnar, a thros ddegawdau'r ugeinfed ganrif a dechrau'r Mileniwm ymddangosodd nifer o sêr ifanc y Clwb ar lwyfannau sirol, cenedlaethol a rhyngwladol.

Newidiwyd Rheol 12 (oedran ymuno â'r Clwb) nifer o weithiau dros y blynyddoedd ac erbyn heddiw caiff plant wyth oed ymuno. Fodd bynnag, caiff plant iau na hyn gymryd rhan yn y sesiynau hyfforddi a gynhelir yn y Clwb. O'r tridegau hyd at y chwedegau, dim ond 10/6d fyddai tanysgrifiad i'r Adran Iau, a thros y degawdau dilynol cedwid y tâl yma mor isel â phosib er mwyn annog y boblogaeth ifanc i ymuno.

Cyn ac ar ôl yr Ail Ryfel Byd, o ganlyniad i nifer fawr o blant ennill arian trwy gadio yn y Clwb, daeth golff yn boblogaidd a chafwyd cystadleuaeth gref a brwdfrydig rhwng swm niferus o ieuenctid lleol a rhai ymwelwyr yn y pumdegau a'r chwedegau. Bu nifer o Aelodau Ifanc y Clwb yn llwyddiannus hefyd ym Mhencampwriaeth Sir Gaernarfon a gynhelid yn Nefyn yn flynyddol.

Yn y saithdegau cafwyd gwell cynrychiolaeth o enethod lleol i ymddiddori yn y gêm o ganlyniad i gefnogaeth Adran y Merched ac o'r wythdegau ymlaen edrychwyd ar ôl yr Adran Iau yn swyddogol gan Drefnydd. Erbyn heddiw mae sawl cynllun hyfforddi i hybu golff yr ifanc ac mae yn agos i gant ac ugain o Aelodau yn yr Adran Iau.

THE EARLIEST JUNIORS

Junior golf is the very life-blood of every golf club and Nefyn and District Golf Club is no exception. As early as 1914, the issue of Junior Membership had been discussed at Club Meetings and the Club had agreed that Juniors should be encouraged and competitions should be organised for them.

In the early years there were many references to Rule 12 [Membership] and various amendments were made at AGMs regarding Junior Membership.

> *August 22nd 1914 (AGM):*
> *Proposition passed: Members' children over 15 & under 18 years of age may become members of the Club on being duly elected, & shall pay half the annual subscription. They shall not be qualified to play in competitions or to vote... It was further agreed that they could play in the Open competitions in the summer months(sic)*

Very few Juniors are mentioned as having joined the Club in the early years. This may be because the Minutes failed to report new Members accurately, e.g. a Miss could be a Junior or an unmarried Full Member. Occasionally, Juniors were referred to as 'juveniles'.

Some of the earliest Junior Members with the dates of their acceptance by the Club:

1911	Misses Mary and Marjorie Williams, Pwllparc, Edern. [Daughters of Captain Watkin Williams, Club Captain 1913]
1919	Miss N A Price and Miss M Price [Daughters of Capt W E Price (Twmpath) Club Captain 1937]

1926 Mr and Mrs C Buckley [C S Buckley, Club Captain 1936] + 2 Juveniles
1928 Miss C Walde – Juvenile Member
1932 Miss Nancy Williams, Hafod, Edern
1933 Miss Hettie W Jones, Angorfa, Edern
1935 Miss Helen (Nellie) Trenholme, Nefyn and Miss Mary Herbert Jones, [Hettie's sister, of Angorfa, Edern]

The last two named ladies, now in their 80s and 90s, still live in the area. Mrs Mary Herbert Rowlands still lives at Angorfa, Edern. Miss Nellie Trenholme, of Nefyn, is a Life Member of the Club and is still a very active and supportive Member.

> **August 1934 (AGM):** Amendment to Rule 12 ...'Agreed: On and from 16th August 1934, members children over 12 and under 18 may be elected as junior members of the Club and shall pay 10/6 per annum.* On attaining the age of 18 they shall cease to be [Junior] members of the Club but shall be eligible for election as ordinary members in the manner provided in Rule 8. They shall not be qualified to vote.' [*This fee was still applicable in 1958.]

There is no record of boys joining, although we asume that there must have been Junior Males.

THE POST WAR YEARS AND THE FIFTIES

Many Juniors took up golf in the post war years but in 1947, the Executive Committee decided that Junior Members were not allowed to play on the Course on Bank Holidays, in Major Competitions and on Saturdays in July and August.

As the numbers of Juniors increased however, so did the support and the encouragement from the Club. In February 1950, it was agreed 'that every Junior Member (local) be given 12 individual lessons with the Professional at 1/6 per person per lesson.' [This was to be at the Club's expense.]

Many successful Juniors emerged in the 50s. Among them were Brian Hefin and Adrian Williams, Ardwyn, Morfa Nefyn. Their father, Richard Glyn Williams, was very supportive of junior golf and both Brian and Adrian had a great deal of success in competitions, playing off low handicaps. It would appear that Juniors were still allowed to play in Open Competitions during the August Meeting for Brian Hefin was the runner-up in the Tweedale Challenge Cup, in 1954, when his father was Captain.

Brian Hefin Williams receives the Runners-up prize in the Tweedale Challenge Cup in 1954 from Mrs Dilys Parry, the Lady Captain, with his father, Club Captain R G Williams looking on. Partially hidden is Mrs E Seth and both Owen Roberts and Capt Hugh Roberts are seated, deep in conversationon, on the Captain's Left.

THE JUNIOR SECTION - YR ADRAN IAU

In 1955 however there was a decision to allow Juniors to play in all Club Competitions.

> **August 1955 (AGM):** Amendment to Rule 12 : Agreed that Members' children and children sponsored by Members may be elected from 10 years of age up to 18… Those with approved handicaps may enter Club Competitions.

Brian's brother, Adrian, won the Captain's Prize in 1956.

Adrian Williams receives the Captain's Prize in 1956. To Adrian's Right is another junior, David Parsonage and Duncan Seth (later Junior Captain) to his Left. Also in the picture (from Left to Right) are D A Williams, Owen Roberts, Dennis Grace and the Captain, Brig W H Wynne-Finch.

> **May 1958:** Resolved that Junior Members be NOT allowed to enter Senior Competitions. They may join in Monthly Spoon Competitions.

The 50s also saw the emergence of David Parsonage, one of Dennis Grace's many protégés. (His story is told in the Chapter entitled 'I remember…') David won the Tweedale Challenge Cup in 1956 when only 12 years of age!

Other Juniors taking part at this time were Stan Roberts (Stan School), Griff Roberts (Arwel), Wil P Williams (Bwlch), Dafydd Albert Hughes (son of Hubert Hughes), Noel Roberts (son of Owen Roberts) and A N McFee (related to the Buckley family). In the late 50s, Paul Smart emerged as a good junior prospect for the Club and he continued to achieve successes in the 60s.

Juniors became very successful and the issue of them playing in Club Competitions raised its head once more. In spite of strong opposition from some Members of Committee, the Executive reversed its decision of 1955 and Juniors were banned from all competitions apart from the Monthly Spoons. R G Williams resigned from the Committee as a consequence.

North Wales Boys' Team 1956 at Llandrindod.
Front Row: Extreme Left: *Wil G Jones (Wil Bach) of Bangor Golf Club then, now of Porthmadog. Next to him is Brian Hefin Williams.* **Back Row: Extreme Right:** *a very young looking Aled Rees from Criccieth Golf Club.*

THE SIXTIES

Junior Golf at Nefyn flourished during the 60s. A D Grace and Richard Williams were very much involved in arranging Junior matches against other clubs as well as organising all the competitions at Nefyn. Alf Whalley (Captain, 1964) was particularly supportive of Junior golf and presented several trophies to the section. Many Members assisted when Juniors were ferried across North Wales to various competitions, including the Daily Telegraph Junior Opens which were held at various venues, including Pwllheli. This Competition was never held at Nefyn since Nefyn hosted the Caernarvonshire Boys' Championship (see later).

The Junior Section was really flourishing at this time and this made for very competitive tournaments and knockouts. Juniors in the 60s included Paul Smart, Merfyn Lloyd, Roy Portlock, Dewi Morgan Lewis Jones, John Roberts (Gerallt, Nefyn), Wil H Jones, T Gareth Gruffydd, William Lloyd Griffith, Gareth Wyn Jones, Gwyn Hughes, Morus Wyn Parry, Roger W Scott and H Tecwyn Williams. Away Members boosted the numbers during school holidays. In 1962, the Courtenay Lord Cup was transferred to the Junior Section as a Challenge Trophy to be played as a match play tournament involving the whole Junior Section. T Gareth Gruffydd won this Cup on three successive years from 1962 to 1964 and because of this he was allowed to keep the Cup (see Cups and Competitions).

Other competitions which the Juniors played at this time were The Harry Parry Cup (18 Holes Stableford), The Professional's Prize (18 Holes Bogey) and a Medal Round for vouchers presented by E S R Morris of Sale.

17 year old T Gareth Gruffydd receives the Major W E Roberts Trophy (North Wales Junior Championship) at Conwy Golf Club from Mr Bobby Brown, the Chairman of the North Wales Junior Golfing Association in 1964. 15 year old Carey Jones (Maesdu Golf Club) is holding the Trophy for the Best Nett score.

In the mid-60s the Junior Section ran a full week of competitions, ably organised by the then Junior Secretary, Roy Portlock.

The Ladies' Section also helped to promote and encourage the Juniors in the 60s. They arranged Matches against them and afterwards treated them to hot-pot suppers in the Club! Matches were also arranged with the Ladies and Juniors together challenging Men's Teams, followed by the traditional hot-pot!

From the two groups of promising juniors in the 50s and 60s, individuals went on to represent their

North Wales Boys' Team 1964 at Conwy Golf Club.
Front Row: *Centre is Paul Smart, Captain of the North Wales Team.* **Back Row: Extreme Left** *is Merfyn Lloyd of Pwllheli and Nefyn Golf Clubs, and centre is T Gareth Gruffydd.*

counties at junior and senior levels. Brian Hefin Williams in the 50s and Paul Smart, T Gareth Gruffydd and Merfyn Lloyd in the 60s played regularly in the Welsh Boys Championship and represented the North Wales Junior Team when they played the South Wales Junior Team in the Championship.

The Caernarfonshire Boys' Championship

In March 1957, E S R Morris of Sale presented a Junior Shield for a Junior Competition under 16 years of age in the Summer Meeting. At a later date, not minuted, this Shield was presented to an Open Meeting for Juniors at Nefyn, and became known as the Caernarfonshire Boys' Championship.

This Championship became an annual competition. It attracted junior boys from Caernarvonshire and Anglesey and was organised by Dennis Grace and Richard Williams (Captain, 1966) for many years. Mr and Mrs Ormerod of Gateley later presented the Junior Ormerod Cup to the Club and the Craven Family presented the Craven Cup. Subsequently, both these Cups were played for in the Caernarfonshire Boys' Championship.

In 1972, it was resolved, for the first time, to run the Caernarvonshire Girls' Championship concurrently with the Caernarfonshire Boys' Championship at Nefyn. The name changed to Gwynedd at the time of the reorganisation of counties in 1974.

In 1976, it is recorded that the Gwynedd Boys and Gwynedd Girls' Championship were to be held on alternate Saturdays – Gwynedd Girls on July 16th and the Gwynedd Boys on July 23rd.

The County Junior Scratch and Handicap Championship was played in conjunction with the Gwynedd Boys' Championship in the late 90s and Nefyn continued to host and organise the Competition. The Shield and the two Cups continued to be presented (see Section on Cups and Trophies) for the Gwynedd Boys.

Since the E S R Morris Shield was inaugurated in 1958, several Nefyn Juniors have been successful in the Caernarfonshire / Gwynedd Boys' Championship. David Parsonage won in 1960 and 1961, Gwyn Hughes 1964, Richard Taylor 1983, Gwyndaf Jones 1987, Dyfed Parry Thomas 1988, Mark Sanders 1989 and 1990, Mark Pilkington 1992, 1993, 1994, 1995 & 1996, Alwyn Thomas 1999, 2000 & 2001 and Tudur L Evans in 2003 & 2004.

In 2002, largely at the instigation of the Captain, R J (Spud) Taylor, girls were invited to play in the Championship and it became known as the Gwynedd Junior Championship. This was an attempt to boost Girls' Golf in keeping with the climate of the time (see later).

THE SEVENTIES AND EIGHTIES

From the Ladies' AGM of 1970, the Ladies' Section, largely due to the influence of Mrs Pip Smart, County Captain, began to encourage Girls to take up the game and to take advantage of excellent training facilities on offer by the County. Many Club prizes began to appear for Juniors. Miss Bellhouse presented the first in 1970. This was for all Juniors and there were 28 entries. It was a great success and it became an annual event for many years.

In the 70s, many County Matches were played at Nefyn – both Caernarfonshire and Anglesey (C & A) and Caernarfonshire and District (C & D) – both Girls' and Boys' meetings. Nefyn's hospitality was warmly acknowledged and there was no doubt these meetings became a 'spin-off' for our own Members.

Junior Organisers and Special Category Juniors

At the start of the 1980s, the North Wales Junior Golf Organisation suggested that the Club appoint a Junior Organiser to foster

Junior Golf at the Club. The Club agreed, for the previous successful record of the 50s and 60s had declined during the 70s. In December 1984, Patrick McAteer was appointed as the first Junior Organiser. In early 1985, Captain Will Roberts was elected to represent Gwynedd on the Welsh Golfing Union and became a strong voice for Junior Golf in Wales. His experience and his enthusiasm inspired Patrick and the number of Juniors rapidly increased.

Mrs Pauline Lane became the first Girls' Junior organiser in 1986 in response to a request from the WLGU that a Lady Member should be involved with Girls' Junior Golf. During the summer of 1986, it was reported that girls were having coaching on Saturday mornings alongside the boys. In 1987, Jacqui Wilcox took over as Girls' Junior organiser with Shirley Roulston as Assistant.

In October 1984, initial discussions took place regarding 'Special Category Juniors' to encourage more competitive golf among the Juniors. If Juniors possessed an official handicap of 18 or less; paid an increased annual subscription; agreed to always play with a full Member in Competitions and did not enter any sweepstakes, they were allowed to play in all Club Competitions apart from the Tweedale and Captain's Day.

It was not until October 1986, there is the actual first reference to the term 'Special Category Juniors'. Special Category Juniors (Males) could play in all Competitions, apart from Captain's Prize (Captain's discretion), Tweedale Challenge Cup, Club Outings and possibly Invitation Day. Boys qualifying for this category of Membership needed a maximum handicap of 18 while girls needed a maximum handicap of 24.

[Over the years the handicaps limit changed and in 2007, it was agreed to dispense with 'Special Category Juniors'. This was on the recommendation of the Golfing Union of Wales that all Juniors should play in all Club Competitions provided they were in possession of a CONGU handicap of 28 for Boys and 36 for Girls.]

The number of Juniors increased and another group of Junior Boys emerged as a result of all this encouragement. They included Richard Taylor, Nick Wylde, Jonathan Bing, Gwyndaf Jones, Ian Roberts (Wern), John Thomas and Dyfed Parry Thomas. Nick (1986), Richard (1990), Dyfed (1995) and John (2004 & 2005) all went on to win the Club Championship at Nefyn.

In 1985, as a Special Category Junior, Dyfed won both the Muriau Cup and the Courtenay Lord Cup.

Dyfed Parry Thomas receiving the Muriau and Courtenay Lord Cups during the Presentation Evening in 1985 from the Captain, Ioi Williams.

Dyfed and John Thomas became prominent junior golfers and soon got their handicap down to single figures. They attended junior coaching organised by the Caernarfonshire Golfing Union and represented the North Wales

THE JUNIOR SECTION - YR ADRAN IAU

Junior Team in their annual match against South Wales at Holyhead during the Welsh Boys' Championship of 1988.

The North Wales Junior Team in 1988. Second from Right Back Row is Dyfed Parry Thomas and seated extreme right is John Thomas.

In 1989, Dyfed, having only just reached Full Membership at 18 years old, won the Captain's Prize during H D Jones' Captaincy. His wonderful score of 69-4-65, against a SSS of 71, was only marred by a bogey-par-bogey finish on the Old Course!

It was not customary to appoint a Junior Captain on a regular basis at Nefyn but in 1986, Ian Roberts (Ian Wern) was appointed Junior Captain. Ian later went on to try his hand at the professional game (See Megan Roberts' Captaincy, 2006)

The Ladies' Section also had some measure of success! As early as 1979, when Fiona Vaughan Thomas arrived on the scene as a most promising Junior, the Ladies' Section had recognised the need to allow Juniors to play in LGU Medals. However, they would not allow them to play in the Cefnamwlch and Dr Griffiths' Rose Bowl until they reached 18 years of age. (See Fiona Vaughan Thomas' exceptionally fine record as a Junior under her Ladies' Captain's Biography)

Fiona appears to have been very much on her own during this time. No other Girl Junior emerged for many years, in spite of repeated requests from Club and County to try and encourage girls to take up the game.

In 1988, Patrick McAteer was unable to continue as Junior Organiser as he was heavily committed to a College Course studying Greenkeeping. Tom Morris took over with Capt Will Roberts' assistance.

THE NINETIES

In 1990, Capt Will was appointed Junior Organiser for a short period until Dennis Humpherson assumed the position in August 1991. Dennis was instrumental in securing a £150 Golf Foundation Grant which was matched by the Club. In 1995 Dennis organised formal Junior Lessons and received donations from the Club to purchase golf balls. The Golf Foundation forwarded another grant to cover John Froom's coaching costs and the Club once again made a contribution.

Dennis resigned in October 1996 and the Committee expressed their sincere appreciation of his efforts. Temporarily, his position was taken over by Dyfed Parry Thomas until he moved to a teaching post in Brecon in September 1997. In the summer of 1998, Patrick McAteer returned as Junior Organiser. At this time, the junior coaching was carried out by the new Assistant Professional, Paul Bright (son of Porthmadog Professional, Peter Bright) on Saturday mornings rather than Wednesday evenings.

(Right) Alwyn Thomas as a Schoolboy International in the 90s.

At the Ladies' AGM of 1990, Marian Grace, as Secretary, announced that three Juniors had shown a great deal of promise during the year. The youngsters were Misses Pauline and Lea Wilson and Miss Siân Jones (now Mrs Siân Teleri Hughes) who had won the Welsh Northern Counties' Nancy Pearce Williams Trophy at Penmaenmawr.

The 90s saw the emergence of Alwyn Thomas who gained county and national honours. Alwyn won many major competitions at Nefyn and achieved a scratch handicap. He has been Club Champion on three occasions, 2000, 2002 and 2003.

Alwyn spent some time at Abersoch Golf Club while aspiring to become a professional golfer. He remains a formidable amateur golfer today, representing the Nefyn Scratch Team in the Bayonett League.

The 90s also saw the development of the Club's most famous golfer, Mark Pilkington. His story is found in the Chapter 'I remember...'

In March 1999, John Froom organised an Open Day for Ysgol Nefyn pupils to try their hand at golf. The Club covered the cost of cutting down clubs and re-gripping. In the summer of the same year, following the moving of the old shed from the 15th hole on the Point to the gravelled area by the first tee, the Juniors were allowed to use the shed as a Club Room. A pool table was added as well as some lockers for their clubs.

THE NEW MILLENIUM

The Juniors were very active at the turn of the century and the Section began to play in a league with other clubs. The Juniors were granted their own personal tees which were coloured blue and positioned in front of the Ladies' tees. (However, in 2005, green tees were introduced and were designated for use by beginners only. Juniors were allowed to play off red tees once they attained a CONGU handicap.)

Juniors who were active at this time were Gareth Williams, Aron Williams, Iwan Thomas, Dylan Thomas, Sion Parry, Tegid Williams, Neil Kennedy, Alwyn Thomas (see earlier) and Tudur L Evans. Tudur became a single-figure golfer early in his teens. He won the Buckley Trophy as a Special Category Junior in 2001 and, as seen earlier, won the Gwynedd Boys' Championship twice. In recent years, Tudur won the ROC Trophy (2006) and the Club Championship (2006 & 2007) as an Intermediate Member. Tudur is in his final year at Aberystwyth University and has the honour of captaining the University Golf Team.

In January 2002 it was clear that funding would be available from the County to promote Junior and especially Girls' golf. The Ladies' Section was enthusiastic in its support and an Open Day for Girls was planned for the Easter holidays. Due to its success, in June 2002, 15 young girls between 6 and 8 years of age began to receive coaching sessions from John Froom following a successful application for a Local Lottery Community Grant of £750. A by-law had to be created to allow these youngsters to become Junior Members by lowering the minimum age. (The Executive Committee of October 2003 agreed that the qualifying age of Juniors be lowered from 10 to 8, but this was not in fact ratified until a proposal at the AGM of 2006!)

Patrick McAteer resigned as Junior Organiser due to pressure of work in 2001 and from 2001 onwards, all future applicants had to be strictly vetted by law. Arwel Thomas took over the post for a short period between 2001 and 2002, while in the Ladies' Section, Janet Ellwood and Carol Smith were selected to help with Junior Girls. Patrick McAteer was re-appointed Junior Organiser in December 2002 and Dilys Ll Owen and Janet Brown agreed to help with Junior Girls in 2003.

Coaching for Girls continued throughout the Summer on Tuesday evenings while the coaching for Boys continued to take place on a Saturday morning. The Club then, however, adopted a 'no gender' policy and both boys and girls joined for lessons together on Saturday mornings. It is interesting to note that the number of girls dropped by 50% almost immediately. They obviously preferred to be taught separately.

In November 2003, Louise Davies, the Welsh Golf Development Officer attended a meeting to discuss Junior Golf at Nefyn. It was agreed to train 6 Junior Leaders in order to have more structured sessions and give more individual attention. In addition, Gwynedd County Council made a request for the Club to participate in a Primary School Link for Tri-Golf. Grants were again forthcoming and the Club received £750 from the Community Chest towards equipment and the training of helpers.

Six Members did go forward and trained as Junior Leaders and three of these continue to help John Froom, the Professional with the organisation on Saturday mornings, together with some parents. Leaders and other helpers also take beginners out on the Course on Tuesday afternoons.

In 2004, John Froom took over the mantle of Junior Organiser and since December 2006 Janet Brown has taken over the Co-ordination of the Section. In that month, Janet planned, organised and executed a Junior Presentation at the Club, immediately before the Children's Christmas Party. This was hugely successful and was followed by a similar event in 2007 (see later).

THE CENTENARY YEAR

In the summer of 2007, the Chairman of the Club, Chris Gaskell, chaired a meeting of Junior Parents and Junior Leaders with the sole intention of encouraging parents to take a more active interest in their children's golf. A Committee was formed and it is very much hoped that this will become a positive and supportive group to promote Junior Golf within the Club.

Developing and Promoting Junior Golf at Nefyn.
The Junior Golf Passport is a comprehensive, progressive, structured programme which was incorporated into the Junior Coaching in the Club. The Passport covers the 5 core elements of the game – Putting, Short Game, Long Game, Playing and Golfers Code. A series of targets are grouped into 6 levels and a certificate accompanies each level. (Tri-golf, see below, is the very preliminary level of the Passport)

Junior Presentation in December 2007
At the Junior Presentation in December 2007,

the following Juniors were awarded Certificates for having successfully completed various Levels of the Golf Junior Passport:
Bethany Westley, Non Howel, Carwyn Jones, Cai Jones, Carwyn Pierce Williams, Lauren Parry, Tim Parry and Tomos Merfyn Humphreys.

The following Juniors received commendations for their achievements during the year:
Stephen Jones, Henry Gregory, Tom Dennis, Alex Dennis, Danial Vaughan Jones, Ifan Rees Jones, Sioned Wynne Jones, Tom Froom, Josh Westley and Thomas Allman.

Dragon Sport Initiative and Tri-Golf in 2007

Dragon Sport is a Sports Council for Wales initiative funded by the National Lottery. It is designed to offer 7-11 year olds fun and enjoyable activities in eight named sports, golf being one of them.

Eight Volunteers from our Club took part in a training session, as part of the Dragon Golf initiative, before going into the primary schools to introduce the game to small groups of children. The coaching scheme used was Tri-Golf. Tri-Golf is a 'mini' version of golf specifically for use by young children in primary and junior schools. It is delivered through fun-based activity sessions involving groups of youngsters indoors or outdoors.

Six sessions were held at four schools, namely Ysgol Nefyn, Ysgol Edern, Ysgol Tudweiliog and Ysgol Abererch, before the participants were invited to attend further coaching at the Club.

Nefyn is now an official starter centre, recognised by the Golf Foundation and therefore funding is available for these young golfers.

Individual coaching at Abererch School

Children at Abererch School receive Tri-Golf Coaching under the Dragon Sports Scheme from Carys Wyn Jones, Ladies' President and T Gareth Gruffydd.
From Left to Right: Front Row: *Harri, Emily, Awel Haf, Hari, Joni, Alaw, Jack and Rhys* **Back Row:** *Ryan, Joshua, Elen and Tiffany.*

Major Junior Presentations during the Centenary Year

Pictured with Junior Co-ordinator, Janet Brown, are Sioned Wynne Jones, winner of the Club Handicap Competition and Thomas Allman, Winner of the Junior Trophy on Founders' Day, 2007 with 21pts over 9 holes.

Emily Boyman

Emily Boyman, aged eleven, is a name to remember for she is considered a potential star of the future. She started swinging a golf club when she was four years old at her uncle's field in Penrhos, near Pwllheli. Her first tutor when she was five was Stuart Pilkington, Mark Pilkington's younger brother, at Pwllheli Golf Club. She progressed rapidly and at six years of age she won the Welsh Qualifying Round of the Wee Wonders Competition at her first attempt.

[The HSBC Wee Wonders is a national junior golf event for the whole of Great Britain and Northern Ireland. It gives boys and girls aged 5-12 a way to progress from coaching competitions into competitive golf. Playing on a Par 3 Course, in 'flag format', the youngsters have 36 shots to get as far as they can. The winner is the one who finishes the furthest distance. There are 4 age categories: 5-6 years of age, 7-8, 9-10 and 11-12 years of age.]

Emily has won this Welsh Qualifying round on no fewer than four occasions, and in 2006 she won the Wee Wonders Grand Final at St Andrews. As a result of this, she then went on to compete in the final of the World Kids Championship in America. This was held in Pinehurst, North Carolina in August 2006. More than 1,100 players from across the USA and more than 30 countries competed in what is recognised as the world's largest golf tournament for boys and girls aged 12 and under.

Since the directive from the Golfing Union of Wales to allow all Juniors to play in Ladies' Competitions, Emily has thus become eligible to play with the Ladies. She makes a formidable opponent and has achieved success in every Club Ladies' Competition she has entered! At the Handicap Review in February 2008, Emily's handicap was reduced to 17 and within weeks she had further reduced to 15.

Thomas Allman winner of the Junior Centenary Cup (94-34-60) with Runner-up, Emily Boyman (97-24-73)

Matthew Astbury, Winner of the Lane Trophy with 48pts, is pictured with the Club Captain, August 2007.

Emily Boyman tees off the 1st at Nefyn, 2008, having had some advice in 2006, aged 10, from Colin Montgomery at St Andrews.

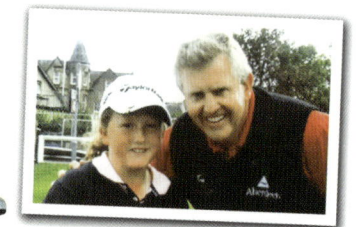

Mathew Jones is congratulated by the Junior Co-ordinator, Janet Brown, on winning the Captain Will Roberts' Trophy with 42 pts in August 2007.

Sam Bolton, Winner of the Ingy Cup with 40pts is presented with the Cup by the Ladies' Captain, August 2007.

THE FUTURE OF JUNIOR GOLF AT NEFYN

Nefyn Golf Club currently has 119 paid up Junior Members on roll, with 46 of them from the local area. It is a promising situation but the Club recognises it cannot afford to be complacent. Members are making a concerted effort through all available initiatives to encourage Juniors and ensure a future for our Club.

The Club Professional and his Assistant together with the Junior Co-ordinator, Janet Brown, her Assistant, Carol Smith, and other helpers, including parents, run a coaching session for children every Saturday morning in the season. Between 20 and 40 children attend, the numbers naturally swelling when Away Members are here for weekends or school holidays. The ages range from 4 to 12/13 and the ratio of boys to girls is 2/3rds to 1/3rd.

Members continue to take Juniors out on the Course after school one day a week and there is currently a powerful drive from the County to encourage Girls' Golf. County coaching is available for Girls and the County Easter Extravaganza and the Halloween Hullabaloo, where girls play with a lady golfer are well supported and hugely successful. We are fortunate that the County Girls' Organiser is our own Junior Co-ordinator, Janet Brown, and consequently as a Club, we are strongly committed to Girls' County Junior Golf.

In January 2008, for the first time, Members were invited to make a voluntary contribution through their subscriptions to create a fund specifically for the Junior Section. The response was overwhelming with over 600 members each adding £2 to their 2008 Subscription.

> **Club Rules 2007 Edition:**
> Rule 12 - Special Categories of Membership
>
> (d) Intermediate Membership; Former Junior Members and other applicants aged between 18 and 32 years may be elected to this category of membership.
>
> (e) Junior Members: Children of members, and others vouched for by full members over 8 years of age may be elected as Junior Members of the Club and shall pay a subscription to be determined annually by the Committee. They shall cease to be a Junior Member on 31st December following the attainment of their 18th birthday but shall be eligible for intermediate membership

In May 2008, the Professional, John Froom and his Assistant, James Salt, are intending to run a ten week Junior Academy for 10 Junior Members in addition to the general coaching on Saturday mornings. It is hoped this may encourage children of secondary school age to remain interested in the game and progress further.

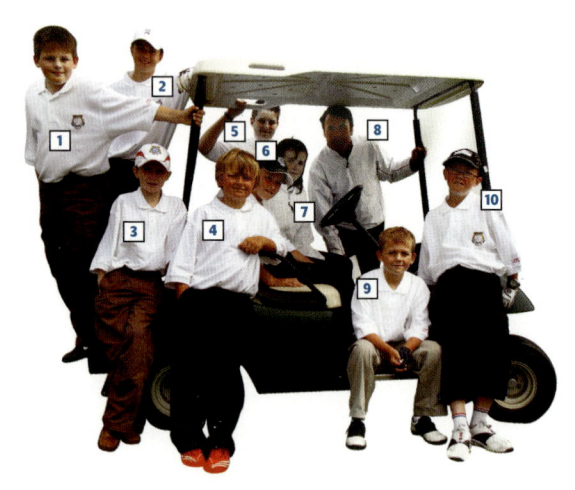

Some Junior Members get ready for the start of the Junior Academy, 2008.
1. Tom Dennis 2. Sam Pascall 3. Cai Jones
4. Tom Froom 5. Tomos Griffith
6. Ifan Rees Jones 7. Hannah Jones
8. John Froom (Professional) 9. Danial Jones
10. Tomos Humphreys

CADDIES

Datblygiad y Cadi yn y Clwb

Ymddengys y cyflogwyd cadis yng Nghlwb Golff Nefyn ers dechreuad y Clwb. Cyfeiriwyd at gwt y byddai'r cadis yn llochesu ynddo mor gynnar ag 1911. Aethpwyd cyn belled a thalu yswiriant am y cadis yn y tridegau a gyda phenodiad Dennis Grace fel Pro a Meistr y Cadis yn y cyfnod yma, sicrhawyd ffioedd teg iddynt.

Y pumdegau hyd y saithdegau oedd cyfnod euraidd y cadis yn y Clwb. Byddai mis Awst yn gyfnod prysur iawn pan fyddai'r hogia lleol yn disgwyl yn eiddgar am yr aelodau o Sir Caer, Sir Gaerhirfryn a thu hwnt i ddod ar eu pererindod blynyddol i Borthdinllaen i chwarae golff. Arferid cadio i'r un rhai yn flynyddol. Bu cadio'n boblogaidd iawn gyda hogia lleol hyd yr wythdegau a'r nawdegau pan eu disodlwyd gan droliau batri.

Earliest references

It is apparent that caddies have been employed at Nefyn Golf Club since the Club's inauguration. The Club's Minutes of August 8th, 1911 refer to alterations to the Pro's Shop and the Caddies' Shelter being approved. At the same meeting it was agreed that girl caddies be retained 'so long as the caddy master is employed and they use the same shelter as the boys'.

August 1930: children were reported caddying in school hours. The Pro to be warned about this habit.

In 1935, in response to the Committee's request to insure caddies, the Secretary, G S Pittman, contacted the Atlas Insurance Company to ask 'whether it would be cheaper to insure a definite number of caddies, say 50 caddies'. The Atlas Company confirmed a rate of £3-3-9 annually for the caddies, providing the caddies were aged between 12 and 16. Following this, the Committee agreed the caddies had to pay the Club 1d each to assist the Insurance cover and a sum of 1/2 per round be charged for caddying: 1/- for the caddie, and 1d each for the Club Insurance and the Caddie Master.

In 1936, with reference to a demand received from certain caddies for increased pay, it was agreed to revise the scale as follows:- Grade A Caddies 1/8, Grade B Caddies to remain at 1/2.

> **August 1937:** *[following the August Competitions] ...It was agreed to have a caddies competition. The Prizes were provided by subscription. (sic)*

Caddying becomes a lucrative business!

In 1945, following the Second World War, caddies' fees were raised to 1/6 for nine holes and 2/6 for 18 holes.

In the late 50s and early 60s, the rate of pay for caddies had risen to 5/- per round. However, certain gentlemen would only pay 4/6 a round! Caddying was in great demand, with many caddies carrying bags or pulling trolleys twice a day.

There was a distinction between bag carriers and *bona fide* caddies. Bag carriers or trolley pullers were very basic and would not assist the golfer at all. *Bone fide* caddies not only carried a bag or pulled a trolley but would select all the clubs for the golfer, spot and find any stray balls, interpret rules, suggest options and egged the golfer on to win competitions. Expert caddies in the early sixties would earn £8 a week, that is £1 for caddying one round per day and an additional £1 as a retainer for assurance of their presence in the morning for the whole week.

During the school summer holidays there could be easily 12 to 15 caddies available from 8am onwards on a daily basis. Very often, more money was to be earned in the August Meeting, when Ladies wanted caddies in the afternoons. These youngsters spent all their free time in the Club and a real sense of camaraderie was built. Little wonder then, that they took to the game and made lasting friendships. Interestingly, there were no girl caddies employed at this time.

Caddying became a very lucrative hobby and certain youngsters were able to buy clubs from Dennis Grace, the Professional and build up to a whole set in their six week summer holiday. (A Dai Rees iron in the sixties cost £4-6-4.)

Caddying continued at the Club into the 80s when the use of battery trolleys became popular and eventually the young earners had to search elsewhere for their pocket-money!

Centenary Junior Presentation
[1] Ladies' Captain, Fiona Vaughan Thomas, [2] Captain, Emyr L Evans, [3] President, Ioi Williams, [4] Ladies' President, Carys Wyn Jones, [5] Junior Organiser/Ladies' Vice-Captain, Janet Brown, [6] Josh Westley, [7] Tom Froom, [8] Tim Parry, [9] Tomos Humphreys, [10] Ifan Rees Jones, [11] Daniel Vaughan Jones, [12] Tom Dennis, [13] Carwyn Williams, [14] Stephen Jones, [15] Alex Dennis, [16] Non Howel, [17] Emily Boyman, [18] Bethany Westley, [19] Henry Gregory, [20] Lauren Parry, [21] Carwyn D Jones, [22] Thomas Allman

I REMEMBER...
DWI'N COFIO...

EMYR L EVANS

Atgofion cynnar Capten y Canmlwyddiant

Y cof cyntaf sydd gen i am Glwb Golff Nefyn ydy cael mynd i'r parti 'Dolig, parti'r plant, a hynny mae'n debyg ddechrau'r 60au pan oeddwn oddeutu 5 i 6 oed. Roedd hwn bob amser yn barti da ac yn rhywbeth i edrych ymlaen amdano oherwydd roedd yr anrhegion a geid gan Siôn Corn y Golff yn rhai gwerth eu cael, yn llawer iawn gwell nag anrhegion Siôn Corn yr Ysgol a'r Ysgol Sul!

Yn y cyfnod yma, adeg yr ysgol gynradd, roeddwn yn rhy ifanc i fod yn Aelod a'r peth agosaf i gael chwarae oedd cael cadio, a dyna oedd tynged Robin ac Aled, fy mrodyr, a finnau. Arferwn gadio naill ai i Nhad, Dyfed Evans, neu'r rhai a chwaraeai gydag ef – H D Jones, John Roberts Williams, Rhys Griffith, John Williams Troed yr Allt, Richard Edgar Jones ...ond i enwi rhai.

Wrth ein bod yn byw ym Mhencaenewydd sydd oddeutu 10 milltir o'r Golff, yr unig adeg y medrwn fynd yno i chwarae (ar ôl dod yn Aelod) oedd pan âi Nhad i chwarae, hynny wrth gwrs ar ôl cael sêl bendith Owen Roberts a dod i oed ysgol uwchradd.

Ei bartneriaid golffio cynnar...

Yn wahanol iawn i'r bechgyn oedd yr un oed â mi ac yn byw yn naill ai Morfa Nefyn neu Nefyn, hogia fel Huw Merfyn, Geraint Hughes ac Emyr Roberts, roedd yn rhaid bodloni ar fynd ella unwaith yr wythnos os yn ffodus ...braidd yn bell i gerdded neu fynd gyda beic! Anodd iawn felly oedd cael ymarfer a chael gwir afael yn y gêm yng nghyfnod fy ieuenctid, yn enwedig wrth chwarae hefo Iwan Edgar oedd yn diflannu ar ôl chwarae rhyw 5 twll i chwilio am flodau gwylltion lawr y clogwyni!

The Centenary Captain, Emyr, with wife, Marian, at the Centenary Ball, August 2007

Cofiaf yn iawn chwarae yng nghystadlaethau fel y 'Gwynedd Boys' a gynhaliwyd yn Nefyn bob haf. Roedd yn gyfnod difyr iawn er na chawsom ni fel plant fynd drwy ddrws y 'Clubhouse'. Dim ond yfed ein hanner o siandi allan ar y lawnt wrth ymyl siop Dennis Grace!

...a'i gynnydd fel golffar

Tros y blynyddoedd bu llawer uchafbwynt ynghlwm â'r bêl fach wen. Roedd y rownd gyntaf erioed o dan par yn eithaf cofiadwy ar y pryd, ond y broblem ydi cofio pryd! Cefais ddwy eleni ym mlwyddyn fy nghapteiniaeth. Tair ergyd yn well na'r safon (68 gros) diwrnod pryd y gwahoddwyd clybiau Cymreig eraill oedd yn dathlu eu canmlwyddiant i Nefyn. Y llall ddwy ergyd yn well na'r safon (69 gros) yng nghystadleuaeth 'Tatws'.

Bûm yn ffodus i ennill llawer o'r prif gystadlaethau yn Nefyn a chael fy enw ar y Byrddau Anrhydeddau. Hefyd cefais y fraint o fod yn Gapten ar y tîm 'scratch' a chael cyfle i gynrychioli'r Clwb ar lawer achlysur.

Yn rhinwedd fy swydd, cefais yr anrhydedd o chwarae y rhan fwyaf o gyrsiau gorau Prydain ac Iwerddon, ambell un gyda seren go enwog. Cefais y fraint o chwarae gyda'r pêl-droedwyr byd enwog Ossie Ardiles a Ricky Villa eleni, yn rhan o ddathliadau cwpan FA Lloegr heb sôn am John Parrott yn Nefyn diwrnod ein Cinio Canmlwyddiant!

...a'r gystadleuaeth efo Tudur

Emyr presents the Club Championship Trophy to Tudur, his son, in September 2007

Er i mi gael ambell i lwyddiant a phleser mawr ym myd y golff tros y blynyddoedd, mae'n debyg mai gweld datblygiad y mab, Tudur, fel golffiwr, sydd wedi rhoi'r pleser mwyaf i mi - ei weld yn cael ei ddewis i chware i Dîm Ieuenctid y Sir, ennill Pencampwriaeth y Clwb ddwy flynedd yn olynol, yn enwedig eleni ym mlwyddyn fy Nghapteiniaeth, a'i weld eleni hefyd yn cael ei ddewis i fod yn Gapten Tîm Golff Coleg Prifysgol Aberystwyth - y ddau ohonom yn Gapteiniaid yn yr un flwyddyn! Yn sicr, un o uchafbwyntiau golff blwyddyn fy Nghapteiniaeth oedd chwarae yn erbyn Tudur yn rownd derfynol Cystadleuaeth Bwrw Allan yr Haf. Creu hanes mae'n debyg? Tudur a orfu!

Ac i orffen..

Anodd iawn ydi meddwl am un uchafbwynt yn benodol, ond yn sicr ddigon, roedd cael ymddiriedaeth Aelodau Clwb Golff Nefyn a'r Cylch i'm hethol yn Gapten Canmlwyddiant y Clwb yn saff o fod yn un ohonynt. Braint ac anrhydedd enfawr oedd derbyn yr alwad hon ac fe fydd y flwyddyn hon yn fythgofiadwy i mi ac i ni i gyd fel teulu. Ymfalchïaf yn fawr o fod yn rhan o dair cenhedlaeth o'm teulu sy'n parhau i gynnal y cysylltiad clòs â Chlwb Golff Nefyn a diolchaf iddynt o waelod calon am eu cefnogaeth trwy'r flwyddyn.

Centenary Captains, Emyr L Evans and Fiona Vaughan Thomas, prepare for the traditional 'Drive-in' on Easter Sunday, April 8th 2007.

The Centenary Captain relates his earliest memories...

My first memory of Nefyn Golf Club was when I went to the Children's Christmas Party in the early 60s when I was 5 or 6 years old. It was always a good party and something to look forward to because the presents we had from Siôn Corn were worth having. They were far superior to Siôn Corn's presents in school and Sunday school!

During my primary school years, I was too young to be a Member and the next best thing to playing was being allowed to caddy. This is what Robin and Aled, my brothers, and I used to do. We caddied for my father, Dyfed Evans, or some of his playing partners – H D Jones, John Roberts Williams, Rhys Griffith, John Williams Troed yr Allt, Richard Edgar Jones - to name but a few. Since we lived in Pencaenewydd which is some ten miles from the Golf Club, the only time I was able to get there to play, after becoming a Member, was when my father himself went to play. I'd had to wait until I was of secondary school age though and then get Owen Roberts' seal of approval before I was allowed on the Course.

His early golfing partners...
As distinct from the boys of my age who lived in Morfa Nefyn or Nefyn, boys like Huw Merfyn, Geraint Hughes and Emyr Roberts, I had to be satisfied with going once a week, if I were lucky. I therefore found it difficult to practise and to get a good grip on the game in my youth, especially playing with Iwan Edgar who, after some 5 holes, would disappear down the cliff to search for wild flowers!

I remember playing in competitions like the Gwynedd Boys' Championship which was held at Nefyn every summer. It was a most pleasant time even though we were never allowed through the Clubhouse door. We used to drink our half of shandy out on the putting green by Dennis Grace's shop!

...his development as a golfer
There have been many highlights concerning the little white ball. The first ever round below par was quite memorable, but I can't remember when this was! I had two sub-par rounds this year in my Captaincy Year. On the day when other Welsh Clubs were invited to celebrate our Centenary, I scored a 68 (3 under par) while I scored a 69 (2 under par) in the 'Tatws' Competition.

Emyr plays 100 holes of golf for the Captains' Charity, Bryn Beryl Hospital, Pwllheli.

Over the years, I have been fortunate to win several of the Club's Major Competitions. I have had the honour of captaining the Scratch Team and have represented the Club on many occasions.

By virtue of my profession, I have been able to play the majority of the top courses in Britain and Ireland, some in the company of renowned stars. I had the honour of playing with the world famous footballers Ossie Ardiles and Ricky Villa this year as part of the English FA celebrations. I also played a round of golf with John Parrott on the day of our Centenary Dinner.

...and the challenge he now faces from Tudur
Even though I've had some personal success and pleasure at golf over the years, it is undoubtedly my son, Tudur's development as a golfer that has pleased me the most - seeing him being selected to play for the County Youth Team, seeing him win the Club Championship at Nefyn two years in succession, especially this year, and seeing him being selected as Captain of the Aberystwyth University Golf Team, both of us Captains in the same year! Without doubt, one of the highlights of my Captaincy year was playing against Tudur in the Final of the Summer Singles Knockout Competition. Tudur was the victor!

In conclusion...
The game of golf and Nefyn Golf Club has always been a part of my life and it was a

privilege and an honour to receive the nod to become the Club's Centenary Captain. If I had to single out a specific highlight over my years at Nefyn, it must be the knowledge that I had the full support and trust of the Members to undertake this important position. The Centenary Year will remain an unforgettable experience for me and my whole family. I am proud to belong to three generations that have such loyal connections with the Club and I thank all of them unreservedly for their support during the year.

(Above Left) *Emyr with Gordon Smith, Vice-Captain rehearse for their performance in the Carol Evening, Christmas 2007.*

(Above Right) *John Froom, the Professional, was not expecting this amorous model in his Fashion Show, May 2007.*

FIONA VAUGHAN THOMAS

Ladies' Captain, Fiona Vaughan Thomas takes her seat in her Chair after her election to Office in April 2007.
Left to Right, *are brother, Stephen, mother Anne, partner Louise Rowley, and father Eirwyn.*

Earliest Beginnings

My first memory of Nefyn Golf Club was joining my mother for tea on a Wednesday afternoon in 1976 when I was nearly five years old. At that tender age, little did I think I would be taking part in Wednesday afternoons over 30 years later and as Ladies' Captain of the Club!

Upon entering that particular Wednesday I made a beeline for Annette Jones (Auntie Annette), who since that day has been an integral part of my life. I immediately felt comfortable in the company of the other Ladies. I recall spending numerous afternoons with the likes of Marian Grace, Pauline Lane, Miss Bellhouse, Miss Roberts (Rhyllech), Miss Annie Williams (Gwynfryn), Mrs Ogwen Jones and Miss Mary Davies to name but a few.

Around this time, my parents began encouraging my golf. Early summer evenings were spent joining them for a game. At this stage, I was just starting to pick up a club and would attempt to caddie for them, if I were patient enough. On the 1st, I would caddie to the marker post and then leave the clubs with Mum or Dad to run down the hill to the bottom. Once they had caught up with me and I was out of sight of the Clubhouse, Dad would bring out an old cut down seven iron, with a masking tape grip, and allow me to hit a few shots to the green. This continued up the second where my little legs would then decide they needed a rest - I think it was more to do with wanting to eat the tube of Smarties in Mum's golf bag! I would then make myself comfortable on the seat by the 3rd Tee, getting ready to watch my parents tee off at the Par 3 Third. I would remain on this seat as they walked down the hill and would then while away the time until they came back down the 7th by talking to any Member who came by.

Christmas Parties

Posh dresses for the girls, matching shirt and ties for the boys, soggy sandwiches, chocolate fingers, and competitive party games are some of my memories from the annual Children's Christmas Parties, held upstairs in the Games' Room. I was always so excited when I heard Siôn Corn's footsteps on the stairs, having just landed from RAF Valley. Siôn Corn during the late 70s and early 80s was Mr Hugh Jones. As a retired local headteacher and having known all our parents for a number of years, he always regaled us with stories about them, which made the occasion even more believable.

Fiona receives a kiss from Siôn Corn (H E Roberts) at the Children's Christmas Party, 2007

Fiona begins to play golf...

The area which is now the 18th fairway (New Course) was where I started my golfing career. Not wanting to be left at home on a Saturday morning, I joined my brother Stephen, at the junior golf lessons run by John Pilkington, the Pro. After these lessons, the boys were allowed to progress to the Course but little old me was left behind. They didn't want a girl ruining their game and would leave me to sit on the putting green wall. This was like a red rag to a bull and concentrated my determination to secure four qualifying cards for a handicap. I would show the boys how to play golf!

This determination meant that Mum, Dad and Auntie Annette were forever on the Course with me in summer evenings enabling me to practise so I could eventually hold my own over 18 holes. Fortunately, Stephen then decided to focus more on his music and passed over to me his old golf clubs. Having already broken numerous windows at the Vicarage whilst playing football, you would think I would be apprehensive about practising my chipping. Not me – and I couldn't get over Dad not being too bothered when I broke a window with a golf ball! He was just glad I was practising!

Fiona performs a newly composed Christmas 'ditty' with Pandy Brodie, Carys Wyn Jones and Sylvia Dennett, December 2007.

...and is encouraged by others.

When I progressed to playing 18 holes and playing in the competitions, I remember as I came up the Old 18th, there would be faces peering out of the Lounge window. Invariably Miss Mary Roberts, Miss Annie Williams, Miss Mary Davies and Miss Bellhouse would be there scrutinising my approach and putt! I remember their encouragement every week and their wild joy when they witnessed the first time

I drove the green! Later, Miss Roberts and Miss Davies actually presented me with their putters!

Seated by the Lounge window and ready to observe play on the 18th green are **Left to Right**, *Nellie Trenholme, Mary Davies and Mary Roberts (Rhyllech)*

Apart from these Ladies, and my parents and Auntie Annette, there were many other Ladies in the Golf Club who encouraged me and helped me on my way. They are far too numerous to mention here but to all of them I offer my sincere thanks. However I am more than indebted to one particular lady – Elsie Hughes. It was Elsie that played with me in the Alternate Day's Competitions and transported me to play in competitions in the early days when my parents were unable to do so, even as far as Liverpool. In addition, she was a very good player herself and I learned a great deal from her.

The practising pays off

During the mid-80s and early 90s my time outside of school and university was filled with many golfing achievements with numerous wins in various Club, County and National Events as well as a few course records. My trophy cabinet was starting to grow. These successes also coincided with my parents' individual Club Captaincies here at Nefyn: my mother Anne, in 1988 and my father Wyn (Rev E W Thomas), in 1995.

The highlights...

Before I received my greatest golfing honour to date of being elected Ladies' Centenary Captain, I was extremely fortunate to hold the post of Non-playing Captain for the Welsh U18 Home International in 1999. We created golfing history at High Post Golf Club by winning the Home Internationals and Triple Crown. I was also Caernarfon and Anglesey County Captain in 2003 and 2004 when the team reached the sub-divisional finals in both years. These wonderful events and experiences strengthened my willingness to hold the post of Ladies' Captain, confident I could fulfil the challenge whilst still continuing with my teaching in Sale.

Fiona with the Club's President, Ioi Williams, at the Centenary Ball, August 2007.

...and finally,

Reflecting back on my Nefyn history has allowed me to recall many cherished memories of which there are far too many to write in this article. My year as Ladies' Captain, falling in such a special year, is so far the pinnacle of all my achievements. I have been truly overwhelmed by the support from everyone at Nefyn Golf Club and look forward to being a part of this fantastic Club for many years to come.

The Prize Winners in her Ladies' Captain's Day
Fiona is pictured with her Ladies' Captain's Day's Prize Winners: **Left to Right:** Runner-Up Siân Teleri Hughes, Winner Kate Norbury and Best Gross Winner, Joan Royle.

Fiona and Emyr let their hair down in the Karaoke at the 100 Year Fancy Dress Party on our Birthday Weekend, 5th May 2007.

HUGH D JONES

1987-2006	-	TRYSORYDD / TREASURER
1989	-	CAPTEN / CAPTAIN
2006	-	AELOD OES / LIFE MEMBER

HD yn cofio'i ddyddiau cynnar yn y Clwb...

Y tro cyntaf i mi roi fy nhroed i lawr ar dir y Clwb oedd ar fore heulog braf ym mis Gorffennaf 1933 fel cadi!

Ar feics y teithiem i gyd i fyny'r allt i'r Clwb. Dysgu'n fuan mai gorchwyl peryglus oedd hwnnw ar y ffordd gyntefig, garegog a garw. Amhosibl marchogaeth i fyny'r rhiw a hunllef bron oedd dod yn ôl i lawr y goriwaered ar wib! Y codymau yn fynych ac ambell un yn cael cryn anaf a dweud y lleiaf.

...ac fel Cadi...

Cofiaf hanesyn bychan pan oeddwn yn cadio ar yr wythfed twll [Dyffryn erbyn heddiw]. Byddwn i a'r cadis eraill yn swatio tu ôl i glawdd [sydd wedi diflannu erbyn heddiw] rhag ofn i'r gwŷr bonheddig sleisio'r bêl i'n cyfeiriad. Gyda llaw, yn y cyfnod yma, byddai dwy radd o dâl am gadio, 1/6 a 2/- sef 1/6 a 6c o dip. Byddai'r cadis yn dod i nabod y gwŷr fyddai ond yn talu 1/6. Fel arfer pan fyddai 'gŵr 1/6' yn troi i fyny, ni fyddai cadi ar gael! Beth bynnag, yn ôl i'r stori. Roedd un cadi ymysg ein criw wedi cadio am wythnos gyfan i un o'r 'gwŷr 1/6' a phenderfynodd dalu'r pwyth. Wrth gwrcwd y clawdd, aeth i boced bag y gŵr a thynnu un o'r peli gorau oddi yno, ei thynnu o'i phapur a'i gwerthu i'r gŵr er mwyn cael ei bres yn ôl!

Dennis Grace oedd y Pro y dyddiau hynny. Cofiaf Dewi Evans (tad M O Evans) yn bennaeth ar y Cadis. Ef fyddai'n dewis y cadis ar gyfer yr Aelodau a byddai Dennis Grace yn gwerthu tocyn am 1/6 i Aelodau oedd angen cadi. Byddai'r cadi yn gorfod cyfnewid y tocyn am arian gyda Dennis Grace a byddai Dennis yn derbyn rhyw geiniog neu ddwy am bob cadi. Ef oedd yn goruchwylio'r trefniant hurio cadis.

Roedd cwt y Cadis (i 'mochel rhag y glaw) yn gyfochrog â Siop y Pro, tua'r un safle â'r adeilad presennol. Adeilad bychan sinc gyda llawr pridd oedd y cwt a meinciau o amgylch y tu mewn fel y gallem eistedd a'n cefnau ar y mur. Yma y clywodd llawer ohonom y straeon amheus cyntaf erioed gan y Cadis hŷn a dysgu smocio ynghyd â gweithgareddau amheus eraill. Hogia Morfa

Nefyn ac Edern yn unig fyddai'n cadio - mae'n siŵr bod Nefyn yn rhy bell yr adeg honno! Cofiaf brynu papur 'emery' am geiniog gan Dennis Grace i loywi pennau rhydlyd clybiau coes bren ein meistri. Llafur cariad fyddai hynny os iawn y cofiaf.

Roedd y cadis, nid yn unig yn waharddedig o'r Clwb ei hun, ond hefyd o'r gwelltglas y tu fewn i'r rheiliau gwyn y tu allan i'r Clwb! Byddai'r cadis yn cael gwobr fechan ar ddiwedd cystadleuthâu mis Awst - fel arfer byddid yn lluchio nifer o fferins 'Quality Street' i'r awyr a byddai'r cadis yn ymgiprys am cyn gymaint ohonynt ag y medrent! Yr unig adeg i mi gael gweld y tu mewn i'r Clwb oedd ar ddiwrnod pan oeddwn yn cadio i Mr Pittman, yr Ysgrifennydd. Cerddai'r Ysgrifennydd yn urddasol yn ei plys ffôrs dros y Cwrs ac roedd hi'n dipyn o fraint i mi gael cadio iddo. Dywedodd Mr Pittman wrthyf, 'Go and see Mrs Edge and get me a pint of draught beer,' a manteisiais ar y cyfle.

Yn gadarn yn y tŷ rheolai Mrs Edge. Yr oedd fel mam i bawb ac edmygid hi gennym oll. Hi oedd Arglwyddes y Tŷ. Ni chlywais i sôn am Mr Edge, ac ni welais ef erioed ond awgrymodd un digrifwr yn y bar unwaith fod ei enw ar y Cwrs, ar gefn y pumed ti, 'Cliff Edge'!

Roedd Capten Owen, Delfryn, yn un o nifer o Gapteiniaid llong yn yr ardal. Yn eu mysg roedd Capten Hugh Jones, Cairn More a Chapten Griffith, Crugan. Byddent yn chwarae dipyn o golff a chyfeirid atynt fel y 'Band of Hope'!

[Ymddengys fod rhywfaint o ddirgelwch ynglŷn â chyfansoddiad cywir y 'Band of Hope'. Mae'n amlwg y gwahoddid Aelodau eraill i yumuno â hwy ar adegau gan fod tystiolaeth yn bodoli fod Capten Price Twmpath, Capten John Williams, Capten Roberts Post Edern, R Ivor Jones a John Evan Roberts wedi bod yn aelodau o'r Grŵp. Yn ogystal, arferid chwarae am Gwpan y 'Band of Hope'.]

Pan fyddai'r 'Band of Hope' yn cychwyn allan, byddem ni, y cadis, yn rhedeg o'r cwt i weld y sioe a chwerthin am eu pen. Credaf fod safon eu golff tua'r un safon â'm golff i! Ni fyddai'r grŵp yma yn llogi cadis. Dim ond pobl gyfoethog o ochr bellaf i Glawdd Offa fyddai'n arfer cael cadis. Arnyn nhw fyddai'r hogia lleol yn hogi eu Saesneg prin.

Roedd Capteiniaid Edern – Capten Jack Roberts, Argraig a Chapten Hugh Roberts, Arwel, yn y genhedlaeth nesaf oedd yn dilyn y capteiniaid hyn o'r Morfa. (Mae'r llun i'w weld ym mhennod y Capteiniaid, 1980.)

Parhaodd y gorchwyl o gadio am rai blynyddoedd nes cael dyrchafiad! Bu dau ohonom yn gweithio shifftiau ar y deuddegfed twll ger Ogof Bebyll. Roeddem yn gofalu am ddiogelwch cerddwyr y llwybr rhag peryglon yr ail ergyd i gyfeiriad y lawnt. Teimlem yn bwysig ryfeddol wrth chwifio'r fflagiau coch a gwyrdd. Byddem yn derbyn 15/- am waith wythnos ar y fflagiau. Gwnaethpwyd y trefniant yma yn sgil rhywun yn cael ei daro ar y llwybr cyhoeddus ger Ogof Bebyll.

...a'i ethol yn Aelod..

Etholwyd fi yn Aelod llawn yn 1948 yn nyddiau Owen Roberts. Tua'r un pryd penodwyd fi yn athro ym Mirmingham, ble bûm am yn agos i ddeng mlynedd. Wrth gwrs, golff yn y gwyliau yn unig fyddai adeg hynny a threuliais wyliau Awst flwyddyn ar ôl blwyddyn ar y maes yn cael llawer o hwyl gydag Aelodau lleol ac ymwelwyr.

Llwyddais i fynychu y rhan fwyaf o'r Cyfarfodydd Blynyddol a chofiaf y rhai cyntaf yn dda. Yr oedd yr ystafell i fyny'r grisiau yn ddigon mawr i'w cynnal! Testun chwilboeth y blynyddoedd hynny fyddai trafod golff ar y Sul. Yr oedd yr areithio yn frwd o'r ddwy ochr a hawdd dychmygu beth fyddai'r canlyniad terfynol wrth weld mwyafrif y rhai yn erbyn yn lleihau yn gyson o flwyddyn i flwyddyn.

Wedi fy mhenodi i Langybi, cefais fwy o gyfle i chwarae a gwneud ffrindiau newydd lu. Mae amryw erbyn hyn wedi'n gadael ond nifer a'u cyfeillgarwch yn parhau. Diolch amdanyn nhw!

...a Thrysorydd,
Ar ddechrau 1987, daeth cais gan y Pwyllgor i mi ystyried ymgymryd â'r swydd o Drysorydd y Clwb. Os cefais sioc erioed, dyma hi! (Rheolwr Banc y Midland yn Nefyn fyddai'n gwneud y gwaith yn draddodiadol hyd ddyfodiad fy rhagflaenydd, I R Williams.) Bu Ioi yn ddigon caredig i ddangos i mi beth fyddai o fy mlaen pe derbyniwn, a llanwyd fi ag ofn a dychryn. Er hynny, penderfynais fentro.

Llwyddais i gyflwyno fy adroddiad cyntaf i gyfarfod cyntaf y Pwyllgor ym mis Ebrill 1987 heb godi gwrychyn neb. Roedd hynny yn galondid ac yn help i mi amgyffred yr hyn oedd o'm blaen. Aeth y flwyddyn rhagddi yn weddol ddidrafferth gan wneud ambell i gamgymeriad a dysgu wrth fynd ymlaen. Rhaid mynegi fy ngwerthfawrogiad o gefnogaeth hael aelodau'r pwyllgorau a fu'n gymorth sylweddol i mi ar hyd y daith.

...a'i Gyfarfod Cyffredinol Cyntaf gyda Robin
Nid anghofiaf fy Nghyfarfod Blynyddol cyntaf yn 1988. Yr oedd y lle yn llawn ac yr oeddwn yn dyheu am gael cyflwyno fy adroddiad mor fuan â phosib. Eisteddwn wrth y bwrdd wrth ochr y diweddar Ysgrifennydd Robin Parry, yn aros i'r amser dechrau ddod, yn orlawn o amheuon a phryderon wrth edrych ar y llu o wynebau a syllai yn ddisgwylgar arnom.

'Do you know?' meddai Robin yn fy nghlust, 'I've been counting.' 'Counting what?' oedd fy nghwestiwn. Daeth yr ateb yn syth gyda gwên o glust i glust. 'The number of people here who have financial connections. I've counted sixteen of them. Bankers, accountants, financial advisers... You name them, they're here. They all live in the financial world.' A godod hynny fy nghalon? Llwyddais i ddweud 'Thank you very much, Robin' cyn i'r Llywydd gyhoeddi fod y cyfarfod ar ddechrau. Curai fy nghalon fel gordd ond pan ddaeth y cyfan i ben, darganfûm fod y pryder wedi diflannu a minnau, er fy mawr syndod, wedi mwynhau fy hun!'

Yn ystod fy mlynyddoedd yn y swydd cefais gyd-weithio â nifer o wahanol bwyllgorau fel y newidient o flwyddyn i flwyddyn, a dysgais lawer. Gwelais lawer o fynd a dod. Cefais weithio gyda 4 Ysgrifennydd, 2 Brif Geidwad y Lawntiau, 2 Bar a chollais gyfrif o'r nifer diddiwedd o olynwyr i Mrs Edge yn y tŷ, yn arlwyo yn y Gegin ac yn gyfrifol am y Bar. Gyda llaw ar fy nghalon, gallaf ddatgan na chollais un Cyfarfod o'r Pwyllgor Gwaith tra bûm yn Drysorydd.

...ac ymddeol yn 2006
Deuthum i gysylltiad â nifer helaeth o bobl yn ystod fy nghyfnod mewn swydd ac mae'r fraint o gael eu galw yn ffrindiau gwiw wedi cyfoethogi fy mywyd. Byddaf yn ddiolchgar byth am hynny.

Fy anrhydedd fwyaf...
Wedi Cyfarfod Blynyddol cyntaf cofiadwy, braf yw cael dweud i fy nghyfarfod olaf fod yn fwy

cofiadwy pan gefais fy anrhegu yn gwbl annisgwyl â thlws mor dderbyniol. Ac yn olaf, y mwyaf amhrisiadwy ohonynt oll, Aelodaeth am Oes o Glwb Golff Nefyn. Wnaeth y Cadi, a gerddodd i lawr y twll cyntaf 73 o flynyddoedd yn ôl, erioed freuddwydio byddai hyn yn digwydd.

HD recalls the early days...

The first time I ever trod on the hallowed turf of Nefyn Golf Club was on a sunny morning in July 1933, as a caddie.

We used to travel up the hill to the Club on our bikes. We soon found out that biking on such a poor, stony and rough surface was dangerous. It was virtually impossible to ride up the hill and it was a nightmare coming back down the descent at speed! There were regular falls with several injuries.

...as a Caddie...

I remember an incident which happened while I was caddying on the present 8th hole [called Dyffryn today]. We used to shelter behind a bank on this hole in case the gentlemen sliced in our direction. During this period, there were two rates of pay for caddying, 1/6 and 2/- i.e. 1/6 and a 6d tip. The caddies soon got to know the ones who only paid 1/6! As a rule, when the '1/6 gentleman' rolled up, there were no caddies available! On this occasion, one of the caddies had been caddying for the entire week for one of the '1/6 gentlemen' and he decided to retaliate. While sheltering behind the bank, he put his hand in the gentleman's bag and pulled out one of the best golf balls. He took the ball from its wrapper and sold it to the gentleman as a 'found' in order to get his 6d tip back!

Dennis Grace was the Pro at the time. I can remember Dewi Evans (M O Evans' father) being the Chief Caddie. He would select the caddies for the Members and Dennis Grace would sell a ticket for 1/6 to Members who required a caddie. The caddie would have to exchange the ticket for money with Dennis. Dennis would receive a penny or two for each caddie in his role as Caddie Master.

The Caddies' Shed, where we sheltered from the rain, was parallel to the Pro's Shop, more or less where the present Shop is sited. The shed was fairly small, made of zinc, with a soil floor and had benches all around the inside so that we could sit with our backs against the walls. This is where a great number of us heard our first shady stories from the older caddies. We also learned to smoke among other things! Only Edern and Morfa Nefyn lads used to caddie – it was likely that Nefyn was too far in those days! I remember buying emery paper from Dennis to brighten the rusty iron heads of the gentlemen's wooden shafted clubs. That was a labour of love, if ever there was one!

August 1931: Passed that a caddie's shelter be erected at a cost of £5. The Pro had raised £3-17-6 through a competition and the Club made up the remaining sum!

The caddies were not only barred from the Club itself but also from the lawn inside the Club's white palings. They used to be presented with small prizes at the end of the Summer Meeting. As a rule, a number of Quality Street sweets were thrown into the air and they would tussle for them. The only time I saw the inside of the Clubhouse was on one occasion when I was caddying for Mr Pittman, the Secretary. It was quite an honour to caddie for him and I can see him now, striding along the Course in his plus-fours. On this particular day, he asked me to go and see Mrs Edge, the Stewardess and bring him out a pint of draught beer.

Mrs Edge ruled the Clubhouse with a rod of iron. She was like a mother to us all and we admired her. She was 'The Lady' of the Clubhouse. I never heard of a Mr Edge and I never saw him. However, one humorist in the bar once said that his name was on a sign at the back of the 5th tee, 'Cliff Edge'!

Captain O G Owen, Delfryn was one of several sea captains residing in the area. Amongst them were Captain Hugh Jones, Cairn More and Captain Griffith, Crugan. They played a lot of golf and they were referred to as the 'Band of Hope'.

[There appears some confusion as to the exact constitution of the 'Band of Hope'. Certain other Club Members must have been invited to join them on occasion, for there is some evidence to support that Captain Price Twmpath, Captain John Williams, Captain Roberts Post Office Edern, R Ivor Jones and John Evan Roberts, to mention a few, also belonged to this group. The photo below, from Iona Roberts' book 'Ail Lyfr Hen Luniau Edern a Phorthdinllaen' (1989) shows yet another composition of the same entitled group!]

'The Band of Hope': Left to Right: Captain William Morris Williams, Hafod Edern, R Ivor Jones, Headmaster of Edern School, Captain John William Jones, Angorfa Edern, and Capten Griffith Roberts, Post Office, Edern.

August 1928: Mrs W Glynne Jones presented a Silver Cup, value £3-0-0 wholesale, for local Band of Hope. 18 entries. No entrance fee. Won by Capt Hugh Jones.

June 1930: The Band of Hope group were asked to appoint their own Secretary to look after their competitions.

I remember when the 'Band of Hope' started their round, we, the caddies, would run out of the shed to witness the show. There was always great hilarity and I recall that their standard of golf was pretty similar to mine! These gentlemen did not hire caddies. As a rule, only rich people from the other side of Offa's Dyke hired caddies and it was with these gentlemen that the local lads used to practise their limited English.

Caddying lasted for a few years until I was promoted! Two of us were appointed to work shifts on the 11th [today's 12th] hole on the Point, near the Pot. We were in charge of protecting the pedestrians from the dangers of second shots towards the green and the arrangement had begun after a pedestrian had been struck close to the Pot. We felt very important when waving red and green flags alternately! I earned fifteen shillings a week working these flags.

August 1934: First report of potential problem with pedestrians on the Point. Proposed that two lads be employed at 15/- a week to keep a look-out on the 11th Hole to prevent injuries to pedestrians walking to Tŷ Coch and Whitehall.

...becoming a Member

I became a full Member in 1948 in the days of Owen Roberts. At around the same time, I was appointed as a teacher in Birmingham where I stayed for nearly ten years. Holiday golf was all I had in those days and I used to spend my August school holidays, year after year, enjoying myself playing golf with Members and visitors. Then, when I was appointed Headmaster of Llangybi Primary School, I had more opportunity to play and made many more friends. Several have by now departed from us but for those that remain, my sincerest thanks to them for their friendship, loyalty and camaraderie over the years.

I managed to attend the majority of the Annual General Meetings and I remember the first ones well. The upstairs room was big enough for an AGM in those days. The usual hot potato was discussing Sunday golf. There were keen discussions from both sides and one was able to pre-judge the eventual result as the majority of the objectors decreased annually.

...and the Treasurer...

At the beginning of 1987, I was asked by the Executive Committee to consider becoming Club Treasurer. If ever I had a shock, this was it! Traditionally, the Manager of the Midland Bank at Nefyn used to do the work prior to my predecessor, I R Williams. Ioi was kind enough to show what was ahead of me if I were to take up the post, and I was filled with trepidation. Even so, I decided to venture and was elected at the AGM of 1987.

I managed to present my first Report to the first Committee, in April 1987, without upsetting anybody. This was encouraging and the year progressed without many problems. Yes, I made some mistakes but I learned from them. I must express my appreciation of the stalwart support of Committee Members along the way.

His first AGM with Robin...

I will never forget my first AGM in 1988. The room was over-flowing and I longed to get it over and done with as soon as possible. I sat next to the late Hon Sec, Robin Parry, waiting for the meeting to start, full of doubts and concerns as I stared at the faces that looked at us expectantly.

'Do you know?' said Robin in my ear, 'I've been counting.' 'Counting what?' I asked. The answer came directly, with a broad smile on his face. 'The number of people here who have financial connections. I've counted sixteen of them - bankers, accountants, financial advisers... You name them, they're here. They all live in the financial world.' I was deflated and just managed to croak, 'Thank you very much, Robin' before the President opened the Meeting. My heart was pounding but when it was all over, I found that my concern had been unfounded and, to my amazement, I had actually enjoyed myself!

...and a record of which he is so proud

During my years as Treasurer, I worked with several Committees as they changed from year to year and I learned a great deal. I worked with four Secretaries, two Head Greenkeepers, two Professionals and I lost count of the Stewardesses and Bar Stewards. I can honestly say I never missed one Executive Meeting in all the years I served as Treasurer and I believe that must be some record!

I met and came into contact with a great number of people in my period as Treasurer and my life has been enriched by their friendship. I am honoured to call them true friends and I will always be grateful for this.

His retirement in 2006
Following a memorable first AGM, it is with pleasure I say that my last, in 2006, was even more memorable when, totally unexpectedly, I was presented with a wonderful gift. And finally, I was given the most treasured gift of all, Life Membership of Nefyn Golf Club. What an honour! The caddie who walked down the first fairway 73 years ago never dreamed that it would have come to this.

At the AGM in April 2006, HD received a standing ovation as he was made a Life Member of the Club. He was then presented with a Silver Salver by the Chairman, Mr Will Lloyd Jones, in recognition of his long and faithful service to the Club.

Pictured, Left to Right: *newly elected Treasurer Richard Rimmington, Life Member H D Jones, Secretary/Manager Barry Owens, newly elected Captain Ian Cooper and Club Chairman Will Lloyd Jones.*

MISS ELLEN TRENHOLME (NELLIE)

1960 -	CAPTEN Y MERCHED / LADIES' CAPTAIN
2001-2003 -	LLYWYDD Y MERCHED / LADY PRESIDENT
2007 -	AELOD OES / LIFE MEMBER

Nellie'n ymuno â'r Clwb.....
Cofia Nellie'r adeg pan gafodd ei chynnig fel Aelod Iau o'r Clwb gan Wing Commander Sleigh (Ysgrifennydd ar y pryd) a thad Robert Holton, (perchennog Siop Newydd, Nefyn yn ddiweddarach). Golffiwr proffesiynol oedd Robert, yn byw yn Cliff Castle ar y pryd. Byddai'r Ysgrifennydd yn ei galw yn Helen bob amser yn hytrach nag Ellen!

Byddai sawl teulu mawr yn Nefyn yn y cyfnod yma, rhai gyda nifer fawr o ferched a fyddai'n mynd i weini i deuluoedd dosbarth canol neu'r byddigions. Cyflogwyd ffrind i mam Nellie gan deulu'r Tweedale.

Fel plentyn, cofia Nellie glywed pobl yn sôn am Gwrs Golff ym Mhentreuchaf ar droad y ganrif. Credai mai cwrs naw twll oedd a'i fod wedi'i osod ar dir yn perthyn i deulu Tanygroes, Nefyn.

Adeiladwyr llongau oedd teulu Tanygroes ar un adeg, fel sawl teulu cefnog arall yn yr ardal. Roedd aelodau o'r teulu'n byw gyferbyn â'r Cecil ym Morfa Nefyn.

...a chofia'r dyddiau cynnar gyda'i ffrind pennaf, y ddiweddar Gladys Roberts (Capten y Merched 1964)...
Roedd Gladys yn briod i Ben, gyrrwr bws Crosville. Cofia Nellie ddiddordeb cynnar y ddwy yn y gêm. 'Yn ystod y rhyfel, pan oedd petrol yn brin, byddai Gladys a minnau'n reidio beic o Nefyn i'r Clwb i chwarae 18 twll. Ambell waith, byddem yn aros i de efo Mrs Edge, chwarae 9 twll arall ac yna beicio yn ôl i Nefyn.' Byddai Nellie'n galw Gladys yn 'Yorkshire Terrier' oherwydd ei hewyllys i ennill. 'Mewn un gêm,' meddai Nellie, roedd Gladys 4 i lawr gyda phedwar i fynd a gofynnodd ei gwrthwynebydd iddi oedd hi eisiau chwarae'r pedwar twll olaf. 'Siwr iawn', meddai Gladys, ac enillodd y pedwar twll!' Roedd ganddi natur gystadleuol. Bu Gladys farw yn naw deg a dwy oed yn ystod ysgrifennu'r llyfr yma.

...ac eraill
Byddai Dennis Grace yn cymryd llawer o ddiddordeb yn y Clwb ac yn y merched oedd yn

chwarae. Byddai'n gwylio'r merched o'i 'gwt' ac yn rhoi pregeth go chwyrn iddynt ar ôl gorffen chwarae os oeddynt yn chwarae'n wael. Byddai'n dadansoddi eu 'swing' a byddai llawer un yn gwella o ganlyniad i'w hyfforddiant.

Yn nyddiau cynnar Nellie fel Aelod, arferai fynd i'r Clwb Golff gyda'r nos i gyfarfod â ffrindiau fel dwy ferch Capten Price (Twmpath) a chwiorydd Parc Stores, Gwyneth a Lena Jones. Byddai'r merched yn treulio gyda'r nosau yn gweu o flaen tân yn y parlwr - lle mae'r gegin erbyn hyn.

Troeon doniol ar y Cwrs...
Cofia Nellie ddigwyddiadau amrywiol fel yr adeg pan oedd yn chwarae gydag Annie Williams (Annie Gwynfryn) un tro. Meddai Nellie, 'Roedd gen i ofn Annie, wyddoch chi! Byddem ni fel merched ifanc yn neidio allan o'n croen pan fydda Annie yn gweiddi.' Cofia Nellie chwarae gêm yn erbyn Annie un tro. 'Roeddem yn chwarae twll a elwir yn 'Heartbreak Hill' (y 9fed heddiw) ac roeddwn i ar y grin ac Annie yn y byncr.' Credai Nellie ei bod am ennill un twll, beth bynnag. 'Aeth Annie i'r byncr, trawo'n wyllt a chladdu'r bêl i ganol y twll ac mi fethais innau'r pyt!'

Cofia Nellie achlysur arall pan oedd yn chwarae'r 10fed twll ar y Penrhyn, (yr 11eg heddiw). Roedd teulu'n cerdded ar ochr yr allt ac roeddynt braidd yn swnllyd. Gofynnodd Nellie yn fanesol iddynt am ddistawrydd tra roedd ei phartner yn chwarae ei hergyd. Yr ymateb gan wraig y teulu oedd, 'Gwrandewch arni hi, mae hi'n siarad fel petai hi'n berchen ar y Cwrs!'. A dyma oedd ateb Nellie. 'Dwi yn berchen ar y Cwrs!' (gan ystyried fod pawb oedd yn talu tanysgrifiad yn berchen ar y Cwrs.) Yn dilyn yr achlysur yma, cyfeiriwyd at Nellie fel Mrs Wynne-Finch, perchennog iawn y cwrs. Felly, ar un cyfnod roedd dwy Mrs Wynne-Finch yn y Clwb!

Roedd 'Mary Rhyllech' (Capten Adran y Merched yn 1939, 1949 a 1966) yn ffrind da arall iddi. Cofia Nellie chwarae efo Mary un tro ar y 14eg ar y Penrhyn (Lifeboat). Dywedodd Mary na chafodd hi erioed 'Dwll mewn Un'. Trawodd ergyd ddigon gwantan nad oedd yn edrych fel y buasai'n cyrraedd y twll o gwbl. Diflannodd y bêl dros y bryncyn bach o flaen y lawnt gan wneud i Nellie a Mary feddwl ei bod wedi dod i ben ei thaith yn fyr o'r lawnt. Mwyaf sydyn, dyma'r bêl yn ail ymddangos ac yn gwneud ei ffordd ar hyd y lawnt ac i mewn i'r twll! 'Oedd, mi oedd yn 'Dwll mewn Un' ond doedd o ddim llawer o glod', meddai Nellie.

Annie Williams (Gwynfryn) left, enjoys a cup of tea in the Lounge with Mary Roberts (Rhyllech).

Nellie joins the Club...
Nellie Trenholme recalls her proud moment of being proposed as a Junior Member of the Club in 1935 by Wing Commander Sleigh [Secretary at the time] and Robert (Bob) Holton's father, a professional golfer, living at Cliff Castle. She remembers the Secretary always insisted on calling her Helen!

In Nefyn, at this time, there were some very large families, some with many daughters who became servants to the middle or upper classes. Nellie's mother's friends were in fact employed by the Tweedale family.

She remembers, as a child, hearing of a golf course in Pentreuchaf at the turn of the century. She believed that this was a 9 hole course on land belonging to the family of Tanygroes, Nefyn. The Tanygroes family were ship builders at one time, like many other affluent families in the area.

...and remembers the early days with her great friend, the late Gladys Roberts, (Lady Captain 1964)...

One of Nellie's closest friends was Gladys Roberts, married to Ben, a Crosville bus driver. Sadly, Gladys died aged 92 during our Centenary Year. Nellie recalls their early interest in the game. 'During the war, when petrol was scarce, Gladys and I would bike from Nefyn to the Club and play 18 holes. Occasionally, we would have tea from Mrs Edge, play another 9 holes and then bike back again to Nefyn.' She described Gladys as a 'Yorkshire Terrier' because of her almost fanatic will to win. Nellie remembers one game particularly. 'Once, Gladys was 4 down with 4 holes to play and her opponent asked her whether she wanted to continue to play the last holes. 'Most certainly I do' she replied and went on to win all four holes - such was her competitive nature.'

...and others

Dennis Grace, the Professional, was very encouraging to the Ladies. He used to watch them play from his little 'hut' and give them a stern telling off if they had played badly. 'I remember he was always keen on analysing our swing! There was no doubt he knew his job and many of us improved through his teaching.'

In the early days, Nellie used to frequent the Golf Club at night to meet up with friends like Captain Price's two daughters and the Parc Store's sisters, Gwyneth and Lena Jones. They used to pass the evening knitting in front of the fire in the lounge – where the kitchen is today.

Some amusing moments on the Course...

Nellie recalls many incidents on the Course. 'I remember once playing with Annie Williams (Annie Gwynfryn). I was always afraid of Annie. We, as young girls, would jump out of our skin when she raised her voice. This particular occasion, I was playing a knockout against her and we were playing 'Heartbreak Hill' (the 9th). Well, I was on the green and she was in the bunker. I was confident I would win the hole but what did she do? She went into the bunker and swung her club really wildly and landed the ball in the hole! I then missed the putt!' [Annie was Lady Captain in 1933 and 1953.]

On another occasion, Nellie recalls playing the old 10th hole on the Penrhyn (now the 11th on the Old Course). On the cliff edge, there was a family of walkers. They were somewhat noisy and Nellie politely asked them to be quiet while her partner played her shot. The female spokesman for the family replied, 'Listen to her! She's talking as if she owns the Course!' As quick as lightning, Nellie replied 'I do own the Course', firmly believing that every one person who paid a subscription was entitled to say they owned the Course. Following this, Nellie was often addressed as 'Mrs Wynne-Finch', the real owner of the Club at the time. 'Thus, for a short time,' she laughs 'there were two Mrs Wynne-Finches in the Club!'

Miss Mary Roberts (Mary Rhyllech) was another good friend. Mary was Lady Captain in 1939, 1949 and 1966. 'I remember playing the 14th on the Penrhyn, the Lifeboat Hole, with Mary. Just before she teed off, Mary said that she'd never had a 'Hole-in-One'. Well, she hit a pretty feeble shot that looked as though it would never reach the green. The ball disappeared over the little hump in front of the green and we thought it must have come to rest there somewhere. But no! Suddenly, the ball reappeared and made its way across the green and into the hole! Yes, it was a 'Hole-in-One' but it really wasn't startling in any way!'

Nellie Trenholme celebrated her 91st birthday in January 2007. Although she does not play golf any more, she is still a faithful supporter of social events at the Club. However Nellie still enters and wins putting competitions and has been caught on camera on the dance floor on many occasions in our Centenary Year.

CARYS WYN JONES

1990 -	CAPTEN Y MERCHED / LADIES' CAPTAIN
2007 -	LLYWYDD Y MERCHED LADIES' PRESIDENT

Mae Carys Wyn Jones wedi bod yn Aelod o'r Clwb am dros ddeng mlynedd ar hugain gan wasanaethu mewn sawl rôl swyddogol dros y blynyddoedd. Mae ei hatgofion yn ddoniol tu hwnt...

...fy nghadi ...gwell oedd ganddo'r moch!

Ym mis Mai 1990 enillodd Carys rownd ragbrofol Cwpan Rover yn Nefyn ac, ynghyd â Katie Hopkinson, teithiodd i Borthcawl gyda dau gadi i Rownd Derfynol y Gystadleuaeth trwy Gymru. Sicrhaodd Katie wasanaeth Jack Trenholme i gadio iddi, tra cytunodd Eirwyn ei gŵr, i dynnu bag Carys. Bu'r holl daith yn dipyn o brofiad, ac roedd clywed ei henw yn cael ei gyhoeddi ar y ti cyntaf, 'And on the tee, Mrs Carys Jones from Nefyn' yn gwneud i Carys deimlo'n nerfus dros ben - a hithau'n hogan o'r wlad o Fynydd Nefyn!

Ni wynebwyd unrhyw drafferthion ar hyd y pedwar twll cyntaf, oedd ar hyd yr arfordir, ond wrth iddynt droi am y pumed, roedd wal yn ffinio ochr chwith y twll. Pan drodd Carys ei phen, ni fedrai weld ei chadi yn unman. Roedd Eirwyn wedi gweld fferm foch yr ochr arall i'r wal ac roedd wrthi'n ddiwyd yn astudio sut oeddynt yn cael eu magu allan yn yr awyr iach. Roedd ei foch ef o dan do yn barhaol! Roedd hi'n amlwg fod golff Carys yn eilradd i Eirwyn, gan fod y moch wedi cymryd ei holl sylw.

...a blwmars enwog pwy?

Mae gan Carys ambell i stori am Aelodau o Adran y Merched. Cofia am Mary Davies gyda'i sgert enwog y byddai bob amser yn chwarae golff ynddi. (Gwelir llun Mary Davies gyda Llongwyr Southampton yn hanes Helen Edgar fel Capten y Merched, 1974.) Pan oedd hi'n oer, byddai Mary yn arfer gwisgo dau bâr o flwmars ffabrig winsiét ei mam i gadw'n gynnes, ac arferai sefyll gyda'i choesau ar led, cyn lleted ag y caniatâi'r sgert iddi sefyll. A dyma fyddai ei safiad ar gyfer trawo pêl. Wrth chwarae'r unfed twll ar bymtheg ar y Penrhyn (Y Pot) gyda Mary, aeth pêl Carys i'r byncr ar y dde ac yn syth i lawr twll cwningen. Daeth Mary i'r adwy - gydag ymbarél a handlen wedi crymanu arni a cheisiodd dynnu'r bêl allan. Gwthiodd yr handlen yn bellach a phellach, ac aeth y bêl yn ddyfnach ac yn ddyfnach, ond ni chafwyd y bêl. Welsoch chi erioed y fath olygfa!

...be sgin ti dan dy gilt?

Marian, o serchog gof - cofia Carys hi'n iawn. Byddai Marian yn hoff o dynnu coes, ond y tro yma, aeth pethau o chwith iddi hi! Byddai bechgyn o'r Alban yn ymweld â Chwrs Nefyn yn flynyddol yn yr hydref ac ambell waith byddent yn gwisgo'u ciltiau. Fel y disgwylid gan Marian, gofynnodd iddynt, 'Dowch o 'na hogia, beth sydd gennych dan eich cilt? Dangoswch i ni.' A dyna'n union a wnaeth un - gan ei gadael yn gwrido'n braf ac yn methu yngan gair!

...dawnsio disgo yn y Clwb...

Mae nosweithiau cymdeithasol yn y Clwb wedi gwella'n sylweddol dros y blynyddoedd. Cofia Carys y sesiynau disgo cynnar yn y saithdegau a'r wythdegau. Y Troellwr Disgiau enwocaf yn Nefyn, wel, a dweud y gwir, yr unig un yn y cyfnod, oedd Gwilym Roberts. Byddai 'Sparky', fel y'i hadweinid, yn troelli disgiau'n rheolaidd yn y Clwb. Chwaraeai'r un recordiau dro ar ôl tro; 'Tie a Yellow Ribbon', 'Tell Laura I love her' a chaneuon Abba. Pan fyddai'r llawr dawnsio'n wag, byddai'n gwaeddi, 'If you don't get up and dance now, I'm going home!' 'Dawnsiwch y 'ffernols', mae gen i record newydd!' Sut bynnag, daeth ei ddyddiau troelli disgiau i ben yn ddirybudd pan adawodd ei holl recordiau ar silff ffenestr gefn ei gar un diwrnod poeth yn yr haf, a chawsant eu toddi i gyd!

...chwarae oddi cartref!

Byddai Carys wrth ei bodd pan drefnid taith i glybiau eraill, un ai i chwarae golff neu i gadio. Mae hi wedi cadio i Rhiannon Ingman ym Mhencampwriaeth Timau Cymru ers i Glwb Nefyn ddechrau chwarae yn y Gystadleuaeth yn Wrecsam yn 1998. Cofia Carys ddigwyddiadau digrif dros ben pan fyddai'r Tîm yn aros oddi cartref! Yn y Fenni, roedd yr holl chwaraewyr a'r cadis yn cael lluniaeth mewn un ystafell wely pan benderfynodd Rhiannon fynd allan am fygyn. Dychwelodd gyda dyn! Mae'n debyg ei bod wedi gweld y dyn yn cerdded o gwmpas yn chwilio am agorwr potel. Dywedodd wrtho fod gan y merched agorwr ac os oedd yn gêm, gallai ddod â'i botel i mewn i'w rhannu efo deuddeg o ferched o Ogledd Cymru. Roedd y cynnig yn rhy dda iddo a chafodd groeso brwd gan y merched pan gyrhaeddodd yr ystafell. Dywedodd na fuasai'i wraig yn coelio ei fod wedi treulio gyda'r nos gyda deuddeg o ferched mewn ystafell wely!

Ar achlysur arall, roedd y merched yn chwarae yn Llangollen ac roedd Sylvia Dennett wedi dod a jin eirin du cryf drybeilig gyda hi. Cafodd un o'r merched, na ellir eu henwi, ychydig yn ormod a dweud y lleiaf o'r jin yma a dechreuodd hiraethu am ei gŵr gartref. Aeth i'r ffenestr a ffoniodd ei gŵr tra roedd yn hanner hongian allan i gael signal ar ei ffôn symudol. Clywyd y sgwrs yn yr ystafell lle roedd sawl un yn piffian chwerthin! Y bore canlynol, roedd yr un wraig yn bryderus iawn gan honni nad oedd wedi ffonio'i gŵr y noswaith gynt - roedd wedi llwyr anghofio'r alwad ffôn roedd y byd yn gwrando arni!

Carys Wyn Jones has been a Member of the Golf Club for over thirty years and served in many official capacities. Her recollections are highly amusing.

...when I lost my caddy to pigs!

Carys recalls winning the Rover Cup at Nefyn in May 1990 when Katie Hopkinson also qualified. The two ladies then travelled with their caddies down to the all-Wales Qualifying Round in Porthcawl, Jack Trenholme caddying for Katie and husband Eirwyn caddying for Carys. It was quite an experience – 'and to hear your name announced over the loudspeaker on the first tee 'And on the tee, Mrs Carys Jones from Nefyn' was quite nerve-racking, especially when you were a country lass from Mynydd Nefyn!'

The first four holes along the coast went well but then as they turned for the 5th, there was a boundary wall running up the left hand side of the fairway. Carys turned around and her caddy was nowhere to be seen. Eirwyn had found a pig farm on the other side of the wall and was more interested in seeing how they were housed outside in the open air, compared with their own pigs which were always under cover! Carys' golf had suddenly appeared unimportant as the pigs took his attention!

...and who could ever forget the famous bloomers?

Carys has many tales relating to Members of the Ladies' Section. Like many long-standing Members, she recalls Mary Davies and her famous skirt in which she played golf. (See photo of Mary Davies with the Master Mariners in Lady Captains' Chapter, 1974.) 'She used to wear 2 pairs of her mother's winceyette bloomers to keep warm and would stand with her legs stretched as far as the skirt would allow and that would be her 'stance' for any golf swing!' Once, Carys remembers playing the 16th Hole (Pot) on the Old Course with her. Carys' ball disappeared into the bunker and straight down a rabbit hole. Mary came to the rescue – with a curve - handled umbrella - and attempted to retrieve this ball. She pushed the handle in further and further ...and the ball went in deeper and deeper, and was never recovered! But what a sight!

...Marian questions the Scots...

Carys remembers Marian Grace with much affection. Marian has been documented elsewhere but Carys recalls a time when the tables turned on Marian herself! There were some Scottish lads who came regularly to play golf at Nefyn in the early autumn and often wore their kilts. Marian, being Marian, asked them 'Come on, lads, what have you got under your kilts? Show us.' And one of them did precisely that – leaving her with a very red face and, for once, lost for words!

...Disco dancing at the Club...

The social events at the Golf Club have improved quite dramatically over the years. Carys recalls the early discos of the late 70s and early 80s. 'The Biggest DJ in Nefyn' [actually the only one at the time] was Gwilym Roberts, 'Sparky' as he was called, and he frequently played at the Club. His records were always the same. 'Tie a Yellow Ribbon', 'Tell Laura I love her' and ABBA hits were played continuously. When the dance floor was empty he would shout 'If you don't get up and dance now, I'm going home' and 'Dance, you 'xxxxxxs', I've got a new record'! His DJ days came to an unexpected end however, when he left all his records, one very hot summer's day, on the parcel shelf of his car and they all became warped in the heat!

...and 'playing' away from home!

Carys enjoyed all Club outings and visiting other clubs either playing or caddying. She has caddied for Rhiannon Ingman in the Welsh Team Championship Competition since Nefyn first entered the Competition in Wrexham in 1998 and recalls some hilarious occasions when the Team stayed away from home! In Abergavenny, all the Team, their caddies and supporters, were in one room in the Travel Lodge Hotel enjoying some refreshments when Rhiannon decided to go out for a cigarette. She returned with a man! Apparently, she had found him wandering about looking for a bottle opener. She told him we had one and, if he were game for a laugh, he could bring his bottle and share the evening with 12 ladies from North Wales. He jumped at the offer and was given a rousing welcome when he arrived in the room! He remarked his wife would never believe he had spent the evening with 12 ladies in one bedroom.

Carys and Rhiannon relax after a gruelling round of golf in thunder, lightning and rain at Carmarthen in June 2007.

On another occasion, the team were in Llangollen and Sylvia Dennett had brought some pretty potent damson gin. One of the ladies, who shall be nameless, had more than an elegant sufficiency and suddenly became homesick for her husband. She phoned him, hanging out of the window for a signal on her mobile, and had a conversation that brought tears of laughter to the eyes of the group. The next morning, the same lady was dreadfully concerned that she had not phoned her husband the previous evening - having clean forgotten the whole phone conversation!

MISS ANNETTE JONES

1978 - CAPTEN Y MERCHED / LADIES' CAPTAIN
2005-2007 - LLYWYDD Y MERCHED LADIES' PRESIDENT

Dyddiau ysgol cynnar efo Owen Roberts

Prifathro Annette yn yr ysgol gynradd oedd Owen Roberts, Ysgrifennydd y Clwb Golff a thrwyddo ef y cafodd hi ei chysylltiad cyntaf â'r Clwb. Yn aml iawn, byddai gwaith ysgol yn eilradd i waith y Clwb Golff pan fyddai Owen yn gofyn i Annette ei helpu i roddi enwau a chyfeiriadau Aelodau'r Clwb ar amlenni a fyddai'n cael eu dosbarthu ar ddiwedd y flwyddyn. Byddai hyn yn digwydd hefyd pan yrrid llythyrau i hysbysebu Cinio Blynyddol y Clwb. Os oeddech eisiau tocyn i'r Cinio, roedd yn ofynnol i chi wneud cais trwy ddychwelyd y llythyr ar ei union oherwydd ni fedrai Gwesty'r Nanhoron gymryd mwy na chant i fwyta. Ar waelod y llythyr bob tro byddai'r geiriau, 'Y Cyntaf i'r Felin gaiff Falu'.

Cael ei chyflwyno i'r Clwb...

Arferai Annette ymweld â'r Clwb gyda G I Hughes a'i wraig, Gwen. GI a'i cynigiodd yn aelod o'r Clwb yn 1959. 10/- y flwyddyn oedd y tanysgrifiad bryd hynny. Fodd bynnag, ni wnaeth Annette gymryd diddordeb go iawn mewn chwarae golff tan 1961 pan ymunodd â'r Merched ar brynhawn Mercher. Chwaraeodd ei gêm gyntaf erioed efo Pip Smart – golffwraig nodedig ac Aelod ers blynyddoedd, cyn Ysgrifennydd Graddnodau – ac roedd Annette wedi cynhyrfu'n lân! Hyd yn oed heddiw, gall deimlo'r nerfau oedd ganddi'r diwrnod hwnnw!

...a dechrau cyfeillgarwch â Marian Grace

Roedd Annette yn gyfaill mawr i Marian. 'Ni oedd babis y Clwb y dyddiau hynny er y gwnes i ddechrau chwarae golff ychydig cyn Marian.' Roedd Marian yn iau nag Annette, ac er ei bod wedi bod yn Aelod o'r Adran Iau ynghynt, ni chwaraeodd Marian lawer o golff. 'Cofiaf fynd i fyny i'r Golff un diwrnod a thad Marian, Dennis Grace, yn gofyn i mi 'Will you take this one in hand and start her playing?' ac i ffwrdd a ni i'r Llain Ymarfer gyda Mr Grace yn dangos i ni beth i'w wneud. 'Don't forget CTD,' fyddai ei hoff ddywediad (Cau Twll Din!).

'Wrth gael ein hatgoffa o'r geiriau yma ganddo drachefn a thrachefn, byddai'r ddwy ohonom yn taro'r peli ymhell.' Mae sawl chwaraewr

yn ein Clwb ni heddiw yn cofio cyngor yr hen Dennis Grace.

Byddai Marian ac Annette yn chwarae golff bob gyda'r nos pan fyddai'r tywydd yn caniatáu a gwelwyd gwellhad mawr yn eu gêm. Cofia Annette sawl digwyddiad doniol tu hwnt ar ac oddi ar y cwrs. Ar un achlysur, dyma'r wraig arall oedd yn chwarae efo'r ddwy ohonynt yn diosg ei dillad i lawr i'w dillad isaf am ei bod mor boeth gan orffen chwarae yn ei 'all-in-one'! Wrth gwrs, ni chafodd yr Ysgrifennydd glywed am hyn! Ar achlysur arall, pan oedd yr un tair yn chwarae mewn tywydd hynod o boeth eto, rhoddwyd gorau i'r gêm, gadawyd y clybiau ar ben gallt y môr ac aeth y tair i'r traeth i nofio. 'Mae'n rhaid bod Marian wedi cynllunio hyn,' meddai Annette, 'gan iddi ddod â'i gwisg nofio gyda hi!'

Cofia Annette y diwrnod pan gafodd Dwll mewn Un. Roedd Annette a Marian i fod i chwarae mewn cystadleuaeth pedwarawdau cymysg yng Ngŵyl yr Haf efo Roy Portlock a Ioi Williams. Fodd bynnag, roedd y ddau wedi gwneud yn dda i gael i'r camau bwrw allan yng Nghystadleuaeth Tweedale a bu rhaid iddynt dynnu'n ôl. Felly, chwaraeodd Marian gyda Jack Wilson ac Annette efo dyn dieithr – 'wnaeth o ddim yngan gair yr holl ffordd rownd. Fedrai'r un ohonom gael sgwrs efo fo. Yna ar yr unfed twll ar bymtheg, Ogof Bebyll, cefais Dwll mewn Un a dechreuodd y dyn yma neidio o gwmpas, yn fy llongyfarch - roedd o wedi gwirioni. Cafwyd ateb parod iawn gan Marian, 'Wel, mae fy ffrind wedi gorfod cael Twll mewn Un i chi ddechrau sgwrsio â hi!'

Bydd y rhai ohonoch sy'n cofio Marian yn cael eich atgoffa o'i fflachiadau o ffraethineb a'i jôcs sydyn. Cofia Annette ennill Tlws Buckley yn 1975 pan oedd Marian wedi marcio iddi. Roedd y ddwy yn eistedd yn y Lolfa yn disgwyl clywed y canlyniadau ar ôl i'r cystadleuwyr olaf ddod i mewn i'r Clwb. Roedd Annette yn cofio Gareth Gruffydd yn dod i'r Lolfa o Far y Dynion ac yn cerdded tuag atynt a Marian yn dweud, 'Drycha ar hwn yn cerdded yma, eisiau gwybod be' da ni wedi'i wneud, mae'n siŵr!' Ond na, roedd Gareth yn dod draw i ddweud fy mod wedi ennill. Cofiaf ei eiriau, 'Llongyfarchiadau ar sgôr arbennig o dda. Ti wedi curo Cresswell o ddwy ergyd!' Ar raddnod o 36, roeddwn wedi cael sgôr net o 65. Yn dilyn hyn, newidiwyd y rheolau a bu rhaid i'r Merched chwarae oddi ar 30 yn Nhlws Buckley o hynny ymlaen!

...a pherfformiadau Marian ar y llwyfan

Fred Smith, gŵr Hilda Smith, fyddai'n paratoi'r gerddoriaeth ar gyfer y cabare a berfformid gan Marian ac Annette. Byddai'r ddwy yn meimio'r geiriau i recordiau Fred! Cofia Annette un noswaith Cinio Gŵyl Dewi pan fu Aled Eames yn difyrru gyda sgwrs am ei ddyddiau mordwyol. Roedd Frank Evans y Post wedi gwahodd Marian ac Annette i roddi perfformiad ar ddiwedd y noson. Cawsant dipyn o fraw, ond yn gyfrinachol, roeddent wedi'u plesio.

Pan oedd y ddwy ohonynt yn newid ar ddiwedd y perfformiad, daeth cnoc ar ddrws eu hystafell newid a Frank yn gofyn oeddynt yn barchus i'w gweld?. 'Siwr iawn, unrhyw adeg,' oedd ateb parod Marian. 'Well, Mr Eames would like to come in and have a chat with you,' meddai Frank, a dyma Aled Eames yn ymddangos. 'Wel am act ardderchog,' meddai Aled Eames, 'roeddwn wedi gwirioni efo chi, mae'n amlwg eich bod yn broffesiynol!' 'Bl..di hel,' meddai Marian dan ei gwynt. Aeth Aled ymlaen i'w gwahodd i Fangor i roddi perfformiad arall iddo fo. Cytunodd Marian ar ei hunion ond gwrthododd Annette. Ceisiodd Marian ei pherswadio, ond wnâi Annette ddim cytuno. 'Tyrd o na 'rhen beth sâl,' erfyniodd

Marian arni. Bu rhaid i Annette ei hatgoffa mai meimio oeddynt ac y buasai angen cael Fred gyda hwy i chwarae'r recordiau, gosod yr uchel seinyddion ac ymlaen. Roedd Marian yn corddi, a dywedodd, 'Fy moment fawr wedi cyrraedd, a chdi'n dweud Na!' a throdd ar ei hunion a dweud wrth Aled Eames, 'Mi nawn ni gysylltu â chi'. Ond wnaethon nhw ddim!

Roedd Marian yn hynod o dalentog a chredai Annette, fel sawl Aelod arall, y buasai Marian yn gwneud bywoliaeth ar y llwyfan. 'Yn y dyddiau hynny, byddem yn creu ein hadloniant ein hunain yn y Clwb. Byddai'r Noson Lawen yn boblogaidd dros ben a Marian fyddai'r seren yn aml. Gwelaf hi'n awr, yn eistedd ar y llwyfan mewn cadair freichiau, gyda'i gin a thonic wrth ei hochr, yn dynwared Dave Allen, gyda'r jôcs yn byrlymu.'

Early school days with Owen Roberts.

Annette remembers Owen Roberts, the Club's Secretary, as her Headmaster in Nefyn School and it was through him she first came in contact with the Club. School work often took second place to Golf Club work and she recalls helping him many times by writing Members' names and addresses on envelopes that were sent out at the end of the year. This also happened when notices went out for example when there was a letter about the Golf Club Annual Dinner. 'If you wanted a ticket (for the dinner) you had to apply by return of post because the Nanhoron could only take 100 Members and at the bottom of the letter from him each time were the words 'Cyntaf i'r Felin gaiff Falu' – First come, first served.'

Annette's first introduction to the Club

Annette used to visit the Club with G I Hughes and his wife, Gwen, and it was GI who proposed her as a Member in 1959. The membership then was 10/-. It was not until 1961 however, that she began to take a real interest in the actual game itself and joined the Ladies on a Wednesday afternoon. Her first game ever was with Pip Smart – an impressive golfer and long-standing Member, past Secretary and Handicap Secretary – and young Annette was terrified! Even today, she can recall quite clearly how nervous she was that day!

Her friendship with Marian Grace...

Annette was a great friend of Marian Grace. 'We were the babies of the Club in those days, although I actually started playing golf a little before Marian.' Marian was younger than Annette and had been a Junior Member but played little golf. 'I remember going up to the Golf one day and Marian's father, Mr Dennis Grace, the Pro, asking me 'Will you take this one in hand and start playing?' and off we went to the Practice Ground with Mr Grace showing us what to do. 'Don't forget CTD' he would say (Cau Twll Din! – Clench the Buttocks!). 'Remember your father's words, CTD every time'.....and we did, and we hit the ball really far!' [There are many of our golfers at the Club today who still remember Dennis Grace's advice when striking the ball!]

Who is the Siôn Corn having words with Alwyn (Dolydd) Roberts at the Sunday morning Golfers' Christmas Lunch?

Marian and Annette played golf every evening whenever weather permitted and gradually their game improved. Annette recalls many hilarious occasions on the Golf Course with Marian. On one occasion, their third playing partner stripped to her underwear after the 4th Green as it was so terribly hot and finished the game in her 'all-in-one'. Obviously the Club Secretary never got to hear of this! On another occasion, the same three, again in sweltering weather, abandoned their game, left their clubs on the cliff edge and went for a dip in the sea. 'Marian must have planned it though', said Annette, 'for she had her bathing costume with her!'

Annette remembers when she got a 'Hole in One'. Annette and Marian had planned to play in the August Meeting's Mixed Foursomes with Roy Portlock and Ioi Williams but both men qualified for the Tweedale Knockout and had to withdraw. So, Marian played with Jack Wilson and Annette with a stranger – 'and he didn't utter one word all the way round. None of us could make any conversation with him. Then, on the 16th, the pot-hole, I had a 'Hole-in-One' and this man started jumping around, congratulating me and was genuinely overjoyed. As quick as lightning, Marian retorted 'Well, it took my friend to get a 'Hole-in-One' before you'd talk to her!'

Those who remember Marian will remember her sparkle, her wit and her fast 'one-liners'. Annette recalls winning the Buckley in 1975 when Marian had marked for her. They were both sitting in the main lounge, waiting to hear the result after the last competitors had come in. Annette remembers Gareth Gruffydd emerging from the Men's Bar and walking towards them and Marian saying, 'Look at this one coming, wanting to know what we've done I suppose!' 'But no! Gareth was coming over to tell me I'd won. I remember his words – 'Congratulations on a really excellent score. You've pipped Cresswell by 2 shots!' On a handicap of 36, I had achieved a nett score of 65. After that, the rules were changed and the Ladies were forced to play off a handicap of 30 in the Buckley!'

...and Marian's stage performances.

Fred Smith, Hilda Smith's husband, provided the music for the famous cabarets performed by Marian and Annette. The two mimed the words to Fred's records! Annette recalls one St David's Day Dinner when the Club had been entertained by Aled Eames who had talked about seafaring. Frank Post (Frank Evans), as Chairman of House, had invited Marian and Annette to perform their act at the end of the proceedings. They were taken aback to be asked but secretly quite pleased too. After the performance, Frank knocked the Ladies' Lounge door, where they were changing, and asked whether they were 'fit to be seen'? 'Oh, yes, any time!' cried Marian. 'Well, Mr Eames would like to come in and have a chat with you' and in came Mr Eames. 'Well', he said 'what a wonderful act! I was thrilled to bits with you and anyone can tell that you're real professionals!' 'Bl..dy hell', said Marian under her breath. He then invited them to Bangor to put on a show for him and Marian immediately agreed but at the same time Annette categorically refused. Marian turned to her and in Welsh tried to persuade her. There was no changing her mind. 'O come on, spoil sport,' she begged. But Annette reminded Marian that they were only miming and they would need Fred with them to play the records, set the speakers etc. Annette recalls Marian getting really cross with her – 'My greatest moment has arrived,' she said 'my First Night and you're saying 'No?' 'and she turned to Mr Eames and said, 'We'll let you know'. They never went!

Marian was tremendously talented and Annette among many other Members believed she should have had a career on the stage! 'In those days we made our own entertainment in the Club. The 'Noson Lawen' was a huge crowd puller and Marian was often the star turn. I can see her now, sitting on the stage in the armchair with her gin and tonic by her side, and taking off Dave Allen, the jokes coming fast and furious.'

Marian's real claim to fame was her very own impersonation of Shirley Bassey and particularly of 'Big Spender'. Annette recalls one occasion in Liverpool, where Enid Evans' Choir, Merched y Glannau, were giving a concert. The time came for Marian to go on stage and perform 'Big Spender'. Laura Wyn Roberts was in charge of the tape and every time Marian got ready to sing, the tape failed. 'Everyone held their breath, many of us seeing the funny side of it but not daring to show it. Marian was furious and she marched down to tell Laura off! And just at that very moment, the tape started and she had to chase back at full pelt to the stage once more! She then performed magnificently and when she finished, a voice cried from the back of the hall 'I'll spend a little time with you, darling, anytime!' and he turned out to be a lad from Nefyn, who was a policeman in Birkenhead!'

Marian arrives at the Ladies' Christmas Cheer

Annette fails to get her Captain's Photo displayed in the Lounge...

In her year of Captaincy, Annette recalls a letter from the Ladies' Committee to the Men's Committee asking whether the Lady Captain's Photograph could be put up in the main lounge alongside that of the Captain of the Club. This was the practice in other golf clubs and visitors had commented on the absence of our Lady Captain. The Lady Secretary received a reply refusing the request. The next day, Captain Will Roberts, the Club Secretary, went to see Annette to explain it was nothing to do with her personally, or her particular photo, but that 'they' did not want the Lady Captain's photo in the lounge. As compensation, Annette was told she could ask a local newspaper to take a photo; she could put that photo in the press; she would be allowed to keep the photo and the Club would pay for it!

...but Marian succeeds!

The following Ladies' AGM, Marian, as the incoming Lady Captain, raised the issue again and it was resolved to approach the Men's Section for the second time. This time the men agreed. Was this Marian's influence? Hers was the first Lady Captain's photograph to appear alongside the Captain and consequently is the first of the Past Captain's Photographs to appear in the Honoured Gallery! Annette recalls it was at the same AGM that it was resolved to pay the Lady Captain's Subscription Fee in her year of office and also pay for her ticket to the Club Official Dinners, St David's Day and the Annual Dinner. Annette remembers telling Marian that she was the lucky one. Annette, immediately before her, had to pay her own fees and had not been able to display her photo! It was a sore point!

It was Marian, at the AGM of 1980, who successfully proposed that the Lady Captain in future only paid for tea for her own guests on her Captain's Day. Up to that time, the Lady Captain paid for tea for whoever signed up to attend. Annette recalls paying £68 in 1978 'and we had beautiful open baps prepared by Rita and Ray Nicholson'. The proposal was agreed, largely because of rising costs but Annette recalls the real reason Marian proposed it, was because some Ladies turned up for the Captain's Tea who rarely frequented the Golf Club. 'On my Captain's Day, Marian had noticed a Member had brought a friend with her and this really annoyed her. 'Wel! Yli ar hon yn dod i fyny a chael te am ddim gen ti a hi byth yn dŵad ar gyfyl y golff' she exploded! ('Well! Look at this one coming up for your tea and she never comes near the Golf Club!')

DYFED O EVANS

Mae Dyfed yn Dad i Emyr, Capten y Clwb yn ein Canmlwyddiant. Cyn treulio cyfnod fel athro yn Ysgol Cymerau, Pwllheli, bu Dyfed yn Ohebydd i'r Cymro am nifer o flynyddoedd.

Fy mhrofiadau cynnar fel cadi...

Ac eithrio ambell i bererin mwy anturus na'i gilydd, dim ond byddigions fyddai'n chwarae golff pan oeddwn i'n hogyn. Doedd y rheini, o angenrheidrwydd, ddim yn wŷr bonheddig i gyd wrth reswm, ond fe fu'n dda i mi wrthynt ar lawer cyfrif. Yn ddeuddeg neu dair ar ddeg oed cawn 1/6, neu ddwy geiniog y twll, erbyn meddwl, am fod yn gadi iddynt yn Abersoch. Ar wythnos lawn o Ddydd Llun tan Ddydd Sadwrn ar gwrs naw twll Abersoch fe enillwn y swm sylweddol o ddeunaw swllt (3/- am 18 twll) - 'run faint yn union ag a gawsai un o f'ewyrthod yn ei joben efo'r Cyngor Sir. Dyna'r oes.

A dyna un fendith o fynd yn gadi. Bendith arall oedd medru cael gafael ar ben hen sbŵn, neu fashi neu fashi-niblic a rhoi coes iddo i chwarae o'r naill werddon i'r llall rhwng y grug ar y rhos ym Mynytho. Bu gwybod rhywfaint am elfennau'r gêm yn gaffaeliad mawr pan ymunais â Chlwb Golff Nefyn ymhen blynyddoedd wedyn.

Ymuno â'r Clwb, Medi 1962

Rhys Griffith, perchennog Garej y Ffôr, a'm perswadiodd i ymuno. Dim ond tair gini oedd y tâl blynyddol bryd hynny. Cyfyngid ar yr Aelodaeth yn ôl y pellter o Borthdinllaen ond roedd Rhys yn ddigon hyderus y cawn fynediad gan ei fod yn llawiach ag Owen Roberts, yr Ysgrifennydd - ac roedd gan Owen Roberts ei reolau ei hun.

Dau chwaraewr brwdfrydig iawn oedd Rhys a minnau bryd hynny. Buom unwaith yn chwarae efo peli oren pan oedd y cwrs dan drwch o eira. Ein partneriaid ambell dro fyddai'r ddau gapten llong o Edern - Capten John Roberts (tad-yng-nghyfraith Rhys) a'i frawd Capten Hugh Roberts, y ddau yn dadau i Aelodau amlwg o'r Clwb. Cawsom lawer o fwynhad yn eu cwmni.

Pan gollai Capten Hugh, rhoddai'r bai ar y bynion ar fawd ei droed! Droeon eraill, byddai Capten John, yn hollol fwriadol yn gwneud rhyw sŵn neu'i gilydd pan fyddai ei frawd yn pytio ac âi pethau'n ffradach wedyn! Mae sôn, wn i ddim ai gwir ai peidio, i Gapten Hugh gael y myll unwaith ym mhen draw'r Penrhyn, rhoi'r ffidil yn y to a cherdded adref.

Un peth a gofiaf yn arbennig amdanynt oedd eu dadlau brwd yn erbyn agor y Cwrs ar y Sul. Efallai mai eu dylanwad hwy sy'n peri na fu gennyf innau erioed awydd i chwarae ar y diwrnod hwnnw er imi orfod ildio ambell i rownd heb gystadlu.

Cael Twll mewn Un
O gyfeirio at ben draw'r Penrhyn gynnau fach, yno, ar y pedwerydd ar ddeg, y cefais y wefr o gael twll ar un ergyd. Lle da hefyd, gan fod modd gweld y bêl yn diflannu i'r twll. Tynnodd John Roberts y Ffôr lun ohonof i'w roi yn y Ffynnon, ein papur bro, a sgwennu stori fach dan y pennawd pryfoclyd, 'Twll-din-llaen'. Yr un John Roberts a welais un tro yn taro ei ddreif mor gam ar y ti cyntaf nes saethodd y bêl drwy ddrws y Clybhows a swatio dan y piano.

Y pennawd uchod gan John Roberts sy'n fy atgoffa hefyd mai'r unig wers golffio a gefais erioed oedd yr un gyffredinol a gynigiai Dennis Grace, y Pro, i egin-chwaraewyr: 'Straight left a cau twll din.'

Fy ffrindiau golffio...
Prin fu fy muddugoliaethau ar y Cwrs ond cefais bleser mawr am dros hanner can mlynedd yn chwarae a chellwair a chyfnewid profiadau. Pan fethodd Rhys â dod i chwarae'n rheolaidd oherwydd i'w fusnes gynyddu, cefais ymuno â John Troedyrallt, Dic Edgar a Dafydd Wyn ar y Sadyrnau. Collais fy lle wedyn pan 'rewodd' fy ysgwydd a methu a chodi fy mraich am dri mis ar ddeg. Ar ôl ail-afael ynddi y dechreuodd y bartneriaeth hir efo Dic Harris Roberts, Hugh D Jones ac Ieuan Ellis. Gwnewch gamgymeriad yn eu gŵydd a chlywch chi mo'i diwedd hi.

Un o'r manteision o chwarae efo Dic Harris yw na raid byth boeni am brinder peli. Gall synhwyro pêl guddiedig o hirbell ac mae'n berchen traed digon mawr i ffagio clewtiau helaeth o dwmpathau gwellt i deimlo'r peli dan y gwadnau.

Rwyf bellach yn tynnu 'mlaen mewn dyddiau, ond mae gennyf sbelan i fynd eto i efelychu'r hen gyfaill John Roberts Williams a ddeuai atom ganol yr wythnos. Roedd ef yn dal i chwarae flwyddyn cyn ei farw yn ddeg a phedwar ugain. Fe dorrodd ei goes wrth lithro ar y pedwerydd pan oedd tua 84 ac yn ddigon penderfynol i ail-ddechrau wedyn. Cyrhaeddai'r maes parcio gydag aml i dolcan newydd yn ei gar a chadwai bawb yn glir.

Ac yn olaf...
Af yn ôl i'r Ffôr i gloi. Wedi cytuno efo Rhys i roi cynnig ar bethau, fe brynais fy nghlybiau cyntaf, rhyw dipyn o gymysgfa, yn siop Edward Jones Williams – Siop Ned – yn y pentref am £2-10-0. Y rheini a fu gennyf am lawer blwyddyn. Galwch fi'n gynnil, os mynnwch, ond prin y medrwn gysgu'r nos pe talwn gannoedd am ddreifar! Rwy'n ffodus erbyn hyn y medraf fynd i garej Emyr yn Llanystumdwy a dewis ambell i glwb ar delerau a alwaf i yn 'fenthyciad parhaol'. Mae'n drefniant delfrydol.

O safbwynt teuluol, rwy'n falch fod fy meibion, Robin, Emyr ac Aled yn golffwyr yn Nefyn, yn falch iawn, yn naturiol, i Emyr gael y fraint o fod yn Gapten ar adeg mor gyffrous yn hanes y Clwb, a'i fod ef a Tudur, ei fab, sbel yn is eu graddnod nag y bûm i erioed.

Dyfed is the father of Emyr, our Centenary Captain. Before spending a period as a schoolteacher at Ysgol Cymerau, Pwllheli, Dyfed was for many years an editor with the Welsh weekly newspaper 'Y Cymro'.

My early experiences as a caddie...
With the exception of the odd character who might have been a little more adventurous than others, only the gentry used to play golf when I was a lad. When I was twelve or thirteen, I

would be given 1/6, or 2d a hole, to be a caddie for them at Abersoch. On a full week, Monday to Saturday on Abersoch's 9 Hole Course, I would earn the substantial sum of eighteen shillings (3/- a day for 18 holes) – the same sum exactly as one of my uncles received for working with the County Council.

That was one of the advantages of my being a caddie. Another advantage was being able to get my hands on an old 'spoon' head, or a 'mashie' or 'mashie niblick' and putting a shaft in it in order to play from one grassy patch to another between the fern on the heathland at Mynytho. Knowing a little about the rudiments of the game proved a great asset for me when I joined Nefyn Golf Club later on.

...and I join the Club in September 1962

I was persuaded to join by Rhys Griffith, proprietor of the Garage at Fourcrosses. The subscription in those days was only three guineas. The Membership was restricted according to the distance from Porthdinllaen but Rhys was confident I would be allowed to join since he was a good friend of Owen Roberts, the Secretary – and Owen had his own rules!

Rhys and I were very enthusiastic players in those days. We once played with orange golf balls when the Course was under a covering of snow. On occasions, our partners would be the two sea captains from Edern – Capt John Roberts, Rhys' father in law, and Capt Hugh Roberts, his brother. Both of them were fathers of respected Members of the Club. We had many pleasurable hours in their company.

When Capt Hugh Roberts lost, he always blamed the bunion on his big toe. At other times, Capt John would intentionally make some noise when his brother was putting and this would cause an uproar. I am told, whether true or not, that Capt Hugh was so irate while playing on the Point on one occasion that he packed up and stormed home.

One subject they would debate at length, and felt very strongly about, was opening the Course on a Sunday. It is perhaps because of their influence that I have not had the desire to play on this day myself, even though I admit I've had to succumb to playing the odd round without competing.

My 'Hole-in-One'

Referring to the Point earlier on, it was on the old 14th Hole that I had the thrill of holing out in one. It's a great hole because you can see the ball disappearing into the hole. John Roberts from Y Ffôr, took my photograph to place in the local paper 'Y Ffynnon' (The Well) under the provocative heading 'Twll-din-llaen' [Ask for a translation!]. It was the same John Roberts whom I once saw hitting such a bad drive on the 1st Hole that it shot through the Clubhouse door and settled under the piano.

It is the above heading from John Roberts which reminds me of the only golf lesson I ever received and Dennis Grace's usual advice for prospective players: 'Straight left and cau twll din.' [Again, ask.]

My golfing companions

Not often did I succeed on the Course but I derived much pleasure for over fifty years from playing, pulling opponents' legs and exchanging experiences. When Rhys failed to play regularly because of his expanding business, I was able to join up with John Williams, Troedyrallt, Richard Edgar and Dafydd Wyn on Saturdays. When I had a frozen shoulder, I lost my place and wasn't able to raise my arm for thirteen months. When I resumed, I started my long partnership with Dic Harris Roberts, Hugh D Jones and Ieuan Ellis. Make an error in their midst and you will not hear the end of it.

One advantage of playing with Dic Harris is that you never need to worry about a shortage of golf balls. He can detect a lost ball from afar and he is the owner of such large feet that he can flatten large patches of thick grass to feel the balls under his soles!

I am now getting on in years but I have a long way to go to emulate my dear old friend, John Roberts Williams, who used to join us for a mid-week game. He was still playing a year before his death at ninety years old. He broke his leg while playing the 4th Hole when he was around 84 years old and he was very determined to resume playing. He used to arrive in the car park with several new dents in his car. Everybody kept clear of him.

And finally...

I shall finish by returning to Y Ffôr. When I agreed with Rhys to give golf a try, I bought my first clubs, an assortment, from Edward Jones Williams' shop (Siop Ned) in the village at a cost of £2-10-0. I played with these clubs for many years. You can say I'm frugal if you like but I wouldn't be able to sleep at night if I paid hundreds of pounds for a driver! I'm fortunate that I can go to Emyr's garage in Llanystumdwy and select one or two clubs on terms I refer to as a 'permanent loan'. It's an ideal arrangement.

Dyfed with son Emyr to his Right and grandson Tudur.

From a family perspective, I'm delighted that my sons, Robin, Emyr and Aled are golfers at Nefyn. I'm even more delighted that Emyr has had the honour of being Captain at such an exciting time in the Club's history and that he and Tudur, his son, have much lower handicaps than I ever achieved.

DR WILLIAM BROADHURST
(1899 – 1982)

Bill Broadhurst or 'Doc Broadhurst' as he was called, will be remembered by many of our senior Members. He was a charismatic character and his effervescent personality filled the Clubhouse as soon as he entered.

Doc Broadhurst was born on the 10th February 1899 in Bolton, Lancs and first came to Nefyn as a baby in 1900, staying at the Three Herrings in Well Street. The family visited Nefyn regularly until 1914.

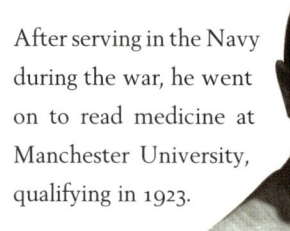

After serving in the Navy during the war, he went on to read medicine at Manchester University, qualifying in 1923.

He then went back to sea as a ship's doctor with Alfred Holt Lines. During this time he became friendly with Mr O H Parry (Captain in 1923) from the Red Garage at Nefyn, who was an engineer on the same ship.

Bill became an orthopaedic surgeon at Salford Royal Hospital and at the same time a general practitioner in Cheetham Hill, Manchester. During the Second World War he served with the RAMC at a number of military hospitals in Lancashire and Cheshire. After the war, when the NHS was formed, he was appointed Senior Consultant Anaesthetist for the West Manchester Regional Hospital Board and was affectionately known as 'Bloody Bill'. He was also a brilliant diagnostician and people came from as far away as Australia and Canada for a consultation.

He became a regular visitor to Nefyn c1949/1950 and joined the Club in 1957. Throughout August he played golf most days in the early morning, spending the afternoon on the beach, while his wife, Maud, played in the afternoons. Moi Parry was his regular caddie and Bill paid him 4/6 a round. In the early evening, Bill would frequent 'The Cabin' in the Sportsman's Hotel in Nefyn, where he would regularly complete the Telegraph crossword with Bob Beswick.

Members remember Bill Broadhurst as a determined character. On one occasion, he was asked by the Secretary, Owen Roberts, not to remove his shirt and exhibit his large frame while playing golf. He agreed he would not do so as he drove off the 1st tee - only to remove his shirt as soon as he had disappeared over the top of the hill, half way down the first!

As a rule, Bill did not drink alcohol but on occasions, he would ask the barman, Owen [Now Ben] Roberts, to drain the dregs from Harry Parry's nearly empty White Label bottles into a pint glass. He would then down the pint in one!

Bill was a fine golfer. He played down to 4 handicap and maintained a handicap of 10 until he was 80. He won the Captain's Prize at Nefyn in 1964 and the Veterans' Competition in the August Meeting on more than one occasion.

Tim Broadhurst, Dr Broadhurst's son, recalls his father's links with Nefyn Golf Club.

'I remember he built up a particular rapport with Mr Grace, the Professional and chose to buy the majority of his golf equipment and clothing from him...

...He was not averse to gamesmanship if he believed he was playing a 'bandit', especially if they were playing for money, pointing out aspects in the fellow's stance or swing which usually had the desired effect. A favourite tactic of his at Nefyn was to draw attention to the view in the setting sun just before the chap was taking his shot and thus spoil his vision.

That said, he was a convivial and generous man, a good loser and a magnanimous winner.'

SUE ASHWORTH
1995 - LADY CAPTAIN

Sue Ashworth is the mother of Simon Dennis, our current Secretary/Manager. Sue now lives in Cyprus but is still very interested in Nefyn Golf Club and welcomes any news from Simon.

Here Sue remembers her golf lessons and her first venture on the Golf Course...

Sue recalls six of them turning up for their first lesson with the new Pro, John Pilkington. The other five were Medi Williams (now Bezemer), Nell Williams, Dorothy Wales, (daughter-in-law of John Wales), Shirley Ives and Ann Partington (now Williams). She remembers every lesson being hilarious, usually due to Medi's dry sense of humour.

Sue recalls the first time she and Shirley Ives went out to play 10 holes. They went out early on the Wednesday morning hoping to avoid the Lady Golfers' Competition. By the time they were coming down the 8th, the Competition was going up the 2nd and 3rd. 'Not knowing about the etiquette of golf, we were shouting to each other from either side of the fairway enquiring to positions of our golf balls, who had the honour, etc. We finally came in after 10, exhausted but so happy!'

That evening, Sue had a phone call from a Member of the Committee, complaining about her lack of etiquette and her behaviour on the Course 'and telling me I was never to set foot on the Golf Course again without being accompanied by a Member of the Committee! I went to see Captain Will but he told me to go and play with someone who knew the etiquette of golf and make sure I didn't open my mouth!' That was when the Greenkeeper of the time, Les Dean, took me under his wing. He marked my 4 golf cards and my handicap came in at 34. I was hooked!'

Her first Lady Captain's Day Competition...

Hilda Smith, the Lady Captain, had put on a special 10 Hole Competition for the beginners, the non-handicappers. Sue and Shirley were nervously waiting to tee off, knowing there were male visitors watching them. Sue went first but as she teed off she had an air shot and somehow, on the down swing, she made contact with the ball which then shot over the practice green. It hit a jug of orange squash which was ready for the half-way drink for the serious competitors. The men laughed and one of them offered her a fiver if she could do it again!

...how long is it supposed to take to play 10 holes?

Sue and Shirley often met up for 10 holes and Sue remembers they 'spent all the time on either side of the fairway, in the rough, hunting for our balls, and of course we would have to call people through. The time would thus easily mount up and we would be out for hours.' On one occasion, Sue recalls, as they came in at dusk, John Pilkington was on the point of sending out a search party for them!

For many years Sue's whole life revolved around Nefyn Golf Club and her handicap fell to 15. She remembers Marian, as Secretary, with great affection and thought the whole Section was wonderful. 'It was very much a Welsh Ladies' Section, one that I was so happy to belong to - such kindness, help and friendliness. In spite of being a non-Welsh speaker, it never mattered, I always felt part of the whole scene!'

WIL PARRY WILLIAMS

Treuliodd Wil Parry Williams (Wil Bwlch) ei gyfnod Coleg yn y Normal ym Mangor, ac yn dilyn cyfnod byr yn yr Awyrlu aeth i'w swydd gyntaf fel athro ym Mirmingham. Dychwelodd i Landudno cyn cael ei apwyntio'n Brifathro Ysgol Treborth, ger Bangor, lle y bu wrth y llyw am un mlynedd ar hugain tan ei ymddeoliad yn 1994.

Ymunodd Wil â Chlwb Golff Nefyn yn y pedwardegau ac yma cawn ei brofiadau cynnar.

Wil yn cael ei gyflwyno i golff...

Yn 1939, ac yntau'n saith oed ar gychwyn yr Ail Ryfel Byd, symudodd teulu Wil o Dudweiliog i Bwlch, Lôn Bridin, Morfa Nefyn. Doedd Wil erioed wedi gweld Clwb Golff na neb yn chwarae golff cyn hyn. Roedd hyn yn rhywbeth dieithr iawn iddo.

Daeth y cyfle cyntaf iddo ar ôl cael tri o hen glybiau golff gan Dennis Grace, Pro y Clwb. Roedd Dennis yn gefnogol a charedig iawn i'r criw o fechgyn ifanc y byddai Wil yn cyd-chwarae â hwy. Y criw yma fyddai'n gweithredu fel cadis ar foreau Sadwrn a hefyd yn casglu peli oedd chwaraewyr wedi'u colli dros allt Henblas neu Borthwen. Byddai'r bechgyn yn ennill arian poced trwy werthu'r peli yma i Dennis Grace.

...ac yn dechrau chwarae...

Cyn i'r bechgyn gael chwarae ar y Cwrs go iawn, byddent yn ymarfer trawo peli ar gaeau Porthdinllaen, gan brofi eu bod yn gyfrifol. Caent ymuno fel Aelodau Iau am 10/- y flwyddyn, a hynny'n cynnwys deg gwers am ddim gan Dennis Grace! Dyna fargen os bu un erioed!

Ar ôl mynd i Ysgol Botwnnog a chyfarfod â Stan Roberts (Stan Elidir neu Stan Scŵl fel y'i hadwaenid yn Edern), mab Prifathro Ysgol Edern, a Griff Roberts, mab Capten Roberts, Arwel, dechreuodd y tri chwarae'n rheolaidd. Mae'n siŵr fod y ffaith fod tad Stan a Griff yn Aelodau llawn yn help ac iddynt hwy eu hannog.

Byddai'r tri ohonynt yn ennill arian poced wrth bysgota, dal cwningod, cadio a chasglu peli a'i gwerthu i'r Pro. Eu prif ddiddordebau oedd beicio a chwarae golff. Cawsant lawer o hwyl a phleser a chwerthin wrth chwarae ar y Cwrs. Roedd Griff yn dipyn o 'waldiwr' a phan ddeuai pen y clwb i gyswllt iawn â'r bêl, byddai'n teithio'n bell iawn i gymharu â pheli Stan a Wil. Fodd bynnag, tueddai Griff i or-waldio! Un tro, cofia Wil i Griff waldio'r bêl oddi ar y ti cyntaf a pheri iddi wneud tro pedol, heibio wyneb y Clwb a glanio ymysg y ceir yn y maes parcio. Sôn am chwerthin, nes eu bod yn wan!

Pan ychydig yn hŷn, byddai'r tri yn chwarae gyda'u hathrawon yn Ysgol Botwnnog, Mr Glyn Owen a Mr Huw Roberts. Weithiau byddent yn mynd i Bwllheli i chwarae, ac ar adegau eraill byddai'r athrawon yn dod adref gyda'r criw i gael te cyn chwarae rownd ar gwrs harddaf Cymru! Dyna esiampl dda o berthynas arbennig rhwng athrawon a disgyblion.

Cofia Wil am un prynhawn arbennig, tua 1950, pan oedd yn helpu Dennis Grace yn y siop. Daeth dyn gweddol fychan o ran taldra, gyda gwallt tywyll wedi'i gribo'n daclus ac yn gwisgo siwt lwyd ddrudfawr, i mewn i'r siop. Nid oedd gan Wil syniad pwy oedd y gŵr bonheddig nes i Dennis Grace ei gyfarch fel 'Mr Rees'. Ie, yr enwog Dai Rees ydoedd, golffar o fri, yn wir un o oreuon ei gyfnod.

Roedd Dai Rees wedi dod i'r Clwb i chwarae gyda Wally Smithers, golffar adnabyddus arall o Glwb Long Ashton ger Bryste, yn erbyn dau Aelod o'r Clwb, y brodyr Robert Davies Owen a Willie Rees Owen, oedd yn olffwyr amatur safonol iawn eu hunain. Dewiswyd pedwar o hogia ifanc y Clwb, gan gynnwys Wil, i gadio am y ddwy rownd i'r sêr. Bu'n ddiwrnod i'w gofio a'i drysori. (Gwelir y bechgyn yn y llun sy'n dilyn, ar tud.244, a dynnwyd ar y diwrnod mawr.)

Y pleser mwyaf a gafodd Wil ar y prynhawn Gwener cyn yr ornest, oedd mynd gyda Dai Rees i'w gerbyd crand, Jaguar mawr llwyd. Agorodd Dai gist y car a rhyfeddodd Wil wrth weld tair set o glybiau golff, tua deg pâr o 'sgidiau a llond bag o beli golff Penfold. Gofynnodd Dai i Wil ei arwain i'r llain ymarfer lle bu'n taro un bêl ar ôl y llall am tua dwy awr, ac yntau wedyn yn mynd i'w casglu. Dyna'r wers golff orau gafodd Wil erioed. Rhyfeddai at gywirdeb y meistr. Cyn taro pêl, gofynnai Dai Rees i Wil, i ba gyfeiriad o'r postyn du a gwyn ar ben y bryn, tua hanner ffordd i lawr y twll cyntaf, y dymunai Wil ei weld yn taro! Byddai Wil yn dweud yn ei Saesneg gorau, 'llathen i'r chwith neu'r dde neu lathen yn fyr neu du draw i'r postyn' a Dai, yn ddieithriad, yn glanio'r bêl ar yr union fan. Welodd Wil erioed y fath gywirdeb!

Atgofion melys am y Clwb....
Cafodd Wil a'r hogia fagwrfa fendigedig ym Morfa Nefyn er ei bod yn amser rhyfel, gyda'r Clwb Golff yn rhan bwysig o'u bywyd. Cofia'r croeso, y pleser a'r boddhad a gawsant fel bechgyn ifanc ac mae'n dal i werthfawrogi'r profiadau pleserus ddaeth i'w rhan.

Dymuna Wil bob dymuniad da i'r Clwb yn y dyfodol.

...a'i dad...
Bu tad Wil, Huw Williams, yn edrych ar ôl Maes Parcio'r Golff yn Uwch-y-Don dros gyfnod yr haf am flynyddoedd gan gychwyn yn 1963. Un siriol iawn oedd Huw gyda'r holl Aelodau a byddai ganddo stori ddiddorol i wrando arni bob amser. Magwyd ef ym Mron Heulog, Bryn Mawr, Meillteyrn. Treuliodd ei oes yn saer maen ar Ystad Cefnamwlch, fel ei frodyr Robin a Tom. Ei swyddogaeth olaf, fel saer maen, oedd codi Bloc Gwyddoniaeth yn Ysgol Botwnnog ar ddechrau'r chwedegau cyn ei ymddeoliad yn 1963. Bu brawd arall iddo, Richie Glyn Williams, yn Gapten ar y Clwb yn 1954.

Wil Parry Wiliams (Wil Bwlch) qualified as a teacher in the Bangor Normal College and following a short period in the RAF, moved to his first teaching job in Birmingham. He returned to teach in Llandudno before being appointed Headmaster of Treborth Special School near Bangor. He was there for a period of twenty one years until his retirement in 1994.

Wil joined the Club in the 1940s and here he recalls his early experiences.

Wil is introduced to golf...
At the onset of the Second World War in 1939, when Wil was seven years old, his family moved from Tudweiliog to Bwlch, Lôn Bridin, Morfa Nefyn. Up to then Wil did not know of the existence of the Golf Club and certainly had never seen anyone playing golf!

Curiosity got the better of him and very soon, he was given three old clubs by Dennis Grace, the Professional. Wil was one of a group of young boys that Dennis encouraged and supported. This group operated as caddies on Saturday mornings as well as ball collectors down the Henblas and Borthwen cliffs!

...and begins to play...
Before the boys could play on the actual Course, they practised hitting golf balls on Porthdinllaen fields to prove they were 'proper golfers'. [Dennis always insisted beginners had to be of a certain standard before he allowed them on the Course.] They joined as Junior Members for 10/- a year and this included

10 free lessons from Dennis Grace!

After moving to Botwnnog School, Wil met Stan Roberts (Stan School), the son of the Edern School Headmaster, and Griff Roberts (Griff Arwel), the son of Capten Roberts, Arwel, Edern. The three of them started to play regularly. The fact that the other boys' fathers were full Members was a great help and they always encouraged the youngsters.

The lads earned their pocket money by fishing, catching rabbits, caddying and collecting golf balls and selling them to the Pro. Their main interests were biking and playing golf. Wil recalls the three lads had tremendous fun and enjoyment on the Course. 'Griff used to give the ball a good clout and if his driver happened to connect squarely with the ball, it went much further than Stan's or my ball. However, Griff used to over-hit and on one occasion he hit a ball off the first tee which made a u-turn in the air around the Clubhouse before landing amongst the cars in the car park. We doubled over with laughter!'

When they were a little older, the three would play golf with Mr Glyn Owen and Mr Huw Roberts, their schoolteachers at Ysgol Botwnnog. Sometimes they would go to Pwllheli to play and at other times, their teachers would come home with them for tea before playing a round at Nefyn. Such was the special relationship between teachers and pupils in those days!

Wil meets Dai Rees

Wil recalls one particular afternoon in 1950, when he was helping Dennis Grace in his shop. A short man with dark, well groomed hair appeared in the shop wearing an expensive grey suit. Wil had no idea who this gentleman was until Dennis Grace greeted him as 'Mr Rees'. Yes, indeed it was Dai Rees, the famous golfer, one of the best and most successful players of his day.

Dai Rees had arrived at the Club to play an Exhibition Match with Wally Smithers, from Long Ashton Golf Club, Bristol, another famous professional golfer. They were due to play against two brothers who were renowned amateur golfers playing off scratch and both

Wil caddies in the Exhibition Match with Dai Rees, June 1950.

I REMEMBER - DWI'N COFIO

Members of Nefyn Golf Club – Robert Davies Owen and Willie Rees Owen. Four local boys were selected to carry the gentlemen's bags, including Wil himself.

In the Photo on the previous page, Dai Rees is preparing to play the 8th Hole - 285 yards [by today, the 9th Hole]. In 1950, this hole was played from the present 9th tee to a green by the black and white marker post, half way up the 10th Hole as it is today. It is not surprising that this hole was called 'Angina Hill'!

In the photograph, Wil is seen in the patterned jumper on the left; Griff (Arwel) is behind him. Immediately to the left of Dai Rees are: Wally Smithers, Stan (School), Herbert Hughes and son David (who caddied for Dai Rees in the morning); Willie Rees Owen is crouching on the left and Robert, his brother is seen leaning on his driver, both of them smoking.

...and has a wonderful golf lesson.

Wil clearly remembers the Friday afternoon before the Match. Dai Rees wanted to practise and Wil was asked to assist him. He accompanied Dai Rees to his large grey Jaguar and when Dai opened the boot, Wil was amazed to see three sets of clubs, around ten pairs of shoes and a large bag full of Penfold golf balls. They went to the practice ground where Dai struck one ball after another down towards the 1st fairway. This went on for around two hours, after which Wil collected the balls. Wil marvelled at the master's accuracy and was enthralled by the experience. Before striking a ball, Dai Rees would ask Wil which direction from the black and white post half way down the 1st Hole would Wil like to see the ball land! Wil would reply in his best English, 'a yard to the right or a yard to the left, a yard short or a yard past the post.' Without exception, Dai would land the ball on the exact spot.

Fond memories of the Club

Wil confesses he and the boys had a wonderful upbringing in Morfa Nefyn even though it was wartime, and the Golf Club became an integral part of their lives. 'I remember the welcome each one of us received as young people. To this day, I still remember and appreciate the happiness we experienced and the opportunities we had. We were very lucky young lads to belong to Nefyn Golf Club.'

Huw Williams, on duty at the Uwch-y-Don Car Park, in the 60s.

Huw Williams, Wil's father

Wil's father, Huw Williams, seen standing outside the shed at the bottom of the Golf Road in the photograph above, was car park attendant for the Club over the summer period for many a year, starting in 1963. He was always cheerful as he greeted the Members and often had an interesting story to tell. He was brought up in Bron Heulog, Bryn Mawr, Meillteyrn (near Sarn). He spent his life as a stonemason with the Cefnamwlch Estate and his last duty as a stonemason was assisting in the building of the science block at Ysgol Botwnnog. This was at the beginning of the 1960s before his retirement in 1963. One of his Huw's brothers, Richie Glyn Williams, was Captain of the Club in 1954.

> **April 1968:** *It was reported that Hugh Williams had been engaged to police the Car Park over Easter and that there was an appreciable decrease in the processions on the 2nd half. (sic)*

DAVID PARSONAGE
1944-1971 - PROFESSIONAL

David's brother, Glyn, now living in Holyhead, relates David's story.

David's father, Stan, was appointed Coastguard at Porthdinllaen Station and was co-opted on to the Golf Club's Committee in September 1957. He remained on Committee until he was posted to Holyhead in late 1961. In the same year, his 17 year old son, David, was asked to deputise for Dennis Grace on Sundays.

David's younger brother, Glyn, was also brought up playing golf at Nefyn but was never up to David's standard. Glyn was happier when he was asked to sing to the Members accompanied on the guitar by Hampton, the Steward (a cousin of Michael Holliday, the pop star).

David, like so many youngsters brought up at Nefyn in the 50s and 60s, was a protégé of Dennis Grace, the Professional, and in fact was his Official Assistant at one time. It was customary for wealthy visitors to ask the Professional if he or any of his assistants were available to play, obviously for a fee! Dennis Grace would suggest that the visitor could play with one of the boys which included David, aged thirteen or fourteen at the time. The visitor would eventually agree to play for a fee of £1 (sponsored by Dennis Grace). David was told to play a close game but lose on the 18th so that the visitor would come back for another challenge!

David won a large Silver Salver in one competition at Pwllheli Golf Club in the early 1960s. This salver has subsequently been presented by his brother Glyn in David's memory to the Junior Section at the Club in the Centenary Year.

Reference is made to David Parsonage's success in the Welsh Boys' Championship at Llandrindod in the Minutes of September 1960. He went on to win several other junior tournaments and, still aged 16, was invited to play with the Welsh Seniors' Squad. On two occasions he broke the course record at Conwy whilst playing with the Welsh Seniors. He also captained the Welsh Junior Team.

Following a period as Assistant to Dennis Grace, David went to the Royal Liverpool Golf Club, Hoylake, as an Apprentice Professional. Thereafter, he served in a number of golf clubs, including Wentworth and was at the Anglesey Golf Club at Rhosneigr for some years. Members at both Nefyn and Rhosneigr still recall some of his quite amazing drives covering incredible yardage!

David generated a great deal of power in his swing as can be seen by the wonderful sequence of stills on the following page.

David at 15 years of age with a number of trophies he won as a junior, including the Silver Salver.

I REMEMBER - DWI'N COFIO

246

This sequence of David's swing was taken at Anglesey Golf Club, Rhosneigr.

David was appointed Professional at Erewash Valley Golf Club, Derbyshire and while there, he competed in the Open Championship at Carnoustie in 1968. He finished in a very creditable 21st position.

During his professional career, David broke course records on a number of courses. He was facing a brilliant future when he tragically died, aged 27, in November 1971.

MARK PILKINGTON
PROFESSIONAL
2007 -   HONORARY MEMBER

Below is a summary of an interview with Mark - by Duncan Smith, the Club's Press Officer.

Mark Pilkington, the eldest child of John and Glenys Pilkington, was born in Bangor on the 17th March, 1978 and brought up in Morfa Nefyn, attending the village school and then Ysgol Glan-y-Môr in Pwllheli. His father was the Professional at Nefyn from 1975 until 1993, and through his early tutoring, Mark went on to become a golfer of international repute at amateur and professional level.

Mark recalls the early years at Nefyn...
It must have been when he was four or five that Mark remembers holding a golf club for the first time. During his school years, his father encouraged him and from the start, he loved practising and experimenting with his swing. 'Nefyn was a great place to learn to play golf,

learning to play in the wind and on fast running fairways, where conditions were never the same two days running. I always loved playing the Point, every hole presenting a different sort of challenge.'

...and the support he received from the Members

Mark remembers the support he had from the Members even at the age of 10 and 11. There was always an invitation from them to play in the Saturday Swindle, until he started winning frequently! He recalls the help he received from members like Bob Entwistle, Dennis Humpherson, the late Derek Clulow, Robin Parry and, of course, Capt Will, 'who was always keen to know how I was getting on, particularly as he was so involved in the Welsh Golfing Union'. Often the Tournaments would be in South Wales and Mark remains grateful to Dennis particularly, as Junior Organiser, and others, who drove him down south after school on a Friday so he could play the following day.

His golf improves by leaps and bounds...

By the age of 13, he was down to single figures and it was at that age, in 1990, he remembers winning his first major Club Competition at Nefyn, the Courtenay Lord Cup. He went on to win this Cup again in 1994 and 1996. Mark also won other Majors at the Club, the Cynfelin Jones Trophy (1992), the Wynne-Finch Cup (1994) and the ROC Trophy (1996).

It was at the age of 12, that Mark had his first taste of competition outside the club scene. This was when he played in the National Junior Under 15s Golf Tournament.

At the age of 15, he was representing Wales as a Junior in the Welsh Boys' Team Championships and at 17, he won the Welsh Youth Championship at Porthmadog with scores of 71 and 68.

At 18, he was selected to represent his country at senior level, which he did for three seasons. 'It was at that time that I met and played alongside amateurs who were subsequently to move, like myself, into the professional ranks - Bradley Dredge, Stephen Dodds and David Park. I also remember playing at that time against the likes of Justin Rose, Paul Casey and on one occasion at Harlech, against Sergio Garcia. He doesn't seem to have changed a bit in fact, since that time I met him at Harlech,' says Mark.

At the AGM of March 1997, Barry Owens, our Secretary/Manager, highlighted some of Mark's achievements during an outstanding 1996 season. He had won the North Wales Four Counties Championship, the Caernarfonshire County Championship, the Harlech Bowl at Royal St David's, the Gwynedd Boys' Championship [5th Time], the Pwllheli Town Bowl, the Peter McEvoy Trophy, the 1996 Golf Foundation Award, had been Runner-up in the British Boys' Championship and had been selected for Full Welsh squad training in Portugal!

The young Mark Pilkington proudly wears his Welsh Boys' Team Championship Blazer.

Young Mark Pilkington partners Nell Hughes in a Mixed Competition with markers James Bentley and Anne Thomas.

...and he joins the Professional Ranks....

Winning the Welsh Amateur Championship at Prestatyn in 1998 was a turning point in Mark's career because he decided to make the transition into the professional ranks. At that time, Mark was in the Walker Cup squad and some people urged him to delay his decision to turn pro in order to represent Britain. 'It would have been an honour, naturally, but selection wasn't guaranteed and so I risked losing a year.'

Mark elected to go to the Qualifying School in Spain in 1998 as an amateur and finished 16th, thereby earning his card. He immediately turned professional. He played for a year on the European Tour but unfortunately lost his card at the end of it.

'It was a massive change from the amateur ranks, not only in the standard of the players, but also the travelling and staying away. There was so much going on around you apart from playing the game, that in spite of having a management company looking after me, it was sometimes hard to stay focused on the golf. As an amateur, if you had a bad tournament, you'd have a couple of weeks, maybe, to sort it out before playing again. On the main tour, there was a tournament somewhere every week and you felt you had to keep playing to stay in touch. I had some good tournaments, but it was overwhelming! The only thing I could do was to keep trying.'

At the Nefyn AGM of March 1999, Mark was presented with a cut glass and silver claret jug by Captain Neville Ingman, to commemorate his success on joining the professional ranks.

...but the competition is intense

In 2000, Mark joined the Challenge Tour and at the end of that year, regained his card for the 2001 season at the Qualifying School.

Extract from http://news.bbc.co.uk):

Wales' Mark Pilkington shrugged off a 4:45am alarm call to fire a brilliant first-round 63 in the Qatar Masters in Doha on Thursday, 8th March 2001. Pilkington was first off at 6:30am local time and arrived with the course still in darkness and floodlights blazing on the practice range..... Starting on the par five 10th, the former Spanish and Welsh Amateur champion hit a four iron to 20 feet to set up an eagle and then added four birdies to be out in 30, with three more birdies coming home.

The following November, Mark and his father John, at the request of the Captain, Spud Taylor, were the guest speakers at the Club's Annual Dinner, at the Nanhoron Arms Hotel in Nefyn. They gave the Members a first-hand insight into 'Life on Tour' as they recounted their many varied experiences.

Mark recalls that 2002 was a good year with a couple of top four finishes and an 80th place on the Order of Merit. 'My fourth place at the Celtic Manor in the Welsh Open was probably one of the most enjoyable results of that year', he adds.

In 2003 however, Mark was not as fortunate. He lost his card and returned to the Challenge Tour for the next three years. He admits the Challenge Tour has changed a lot in the last few years. 'Now, it's played on some fantastic courses with good crowds and, of course, there's more sponsorship available. The season-long challenge of virtually every week a tournament in some part of the world, prepares you very well and the standards are very high now. A higher percentage of players from the Challenge Tour will retain their cards than those who gain it through the Qualifying School.'

2006 - The joys...

The Final of the 2006 European Challenge Tour took place in October at the San Domenico Golf Club in Italy. The top 45 professionals battled it out for the coveted 25 cards available for the main European Tour for 2007 and Mark tied for second place at 11 under par. Not only did he secure his playing privileges but also topped the rankings of the 2006 European Challenge Tour beating his nearest rival and long-time leader of the rankings, Johann Axgren by over 13,000 euros. 'Getting into the top ten had been my initial goal for the year, but to finally come out on top of the Tour rankings after such a long and exhausting season was a real confidence boost. Knowing I've done it will definitely help in the future, when the pressure is on,' commented Mark.

In what was arguably one of the best year in Mark's professional career to date, he achieved three top 20 finishes, two top 10 finishes, three top 2 finishes and that all-important first tour win of his professional career, in Kazakhstan. Here he took the biggest purse of the year on the Tour.

'I couldn't have timed it better, I suppose; it really was something special to get that first professional tour win. The Arnold Palmer-designed Course was fantastic and there were reasonable crowds following the event throughout.'

...and the disappointments

The Challenge Tour at Nefyn in June 2006, brought a different kind of challenge for Mark. Playing in front of his home crowd brought extra pressure as he knew their expectations of him were quite high!

'Obviously, I wanted to do well and felt I ought to do well, so I suppose that made me try a little bit too hard. Naturally, you do feel a bit of pressure in front of your home crowd. Having the support, though, was great. Most other pros had maybe half a dozen people following them, whereas I was lucky enough to have a sizeable entourage with me every day. I did enjoy it, though Saturday was very tough for everyone and a couple of those new tees, particularly at the 2nd - no chance of driving the green these days - and the 15th have made quite a difference!'

Mark was disappointed in not making the cut at The Open at Royal Liverpool G C in Hoylake, in July 2006. In the first round, he shot 4 over Par and in the second, 4 under to bring him in at Even for the two days. He came within just one shot of qualifying for the last two days. 'I played brilliantly to qualify and Thursday was really disappointing. I then played well on the Friday, going out last. It was frustrating not to make it and I felt a bit down, but that's the way it goes.'

2007

Mark returned to the Main Tour in 2007 feeling that the tough experiences of the Challenge Tour would stand him in good stead. Having finished top of the Order of Merit on the Challenge Tour, he was assured of invitations to almost every big event on the European Tour.

His 2007 season began well (actually in early December 2006) with a top 10 finish at Leopards Creek, South Africa. Unfortunately, Mark's golf was inconsistent during the season and he was unable to make the cut in several European Tour Events. As a result, he sadly failed to retain his card for the 2008 season. He will now concentrate on the Challenge Tour and will have invitations into some of the European Tour Events.

And the future?...

Mark would welcome the opportunity to play in the States at some time, but recognises that it is something to which one has to commit fully to be successful. 'Splitting oneself across the Tours would be difficult and would be a big upheaval. However, I believe my long and high game would be suited to the American courses.'

Mark Pilkington with his father John, at the Open in Hoylake, July 2006.

Mark's father has been his mentor, coach and caddie for many years and Mark gratefully acknowledges 'the massive support I've had from my dad, even through the years when I've been struggling. Being a pro and a coach, the approach has been a little different, but on the course, it's not so much father and son, more player and coach, and it works for us. It's been great over the years having him there.' Carrying the massive pro's bag in the 30 degree heat of Leopards Creek however, may have had something to do with the fact that although John will continue as Mark's coach, he will no longer caddy for Mark.

Mark is looking forward to the new 2008 season. At the time of writing, he feels happier with his game than he has in a long time. All of us at Nefyn follow his career with interest and pride and wish him well in the future.

The Club still displays the two record breaking rounds Mark shot around Nefyn. The first was in 1995 at the age of 17, when he had a 67 nett off a handicap of 1 on the New Course [opened 1994]. The second was in 1998, when he had a remarkable Gross 64 off a handicap of +3 (67 nett) in the Tweedale Cup. In this particular round, he scored a record nine birdies.

At our 2007 AGM, as we brought in our Centenary Year, Mark was elected an Honorary Member of Nefyn Golf Club.

I Remember - Dwi'n Cofio

CLUB PROFESSIONALS 'Y PROS'

Gwŷr Proffesiynol Nefyn

Roedd ychydig o ddirgelwch ynglŷn â'r gwŷr yma ar y cychwyn, gan y cyfeiriwyd at y rhai cynnar fel 'y Pro'. Yng Nghofnodion y Clwb cyfeiriwyd at ddau 'bro' o'r enw Jones yn y blynyddoedd cynnar. Tybed ai'r Tom Jones a fu'n 'Bro' am hanner can mlynedd yng Nghlwb Maesdu yn ddiweddarach oedd un ohonynt? Yn dilyn J H Jones, a edrychai ar ôl y cwrs ynghyd â gwerthu peli trwy'r degau a'r dauddegau, penodwyd L A A Riley am gyfnod byr yn 1931.

Yn Hydref 1932, penodwyd Dennis Grace yn 'Bro' gan gychwyn ar gyfnod ymestynnol iawn. Dan adain Mr Grace, magwyd cenedlaethau o olffwyr ifanc ac yn sgil hyn, etholwyd ef yn Aelod Anrhydeddus o'r Clwb yn 1976.

Dilynwyd Dennis Grace gan John Pilkington yn 1975 ac arhosodd John gyda ni tan y penodwyd John Froom, ein 'Pro' presennol, yn 1993.

Earliest References to a 'Pro' 1908 - 1911
The mysterious 'Jones'

There appears to be some mystery surrounding the early years in relation to the appointment of a Professional. It is not reported who he was or whence he came. The first reference to a Pro was in a Balance Sheet for the AGM in 1908 showing 'The Wages of the Professional and extra labour' for the year standing at £53-10-3. The next reference to a Pro was in a Committee Meeting of Sept 1909, where it was resolved that 'the pro be kept conditionally till November and that the pro's shop should be rebuilt'. The Pro, still un-named, attended the Committee Meeting that November and it was decided that his services should be retained.

In October 1909, we find there was indeed a Pro named Jones who played against Bowman, the Pwllheli Pro, in a return Match at Home against Pwllheli.

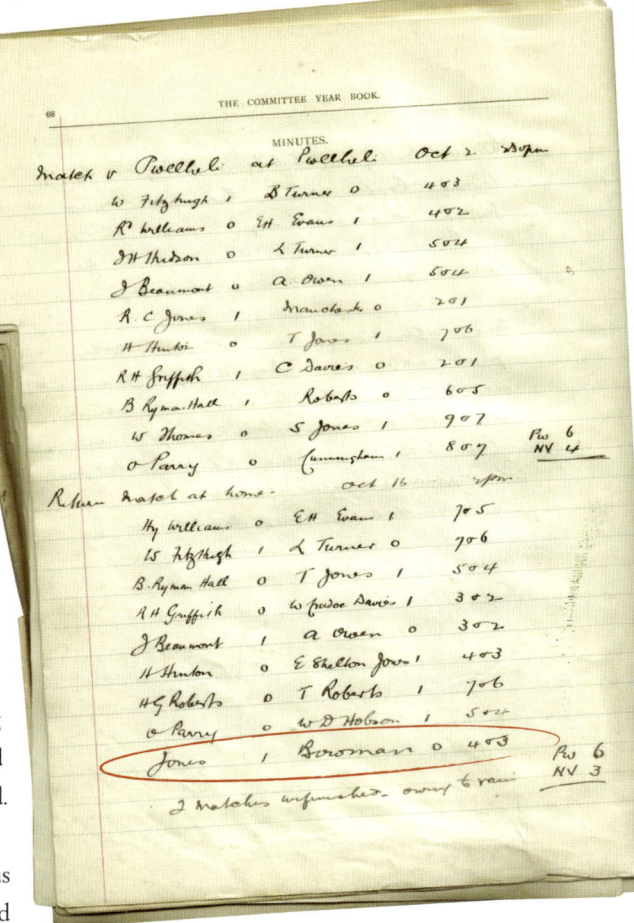

Results of the Return Match with Pwllheli, October 16th 1909, showing Jones winning 4 & 3

These matches continued at Home and Away in 1910.

But who was the mysterious Jones? Had he been in position from the inauguration of the Club? There is every reason to believe that he was in fact a certain Tom Jones who began his apprenticeship at the Great Orme Club, Llandudno and then, according to his daughter and grandson, he moved to Nefyn, where he served as Pro for 3 years. (His daughter is Elsie Brown, a former Welsh International Golfer and his grandson is Clive Brown, ex-Welsh Amateur Champion, Welsh International and Captain of the successful Walker Cup side at Porthcawl, in 1995).

Tom Jones in later years as Captain of the PGA

The following is an extract of a conversation with Clive Brown:

'In 1912, Tom moved to Nefyn to serve as the Pro for three years. He returned to Llandudno, to Maesdu Golf Club in 1915 where he was instrumental in designing and building that Course. In 1929, a prize of £3-3-0 was given to him in a Best Course Improvement Suggestion Competition sponsored by Nefyn Golf Club. Following this, Tom Jones was asked to visit Nefyn to advise on course design. He was the first Golf Professional in Wales to be elected Captain of his own Club, at Maesdu. He died in 1967 at the age of 74.'

Much of Clive's information is confirmed in the Minutes and very much later, in March 1965, it is reported that '£10 be sent from the Club to Tom Jones' Testimonial Fund, on the occasion of his retirement from Maesdu'.

There is however, no mention in the Minutes of a Tom Jones being in employment at the Club between 1912 and 1915 in spite of discussions regarding the appointment of a Pro being reported at that time. His daughter and grandson are equally adamant that Tom Jones was the Professional at Nefyn for three years and the only possible explanation is that his three years spanned 1908 - 1911 when 'Jones the Pro' was very much in evidence.

(See Photo of the newly built thatched-roof Clubhouse of 1908 with the lean-to Pro's 'Shed' visible in the foreground in the Captains' Chapter, 1909, B Ryman-Hall.)

1911 – 1913

In February 1911, 70 applications were received for the position of Pro of which two were short-listed. Both then withdrew and it was agreed to appoint an apprentice from Hoylake (un-named) on a month's trial, after which he was retained.

When the new Clubhouse was opened in the summer of 1911, it was reported that the separately constructed Pro's 'Shop' had undergone improvements and the insurance on the Shop was £40 with £10 for the Pro's effects. However, by September, it had been decided to dispense with the services of the Pro for the time being and in February 1912, the Committee confirmed yet again there was no need for a Pro.

CLUB PROFESSIONALS - 'Y PROS'

First named Professional
J H Jones - 1913 - 1931

A year later however there was a change of opinion and in June 1913, John Henry Jones, who was the current Greenkeeper was asked to undertake the duties of 'Professional' for the summer season, until September 30th. His wages were to be one guinea (£1-1-0) per week and he was allowed to profit on the sale of golf balls and clubs. A boy was retained to work on the Course for 6/- per week together with a Griffith Davies at a £1 per week.

J H Jones had come to Nefyn originally as Greenkeeper in September 1911 from North Wales Golf Club, Llandudno, on the recommendation of Collins, (the Pro at North Wales) to work on the extension of the Course to the 18 holes that Collins had designed. As Greenkeeper, his wage in 1911 had been £1-7-0 per week and so he actually took a decrease in wage to become the Pro!

J H Jones is the first person to be actually appointed and named as a Professional at the Club. In September 1913, he reverted to the position of Greenkeeper for the winter and spring months, from Oct 1st to April 30th, and this at his previous wage of £1-7-0.

The war years intervened and the Course was closed. All eligible and able-bodied men were serving in the armed forces and other staff were laid-off. It was not until 1919 that the desirability of having a Pro was again discussed but the Committee found it impossible to pay for one. Thus, in April of that year, it was suggested that J H Jones be re-employed as Groundsman (change of terminology from Greenkeeper) and permitted to mend clubs etc. outside working hours. This continued until 1922, when on July 24th, it was resolved 'that J H Jones be placed in the position of Professional in same terms as Bowman, Pwllheli for the months of July and August.' (sic)

In September 1925, it was passed that J H Jones 'sweep out the Club room when required.... and remove all dogs he has at the Club House with the exception of one and if he wishes to breed dogs, he is to do so at his home' (sic).

'...to remove all dogs he has at the Club House...'

In 1926, J H Jones' Pro's wages were raised to £2-10-0 per week 'all year round'. In December 1928, a second fire totally destroyed the Clubhouse, the outbuildings and the Members' and Pro's effects. A new Clubhouse, on the present site, was opened in August 1929 and the Pro was given a purpose-built shed to continue his work.

> **July 1922:** *Proposed and seconded that if Jones (Pro) should see anyone playing on the links on Sundays, that he takes their name and that they be prosecuted.*
>
> **August 1929:** *Passed that J H Jones (The Pro) be admitted to the Club House when invited by a member during July and August only and in his capacity as Pro and not as the Greenkeeper.*

L A A Riley - 1931 - 1932

In March 1931, J H Jones tendered his resignation and L A A Riley, 'late Pro of Penmaenmawr' was offered the position of Pro in April 1931.

The Course (17th and 1st Greens) in the 30s showing poor state of the Course.

By June 1931, numerous complaints had been received by the Committee concerning the poor state of the Course and it was obvious that Riley was a complete disappointment. There followed 18 months of unrest and dissatisfaction. Finally, in September 1932, the Green Committee recommended the termination of his employment and he was dismissed, in spite of an appeal.

Dennis Grace - 1932 - 1940

29 applications for a 'working Professional' were then considered and four were called for interview on 6th October 1932. Dennis Grace, aged 24, from Maesdu Golf Club was appointed after a unanimous vote from the Committee. It may have been due to the problems with Riley, and his lack of understanding and interpretation of his role, that led to the drawing up of a Contract for Grace.

There is only a draft version available but this laid down quite clearly what his duties were to be. His commitment as a working Professional was spelled out, from his work on the Course under the direction of Chairman of the Green Committee to the number of hours he was expected to open his shop and be available for Members. 'Any insubordination, misconduct or deliberate breach of trust shall be subject to instant dismissal', otherwise any termination of contract was to be one month's notice from either side. Wages, sick pay, holiday entitlement – all were clearly explained and documented and it was 'agreed that the said Dennis Grace is prohibited in the use of the Clubhouse'!

Dennis Grace's starting wage is not known but 3 months later, in January 1933, it is documented his wages were increased to £2-0-0 per week.

Grace was actively involved in working on the Course under the direction of the Green Committee e.g. on March 24th 1934 Grace was instructed 'to make a very light dressing of ICI fertiliser on the greens and to use the Atco mower for the first cutting after which only the hand mower was to be used on the greens'.

In September 1934, there was reported a criticism of Grace's work and his 'flagging interest in the welfare of the Course'. This, however, appears to be have been amicably resolved.

The mid 1930s saw a considerable amount of work undertaken on the Course under the direction of the Greens' (now changing from Green) Committee and the supervision by Grace. Grace frequently attended Committee Meetings and his opinion was obviously valued. He succeeded in getting his Assistant put on the Pay Sheet of the Club and in April 1936, in getting 'an extra man put on for weeding greens' – a practice that continued each summer for many years. He also succeeded in getting the Committee to agree that any employee finding golf balls on the Course 'must only dispose of them to the Professional' and not sell them for private gain!

> **September 1936:** *The Greens' Committee reported many routine matters such as condition of bunkers, position of Tee Boxes, uncut rough etc. came under notice and the attention of the Professional in charge of the workmen was verbally directed to the omissions. (sic)*

It was acknowledged that much of Grace's time was involved with Members and visitors in the vicinity of the Clubhouse during the busy summer period. From the following year, he was relieved of the work of cutting the greens near the Clubhouse to give him more time to inspect the Course.

In 1937, Grace played in two Golf Professional Competitions, at Rhyl and Conwy. In the same year, he was given the use of part of the 9th Fairway (today's 11th hole on the New Course), near the hedge, for giving lessons to non-members at a charge of 4/- with 1/- to go to the Club! In October, the Committee paid for Grace to attend a 6 day Greenkeepers' Conference.

> **June 1938:** *Committee agreed to allow Seth Jones, Grace's assistant, to practise golf on the course at suitable times and, if desired, to play games with local members of the Club. The lad is not allowed to play with visitors for money until such time that the Committee are satisfied that he is sufficiently proficient at the game!*

In October 1938, Grace's two year old son, Albert, died and this had a profound effect both emotionally and physically on Grace. By January 1940, it was reported that he was no longer capable of undertaking physical work. There followed much discussion over the ensuing months and finally in April 1943 Grace was dismissed.

Sidney Ball and Pierce Hughes · 1940 - 1945

On April 12th 1940, Sidney Ball from Manchester was appointed as a combined Professional/Greenkeeper, to cover Grace's work. There were a few problems with Ball and he finally resigned in March 1943.

Mr J Pierce Hughes, Groundsman, was then given the opportunity to 'carry out repairs to clubs of Members and visitors during the evenings and on Saturday afternoons, in his own time, and for this purpose he would be allowed the use of the Professional's Shop'.

Grace Returns as Professional · 1945 - 1975

J Pierce Hughes continued this practice for many months but in September 1945, the Club again gave serious thought to appointing a permanent professional and A D Grace was re-appointed. His contract was again clearly laid out and at the AGM of 1946, the retiring Captain, Wing Cmdr Horatio Sleigh, referred to the appointment of A D Grace as Professional and stated '...the present excellent condition of the Course more than justifies his appointment and testifies his capabilities'.

> **November 1954:** *Resolved that the Club donate £2 without prejudice towards the Professional's broken dentures!*

Dennis Grace practising his putting in 1957

Ironically, Grace's Contract still did not allow him in to the Clubhouse except while on duty! He had to wait until February 1959 when, 'as a token of appreciation of the Professional's loyalty and devotion to the Club, it was unanimously agreed to allow him the use of the Clubhouse and all the privileges there-in – well knowing that such a favour would not be abused'!

In 1949, Grace suffered a long illness but recovered and during the following years he continued to work diligently for the Club.

In 1960, Grace's Contract was reviewed. It was agreed he be offered £9-10-0 per week in winter (with one day off) and £6 per week with no manual work in the summer. As a comparison, Donald and Evan Williams, the groundsmen, were on £10 a week!

There followed some fiery moments in the 60s with some disagreements between Grace and the Committee. It was at this time that he was admitted to the Llangwyfan TB Sanatorium in Denbighshire (1964). When he returned, Grace was offered a twelve-month 'Pro only contract' which he welcomed. Twelve months later, he was offered his former Contract as he 'had given satisfaction to a good degree'!

> **July 1971:** *It was reported that a child had taken a Member's golf ball off the fairway and sold it to the Professional, who, on being asked to return it to the player by the Captain and Lady Captain, refused unless he was reimbursed with the 9d he had paid for it!*

It is unclear what took place between 1965 and his retirement in May 1975. It is known he had another long illness. He was reported to have been taken ill in Blackpool in 1967 and a relapse occurred within months. How long he was off work is unclear but, we are told, at the AGM of 1975, that 'Dennis Grace was welcomed back after his prolonged illness'.

Dennis Grace in a familiar pose, observing an Exhibition Match in 1970

CLUB PROFESSIONALS - 'Y PROS'

In recognition of his long service to the Club (although far short of the 45 years he himself claimed!) a Testimonial Fund was set up. In October 1975, this Fund stood at £1647. It was decided at Committee that the Club would increase this by a further £1000 from Club Funds. At the AGM of 1976, Dennis Grace was elected the first (?) Honorary Member of Nefyn and District Golf Club, an honour he held until his death in 1980.

[It was minuted that Honorary Members were introduced for the first time in 1975. However, research shows that Gwynedd Jones was elected Honorary Member in 1930 and before him, the local District Nurse had been elected an Honorary Member on December 5th 1922!]

Outside Nefyn, Dennis Grace played in the Caernarfonshire and District Golfing Union Championship but nothing much further afield. He became an established Starter at prestigious North Wales events and he nurtured and encouraged David Parsonage, his Assistant, who had success at the Welsh Boys' Championship in Llandrindod Wells in 1960.

Members remember Dennis Grace with great affection. He was a cheery little fellow and was very much a Members' Pro. His personality and sense of fun made him friends with everyone with whom he came into contact – from all over the world. During his time at Nefyn, he had suffered many serious illnesses but always with dignity and courage.

Many of our present golfers owe much to his teaching skills and encouragements. Leslie Edwards, writing in 'The Game that was Golf' (Fore Golf Publications, Ltd, Dovercourt, 1992) reports that the celebrations to mark his retirement lasted over several days:

'The juniors opened their piggy banks and presented him with a pen and pencil set (to work out his racing bets); the senior juniors threw a champagne party and gave him a solid silver fruit dish, a member from Chester had a special cake baked for the occasion and the ladies contributed a silver table lighter.'

Members turned out en bloc for his retirement party and he was presented with a cheque for £2,647. Merched y Glannau sang and included one song with words parodied to the tune of 'Amazing Grace'. It was a truly memorable evening.

The Era of the Modern Professional
J R Pilkington · Aug 1975 · May 1993

In August 1975, John R Pilkington was appointed Pro at £30 per week (£10 more than the minimum recommended by the PGA) with a 2.5% commission on Green Fees. Although Steven R Griffiths had been appointed Head Greenkeeper in July 1976 on a salary of £2,500 per annum, in September 1978, it was John who was designated Course Supervisor, to liaise between the Committee and the Greens Staff. After Griffiths resigned in 1987, John was asked to take on the role of Advisory Head Greenkeeper while Patrick McAteer, the Head Greenkeeper designate, was qualifying at College. In November 1989, John was relieved of this duty when Patrick was formally appointed Head Greenkeeper.

Before he accepted the post at Nefyn, John had been the Professional at Wirral Ladies' Golf Club and had been heavily involved in teaching. He had also been offered the post at Royal Liverpool

Golf Club but he chose Nefyn because he had always wanted to live in Wales!

While at Wirral Ladies' Golf Club, John had made a name for himself as an extremely gifted teacher and had his own regular Golf Lessons' Column in both the West Cheshire and the Liverpool Echo Newspapers. He was also featured in a Welsh medium book about the art of playing golf, entitled 'Cerdd Daro' which was written by William Lloyd Griffith who hails from Edern. This book won first prize in the National Eisteddfod of Wales (1979) in the category 'Coaching Book for any Game'. In acknowledging John's contribution to this book, Wil Lloyd described him as 'Nefyn and District's Professional and one of Wales' leading golf coaches'.

From Left to Right: Gareth Wyn Jones, G S Owen (Griff Bodelen), John Pilkington and Patrick McAteer in a Pro-Am at Nefyn.

(Right) Mark Pilkington, with his father John, on the 4th at Nefyn, during the Challenge Tour, June 2006.

Because of his commitment to teaching, John did not play a great deal of tournament golf. He did, however, have some success in the professional ranks with his greatest win being the Euro Challenge at Royal Birkdale in 1976.

He continued his teaching commitment at Nefyn and was particularly involved in Junior Golf. His Junior Protégés included John Thomas, Dyfed Parry Thomas and our Centenary Ladies' Captain, Fiona Vaughan Thomas. He was also instrumental in getting both his sons, Mark and Stuart, interested in golf from a very early age.

In the early 90s, John became involved with coaching on the European Tour. In February 1993, he tendered his resignation and although the Committee requested he should reconsider his decision, he finally departed from the Club in May of the same year.

He moved on from Nefyn to take on a dual role in coaching with the Tour and teaching privately at the Pen-y-Berth Driving Range at Penrhos near Pwllheli. He later became the Professional at Pwllheli Golf Club, where his son Stuart is now the Teaching Professional. Stuart follows in his father's footsteps and is gaining a similar reputation as a first rate teacher.

John is now very much involved with coaching on the European Tour as well as the Challenge Tour. Philip Price (Pontypridd) and David Howell (Swindon) are two of his tutees from a long list of professionals on the European Tour. He has also been caddying for son Mark on both Tours but now concentrates more on the coaching side.

CLUB PROFESSIONALS - 'Y PROS'

J A Froom - May 1993 -

In April 1993, eight professionals were interviewed from 32 applicants, and John Andrew Froom of Solihull was appointed Professional at Nefyn.

John started his professional career in 1983 as a Junior Assistant at Kings Norton Golf Club, Wythall in the Midlands. Following periods as Assistant at South Herts London, and Ladbroke Park in Warwickshire, he joined the Robin Hood Golf Centre, Cheltenham, as Professional Manager in 1987. After returning as Head Professional to Ladbroke Park, he took on teaching positions at both Schloss Ludesburg and Gottingen Golf Clubs in Germany before returning to the UK in 1993.

John's golfing prowess was apparent at an early stage when he was a Member of the Warwickshire County Boys and Youth Teams. As a Professional, he became a leading area qualifier for the Peugeot National with a score of 68, and a National Qualifier (Blackwell Heath) for the British Open with a score of 69. Locally, his wins have included a Course Record Score of 68 in a Pro-Am at Abergele, a 69 at Rhuddlan when he won the Pro-Am and a 68 at Royal St David's, Harlech. He thoroughly enjoys a challenge from Members and visitors alike on the Nefyn Course and plays regularly in the North Wales Alliance throughout the winter.

In recent years John has maintained his Class AAA status as a Professional through residential courses at the Belfry. He is a qualified Tri golf tutor, a recognised teacher for HSBC Bank and has been a commentator for an American Golf Channel.

John's contribution to the Junior coaching at the Club is discussed in the Junior Section Chapter.

At the end of 2006, John worked alongside the Ladies' Section to promote Ladies' and Girls' Golf at the Club. The scheme known as the 'Ladies' Taster Scheme', sponsored by Golf Development Wales, was set up in response to dwindling numbers of lady golfers in a national trend. It was a concerted effort to introduce golf to ladies who had never shown any prior interest in the game. It involved John teaching groups of novice lady golfers over a period of twelve months, ably assisted by some Lady Members and the occasional Male Member. The Club responded by offering various packages and the scheme has successfully resulted in an influx of 17 new Lady Members to the Club.

John has other interests apart from his golf. He is keen to keep fit and regularly attends the gym. He enjoys table tennis and has played for the England Schoolboys' Team and the Birmingham Seniors' Team. He also enjoys football and in his youth played for the South Birmingham under 16s.

Happily married to Ali, John has three young children, Harriet 12, Hannah 10 and Tom aged 8.

Hannah and Tom have both shown an interest in golf. Hannah won an Open Junior Competition in her age group at Porthmadog and Tom is beginning to bring in some awards. In the 2007 Junior Presentation, he was praised for reducing his Club handicap by 12 and being Runner-up in the new Bannau Trophy.

He was also named the Best Putter among the Juniors for the second year running, which will not surprise Members who see him regularly on the Putting Green!

John, with his wife Alison and children Tom, Hannah and Harriet

The Assistant Professionals
John Pilkington's Era
The following were appointed as Assistant Pros between 1975 and 1993, during John Pilkington's Era. Ken Lamb left to become a Pro at Warren Park, Wallasey; Mike Bradley went to teach in Germany and Austria; Steven Laidler was also a Barman at the Club at the time but his destination is unknown; and Alan Drosinos Jones, is currently the Pro in Abersoch.

John Froom's Era
Since John Froom's appointment, the following have served as Assistant Pros from 1993-2005: Mathew Tomlinson, now teaching in Berlin; Gwyndaf Jones, now Manager, Oriel Glyn-y-Weddw, Llanbedrog; Paul Bright, PGA Qualified, now teaching in Austria; Gareth Dobson Jones, Teaching Pro at Sandiway; and Danny Martinez-Perez, PGA Qualified, and now Teaching Pro at Fore Golf, Chester.

James Salt, was appointed in March 2007. James was a Member at Nefyn for many years and won the Club Championship in 1999 and 2001 together with the Tweedale Challenge Trophy in 2000. He achieved a handicap of +2 as an amateur before taking up a golf scholarship in the USA. He then became a Tournament Pro in Doha Golf Club in Qatar before joining us at Nefyn as a PGA Trainee. James continues to play in the Regional Assistants' Tournaments.

CUPS AND COMPETITIONS
CWPANAU A CHYSTADLEUTHAU

Un cais a gafwyd gan sawl Aelod, wrth hel manylion a chofnodion am hanes y Clwb, oedd sut y daeth y gwpan yma a'r tlws acw i feddiant y Clwb a pha fath o gystadleuaeth oedd yn bodoli wrth chwarae amdanynt yn yr hen ddyddiau. Isod, ceir hanes y cwpanau, pwy a'u cyflwynodd hwy i'r Clwb, sut gystadleuaeth a chwaraeir amdanynt a pha amodau a chwaraeir. Cyfeirir at ambell i orchest a doniolwch wrth i Aelodau droi ati i frwydro am y tlysau.

While carrying out research and collating materials for this history of the Club, the most frequently asked questions by Members concerned the Club's cups and trophies. Members were interested in the history surrounding these and the format of play that had developed over the years. Over the last one hundred years, the majority of cups and trophies at Nefyn Golf Club have been presented to the Club by Members.

There follows therefore a history of the cups and trophies and some references are made to quite extraordinary successes of some individuals.

When the Club was founded in 1907, Members used to turn up for competitions at a stipulated time and the Club would arrange the pairings. In October 1911, due to a loss of interest in competitions, it was decided to allow cards to be taken out anytime during the day rather than the practice of fixing a starting time for all competitors.

Very few details are available regarding Ladies' Golf at this time and the rare mention in the Minutes confirms very few ladies actually played golf.

In 1951 it was resolved that a draw be made for all competitions apart from foursomes and fourballs. Entries for the competition would be received up until 5pm the previous evening, when the draw would take place. This practice did not last for long and the tried and tested custom of members making up their own pairings re-emerged, a custom which is still in existence today. The exception to this is the Captain's Day, when a draw is made.

Handicaps

In June 1969, it was decided to have a handicap limit of 18 for all major competitions. Monthly Medals would remain at 24. However, while H M Williams was Chairman of the Match and Handicap Committee (1998-2004), the handicap limit for Gents was raised to its limit, 28 for all competitions, including the August Meeting.

The Ladies' handicap limit was 36. Many Members will recall the 36P or 36* and the P or * would only disappear after you proved your game and could play to 36. In the August Meetings in the 70s and 80s, the playing handicap for competitions was reduced to a maximum of 30 for all competitions. In February 1998 however, the Ladies' maximum handicap was increased to 45, only to reduce again to 36 in January 2004. [This was the second time the ceiling had been raised to 45 for a decision had been made in October 1910 to raise the handicap limit from 36 to 45 but it is unclear whether this might have been an internal Club ruling.]

CUPS AND TROPHIES OF THE MENS SECTION

THE EARLIEST CUPS & TROPHIES

1. *Muriau Challenge Cup* 2. *Wynne Finch Challenge Cup*
3. *Tweedale Challenge Cup* 4. *Festival Cup* 5. *Victory Cup*
6. *Courtenay Lord Cup* 7. *R A Pugh Captain's Prize 1929 / O H Parry Cup*

1 Muriau Challenge Cup

A certain Mr Pritchard donated the Muriau Cup to the Club on September 24th, 1925 and expressed his wish 'it be named 'Muria Cup' – to be played for by the resident members of the Club only' (sic - Club's Minutes). [Muria is the way the local people of Llŷn would pronounce Muriau - meaning walls.] It was finally agreed that the Competition should be an 18 Hole Medal and should be played annually, on the Saturday preceding Easter. The Cup was first presented in 1927 and the Winner was Capt J D Griffith.

Details of formats of competitions were rarely minuted but exceptionally in 1937, and again in 1954, it is reported that the Muriau Cup was played for in a Singles Knockout format. By the early 60s however, the Competition appears to have reverted to the 18 Hole Medal and it is played in this format today.

2 Wynne-Finch Challenge Cup

On February 3rd 1928, the Club Captain, Major Wynne-Finch, presented the Club with a Cup to be played for in the month of August as an 18 Hole Medal for Gentlemen. However, it was not played until 1929 when the Winner was C H Buckley. From 1939 onwards, the Wynne-Finch Challenge Cup continued to be an 18 Hole Medal Competition but was changed to be played in September.

3 Tweedale Challenge Cup

The Tweedale Challenge Cup is the 'Blue Ribbon Competition' of the Club.

Ernest Tweedale (Captain 1921 and 1922) presented this Cup in 1927, the Inaugural Winner being J H Millar. Originally, the Cup was played for in a Knockout format by Members only. In 1931 however, Ernest Tweedale requested that the Competition for his Cup become an Open Competition instead of restricting it to Club Members and it has remained in this format ever since.

This prestigious Cup is rarely won by the same person more than once but there are some exceptions. C H Buckley won the Cup twice, in 1930 and 1937; Edwin Jones won in 1945 and 1946 and T Gareth Gruffydd has captured the Cup on 6 occasions - 1971, 1978, 1980, 1985, 1987 and 1989.

4 Festival Cup

To celebrate the Festival of Britain, Wing Commander Sleigh, as Chairman of the Handicap Committee, in January 1951 proposed a Major Competition to be held on June 9th and 16th, called 'The Festival of Britain, Nevin and District Open Meeting'. At the same meeting, he proposed a Wynne-Finch 'Festival of Britain Cup' be played as a Medal on July 7th, the best 4 scores to qualify for a Knockout Competition.

From 1952 onwards, this Cup was played for annually and was named The Festival Cup. The Inaugural Winner in 1951 was H G Atherton.

In the Presentation Ceremony at the end of the August Meeting in 1988, the Festival Cup, which had been won by John C Blore, and ironically the first trophy he had won at the Club, was presented in error to another Member! John was officially presented with the Festival Cup during the ensuing Wednesday Night Presentation by the Captain, R M Williams.

5 Victory Cup

On June 1st 1946 it was decided to have a Victory Day Competition to take the form of a Medal round. It is unclear what it meant by the following – 'and when conditions permit, it was agreed that a trophy be purchased from prize monies accumulated from ex-captains during the war years' (sic Club's Minutes). It was to be played for annually on Whit Saturday.

On September 6th of the same year, it was agreed that the Victory Cup would be purchased for the sum of £37-10-0. It is claimed that Wing Commander Sleigh, Owen Roberts and J E Roberts journeyed to Llandudno to purchase this Cup. The Club agreed to pay for a plinth and suitable engraving. It is unclear exactly when the Competition was played but the Inaugural Winner in 1946 was A Blaney Jones.

6 Courtenay Lord Cup

In the Club's first recorded minutes (14th March 1908) held at the Tŷ Coch Inn, reference is made to a Courtenay Lord Cup and it is assumed that this Cup was presented to the Club by J Courtenay Lord, a Member of the very first Committee. After much discussion at Committee, it was agreed The Courtenay Lord Cup should remain a Challenge Cup and be played for on four occasions annually – specifically on the 3rd Saturday of the month in April, July, October and January. The Cup was to remain the property of the Club and mementoes were to be purchased for the winners. The winners in 1908 were W Fitz-Hugh (twice,) J N McCurdy, and J Beaumont.

The January, April and October 1910 Mementoes won by Richard Williams Porthdinllaen Farm, Uncle to Richard Williams (Captain 1966), and presented by J Beaumont.

This Cup has a varied history.

1913: It was decided it should be played for only once a year;

1927: It was stipulated it should be played at Whitsuntide;

1952: It was decided that the Courtenay Lord Cup would be used as the Challenge Trophy for the annual Edern and Morfa versus Nefyn matches.

1962: It was agreed that the Cup should be transferred to the Junior Section as an Annual Challenge Trophy. When T G Gruffydd won the Cup on three successive occasions, it was presented to him outright.

1972: The Club requested the Cup back from its owner and it has been played for ever since by the Gent's Section as an 18 Hole Medal, early in the season.

7 R A Pugh Captain's Prize 1929 / O H Parry Cup

In 1929, O H Parry won the Captain's Prize and was presented with a Silver Cup, engraved with 'Captain's Prize, Presented by R A Pugh 1929'. The Captain's Day was played in the August Meeting, at the end of R A Pugh's Captaincy, prior to the AGM.

In September 1989, this Cup was offered to the Club by O H Parry's two granddaughters and it was resolved to accept this generous gift. The following inscription (sic) was written on the new plinth:

'PRESENTED TO NEFYN AND DISTRICT GOLF CLUB IN 1989
BY MRS GLENYS SYCAMORE AND MRS MELITA EVANS,
THE GRAND-DAUGHTERS OF THE LATE O H PARRY, ESQ,
WHO WAS CAPTAIN OF THE CLUB IN 1923.'

Thus, since 1989, this has been known as the O H Parry Cup. It is played for at the very end of the season and is one of the most coveted Cups in the Section. Only male competitors who had either won or finished runner-up in the Club Major Competitions qualified to play in this 18 Hole Medal. In its inaugural year in 1991, the Cup was won by Don Schofield. [Since 2005, when Ladies and Special Category Juniors were invited to play in the Cynfelin Jones Cup, if they were to win that Trophy, they too would be eligible to play in the O H Parry Cup.]

CUPS & TROPHIES 1953-1985

8 *Wynne-Finch Mixed Foursomes' Bowl*
9 *Buckley Trophy* **10** *Barbet Salver*
11 *Club Championship Trophy +* **12** *Club Championship Shield*
13 *Tlws Bwrw Allan yr Hynafgwyr Rover Seniors Doubles Knockout Trophy*

8. Wynne-Finch Mixed Foursomes' Bowl

In November 1961, the Club accepted a Challenge Bowl kindly presented by Sir William and Lady Wynne-Finch for a Mixed Foursomes' Competition. The Bowl was to be engraved 'Sir William and Lady Wynne-Finch Bowl, Mixed Foursomes'. This Competition is held annually and is the major Mixed Foursomes' Competition of the Summer Meeting.

9. Buckley Trophy

In August 1953, Charles Buckley, who had been associated with the Club for over 30 years, offered a Challenge Trophy for both Gentlemen and Ladies. The Competition was to take the form of an 18 Hole Medal Round and in its first year, 1954, the Challenge Trophy was won by Mrs R D Owen.

During its 54 years' existence, the Buckley Trophy has been won by Ladies on 10 occasions. In the years when Ladies did not win the actual trophy, a Prize was awarded to the Leading Lady by Mrs C H Buckley. This custom has been continued in her memory by Mrs Claire Cooper, her daughter.

In the 90s, the Ladies were granted courtesy shots due to the differences in the SSS between the Men's and the Ladies' Courses. The Ladies received 4 courtesy shots due to the SSS being 71 for Men and 75 for Ladies. In 2007, when the Men's and Ladies' SSS were re-assessed (Men's 72 and Ladies' 74) the Ladies received only two courtesy shots.

J R Williams has won the Buckley Trophy on 2 occasions (1999 and 2004), the only Member to achieve this.

10. Barbet Salver

In March 1980, a Silver Salver was presented to the Club by Laurence Barbet. It was referred to as The Barbet Salver and it is played for by the Gentlemen in the August Meeting as an 18 Hole Stableford Competition. Its Inaugural Winner was S R Cresswell.

11. Club Championship Trophy + 12. Club Championship Shield

On November 2nd, 1968, J E Roberts' offer of a Shield for the Club Championship was duly accepted by the Club. The first Club Championship Competition was played in 1969. Initially, it was a 36 Hole event, the first round being played in conjunction with the Festival Cup and a week later, the second round in conjunction with the Victory Cup. The Inaugural Winner was T Gareth Gruffydd.

In 1984, it was decided that the Championship would be played as a 36 Hole Medal Competition on consecutive days. Since 2003, the 36 Hole Championship has been played on one day at the beginning of July. In 2002, the Club purchased a new Club Championship Trophy.

T Gareth Gruffydd has won the Club Championship on 17 occasions: 1969 to 1971, 1974 to 1981, 1985, 1987, 1989, 1991, 1993 and 1996. In 1974 he recorded the lowest 36 holes aggregate in the history of the championship: $64 + 68 = 132$ (the SSS for the Old Course being 69). The 64 constituted the Old Course Record. Other multiple winners have been John Richardson (1982, 1983 & 1984), Geraint W Hughes (1988, 1994 & 1998), Alwyn Thomas (2000, 2002 & 2003), James Salt (1999 & 2001), John Thomas (2004 & 2005) and Tudur L Evans (2006 & 2007).

13 Tlws Bwrw Allan yr Hynafgwyr
Rover Seniors' Doubles Knockout Trophy

In 1985, Jack Trenholme donated the 'Rover Cup' to the Club. It was to be played for as a Foursomes' Competition with the Winners going forward to an Area Final. In 1990, however, Pentraeth Motors, Anglesey (Rover) confirmed that the Rover Competition had been withdrawn.

In 2006, with Jack Trenholme's consent, this Rover Trophy was transferred to the Senior Section to be played for in the Senior Doubles Knockout. Tony Connolly, Senior Organiser, was responsible for alterations made to the inscription on the glass trophy and a new plinth was added. The Inaugural Winners were Paul Denston and Ian Cooper (the 2006 Captain).

CUPS & TROPHIES 1985 - 2006

- 14 Cynfelin Jones Cup
- 15 Seniors' Scratch Trophy
- 16 Cwpan Siop Bryn 'Raur
- 17 Tudur Roberts Cup
- 18 Tatws Team Trophy
- 19 Parry Goblet

14 Cynfelin Jones Cup

The Cynfelin Jones Cup was presented to the Club in 1987 by the family of the Rev Cynfelin Jones who was Captain in 1914 and one of the Founder Members of the Club. It was decided that the Cup would be played for in a Stableford format. On June 26th 1987, however in its first year, it was played in error as a Medal. It was resolved to re-play the Competition under the correct rules in July. Lt Col R W Parry won the Cup in its Inaugural Year and repeated the feat the following year.

From 2005 onwards, Ladies and Special Category Juniors were allowed to play in the Cynfelin Jones Trophy.

15 Seniors' Scratch Trophy

In 1985, the Captain, J P Bentley, presented a trophy to be played in perpetuity as a Seniors' Championship. The Competition was initially played as a 36 Hole Championship over 2 days and the age limit was 60. The Inaugural Winner in 1987 was S R Cresswell.

In 2001, the age limit was brought down to 55 to comply with WGU regulations and in 2003, the Competition was changed to an 18 Hole Championship.

Multiple winners of the competition are Don Schofield (1989, 1991, 1992, 1993), John Richardson (1988, 1990, 1996, 2006), Roger Ellwood (1998, 1999, 2000, 2001, 2005) and T Gareth Gruffydd (2002, 2003, 2007).

16 Cwpan Siop Bryn 'Raur

In May 2000, the Club accepted a Cup from Capt Hugh and Mrs Laura Wyn Roberts, Dolydd, named *'Cwpan Siop Bryn 'Raur'*. 'Siop Hamdden Bryn 'Raur – Sports' was the name of the shop they ran on Lôn Uchaf, by their home. [Bryn 'Raur, shortened from Bryn yr Aur – meaning Golden Hill, was the area around the shop.]

The Cup was to be played for in the Summer Meeting as the Veterans' Competition. The Competition was extended to 18 Holes from the traditional 10 Hole Competition and was to be played in a Stableford format. It is a Competition for both Ladies and Gentlemen (Members only) over 60 years of age.

17 Tudur Roberts Cup

Two Silver Cups were bought by the Club from an antique shop in Criccieth in October 1996. (See also under Ladies' R A Pugh Cup, P.289) One of these Cups had the inscription 'Captain's Prize, Nevin Golf Club, 1946'. The Captain at the time had been Ellis Tudur Roberts.

The Club contacted Stan Roberts (Ellis Tudur Roberts' son) and it was agreed that the Cup could be played for annually, with the stipulation that it would never become a major competition. Ever since 1996, the Tudur Roberts Cup has been played for at the beginning of the golfing season.

18 Tatws Team Trophy

In August 1986, R J (Spud) Taylor (Captain, 2001) presented a trophy together with an annual sum of money for a competition to be played in an AM-AM format at the end of the Summer Meeting. It was to be called the 'Tatws Team Trophy' (*tatws* meaning potatoes). Spud donated further money to pay for prizes until the end of the century – in the event, until the end of his Captaincy. Spud set £100 aside each year in the event of someone scoring a Hole-in-One. On the 16th Year of the Competition, Spud's final year of sponsoring the event, Chris Gaskell holed his first shot of the day on the 11th Hole. Spud duly presented him with the £100 which Chris immediately donated to the Captain's Charity!

The following year, 2002, saw Chris Gaskell taking over the sponsorship of the Tatws Team Event and he has continued to do this to the present day.

19 Parry Goblet

In September 2004, Lt Col R W Parry donated a Cup to the Club in memory of his grandfather and father, who, along with himself, had all been Captains of Nefyn. In fact, the R&A wrote to Lt Col Parry to congratulate him and his father and grandfather on attaining a unique feat. The R&A stated that very few golf clubs have been honoured to have three generations of Captains at their clubs.

The Cup, named 'The Parry Goblet' is listed as one of the Club Major Competitions. It is played for annually in May and is in Medal format. The Inaugural Winner in 2005 was Lee Coppin.

CENTENARY CUPS & FOUNDER'S TROPHY

1. *Cwpan Canmlwyddiant Adran y Merched - Ladies' Centenary Cup*
2. *Tlws y Sylfaenydd John Wales Founder's Trophy*
3. *Cwpan Canmlwyddiant y Dynion - Gent's Centenary Cup*

1 Cwpan Canmlwyddiant Adran y Merched - Ladies' Centenary Cup

The Centenary Ladies' Captain, Miss Fiona Vaughan Thomas, presented Cwpan Canmlwyddiant Adran y Merched / The Ladies' Centenary Cup to be played for on the May Bank Holiday Weekend as part of our Centenary Birthday Celebrations. This is a Major Competition, in Medal format, and is to be played annually on the same weekend. The Inaugural Winner on 5th May 2007 was Dilys Llewelyn Owen, 102-28-74.

2 Tlws y Sylfaenydd John Wales Founder's Trophy

In January 2005, Valerie Dunmore, offered The John Wales Founder's Trophy to the Club in memory of her grandfather, John Wales. [Mrs Dunmore conceded that her grandfather was actually a founder member of a golf course on Porthdinllaen Point rather than founding Nefyn Golf Club itself.]

The Wales' family accepted the Club's invitation to attend the Trophy's Presentation on June 16th 2007 and they themselves presented the Trophy. The Inaugural Winner was Tony Smith with a score of 79-11-68, having won on a card play-off from the Club Chairman, Chris Gaskell 83-15-68. An additional Trophy was presented to the Junior Competitors and was won by Thomas Allman. Suzanne Hemphill won the Ladies' Prize.

3 Cwpan Canmlwyddiant y Dynion - Gent's Centenary Cup

In May 2007, during the Club's Centenary Celebrations, the Captain, Emyr L Evans, presented the Club with Cwpan Canmlwyddiant y Dynion / The Gent's Centenary Cup. This, along with the Ladies' and Junior Centenary Cups, is to be played annually on the May Day Weekend to celebrate the Club's Founding. It is one of the Gent's Major Competitions and was won in its Inaugural Year by D A L Thomas with a score of (92-24-68) after a card play-off from T Gareth Gruffydd (74-6-68).

ADDITIONAL CUPS, TROPHIES AND PRIZES PRESENTED DURING THE CENTURY

Morfa Nevin Cup

It is believed that this Cup was presented to the Club by a person/persons unknown on September 17th 1910 and it was intended to be played for annually in a three cornered competition between Nefyn, Morfa Nefyn and Edern. However, on the 5th October 1912, the Secretary stated that as Morfa Nefyn had lost two of its best players, the original spirit of the competition had evaporated and that a general competition including all the subscribers should be held to play for its final disposal! There is no record of when this was played and no record of the eventual winner! In 1920, however, there was a match between Nefyn v Morfa Nefyn and Edern.

Saturday Sep 24th 1920:
Match; Nevin v Morfa & Edeyrn

W Fitzhugh	0	R Williams	1	1 up
O H Parry	1	J H Hudson	0	7 & 5
Rev Cynfelin Jones	1	J Beaumont	0	4 & 2
W Thomas	0	J McCurdy	1	3 & 1
R Lewis	1	H G Roberts	0	2 & 1
R H Griffith	0	H Hinton	1	4 & 2
	3		3	

Result: A Draw

Varley Cup
In July 1927, Dr S C Varley (Club Captain, 1932) presented a Cup to be played for at the Summer Meeting. This was won outright and no records are to hand.

J Axon Winter League Trophy
In September 1966, the Club accepted a trophy from Mr Jim Axon, of Plas Pistyll Hotel, to be presented to the Winner of the Winter League Competition annually. This Cup has disappeared.

Lane Cup
In November 1976, the Club accepted a Cup from Peter Lane of the Linksway Hotel, to be played for on Club Outings. It was named the Lane Cup. Sadly, in 1989, the Cup was mislaid and consequently never played for after this date.

Tlws Llŷn
In 1979, a 36 Hole Scratch Competition called *Tlws Llŷn*, Llŷn Trophy was initiated by T Gareth Gruffydd. The Trophy was played in conjunction with Pwllheli Golf Club. 18 holes were played at Pwllheli and 18 at Nefyn with the main prize presented to the 36 Hole Champion. There were also nett prizes. In its Inaugural Year, the Trophy was won by T Gareth Gruffydd with a score of 139 (70 at Pwllheli and 69 at Nefyn). The Nett Prize was won by Gareth Wyn Jones of Nefyn. After three years, the Trophy was withdrawn due to a congestion of fixtures at both Clubs.

President's Putter
The President's Putter was presented to the Club on the occasion of Owen Roberts' election as President in 1984. It used to be displayed on the wall by the window in the Bar but at present is under lock and key at the Club! It was not played for until 1989, the Winner being Gordon Smith. It was originally an 18 Hole Medal Competition at the beginning of the Summer Meeting. Several Presidents of the Club have suggested that the President's Putter should be played for on a President's Day, but it was not

until 2007, that I R Williams, the President, initiated a specific President's Day. Currently, there is an intention to play for the Putter on President's Day in September 2008.

Derek Clulow's Prize

In May 1977, Derek Clulow presented a Prize to the Club for the August Meeting. This Prize was originally the R Brown's Prize and Derek continued to donate the Prize in R Brown's memory until 2008, when Derek himself passed away. The Prize was awarded to the best aggregate nett score by a Gentleman Member in the Buckley Trophy and the Qualifying Round of the Tweedale Challenge Cup. Derek's wife, Jean, continues to provide the Prize in Derek's memory.

Professional's Prize

In the following year the Professional, John Pilkington presented a Prize for the August Meeting. It was to be a similar format to the Clulow Prize, except that it was presented for the gross aggregate of the same two competitions. John Froom, our present Professional, continues to present this Prize today.

ADDITIONAL MEN'S COMPETITIONS PLAYED DURING THE CENTURY

Gŵyl yr Haf Summer Meeting

August Meeting competitions are discussed specifically in another section.

Captain's Prize

The earliest reference to a Captain's Prize is in the Minutes of August 1909 when it was recorded 'Captains Prize – 10 entries – Won by R Cynfelin Jones' [sic]. In 1910 and 1916 mention is made that a Captain's Prize was presented but there are neither details of the competition nor a winner.

On July 24th 1925, it is minuted that an 18 Hole Stroke Play Competition was played for the Captain's Prize (W Glynne Jones). The best 16 qualified for the Knockout Tournament which took place in the fortnight preceding the August Meeting and the Final took place during the August Meeting itself.

In 1926, the Captain, Charles Richards, however, presented a Prize which was to be won outright. At the same time as the Members played for this Prize, a Special Prize was given by the Club to the 'Long Handicap Members, 18 to 36'. It appears the format then reverted back for many years to the qualifiers playing a knockout to decide the eventual winner.

In 1964, the Captain, Alf Whalley, expressed his desire for the Captain's Prize to be played over 2 Medal Rounds. Capt Will Roberts continued this custom the following year.

In 1967, the Captain, C I Murray, expressed his wish to play for his Prize with a Qualifying Round and then 4 only to qualify for Match Play. In ensuing years, the Captain's Prize was regularly played as a Qualifying Round and a subsequent Knockout Competition.

In 1985, the Captain, I R Williams, decided to have a day specifically for the Captain's Prize – 'The Captain's Day' and this was held during the Summer Meeting in August 1985. This is still the custom today.

S B Murray has won the Captain's Prize on three occasions (1973, 1974 and 1981), the only one to do so.

Coronation Competition

On Saturday, May 5th 1953, a Coronation Competition was held. The Men's Prize was donated by Mr W H Owen of Chester, the Ladies' Prize was presented by the Club, the Junior Prize was presented by Mrs Jones, Marvan, Nefyn, and the '60 and over Prize' was presented by Mr R Glyn Williams. (See photo of winners, Captain Price (Twmpath) and Brian Hefin Williams in Chapter on Captains, 1937.)

Jubilee Competitions (50th Anniversary of the Scouts' Movement)

In September 1957, the Jubilee Competitions were held. These were an 18 Hole Individual Medal Competition and a Fourball Best Ball Bogey Competition.

Nefyn Scratch Trophy

In 1973, the Management Committee instigated a new major tournament for the Nefyn Open Scratch Trophy. It was hoped that the tournament would become a permanent fixture. The inaugural event was staged on June 24th 1973 but due to clashes with Welsh Golfing Union fixtures, the turnout was rather disappointing.

However, the 36 Hole Competition did attract 33 of the ablest golfers in North Wales, Cardiganshire, Cheshire and Lancashire. Among the competitors were three Welsh Internationals – J Roger Jones Conwy, Dave McLean Holyhead and Ted Davies Prestatyn, the 1972 Welsh Amateur Champion.

Many of the entrants had never played at Nefyn before and the Club Professional, A D Grace, and his staff were highly complimented on the fine state of the course.

J Roger Jones, who won the Trophy, equalled the course record of 66 held by T Gareth Gruffydd and Paul Smart (Nefyn).

Results:

J R Jones Conwy (Scratch)	66 + 70 = 136
E N Davies Prestatyn (+1)	71 + 69 = 140
T G Gruffydd Nefyn (1)	72 + 70 = 142
D McLean Holyhead (Scratch)	70 + 72 = 142

Due to competition from other Scratch Events in North Wales, The Nefyn Scratch Trophy was only played for three years.

Cynghrair Golff Haf Eryri Summer Golf League

In September 1974, T Gareth Gruffydd was given support to set up an organised programme of local area Inter-Club Matches from 1975 onwards, called the Cynghrair Golff Haf Eryri / The Eryri Summer Golf League. Nefyn lost the League to Porthmadog Golf Club on a fraction of a point!

Over a hundred golfers took part in the End of Season League Meeting at Nefyn and the event was hailed a great success.

Due to Nefyn's lack of success in the League and last minute cancellation of some matches, Nefyn decided to withdraw from the League in the mid-80s although the League itself continued for a few more years.

Wednesday Night Competition

The Wednesday Night Competition was initiated in 1975 by the Captain, Evan Hughes. Originally, it was played as a Nine Hole Competition but when the new holes were constructed at Abergeirch in 1977, the Competition changed to a 10 Hole Competition. For many years the Competition was played as a 10 Hole Medal, but recently a Stableford Competition alternates with the Medal.

Initially, Members used to donate a prize to be presented to the winner on each Wednesday evening. Prizes were attractive and included items such as an electric shaver, a watch, vouchers, etc. Later, the entry fees were used to buy vouchers and golf balls from the Professional's shop.

The Wednesday Night Competition is a very popular event. Up to 50 Members compete on sunny summer evenings and this is usually followed by a meal and a few drinks while socialising in the Clubhouse. Together with the 'Pacyrs', who played on Sunday evenings, the Wednesday Night Competition has been at the forefront of encouraging New Members to play in competitions.

Some incredible scores over 10 holes have been recorded over the years, but one which deserves a mention is the Stableford score of 34 points by Neil Kennedy in July 2007. Most of us would be pleased with this total for 18 holes! Members' handicaps have not been regularly adjusted over the years in the Wednesday Night Competitions with the exception of a period when a certain Mr Entwistle was yielding the axe as Match and Handicap Secretary!

In October 2007, in a Wednesday evening competition, Bobby Jones (Bobby Ceidio Bach) was playing the 3rd Hole. He stopped his buggy (soft top style) in the rough on the left hand side of the hole in order to search for his lost ball. All of a sudden, the buggy sprung into life and started careering towards him. He jumped out of the way, and started chasing after it to stop it, but to no avail!

The buggy had other ideas and sped along, veering right immediately in front of the 3rd Green and disappeared over the cliff edge. It was found on the rocks with a broken front axle, but Bobby's clubs, except for one which he picked up by the cliff edge, were all intact. His playing partners - T Gareth Gruffydd, Eirwyn Jones and the late John Alun Jones had one huge laugh at Bobby's expense. It was rumoured that the lifeboat was launched because of a sighting of a car near the cliff edge! The Greens' Staff recovered the buggy the following day.

The buggy had other ideas... and disappeared over the cliff edge.

Pro-Am Tournaments

On September 19th 1982, the Captain, Laurence Barbet and the Competition Committee arranged the Club's first ever Pro-Am Tournament. It proved to be a great success. The Professional's Prize was won by Andy Griffiths of Llanymynech with a score of 71 (after a play-off with John Barnet of Royal St. David's Golf Club). T Gareth Gruffydd won the Amateur Gross Prize with 69.

In June 1983, it was proposed to have another Pro-Am in 1984 and thereafter bi-annually.

> **May 25th 1984:** The Committee felt that the format should be for 5 team prizes for Amateurs and no individual prizes except for Professionals. Scoring would be by Better Ball Medal – the best two scores at each hole to be aggregated. The amateur prizes should take the form of a small trophy and cheque for the winners and vouchers for the Runners-up...

There is no record of any preparations for the 1986 Pro-Am. Members however, do recall the event and Ian Woosnam broke the Professional Course Record with a 67. (See Chapter on Course Records)

In September 1987, it was decided that an AM-AM be held in 1988 instead of a Pro-Am and the Club has not held a Pro-Am since 1986.

CUPS AND COMPETITIONS - CWPANAU A CHYSTADLEUTHAU

Pencampwriaeth Dros 25 UGC - WGU Over 25s Championship

In December 1991 it was resolved to accept the Welsh Golfing Union's request of hosting the Welsh over 25 Championship at Nefyn in 1995.

WGU Report, 1995

'The 1995 Welsh over 25s Championship was held for the first time at a weekend and the spectacularly beautiful Nefyn and District Golf Club was the venue. The weather was on the whole kind, a cool wind for the first round reminding everyone of how exposed the course is.'

The Leading Scores were:

1st	R Emmanuel	Cardigan	78	74	72	=	224
2nd	C J Davies	Llandrindod Wells	74	74	78	=	226
3rd	B Griffiths	Llanymynech	73	74	80	=	227
9th	G W Hughes	Nefyn & District	77	78	80	=	235

Cynghrair Safonol Bayonett Scratch League

The Bayonett Scratch League is a winter scratch golf league where Clubs play Home and Away matches against other Caernarfonshire, Merionethshire and Anglesey Golf Clubs. The League commenced on October 23rd 1992 when Nefyn hosted Bangor in the first match. Until recently, Nefyn has not been that successful in the League due mainly to several low handicap Members living away and not being available on a regular basis. However, apart from a couple of years, Nefyn has regularly supported the League since its inception.

The League comprises 3 Divisions, Nefyn languishing in the second, or more frequently the third division. In March, 2003, Nefyn was promoted from the Third to the Second Division.

The Nefyn Scratch Team has played in several Welsh Team Championship over the years, but has not enjoyed a great deal of success. When the Finals of the Welsh Team Championship were held at Nefyn in 1999, Nefyn were beaten by Bargoed in the Third Round. (See Photo of 1999 Scratch Team in Chapter on Teams and Groups)

The Whitbread Texas Scramble

This Competition, proposed by T Gareth Gruffydd, began in 1995. It was sponsored by Whitbread (through Mike Robinson, H R Manager) for the first five years. Not only did Whitbread present a beautiful cut-glass Trophy and an extremely generous table of prizes, the company also gave vouchers to the winning teams. The Texas Scramble Competition became the opening competition of the August meeting, a tradition which still exists.

One of our more observant Members, Alex Brown, noticed an engraving error on this trophy. Aptly or not, the engraving showed 'The Whitbread Scamble Trophy'! In recent years the Competition has been sponsored by Caribbean Connections (Drew Foster), Coors Beers, the Bass Brewery and lately the Carlsberg Brewery.

In 2007, the Executive Committee agreed the 'Whitbread Scamble Trophy' could be presented to the Ladies' Section for use as one of their Major Trophies. The inscription has been professionally covered by a golf ball sitting on a tee peg and it is now the Ladies' Club Championship Trophy.

NATIONAL CHALLENGES

1. *Her Geltaidd - Celtic Challenge*
2. *Her y Bedair Gwlad - Four Nations' Challenge*

1 Her Geltaidd - Celtic Challenge

'*Her Geltaidd*' or the 'Celtic Challenge' Competition was launched in 2001. The Celts play the Rest of the World for the Trophy. Members have to declare their nationality before play!

2 Her y Bedair Gwlad - Four Nations' Challenge

In October 2003, Gareth and Shan Gruffydd proposed an International Competition named 'Her y Bedair Gwlad' or 'The Four Nations' Challenge', for which they presented a clock trophy representing the four nations. Members elected for which of the four nations they would play. Four Competitions were held as close as possible to the four Saints' Days.

In its inaugural year, the winter of 2003-04 witnessed extreme weather conditions - rain, snow, wind and frost and without exception, each selected day was doomed by the weather! In 2005, the Competition was changed to a one day event. Tony Connolly captained the Irish side which won both in 2004 and 2005. However, due to busy golfing schedules and consequent difficulties in raising teams, The Four Nations' Challenge has not been played since 2005.

Other Championships played at Nefyn

June 2002	British Universities' National Golf Championship
June 2004	British Universities' Home International Tournament
June 2005	North Wales Regional Finals of Welsh Handicap Team Championship
July 2006	Ryder Cup Wales European Challenge Tour
Sept 2006	North Wales Counties' Match v Cheshire
July 2007	Welsh Boys' Championship
Sept 2007	North Wales Counties' Golf Assoc Youth Championship

County Competitions

2002	Nefyn 7 a side Knockout Team were Runners-up to Caernarfon in the Final at Royal St David's Golf Club, Harlech.
2006	Nefyn 7 a side Knockout Team were Runners-up to Royal St David's in the Final at Caernarfonshire Golf Club, Conwy.

CUPS AND TROPHIES OF THE LADIES' SECTION

CUPS AND TROPHIES OF THE LADIES' SECTION

1 Dorothy Wood Memorial Cup **2** + **5** Marian Grace Memorial Trophy
3 Tlws Môr a Mynydd **4** Tlws y Lôn Goed **6** Arfaes Trophy

1 Dorothy Wood Memorial Cup

In February 1978, the Ladies' Committee received a letter from a N J Acres offering to present a Cup to the Ladies' Section in memory of his aunt, Mrs Dorothy Wood. He would also provide a prize for the winner and the Cup was to be called 'The Dorothy Wood Memorial Cup'. Mrs Dorothy Wood had donated prizes for an Open Ladies' Medal Competition in the Summer Meetings and it was decided to continue this tradition in her memory.

The Cup was first presented in the Summer of 1978 and the Inaugural Winner was Christine Benny, a remarkable young golfer, playing off a handicap of 9. 'Miss Benny swept the board during the summer meeting [of 1978] winning many competitions, including the Buckley Trophy and the Dorothy Wood Memorial Cup' (Ladies' AGM Minutes, 1978).

Both M Lawton and Janet Ellwood have won the Dorothy Wood Memorial Cup on three occasions.

2 + **5** Marian Grace Memorial Trophy

Marian Grace died in 2003 and four of her closest friends, namely Sylvia Dennett, Elsie Hughes, Rhiannon Ingman and Carys Wyn Jones donated a Trophy in her memory. It was decided to have a 4BBB Medal as this was one of Marian's favourite format of playing. As Marian knew so many of the Away Members, it was deemed appropriate to have this played during the Summer Meeting.

The Trophy was presented for the first time in August 2005 and the Winners were Chris Whittaker and Jill Saunders.

3 Tlws Môr a Mynydd

Carys Wyn Jones (Past Ladies' President and Past Ladies' Captain) and her husband, Eirwyn (Past Captain) presented this Cup to the Ladies' Section in 1999.

It was to be played as a Medal Competition during the August Meeting. The Inaugural Winner was June Simpson.

4 Tlws y Lôn Goed

This Trophy was presented at the end of the Centenary Year by Rhiannon Ingman (Past Lady Captain, 1998). It is to be played on the last Friday of the Summer Meeting and the format will be the traditional Ladies' Stableford Competition.

6 Arfaes Trophy

This was presented by Sylvia Dennett in 2005 for a Ladies' Open Stableford Competition in the Summer Meeting. The Inaugural Winner was Marion Hall.

KNOCKOUT COMPETITIONS AND THE OUTING SHIELDS

- **7** Whitfield Salver
- **8** Ladies Outing Trophy, presented by Mrs K Magee
- **9** Dr Griffiths' Rose Bowl
- **10** Ogwen Jones Trophy (Club Championship)
- **11** Roulston Rose Bowl
- **12** O G Evans Shield – Autumn Outing
- **13** Cefnamwlch Challenge Cup for Ladies

7 Whitfield Salver

In November 1983, a cousin of Peggy Whitfield (Lady Captain 1982), approached the Ladies' Section and said she and her husband wished to donate a silver salver in Peggy's memory. At first, the Salver was presented for a Winter Foursomes' Knockout and it is believed that the Inaugural Winners were Marian Grace and Enid Evans.

The Whitfield Salver took many different formats over the following years. In 1995 however, it was agreed that the format should be a Singles Knockout and was to be played in the Spring and Summer months.

8 Ladies' Outing Trophy, presented by Mrs K Magee.

The first Outing Shield was bought by the Ladies' Section and ran from Shirley Roulston's win at Rhuddlan in 1982 to 1988.

In 1989, Mrs K Magee, an Away Member, presented this Shield for the Ladies' Spring Outing, the first Winner's name engraved being that of Anne Thomas, at Betws y Coed.

9 Dr Griffiths' Rose Bowl

There is no record of when exactly Dr Griffiths (Captain 1911) donated the Silver Rose Bowl to the Ladies' Section but it is reported that a Miss K O Jones won 'the Rose Bowl', as it was simply called, as early as 1927.

In June 1946, it was decided to play the 'Griffiths' Rose Bowl by knockout match play to commence June 19th to be completed by July 3rd.' (Ladies' Committee Minutes). One year later, in May 1947 it was agreed that the

Dr Griffiths' Rose Bowl be changed to a Medal first round, with the best 4 nett players qualifying for Match Play. Eileen Seth was the Winner in this new format which is still played today.

Eileen Seth won the Rose Bowl on 3 occasions. Others who won on more than one occasion chronologically were Annie Williams (6 times), Gladys Roberts (5) Pip Smart (3), Ena Bellhouse (2), Mary Roberts (2), Elsie Hughes (3), Laura Wyn Roberts (2), and Shirley Roulston (2).

10 Ogwen Jones Trophy (Club Championship)

In 1981, Win Ogwen Jones (Lady Captain, 1956) presented a Crystal Bowl for the Best Gross on her daughter Bethan's Lady Captain's Day. The Winner on that day was Dr E Buchanan.

Mrs Ogwen Jones then decided to develop this idea into an annual Club Championship Competition, away from Lady Captain's Day. The format was changed to a Medal round with the 4 best gross scores then competing for the title in a Knockout Competition. Win provided the prizes each year and the Ladies' Section bought a shield to record the winners. Laura Wyn Roberts, in 1982, was the first Club Champion and she received a Royal Worcester Biscuit Barrel.

This format continues to the present day and her daughter, Bethan Rees-Jones, presents prizes each year in memory of her mother.

In 2007, the Ladies' Section inherited a beautiful Crystal Trophy from the Men's Section. This had originally been presented by Mike Robinson of Whitbread, for the first Texas Scramble, sponsored by Whitbread for the August Meeting in 1994. This has now become the official Ladies' Championship Trophy and the names of all winners appear on the Honours Board.

An incredible record has been set by Miss Elsie Hughes (Past Lady Captain, 1996) who has won the Ladies' Club Championship on no fewer than 12 occasions. Fiona Vaughan Thomas has won on 3 occasions.

11 Roulston Rose Bowl

In 1999, Past Lady Captain Shirley Roulston presented a Crystal Rose Bowl for a Knockout Competition for the Bronze Division players. This Rose Bowl is competed for annually to this day and Shirley continues to provide prizes.

12 O G Evans Shield – Autumn Outing

O G Evans, the owner of Evans Coaches, Llaniestyn, has driven the Club's Members to many outings both near and far for many years.

In 1997, during the Presentation of Prizes in the Ladies' Outing to Holywell, OG, as he is called, announced he would give a shield for the Ladies' Autumn Outing, beginning that same year.

Sylvia Dennett won the Competition and she was presented with the O G Evans Autumn Outing Shield at the AGM of 1997.

13 Cefnamwlch Challenge Cup for Ladies

At the AGM of August 1946, Colonel Wynne-Finch of Cefnamwlch Estate, had been elected President of the Club and in February 1948, the Ladies' Section received a letter from his wife offering a Cup to be played for annually.

In July 1947, Mrs Gladys Wynne-Finch was invited to the Club to present her Cup and have tea with the Committee. Little is documented about the actual format of the Competition but a 'Qualifying Round for the Cefnamwlch Challenge Cup was to be played on July 21st and the Final on July 28th', (Ladies' Committee Minutes) followed by the Presentation. The Inaugural Winner was Mrs W P Y Seth, who was to win it on two other occasions in the following 10 years.

Today, the Competition takes a similar format to the Dr Griffiths' Rose Bowl with the first round played as a Qualifying Medal round with the best 4 nett players going on to a Knockout Competition.

Multiple winners of the Cefnamwlch Challenge Cup, again chronologically, are Mary Roberts (on 3 occasions), Annie Williams (4), Gladys Roberts (4), Pip Smart (4), Pauline Lane (3), Eileen Seth (3), Elsie Hughes (2), Shirley Roulston (3) and Fiona Vaughan Thomas (3).

CUPS AND TROPHIES PRESENTED 2000 ONWARDS

14 *Beaumont Trophy*   **15** *Tlws y Penwaig*   **16** *Tlws yr Eifl*
17 *R A Pugh Cup*

14 Beaumont Trophy

This is one of the earliest trophies ever presented to the Club. It was presented in 1908 by the first ever elected Captain of Nefyn, John Beaumont.

In 2007, the Ladies' Section inherited this Cup and it was decided to have a Stableford Competition. On June 6th, 36 Ladies competed for the Trophy for the first time and the Winner was Christine Smith.

15 Tlws y Penwaig

This was a new Trophy for the Centenary Year. It was presented by the retiring Ladies' President, Annette Jones (Lady Captain, 1978), the format being the best 3 aggregate scores from all the Major Trophies. Annette Jones also donated prizes for the Winner and Runner-up. The Inaugural Winner was our Ladies Captain – Fiona Vaughan Thomas, playing off 1 handicap - Aggregate Score 217   (71 / 72 / 74)

16 Tlws yr Eifl

In 2005, the Ladies' Section put in a request to the Executive Committee for a Trophy to equate with the Men's O H Parry Cup. The Competition was to be an 18 Hole Medal and only the Winners and Runners-up of the Ladies' Major Competitions would qualify to compete. The Executive agreed to the request and Tlws yr Eifl was presented for the first time in the Autumn of 2005. It was won on that occasion by Suzanne Hemphill.

17 R A Pugh Cup

On March 26th 1929, the Captain, Rennell A Pugh presented a Cup to the Club. It was to be played over Easter in an Open Event to celebrate the opening of the new Clubhouse in its present position, following the fire which completely destroyed the previous Clubhouse in December 1928.

In October 1996, the Secretary (J Barry Owens) was given consent to buy two Competition Cups with the Club's name engraved thereon from a shop in Criccieth for £120. It appears that these two Cups were won outright by Members at one time and, having been passed down within families, were subsequently sold to the antiques shop at Criccieth. One of these Cups was the Rennell A Pugh Easter Cup, and from 2007 onwards it was placed on a new plinth and donated to the Ladies' Section in a Fourball Competition. The Inaugural Winners were Katie Hopkinson and Christine Smith with 38pts.

ADDITIONAL TROPHIES

1 *Lady Captains' Shield*
2 *The Dennis Grace Cup and* **3** *The A D Grace Trophy*

1 Lady Captains' Shield

In 1969, The Lady Captain, Eve Worrall, presented an Honours Board for the Ladies' Lounge entitled 'The Lady Captain's Prize Board' and in the same year, her husband, Sam Worrall presented this Shield to record the names of the Lady Captain's Prize Winners. For many years, this Shield had pride of place in the Ladies' Lounge.

2 The Dennis Grace Cup and 3 The A D Grace Trophy

In 1984, Marian Grace (Lady Captain, 1979) presented a Cup in memory of her father, Dennis Grace, long-serving Professional at the Club. This was for a Winter Eclectic Competition over 9 Holes, the winner of the Silver Division to play the winner of the Bronze Division in a Knockout to determine the overall winner. The Inaugural Winner was Jacqui Wilcox.

Marian also provided the replicas and since her death, Dennis Grace's family continue to provide prizes for the Winner and the Runner-up.

The Shield, named the A D Grace Trophy, recorded the names of the Winners of the Cup and was bought by the Ladies' Section in June 1989.

ADDITIONAL CUPS, TROPHIES AND PRIZES PRESENTED DURING THE CENTURY

Ladies' Challenge Cup
There is a reference in the Club's Minutes to a Ladies' Challenge Cup being played in May 1909. It was won by a Miss Roberts – 8 down. It was played for again in the August Meeting of 1909 when it was reported that there were 5 entries and the Cup was won by Miss E Gray – 6 down. It would appear that this Cup was played for quite regularly in the early days and alternated with a Ladies' Medal.

> *Nov 20th 1909: A decision was made to allow Ladies to play for a Medal each month, except those in which the Ladies' (Challenge) Cup is played for. The Captain [B Ryman Hall] would present a set of buttons to winners. [sic]*

The Seniors' Salver
The Seniors' Salver was originally confined to 'Local Ladies aged 55 and over'. It was presented by the Lady Captain, Enid Evans, in September 1987 for the Best Aggregate Score for LGU Medals from April to October. Megan M Williams was the Inaugural Winner.

In 1995, it was agreed that this Trophy be open to all Ladies over 55 years of age. The age was brought down to 50 at one time to encourage more Ladies to compete but as the average age of the Ladies increased, the age-limit was put back to 55!

The Ashworth Cup
During Sue Ashworth's year as Lady Captain, 1995, she and her husband Geoff presented the Ashworth Cup for a new 18 Hole Mixed Foursomes Knockout, with a draw for partners. The Inaugural Winners were Rhiannon Ingman and H E Roberts.

At first, this Competition was very popular but it became increasingly difficult to organise. As a result of poor support, the Cup was withdrawn in 2001 and from 2002 onwards the Ladies' Section have organised a Mixed Foursomes Knockout Competition where Members form their own pairings. The Ladies' Centenary Vice-Captain, Mrs Janet Brown, as she came into Office at the very end of the Centenary Year, signalled her intent to provide a Trophy for this increasingly popular event, to be called Tlws Delyn – The Delyn Trophy.

LADIES' COMPETITIONS

[Please also refer to the Chapter on 'Lady Captains and Development within the Ladies' Section' where most of the Ladies' Competitions are discussed chronologically.]

Festival of Britain Competition

In response to an appeal from H M Government to all local authorities, the Golf Club decided to participate in the Festival of Britain. The Ladies' Committee received a letter from the Men's Secretary (07.02.51) asking the Ladies to hold a Competition to celebrate the Festival of Britain week in June 1951. An Open Ladies' Stableford Competition was therefore arranged for June 16th. The Entry fee was 2/6 inclusive of green fee. Prizes were £3-3-0 and £1-1-0. [The Ladies however, were not presented with a Festival Cup – see above under Men's Cups!]

Eclectic Competitions

Winter and Summer Eclectic Competitions are popular within the Ladies' Section. It would appear that the Winter Eclectic Competition began as early as 1949, when it was minuted that Ladies could take out as many cards as they wanted at 3d a card for the new Winter Eclectic Competition.

County Competitions held at Nefyn

April 1954	County Championship
April 2004	County Championship, when Fiona Vaughan Thomas was the Ladies' County Captain. Fiona won the Championship for the 4th time.
May 2004	County Match – Win against Shropshire, by 6 matches to 5
June 2007	County Match – Win against Mid Wales, by 7½ to 1½, when Laura Wyn Roberts was the Ladies' County Captain

Ladies' Championships at Nefyn

Sept 2005	Welsh Senior Ladies' Championship

JUNIOR COMPETITIONS

CUPS AND TROPHIES OF THE JUNIOR SECTION

[1] *The Lane Junior Trophy* [2] *The Lane Junior Trophy*
[3] *Captain William Roberts' Trophy*
[4] *Cwpan Canmlwyddiant Yr Adran Iau - Juniors' Centenary Cup*
[5] *Hugh Hefin Williams Memorial Shield* [6] *Ingy Junior Cup*

1 The Lane Junior Trophy

This Trophy is presented to the Leading Non-Member in the Lane Junior Trophy Competition (see below).

2 The Lane Junior Trophy

In May 1982, Mrs Pauline Lane, herself a Life Member of the Club, a Past Ladies' President and Past Captain, offered a Trophy to the Junior Section in memory of her late husband, Peter Lane. The Competition is traditionally played on the middle Sunday of the Summer Meeting and is an Open 18 Hole Stableford Competition for Girls and Boys aged 14-17. The Lane Trophy is awarded to the Winning Junior Member.

Peter, who was Captain in 1960, had been a strong supporter of Junior Golf at the Club. Pauline continues to present generous vouchers every year to the Winner of the Trophies.

3 Captain William Roberts' Trophy

In June 2001, an offer was accepted from the Nefyn Branch of the British Legion to present the Club with a Cup for a Junior Competition in the name of Capt Will Roberts. The British Legion still provides replicas for the Winner and the Runner-up. The Competition is an 18 Hole Stableford for Junior Members. Captain Will, Club Captain in 1965, was another strong supporter of Junior Golf. The Inaugural Winner in 2002 was Iwan Thomas.

4 Cwpan Canmlwyddiant Yr Adran Iau / Juniors' Centenary Cup

The Juniors' Centenary Cup, which was played on Saturday, May 5th 2007 was bought by the Junior Section with funds augmented annually by an anonymous benefactor. It was very recently disclosed that this benefactor was Peter Ingham, who sadly passed away in September 2007. It is understood that it was Peter's expressed wish that his annual generous gift should be continued to be donated by his widow, Helen, and she is proud to do so in his memory. The Junior's Centenary Cup winner was Thomas Allman.

5 Hugh Hefin Williams Memorial Shield

This Trophy was presented in 2000 in memory of Hugh Hefin Williams (Hugh Dŵr) by Eira, his daughter in law. It was intended for Junior Members of secondary school age and in its Inaugural Year, it was won by Gareth Williams (Gelli Wen), Junior Captain.

6 Ingy Junior Cup

The Ingy Cup was presented in 2003 by Peter Ingham for an 18 Hole Stableford.

The Bannau Trophy *(Pictured Left)*

This was presented by Dorothy Humpherson for the most improved Non - Handicapped Junior. The Inaugural Winner in Dec 2007 was Josh Westley.

GWYNEDD JUNIORS

1 *Ormerod Junior Cup* **2** *E S R Morris Shield*

1 Ormerod Junior Cup

It is unclear as to when the Ormerod Cup was presented to the Club. What is known however, is that it was presented as a Junior Cup by a Mr & Mrs Ormerod, from Gateley, Norfolk who became Members at the Club in October 1957.

The Cup is now presented in the Gwynedd Juniors' Competition to the Winner of the 9 Hole Handicap Competition.

2 E S R Morris Shield

In March 1957, it is minuted that E S R Morris of Sale was to be 'warmly thanked for his presentation of a Junior Shield to be played for by Juniors under 16 in the Summer Meeting'.

This Shield has for many years been played for by the Gwynedd Boys' Competition, hosted and organised by Nefyn and since 2002, for the Gwynedd Juniors' Competition. It is presented to the Winner of the 18 Hole Scratch Competition.

The Craven Cup

This was presented by the Craven Family as a Junior Cup for the Club but the year is uncertain.

During the research for mementoes and such like for the Centenary Book, this Cup was found in a bank-vault box alongside the broken ROC Trophy. It is a mystery how both have lain undiscovered for so many years. The latter has been sent for repair and the Craven Cup will once again be presented at the Gwynedd Juniors' Competition, in 2008, to the Winner of the 18 Hole Handicap Competition.

REFEREES AND STARTERS
DYFARNWYR A CHYCHWYNWYR

Dros y blynyddoedd mae nifer o Aelodau'r Clwb wedi cynorthwyo fel dyfarnwyr mewn rowndiau terfynol cystadleuthau, yn arbennig yng Nghystadleuaeth Rhuban Glas y Clwb - Cwpan Her Tweedale. Erbyn heddiw mae rhai Aelodau wedi dilyn cyrsiau dyfarnu a drefnir gan Undeb Golff

Cymru (GUW). Mae ein Cychwynnwr Swyddogol presennol, Bob Entwistle, i'w weld ym mhob drycin ar y ti cyntaf yn sicrhau tegwch i bob chwaraewr a chystadleuwr.

Referees

Over the years, certain Members have refereed final knockout matches at the Club. In the 50s, the two Owen brothers, Willie Rees and Robert Davies were in charge, unless they were competing themselves when J H Leach would then deputise for them. In the 60s, 70s and 80s, C H Buckley, Richard Williams, T Gareth Gruffydd and Don Schofield were often invited to referee and they were joined by Capt Will Roberts and Lt Col R W Parry in the 90s. In recent years, the duty has been carried out by the Club's qualified official Referees, Geoff Simpson, Terry Evans and Howard Dennett.

The Ladies' Section as yet have no qualified referees and refereeing has usually been undertaken by Silver Division players or those with many years of golfing experience.

Starters

June 1945: J P Hughes – one of the greens' staff to act as starter when required [1st reference to a Starter at the Club]

Until 2002, there was no officially recognised starter at the Club. Certain competitions, e.g. Captain's Day, merited a starter because of the number of competitors taking part. On those occasions however, Members or the Pro volunteered to act as a starter for the day.

In 2002, Bob Entwistle was appointed the Official Club Starter and since that date, Bob has been seen on the 1st Tee supervising the start of Club Competitions, for both the Ladies' and Men's Sections, and all Charity and Open Competitions.

Bob recalls a real highlight of recent years when he was asked to be the Official Starter for the Ryder Cup Challenge Tour in July 2006. At the young age of 82, he was one of the first to arrive in the Clubhouse, reporting for duty daily at 6.45am... and never once complained of the long hours involved!

Before coming to Nefyn, Bob was a long-standing Member at Saddleworth, being a past Captain and Match and Handicap Secretary there for a number of years. It will not surprise our Members to learn that he gained a reputation for being the snappiest dresser at Saddleworth for Bob is always immaculate on the 1st Tee at Nefyn.

Bob is proud of the position he holds and thoroughly enjoys welcoming both Members and visitors alike to the 1st Tee. He quite correctly keeps competitors on their toes – he does not tolerate late arrivals and his favourite instruction of 'Can you please identify your balls and have you exchanged your cards?' always goes down well!

Thank you Bob for all the hours you put into being our Starter.

Cups and Competitions - Cwpanau a Chystadleuthau

SOME MEMBERS' GOLFING SUCCESSES DURING THE CENTENARY YEAR
LLWYDDIANNAU GOLFFIO RHAI O'R AELODAU YN YSTOD Y CANMLWYDDIANT

Yma, cawn ddetholiad o Enillwyr Cystadleuthau 2007 mewn lluniau, gan gynnwys Tlysau newydd y Canmlwyddiant, sef Tlws y Sylfaenydd a Chwpanau Canmlwyddiant y Dynion, y Merched a'r Adran Iau.

There follows a photographic selection of 2007 Competition Winners, including Winners of the new Centenary Trophies - the Founder's Trophy and the Centenary Cups for Gentlemen, Ladies and Juniors.

The Captain with the Winner of the Centenary Cup, D A L Thomas (92-24-68)

Roger Ellwood (right) and Chris Houscroft, Winners of the Seniors' Centenary Open

Tony Smith, Winner of the Founder's Trophy, with 79-11-68. Pictured with Tony is Mrs Marion Wales, John Wales' daughter-in-law, aged 101 years!

Carol Smith (Handicap 13), Winner of the Arfaes Trophy with 41 pts

Ladies' President, Carys Wyn Jones, presents the Dorothy Wood Memorial Cup to the Ladies' Centenary Captain who achieved a new Course Record with 73-2-71 (CSS 77)

Cwpan Siop Bryn 'Raur Winner, John Davison with 39 pts

Winner of the Buckley Trophy, O Darby (78-10-68)

The Centenary Captain presents his Captain's Day Main Prize to Dylan Thomas, (84-16-68)

The Wynne-Finch Challenge Bowl was won by Paul and Sue Bentley (89-21.5-67.5)

M Emms (10) proudly holds the coveted Tweedale Cup.

GOLFING SUCCESSES IN 2007 - LLWYDDIANNAU GOLFF YN 2007

Jonathan Abbott (Handicap 11), Winner of the Barbet Salver with 38pts

Carys Wyn Jones presents her Ladies' President's Runner-Up Prize to daughter Siân Teleri Hughes (84 nett). The Winner was Christine Smith (83 nett)

The Annual Presentation Table complete with the Centenary Crystal Obelisks

Dylan Humphreys, Winner of the President's Putter (84-17-67)

Jean Cooper and son-in-law John Thomas, Winners of Charity Mixed Competition and the Woodlands Cup, repeating their success of 2005.

Christine Smith is presented with the Dr Griffiths' Rose Bowl

GOLFING SUCCESSES IN 2007 - LLWYDDIANNAU GOLFF YN 2007

Hilary Taylor is presented with the Cenfamwlch Cup

Dilys Ll Owen and Janet Ellwood share the Seniors' Salver

The Ladies' Club Championship presented to Fiona Vaughan Thomas

Christine Smith and Katie Hopkinson, Winners of the R A Pugh Cup with 38pts

Jean Cooper is presented with the Roulston Rose Bowl

Shan and Gareth Gruffydd, Winners of the Summer Mixed Knockout Competition

GOLFING SUCCESSES IN 2007 - LLWYDDIANNAU GOLFF YN 2007

Lee Coppin, Winner of the O H Parry Cup (77-11-66)

H T Williams, Winner of the Victory Cup (90-16-74)

R J Spud Taylor Winner of the (missing!) ROC Trophy (85-16-69)

Jonathan Richards, Winner of the Festival Cup (82-10-72)

T Gareth Gruffydd (5) and Wil H Williams (12), Winners of the Summer Doubles Knockout Competition

The Wynne-Finch Trophy was won by Terry Evans (82-13-69)

GOLFING SUCCESSES IN 2007 - LLWYDDIANNAU GOLFF YN 2007

Golfing Successes In 2007 - Llwyddiannau Golff Yn 2007

MEMORABLE GOLFING OCCASIONS
A SELECTION OF VISITS OF PROFESSIONALS TO NEFYN GOLF CLUB OVER THE YEARS

DYDDIAU GOLFF COFIADWY
DETHOLIAD O YMWELIADAU GWŶR PROFFESIYNOL Â'R CLWB DROS Y BLYNYDDOEDD

Dros y ganrif ddiwethaf, ymwelwyd â'r Clwb Golff gan nifer mawr o wŷr proffesiynol ac enwogion eraill. Cafwyd ymweliad gan ambell i berson ar ben ei hun ond yma edrychir ar ymweliadau grwpiau o enwogion y byd golff.

Mor gynnar ag 1920, estynnwyd gwahoddiad i'r enwogion James Braid a J H Taylor a dilynwyd hyn gydag ymweliad Dai Rees a Walley Smithers yn 1950. Yn 1970, cafwyd ail ymweliad gan Dai Rees a'r tro yma, ei gyd-chwaraewyr oedd Dave Thomas, Bernard Hunt a Peter Alliss. Cychwynnwyd Cystadleuthau Pro-Am gan Laurence Barbet yn yr wythdegau pan gafwyd ymweliadau lu gan wŷr proffesiynol, gan gynnwys Ian Woosnam yn 1986.

Cwblhawyd yr ymweliadau hyn gyda gwahoddiad Taith Her Cwpan Ryder Cymru i Nefyn yn 2006 pan enillwyd y twrnamaint gan y Cymro, Sion Bebb.

The Visit of Braid and Taylor 1920

James Braid (1870-1950) was a Scottish professional golfer and one of the 'Great Triumvirate' of golf alongside Harry Vardon and John Henry Taylor. He won the Open Championship on five occasions between 1901 and 1910; four British PGA Matchplay Championships between 1903 and 1911 and the French Open in 1910. He was also a renowned golf architect and designed and remodelled courses all over the country including Gleneagles and Carnoustie. In 1912 he retired from professional golf and became the Club Professional at Walton Heath.

James Braid pictured pre-1920
Photo courtesy of James Braid's granddaughter

John Henry Taylor (1871-1963), known as J H Taylor, was an English professional golfer who was Club Professional at Royal Mid Surrey Golf Club from 1899-1946. Like Braid, he also won the Open Championship on five occasions, between 1894 and 1913. He won the French Open twice and also won both the German and Dutch Opens. Again like Braid, Taylor was also involved in designing courses, mainly in the south of England but also travelled north and designed for example Heaton Park, near Manchester and Royal Birkdale.

In June 1920, it was proposed that 'Messrs Braid and Taylor be engaged to play an exhibition game on Nefyn links' (Club Minutes 12.06.20). One month later, Messrs J Beaumont, Rev R C Jones, O Williams and Dr R H Griffiths were elected caddies for the afternoon match between Braid and Taylor.

The Exhibition Match took place on July 29th 1920 and according to James Braid's granddaughter, who has Braid's old ledgers, the entry for Nefyn Golf Club showed his fee was £17-2-0 and his expenses £4-8-0. (At the time, annual Subscriptions were Gents £1-10-0 and Ladies 15/-!) The Captain, Mr Rees Thomas entertained both Braid and Taylor at his own expense at the Bryn Awel Hotel and the Club provided a celebratory lunch the following day.

The visit of Braid and Taylor to the Club in 1920. Seen standing fourth from Left is James Braid and fourth from Right is J H Taylor.

In July 1963, Henry Parry (Captain, 1941) presented the signed cards of the Exhibition Match between Braid and Taylor. (See Chapter on Captains, 1920)

The Visit of Dai Rees 1950

South Walian D J Rees (1913-1983) was one of Britain's leading golfers from the early 1930s onwards. He captained the Ryder Cup Team to victory against the US in 1957 (their first win since the famous 1933 victory captained by J H Taylor). Following this he was awarded the BBC Sports Personality of the Year and in 1958 was made a CBE. Dai Rees played in nine Ryder Cups in total between 1937 and 1961. He was Runner-up in the Open on three occasions and won the News of the World Match Play on four occasions between 1936 and 1950.

In February 1950, it was reported that 'the Club was attempting to secure the services of D J Rees, South Herts Golf Club, for an exhibition match on Saturday, June 17th 1950 and resolved to engage Mr Rees at the stipulated fee of 50 guineas'.

The Captain, R Davies Owen, and his brother, Willie Rees Owen, were extended an invitation to play with Dai Rees, and Wally D Smithers (Professional), a colleague of R Davies Owen, made up the fourth player. Dai Rees' caddy was Stan Roberts (son of Ellis Tudur Roberts), while Wil Parry Williams caddied for Wally Smithers. (See Wil's reminiscences in the Chapter 'I remember...') W Rees Owen's caddy was David Hughes (son of Herbert Hughes, brother of Kathleen Bentley) and Griff T Roberts (Arwel) caddied for the Captain, R Davies Owen. Griff recalls that on reaching the 18th Green, Robert Davies Owen emptied all the golf balls from his bag and gave them to him in recognition of his expert caddying advice!

Dai Rees chipping on to the second Green during the Exhibition Match with Walley Smithers, Robert Davies Owen and Willie Rees Owen in 1950. On the Left can be seen Alec and Pip Smart and on the Right, Richie Glyn Williams.

The Visit of Bernard J Hunt, Dave Thomas, Peter Alliss and Dai Rees in 1970.

Bernard J Hunt MBE (b.1930) was a leading English golfer on the European circuit in the 50s and 60s. He topped the Order of Merit in 1958, 1960 and 1965. He was selected for the Ryder

Cup Team eight times between 1953 and 1969 and was non-playing Captain in 1973 and 1975. He represented England on seven occasions in the World Cup and during his competitive golfing career he won no fewer than 33 titles world-wide and twice captained the PGA.

Dave Thomas (b.1934), another renowned professional of the 50s and 60s, won over a dozen tournaments in Europe and Britain and on two occasions, 1958 and 1966, was Runner-up in the British Open. He was awarded the Braid-Taylor Memorial Medal at Muirfield in 1966 when he was beaten by Jack Nicklaus. He also was a Ryder Cup Player and represented Wales in the Canada Cup on nine occasions in the 50s and 60s and also twice in the World Cup in 1969 and 1970. During the 70s, golf course design became his main focus.

Peter Alliss (b.1931) was born in Berlin where his father, Percy Alliss, another renowned golfer of his time, was a club professional. He left school at 14 and began his career as a professional golfer in 1947, aged 16. Between 1954 and 1969, he won 20 professional tournaments - including three British PGA championships - and was twice winner of the Vardon Trophy. He represented Gt Britain and Ireland in the Ryder Cup on eight occasions between 1953 and his retirement from the professional golf circuit in 1969.

Peter's retirement at the early age of 38 led to a successful new career as a broadcaster, writer and golf course design consultant. Working alongside partner Dave Thomas, above, he created over 50 courses including The Belfry at Sutton Coldfield, National Headquarters of the PGA and a Ryder Cup venue.

Peter made his first broadcast in 1961 as part of the BBC team covering the Open Championship at Birkdale which was won by Arnold Palmer. By 1978, he was the BBC's chief golf commentator following the death of his co-host and great friend Henry Longhurst. Modesty would prevent him saying that Golf Digest described him as 'the greatest golf commentator ever'- but to many that is precisely what Peter is.

It is not only as a commentator that Peter is revered however. He became a part of TV history, fronting 140 episodes of the popular BBC series Pro-Celebrity Golf, between 1974 and 1988, and progressed to an informal chat show on the fairways, 'Around with Alliss'.

> *September 1969:* Resolved that we accept the Proposal of the Forces Help Society and the Lord Roberts Fund, to nominate Nefyn Golf Club for their customary 1970 Exhibition Match. [sic]

Thus it was not at the instigation of the Club that the Exhibition Match between Bernard Hunt, Dai Rees, Dave Thomas and Peter Alliss actually took place. The organization must have been in the hands of outside organisers for there is very little recorded in the Minutes. In November, the date for the Match was confirmed as Sunday, July 26th 1970 and in June 1970 it was confirmed there would be no 'main catering' undertaken on that day. Tenders were to be invited from 'travelling caterers' and the number of 'diners to sit with the professionals be kept down in numbers'. Eventually it was agreed that 'those invited to dine with the Professionals to be the President and Lady President, The Captain and his lady, Lady Captain and Mrs Fenwick and our Professional' (Minutes July 18th).

Surprisingly, there is no report or comment on the match in the Club's Minutes but photographs are displayed in the Club's foyer.

Peter Allis, Dave Thomas and Dai Rees admiring Bernard Hunt's tee shot on the First Hole at the Exhibition Match, July 1970.

Dave Thomas admires his second shot to the second green. **From Left to Right,** *in the background, can be seen William Lloyd Griffith, Bethan Rees-Jones (with Val Leigh-Morgan behind her), Albert Portlock Junior, Dennis Grace, Stan Fray, Gresham T Owen, Dai Rees (partly hidden behind Dave Thomas) and Richard Williams (Porthdinllaen).*

The First PRO-AM at Nefyn

It was Laurence Barbet, as Vice-Captain, that proposed in July 1981 that the Club should run a sponsored PRO-AM the following year. The date was set for Sunday, September 19th 1982.

The PRO-AM was a great success. The Pro's Prize finished in a tie between Andy Griffiths (Professional at Llanymynech and childhood friend of Ian Woosnam) and John Barnett (Professional at Royal St David's, Harlech) on 71. Andy Griffiths then went on to win the sudden death play-off. T Gareth Gruffydd won the Amateur Gross with 69.

The 2006 Ryder Cup Wales Challenge Tour

This Tournament was played at Nefyn at the end of July. The Course had been lengthened by over 200 yards, with the hope of presenting a challenge to the up and coming professionals. But, as Jean Baptiste-Gonnet's wonderful 62 in the Second Round showed, a benign day at Nefyn is no test for such players. (See his scorecard in the Course Records Chapter.) However, in the Third Round on the Saturday, there was a strong wind and only four players managed to equal the

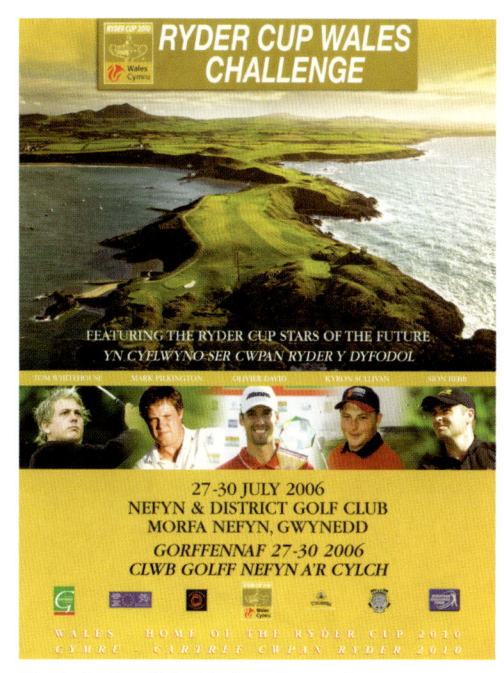

The Ryder Cup Wales Challenge Poster advertising the Tournament

par of 71. There were no scores under par. When Nefyn shows its teeth, it proves it is a match even for quality players! Jean Baptiste-Gonnett from France, besides creating a new professional record off the Blue Tees, also finished runner-up in the Tournament to Welshman, Sion Bebb.

MEMORABLE GOLFING OCCASIONS - DYDDIAU GOLFF COFIADWY

Final Positions in the Ryder Cup Wales Challenge Tour held at Nefyn Golf Club 27-30 July, 2006.

Nefyn Golf Club: Course Par: 71 Total yards: 6718 Total metres: 6152

Position	Name	Country	To Par	R1	R2	R3	R4	Prize Money
1	Bebb, Sion E	Wales	-10	68	64	73	69	£20,800.00
2	Gonnet, Jean-Baptiste	France	-9	69	62	71	73	£14,300.00
T3	James, Lee S	England	-7	68	68	73	68	£8,450.00
T3	Manley, Stuart	Wales	-7	68	69	71	69	£8,450.00
T5	Echenique, Rafael	Argentina	-6	68	67	75	68	£5,850.00
T5	David, Olivier	France	-6	65	64	80	69	£5,850.00
7	Hugo, Jean	RSA	-5	67	66	75	71	£4,160.00
T8	Urquhart, Murray	Scotland	-4	68	70	73	69	£3,380.00
T8	Williams, Craig	Wales	-4	67	68	74	71	£3,380.00
T29	Pilkington, Mark	Wales	+1	68	71	78	68	£1,092.00

Sion Bebb approaching the 14th Green during the Final Round.

Sion Bebb driving at the 15th, Final Round

Sion Bebb's approach putt on the Final Hole

Sion Bebb proudly holds the Ryder Cup Wales Challenge Trophy, 2006

Mark Pilkington tees off from the 5th Tee. Photo taken from the other side of the river mouth at Abergeirch.

Jean Baptiste-Gonnet driving at the 18th, Final Round

Jean Baptiste-Gonnet is congratulated by Club Captain, Ian Cooper and Ladies' Captain Megan Roberts, on creating a new Professional Course Record (62) and finishing Runner-Up

MEMORABLE GOLFING OCCASIONS - DYDDIAU GOLFF COFIADWY

COURSE RECORDS
COFNOD O'R SGORIAU GORAU AR GWRS NEFYN

Dros y degawdau bu llawer o newidiadau ar ffurf Cwrs Golff Nefyn ac, o ganlyniad, cofnodwyd sawl sgôr arbennig gan amaturiaid a gwŷr proffesiynol yn eu tro. Erbyn heddiw, mae dau gwrs gwahanol i'w gweld, ond gan na chwaraeir cystadleuthau ar yr Hen Gwrs mwyach, (y deg twll cyntaf a'r Penrhyn), mae cofnod y sgôr gorau ar y Cwrs yma'n dyddio'n ôl i 1977.

Isod, fe welir ddetholiad o'r sgoriau gorau a gyflawnwyd dros gyfnod yn ymestyn o 1920 i 2007, gan wŷr a gwragedd. Yn ogystal, cyfeirir at sgoriau arbennig gan aelodau hŷn sydd wedi taro'r bêl fach o amgylch y cwrs mewn sgôr sy'n gyfartal neu yn llai na'u hoedran!

Over the decades there have been many alterations to the actual Course and, as a result, over the years several notable Course Records have been achieved by amateurs and professionals alike.

There have been two Courses available for play since 1994. The Record for the present Old Course (the First 10 Holes and the Point) dates back to 1977 and is not likely to be bettered as we no longer have any official competitions on this Course.

Below we see the Course Records which have been achieved over a period extending from 1920 to 2007 by gentlemen and ladies alike. In addition, references are made to particular records where the more senior members have achieved scores equal to or below their ages!

The first ever recorded Course Record was achieved by James Braid. (Please see Braid's score card in the Captains' Chapter, 1920.) Braid's 69 was probably the first time anyone had officially broken 70 around Nefyn.

The Amateur Course Record of 64 for the Gents' Pre-1977 Course, was achieved on July 7th 1974 by T Gareth Gruffydd. Prior to this the record stood at 66 and was held by three individuals: Paul Smart and T Gareth Gruffydd from Nefyn Golf Club and John Roger Jones (Welsh International) from Caernarfonshire Golf Club (Conwy).

T Gareth Gruffydd also holds the Amateur Course Record of 67 for the Post 1977 Course (the current Old Course). The Card shows 13 pars and 5 birdies and is the only occasion in any competition that TG has played a full round without dropping a shot on any hole!

(Both the 1974 and 1977 Amateur Course Records can be seen in the Chapter on Captains - 1990)

Professional Course Record on the Pre-1977 Course held by Bernard Hunt with a 65. This score was achieved in an Exhibition Match played with Dai Rees, Peter Allis and Dave Thomas on July 26th 1970.

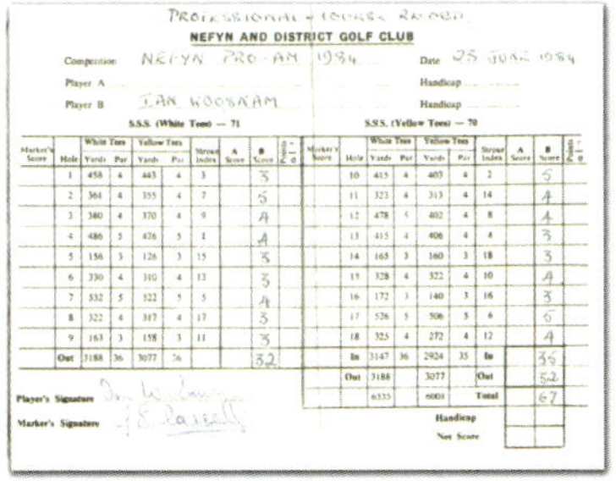

Professional Course Record of 67 on the Post 1977 Course held by Ian Woosnam, June 23rd 1984.

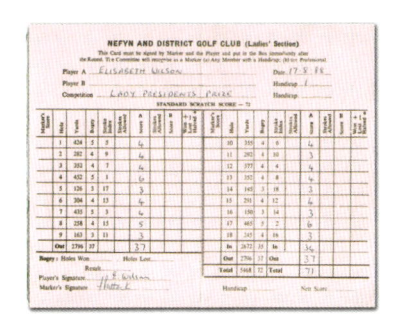

Post 1977 Ladies' Course Record of 71 set by Elisabeth Wilson (Cheshire County Champion) on August 17th 1988 playing off a handicap of 1. (SSS 72)

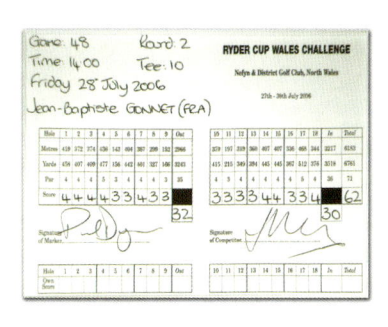

Jean Baptiste-Gonnett from France, created the new Professional Record of 62 during The Ryder Cup Wales Challenge Tour on July 28th 2006, playing off the blue tees which extended the Course by 200 yards.

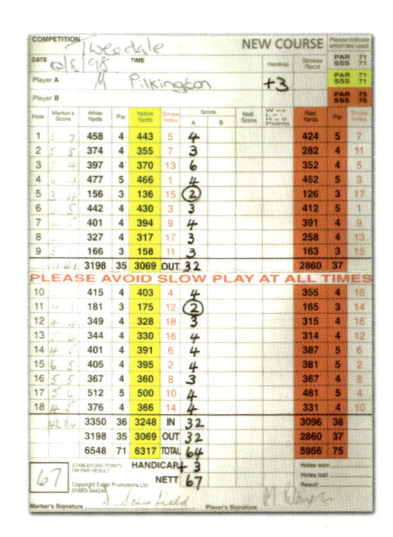

(Amateur) Mark Pilkington broke the 'New Course' record on August 10th 1998 with a 64, which included 9 birdies and one double bogey, playing off a handicap of +3.

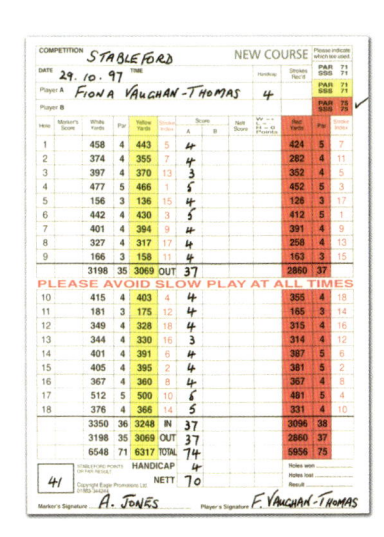

Ladies 'New Course' Record (Post 1994 Course) of 74 set by Fiona Vaughan Thomas on October 29th 1997, playing off a handicap of 4. (SSS 75)

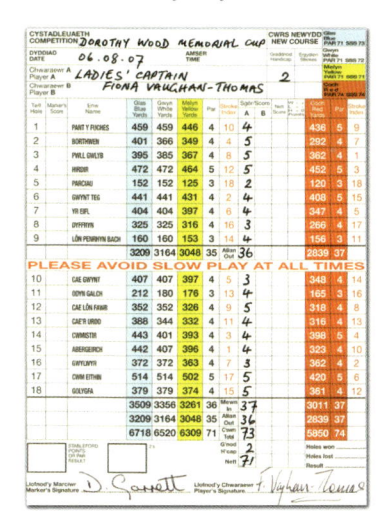

Ladies 'New Course' Record of 73 set by Fiona Vaughan Thomas on August 6th 2007. (New GUW Course Rating and new SSS of 74 in 2007.)

NEFYN COURSE RECORDS - SCORIAU GORAU AR GWRS NEFYN

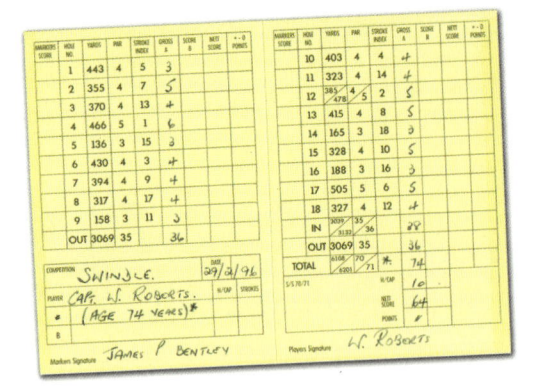

This wonderful score was achieved by **Captain Will Roberts** *on February 29th 1996 at the age of 74.*

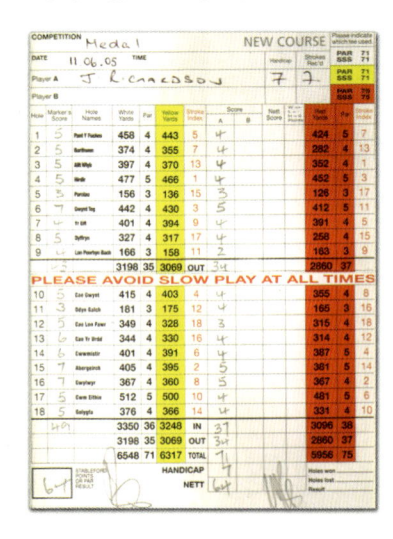

John Richardson's fantastic level par score of 71 was achieved on June 11th 2005, at the age of 77. The following year John repeated this score in the Senior Scratch Trophy!

CENTENARY SCORECARDS
CARDIAU SGORIO'R CANMLWYDDIANT

Cynlluniwyd cardiau newydd ar gyfer y Canmlwyddiant trwy nawdd Cwmni Jewson, Cyflenwyr Adeiladu. Ychwanegwyd fesuriadau newydd o'r Tîs Glas ar gerdyn y Cwrs Newydd. Dilynwyd patrwm o enwi'r tyllau ar y cardiau newydd, arferiad a ymddangosodd ar sawl fersiwn o gardiau'r cwrs dros y blynyddoedd.

New Scorecards, sponsored by Jewson were designed for the Centenary Year with the Blue Championship Tees appearing for the first time. Many Members and visitors regularly enquire about the names being given to the holes on the new versions of both the New and Old Course Scorecards. Many names were present on previous scorecards and these have been resurrected. [See Fiona Vaughan Thomas' Scorecard of August 2007 on the previous page.] There follows some brief explanations about the derivation and translations of the Welsh names:

THE NEW COURSE
Y CWRS NEWYDD

1 **Pant y Fuches**

Pant = hollow; *Fuches* = herd
(The bottom of the slope on this hole used to be a retreat for herds of cows in storms.)

2 **Borthwen**

wen = white; *Borth* = harbour/bay

3 **Pwll Gwlyb**

Gwlyb = wet; *Pwll* = pond or mere
(The wet area is where a sliced drive finishes.)

4 **Hirdir**

Hir = long; *dir* = land (Name of original field)

5 **Parciau**

= Parklands
(belonging to Pwll Parc and Porthdinllaen Farms.)

6 **Gwynt Teg**

Teg = fair; *Gwynt* = wind
(a following southwesterly wind)

7 **Yr Eifl**

= The Rivals

8 **Dyffryn**

= Valley

9 **Lôn Penrhyn Bach**

Lôn = Lane; *Penrhyn Bach* = little promontory
(Lane/footpath to the Point.)

NEFYN COURSE RECORDS - SCORIAU GORAU AR GWRS NEFYN

10 Cae Gwynt

Gwynt = wind/y; *Cae* = Field

(Name of original field)

11 Odyn Galch

Galch = Lime; *Odyn* = Kiln.

12 Cae Lôn Fawr

Fawr = Big; *Lôn* = Lane; *Cae* = Field

(Original name of Field)

13 Cae'r Urdd

Urdd = Welsh League of Youth; *Cae* = Field

(The Urdd used the field on the left hand side of 15th Hole for their youth camp.)

14 Cwmistir

Cwm = valley; *is* = below; *tir* = land

(Name of farm in the distance)

15 Abergeirch

Aber = mouth of; *geirch* = River Geirch

16 Gwylwyr

Gwylwyr = sentry / observers

(Mountain with three quarry levels above Nefyn)

17 Cwm Eithin

Eithin = gorse; *Cwm* = valley

(Recently named because of abundance of gorse)

18 Golygfa

Golygfa = Scenery / vista - Say no more!

THE OLD COURSE
YR HEN GWRS

1-10 As for New Course

11 Henblas

Hen = Old; *Blas* = palace

(Name of house below the cliff on the beach)

12 Tŷ Coch

Coch = red; *Tŷ* = House

(Named after the Pub)

13 Land's End

14 Lifeboat

15 Pen Cei

Pen = Head of / tip; *Cei* = Quay / jetty

(Named after the house below the 15th Green)

16 Pot

The 'Pot' refers to the geographical 'blowhole' between Tee and Green.

17 Long

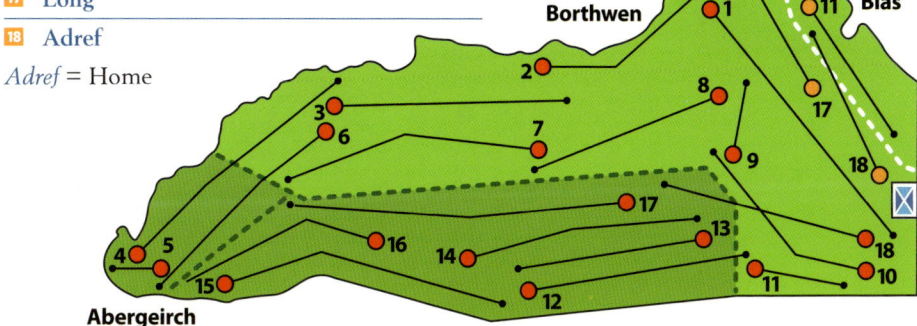

18 Adref

Adref = Home

NEFYN COURSE RECORDS - SCORIAU GORAU AR GWRS NEFYN

TEAMS AND GROUPS - TIMAU A GRWPIAU

TEAMS AND GROUPS
TIMAU A GRWPIAU

Isod, cawn gasgliad o ffotograffau sy'n portreadu timau a grwpiau o Adran y Merched ac Adran y Dynion a gynrychiolodd y Clwb dros y blynyddoedd.

LADIES' SECTION

The North Wales Shield Association

The first Team to be entered in the North Wales Challenge Shield Association, Holyhead 1986. **Back Row, Left to Right:** Elsie Hughes, Shirley Roulston, Leah Fray, Carys Wyn Jones and Pam Cresswell with their respective caddies, Marian Grace, Nell Hughes, Lady Captain Dorothy Roberts, Åse Richardson and Megan M Williams.

The Ladies' A Shield Team, 1997. One year after being promoted to Division 3, the Ladies of the A Shield Team win Division 3 and are promoted to Division 2! **Back Row, Left to Right:** Janet Ellwood, Shirley Roulston, Dorothy Roberts (Shield Match Secretary), Laura Wyn Roberts and Elsie Hughes **Front Row:** Carys Wyn Jones, Rhiannon Ingman, Lady Captain Helen Griffith and Janet Brown.

The Ladies' B Shield Team enter the Competition for the first time in 1997. **Back Row, Left to Right:** Jean Coppin, Sylvia Dennett, Dorothy Roberts (Shield Match Secretary), Dilys Ll Owen and June Simpson. **Front Row:** Dorothy Barton, Liz Mangham, Lady Captain Helen Griffith, Mary J Williams.

The Ladies' A Shield Team, Winners of the Division 2 Shield, 2000. **Back Row, Left to Right:** Elsie Hughes, Laura Wyn Roberts, Sylvia Dennett, Jacqui Gill, Suzanne Hemphill and Rhiannon Ingman. **Front Row:** Åse Richardson, Lady Captain Dorothy Barton, Janet Brown and Janet Ellwood. [The following year they won the Division 1 Shield, see Ladies Captain's Chapter, 2001]

PHOTO: Courtesy of Dewi Wyn (Pwllheli)

The B Shield Winning Team – who were promoted in 2004 **Back Row, Left to Right:** Christine Smith, Shan Gruffydd, Dilys Ll Owen, Yvonne Wray, Liz Mangham, Jean Cooper and Barbara Parsons. **Front Row:** Pat Metcalfe, Megan Roberts (who played in every match and won!), Ladies' Captain Janet Ellwood, Carys W Jones and Dorothy Barton

Welsh Team Championship

During her Captaincy, Rhiannon Ingman persuaded the Ladies' Committee to enter the Welsh Team Championship for the first time, in 1998. The Championship was held at Wrexham Golf Club and our Team consisted of Janet Brown, Janet Ellwood, Elsie Hughes, Rhiannon herself and Laura Wyn Roberts. They arrived at Wrexham to find they had been drawn against Rhuddlan, who had brought a full coach of supporters with them. Nefyn were every much the underdogs, extremely naïve and inexperienced in playing at this level and Rhiannon recalls they were terrified standing on the first tee! However, it was a beginning and with the exception of 1999, Nefyn has since sent a Team to compete every year. Ironically, the Team has met with more success when the Championship has been in South Wales rather than in the North.

At the time of writing, plans are being laid for hosting this Championship at Nefyn in June 2008, and we hope the Nefyn Ladies will meet with more success playing on their home ground!

The Ladies' Team at the 2000 Welsh Team Championship at North Wales Golf Club.
Left to Right: *Sylvia Dennett, Janet Ellwood, Janet Brown, Elsie Hughes and Rhiannon Ingman.*

The Team and their Caddies, Welsh Team Championship, Monmouthshire Golf Club, Abergavenni 2005. **Left to Right:** *[Team (T)] Shan Gruffydd, Megan Roberts, Sylvia Dennett (T), Carys W Jones, Laura W Roberts (T), Janet Brown (T), Joan Royle (T), Dilys Ll Owen, Rhiannon Ingman (T) and Dorothy Barton.*

The Team and their Caddies, Welsh Team Championship, Carmarthen 2007
Standing Left to Right: *Rhiannon Ingman (T), Joan Royle (T), Jean Cooper, Shan Gruffydd, Janet Brown (T), Åse Richardson, Janet Ellwood (T), Megan Roberts, Carys W Jones and Sylvia Dennett (T).*

MEN'S SECTION

Nefyn Scratch Team, WGU Welsh Team Championship, Nefyn August 1999. **Standing, Left to Right:** *Alwyn Thomas, Jamie Salt, Roger Ellwood, Ieuan Ellis (Non-playing Captain), Stephen Murray (Club Captain), Geraint W Hughes and T G Gruffydd with Stuart Williams kneeling.*

Final of the Caernarfonshire Seven a Side Competition, Conwy Golf Club October 2006. (*Nefyn were Runners-up to Royal St David's Golf Club.*) **Left to Right:** *Paul Denston, John Thomas, Ian Hamilton, Dave G Jones, Ioi William, Ian Cooper (Club Captain), Tony Smith, Emyr L Evans (Club Vice-Captain) and Tudur L Evans.*

2007 Scratch Team v 70s Scratch Team, June 2007. **Standing Left to Right:** *Geraint W Hughes, Aled Warren-Rees, Gresham T owen, Paul Smart, T Gareth Gruffydd, Merfyn Williams, Jonathan Richards, Clive Brown, Sion Williams, Emyr L Evans.* **Seated:** *Wil G Jones, Owi Ward, Ian Hamilton, John Thomas and John Alun Jones.*

Nefyn Scratch Team, WGU Welsh Team Championship, Maesdu 2006. **Standing, Left to Right:** *H Merfyn Williams, Ian Hamilton, Emyr L Evans, Tudur L Evans and Sion Williams*

The successful Club Snooker Team, formed in 2007, Llŷn Division 3 Champions, Easter 2008.
Left to Right: *Pat McAteer, Ian Hamilton, T Gareth Gruffydd, Bobby Jones, Eirwyn Jones and the late John Alun Jones (inset).*

TEAMS AND GROUPS - TIMAU A GRWPIAU

GROUPS

The Bells' Society

In the late sixties, a number of people met to consider whether it was possible to combine Scotland's two greatest gifts to the world, namely golf and whisky! They came up with the concept of fourball matchplay, with a drink for every hole won.

In 1970, they formalised the idea by founding the Bells' Society with the first Captain being Horace Barber. The Society originally consisted of Away Members who booked a week's holiday every year and played a competition every day for a variety of trophies with 'Bells Day' being on the Wednesday. On Thursday night, in the hope that they would be allowed to play the following year, they invited their wives to the annual dinner.

Over the years many Club Members and non-members have joined the Society and though it has diminished in number, it continues to thrive and uphold the old traditions.

'The Bells' Society', 1985-1986.
Left to right: *Horace Barber, Tony Copeland, Jim Axon, C Dale, Roland Grimes, Dave Needham, Derek Clulow, Bob Beswick, Ken Birchenough, M Chapman, Bob Cooper, Jack Lines, Fred Goosey with Dennis Urion, Captain, kneeling.*

Hogia Pnawn Dydd Mawrth
Retired gentlemen (mostly teachers) who began to play regularly on Tuesday afternoons.
Back Row, Left to Right: *Hugh Williams, John E Jones, Hugh D Jones, Robert G Humphreys, Cledwyn Rowlands, Ieuan Ellis, Harri Noel Williams* **Front Row:** *Richard Edgar Jones, John Roberts Williams ('Dros fy Sbectol'), Dyfed Evans, John Williams, Hugh E Roberts, Dafydd Ogwen Williams, a Hugh E Davies.*

Y Pacyrs (The Packers Golf Group)

This group was formed in the late 70s and so named after Kerry Packer, an Australian who founded the Cricket World Series in 1977. The Pacyrs initially played regularly on Sunday afternoons, retiring to the Clubhouse for refreshments after 10 holes. The group's organisers were Owie Roberts and Edward Jones. In addition to the Sunday play, they organised outings e.g. Hawkstone Park and played several mixed competitions with the Ladies' Section.

Many locals were introduced to golf by this group and have since become regular competitors at the Club.

The Pacyrs in the 80s on one of their annual outings.

Teams and Groups - Timau a Grwpiau

HELPING OTHERS
THE CLUB HELPS LOCAL CHARITIES
HEPLU ERAILL
Y CLWB YN HELPU ELUSENNAU LLEOL

Mae Aelodau'r Clwb wedi bod yn cefnogi elusennau ers dros ddeugain mlynedd ac yn ddiweddar, mae'r swm a gasglwyd yn flynyddol wedi esgyn i gyfansymiau syfrdanol. Cyflwynwyd Cystadleuaeth 'Y Neidr' i'r Clwb yn yr wythdegau a thros y bum mlynedd ar hugain ddilynol, bu Aelodau a'u ffrindiau oll yn cystadlu yn ystod Gŵyl yr Haf i gasglu arian mawr.

Yn y blynyddoedd diweddar, chwaraewyd cystadleuaeth ar un diwrnod yn flynyddol at elusennau fel Tŷ Gobaith ac ar Ddydd Sul Gŵyl Banc mis Awst, chwaraeir y Gystadleuaeth Pedwarawdau Cymysg at Elusen, cystadleuaeth sy'n hynod o boblogaidd gydag Aelodau ac ymwelwyr lu.

Mae elusennau lleol a thu hwnt wedi elwa'n fawr o ymdrechion Capteiniaid ac Aelodau'r Clwb dros y blynyddoedd.

Members of the Club have been supporting charities for over forty years and in recent times, the amount raised per annum has reached a staggering height.

As early as July 1967, the Ladies' Section had begun playing an RNLI Spoon Competition. The Competition Entry Fee was donated to the RNLI and we are told 'the money was given to the men's section who made it up to a £5 donation.' Since then, this has become an annual competition and from 2007 donations are given in lieu of the Competition Fee.

In July 1983, the Ladies began playing the Macmillan Cancer Relief Spoon Competition and this also has become an annual competition. Like the RNLI Spoon, all Entry Fees were donated to the Charity until the 2007 decision to ask for donations. Both charities have benefitted financially from this decision.

The 'Snake' Competition

The 'Snake' Competition was introduced to Nefyn in 1980 by Shan and Gareth Gruffydd who had seen this fun competition played at Padeswood and Buckley Golf Club. The idea was to form teams of 5, each person with a selected club, to play 2 holes on the Course – 1st Tee to the 4th Green and the 6th Tee back to the 18th Green. This was arranged for the Sunday evening, in the middle of the August meeting.

August Meeting 1991: *Members and guests await their instructions from Derek Clulow, with his famous whistle and 'People' call for order!*

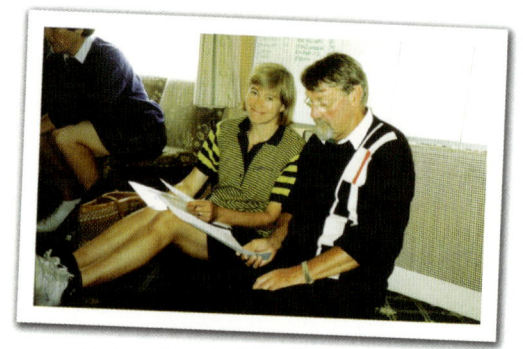

Hilary Taylor and Derek Clulow check the scores in the 'Snake' Competition of 1991

In 1981, Hilary Taylor took over the running of this Competition for a total of 16 years, ably assisted by Derek Clulow. Any profit in those early years, however small, was always donated to the local Lifeboat.

During the Summer of 1985, Bob Geldof and Midge Ure had organised 'Live Aid' – a multi-venue rock music concert held on July 13th to raise funds for famine relief in Ethiopia. A few weeks later, some youngsters taking part in the Snake at Nefyn, asked Hilary if they could collect money for Live Aid. They went around with a bucket and £50 was raised for the cause. This was the turning point in the Snake Competition and from 1986 onwards the competition became a charity competition, money so raised going to the Captain's chosen charity.

Sally Jones and Richard Harvard followed Hilary in organising the Competition and more recently Vicky Lyons has assisted Richard. In 2001, there was another money-spinner added to the Snake when the Captain, Spud Taylor, donated and auctioned two leather coats and since that year, an annual auction has been a regular feature of the evening's entertainment.

The Snake is hugely successful. It is the only competition in the golfing year where families and friends, young and old, compete and then socialise together. It now raises in excess of £3000 in one evening and since 2003, the sum raised has been shared between the two Captains' charities.

A Nominated Day for Charity and the start of the Charity Mixed Open Competition

The specifically appointed day for a Charity Competition started with a Competition organised by the Treasurer, Mr H D Jones, on August 18th 1988. The Executive Committee released the full day and Members raised £252.55 for the Local Branch of MENCAP.

This inspired the Ladies' Committee and particularly Marian Grace, the Lady Secretary, and together they began organising Open Mixed Foursomes for Charity at the end of the summer. The Executive Committee did not allow them a date in August and for the first four years, these charity competitions took place in September, before moving to the August Bank Holiday Sunday.

Members were generous in the extreme. Beautiful and expensive prizes were donated resulting in less expenditure. After a few years, raffle books were printed for selling before the main Competition Day and this had an enormous impact on profits. The Executive reduced green fees and eventually abolished them altogether.

Below is a tabular summary of the achievements of the Charity Mixed over the years. The chosen charity was always nominated by the incoming Lady Captain for her year of Office.

1988 - £224.04
The Bryn Beryl Special Care Unit 1st mention of Ladies organising an Open Mixed Foursomes for Charity. (Sunday, Sept 18th) Ladies wrote to the Men to ask if this could be an annual event.

1989 - £342
Nefyn and District Physically Handicapped and Nefyn and District Diabetic Society Also held in September (24th)

1990 - £564.50
NSPCC (Local Branch) and Gwynedd Hospice at Home Renamed 'The Charity Mixed' (Sept 9th)

1991 - £705.20
Llŷn Asthma Group and Llŷn Cancer Group

1992 - £1172.39 (Actually gave £600 each)
1) Haematology Unit at Alaw Ward Bangor
2) Apnoea Monitor for Sudden Infant Death Syndrome (SIDS) Raffle Books printed to help boost fund (£50, £20 and £10 prizes). 1st time Competition was played on August Bank Holiday Sunday.

HELPING OTHERS - HELPU ERAILL

1993 - £1005
Pulse oximeter for Pwllheli Ambulance Service
Raffle books printed annually.

1994 - £1385
Accident equipment for Pwllheli Fire Service

1995 - £1256
Satellite Navigator for RNLI

1996 - £1657.50 (£1700)
ECG Machine for Nefyn Doctors' Surgery

1997 - £1397.91 (£1400)
Air Support Helicopter Service

1998 - £2733.26
Spirometers and Syringe Drivers for Nefyn, Botwnnog and Pwllheli Surgeries and Hospice at Home.

1999 - £1962.15
Physiotherapy Dept Pwllheli (£2000 + £1000 gift from Captain, S B Murray) Executive asked to reduce green fees for Charity Mixed

2000 - £2256
Flowtron Machine for Bryn Beryl Hospital + Defibrillator for the Golf Club

2001 - £2,500
Hospice at Home Raffle abandoned. Fees increased.

2002 - £4,646
Hope House, Conwy Charity Account now includes all fund raising activities during the year

2003 - Over £4000
Tŷ Gobaith yng Nghymru (£1974 in Charity Mixed) Merchandise sold in Club on every possible occasion.

2004 - £5002
Air Ambulance, North Wales (Please see photo of Cheque Presentation under Ladies' Captains' Chapter, 2004)

Additional fund-raising occasions...

From 2001 onwards, a conscious decision was made to try and boost the Charity Funds (both the Captain's and the Lady Captain's) by holding specific social events aimed at raising money. 10 Hole Friendly Mixed Competitions (followed by equally friendly meals in the Clubhouse) became very popular! Any profits from concerts, occasional dinners like a Valentine's Dinner, carol evenings, quiz nights and coffee mornings were donated to the Charity Funds. One-off fun events like a Tug of War (2001) and annual events like the 'Guess the Combined Yardage of the Captains' Drive-in' (2003 onwards) helped to boost funds. Some Captains even saw fit to charge a £1 if a golfer landed in the green-side bunker on the 18th but this proved not to be quite so popular among some Members! Others raised a voluntary contribution on their traditionally 'free' Captain's Day Competition! Recently, the Captains have run a specific Captains' Charity Competition to swell the charity fund.

In 2001, the Captain, R J Spud Taylor, responded to an appeal to support the Special Care Baby Unit at Glan Clwyd Hospital. A local Doctor's son had been cared for at the Unit after a premature birth and the Doctor had started an appeal for funds. In all, the Captain raised £3500.

John Davison, Captain in 2003, chose the Air Ambulance for his chosen Charity. A total amount of £5350 was raised.

In 2004, the Captain, H Eirwyn Jones, named The Child Development Centre in Pwllheli as his chosen charity and raised over £6000. (Please see photo of the Cheque Presentation under Captains' Chapter, 2004)

Presentation of 2 cheques in excess of £8000 to Tŷ Enfys, [Rainbow House] Ysbyty Gwynedd in 2006.
Pictured clockwise from front Left, Ladies' Captain Dorothy Humpherson, Vice-Captain Ian Cooper, Captain Richard Rimmington, Match and Handicap Secretary T Gareth Gruffydd, Ladies' President Annette Jones and Mrs Val Moulds, Chairman of Tŷ Enfys

In 2005, the Captain and Lady Captain decided to combine their efforts and support the one single charity and this trend has continued to the present day. In 2005, that Charity was Tŷ Enfys and a total of £8202 was raised.

Representatives of the Doctors' Surgery in Nefyn receive a cheque for over £5,300 in 2006

Lois Angharad Owens receives a £2000 cheque for the Star Fish Appeal, King's College Hospital, London, from Captain Ian Cooper and Lady Captain Megan Roberts

In 2006, two charities were selected, namely The New Doctor's Surgery in Nefyn and The Star Fish Appeal, [the Paediatric Liver Unit at King's College Hospital London]. £7320.76 was raised.

The Centenary Year saw a staggering £12,525 raised by the Centenary Captains towards buying Specialist Equipment for Ysbyty Bryn Beryl, Pwllheli.

The Centenary Captains are pictured presenting the cheque to the representatives from Ysbyty Bryn Beryl.
Pictured Left to Right: *Jayne Cotgrove Community Physiotherapist, Judy Jones Team Leader, Sharon Parry Senior Nurse, Arwel Hughes Chairman of the League of Friends, Hannah Williams Occupational Therapist and Ward Sister Sarah Jones*

From time to time the Club has supported Open Competitions for Charity by releasing the Course free of green fee charges. In 2005, for example, an Open Charity Team Competition was organised by the Professional, John Froom and Barry James, a Club Member. This took place on Easter Sunday and £1,155 was raised towards Tŷ Gobaith (Hope House) at Conwy and the North Wales Air Ambulance. Thus it is all the more remarkable that during this same year, the Captains also raised over £8000 for Tŷ Enfys! In May 2008, two past Captains, Hugh and Laura Roberts, Dolydd, have been given the courtesy of the Course and plan to run another Open Competition in aid of Tŷ Gobaith.

...and reponse to Disasters

Apart from the annual charity fund-raising, the Club Members willingly respond to local or international disasters or appeals. Live Aid has already been mentioned but two others spring to mind. In February 1990, when the sea floods devastated the Towyn area on the North Wales Coastline, the Captain immediately nominated the Towyn Appeal as his Charity and generous donations were added to the sum already raised during the year. On New Year's Eve, 2004, over £1200 was raised for the Tsunami Appeal in a spontaneous response to the Asian disaster.

SOCIAL EVENTS OVER THE YEARS
DIGWYDDIADAU CYMDEITHASOL DROS Y BLYNYDDOEDD

Yn ystod y degawdau ar ôl yr Ail Ryfel Byd ychydig o nosweithiau cymdeithasol a drefnwyd yn y Clwb ar wahân i Ginio Gŵyl Dewi a'r Cinio Blynyddol. Yn ddiweddarach, ychwanegwyd nosweithiau llawen pan fyddai'r Aelodau'n cynnal nosweithiau o ganeuon a sgetshis i adlonni'r gynulleidfa. Trefnwyd y rhain gan Adran y Merched.

Arferid chwarae ping-pong yn yr ystafell i fyny'r grisiau nes i rywun gael benthyg y bwrdd am gyfnod! Trefnwyd y Parti 'Dolig cyntaf i'r plant yn 1951. Ychydig o nosweithiau Cymraeg a drefnwyd ar wahân i ambell i gyngerdd gan Hogia'r Wyddfa, Celt ac, yn ddiweddar, Mynediad am Ddim a Chôr Glanaethwy dan arweiniad Cefin Roberts.

Yn dilyn Dawns y Mileniwm, trefnwyd nifer o ddawnsiau a nosweithiau o adloniant amrywiol, fel jas a chanu gwerin a chloriannwyd y sîn gymdeithasol gan Ddawns Fawreddog y Canmlwyddiant ym mis Awst 2007.

The Men's Committee over the years rarely discussed social events unless a House Committee report suggested a price and venue for an Annual Dinner or a St David's Day Dinner. The former, originally set in February, became an 'Annual Dinner and Guest Speaker' and moved to November while the latter was always on the Saturday closest to St David's Day.

Ladies tended to arrange a Ladies' Dinner annually, after their AGM and this was minuted.

Oct 1950: Dinner to be arranged after the AGM at the Cecil Court Hotel.

Oct 1951: Dinner at the Crown Hotel Pwllheli at a cost of 7/6 to be arranged after the AGM.

Oct 1952: Dinner to be arranged at the Nanhoron Hotel after the AGM. Cost 8/-. Mrs Edge [Stewardess] to be invited and her dinner paid for by the Ladies' Fund.

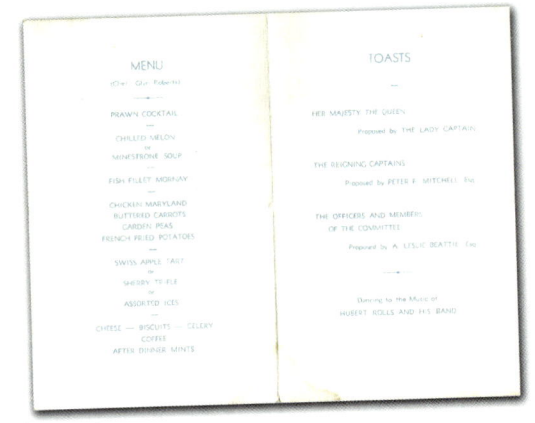

Annual Dinner and Dance Menu at the Woodlands Hall Hotel, Edern in February 1971. Ticket: 30/- (Proprietors Richard and Dorothy Roberts, Past Lady Captain and Lady President)

Occasionally praise for a concert or some entertainment was minuted in the Executive Minutes but it was left to the Ladies' Section's Minutes to reveal to us what really took place at the nineteenth hole in the Clubhouse or elsewhere.

> *Aug 1933:* The [summer] meeting wound up on Thursday 24th August by a ping-pong tournament in the afternoon and a very pleasant dance [at Madryn Hall]. (sic)
>
> *Dec 16th 1933:* Mixed Foursomes Competition - 18 holes. After the competition, tea was served and then a Whist Drive and Supper. The whole day was a great success. (sic)

Afternoon Whist Drives and Bridge Drives followed by tea or supper became extremely popular but there were constant complaints about the tea not being up to standard! Bridge Drives continued up to 2005 and the Whist Drives continue to this day on Friday evenings.

The upstairs room in the 1929 Clubhouse became a Games Room where the Club's Ping-Pong Table was erected. Ping-pong became a regular pastime especially when bad weather caused the cancellation of golf! In 1946, there was uproar because the Ladies discovered the Men's Section had given the table to a Club Member without asking their permission!

> *April 1946:* A letter was read from Captain Hughes (Nat Pro Bank) saying that the table tennis table which had been given to him by the Club could now be returned if the members so wished.

The table was duly returned and ping-pong resumed! (See photo in Chapter on Captains, 1946)

In 1971, Frank Evans, the Chairman of House, produced a Calendar of Social Events for the Winter Months as follows:

The Children's Party in December, with coffee morning in November to raise funds for it!
New Year's Eve Function
Golf Dance in February
St David's Day Function in March
Whist Drive on Nov 3rd
Noson Lawen Nov 13th with buffet supper and another one on January 15th (when Hogia'r Wyddfa, a Welsh Folk Group, would entertain).

The November 13th Noson Lawen [Merry Evening] was intended to give Club Members a chance to show their talents in music, prose, poetry or acting. The evening was hugely successful and this much valued cultural tradition continued for many years. Some real stars emerged (See Annette Jones' and Carys Wyn Jones' reminiscences in the Chapter 'I Remember...')

Social golf became a relief from the constant competitive element that was emerging. Ladies arranged matches with the Junior and Gent's Sections and followed these with hot-pot suppers. Relaxed mixed competitions were welcomed and the 'Pacyrs' (see under Groups and Teams) v the Ladies became quite a fiercely contested fun competition!

Mixed Foursomes were always fun and here the Vicar, third from the left, was relieved to find he did have a female (?) partner after all! **Pictured Left to Right:** Geraint Hughes, Mary J Williams, the Vicar and Les Gill in the late 80s.

SOCIAL EVENTS - DIGWYDDIADAU CYMDEITHASOL

These competitions, recently renamed as 'Friendly Mixed 10 Hole Foursomes', are still played regularly today.

In the 80s, pub quizzes became popular and the Golf Club followed suit. There were General Knowledge and Rules of Golf Quizzes and Forums and these have continued to the present day.

The Children's Christmas Party

The first documented evidence of a children's Christmas Party is in the Ladies' Minutes of September 1951 when it was reported that the party was to be arranged for December 22nd that year.

The Children's Christmas Party, 1971.

(Above): The Children's Christmas Party, 1986 with Club Captain, Gresham Owen and the Lady Captain, Margaret Chafe standing at the rear.

(Left): The Children's Christmas Party December 18th 1952. Next to Sion Corn on the Left is the Immediate Past Captain, W L Davies and Peter Lane is on the extreme Right. Note there are no ladies present in the photograph, although they organised the party, bought the presents and decorated the Clubhouse!

THE NEW MILLENNIUM

Members enjoy the Millennium New Year's Eve Party at the Golf Club.

Max Boyce MBE, the Welsh Comedian, Singer and Entertainer at the Millennium Ball.
(Inset): ..."I know 'cos I WAS THERE!" Welsh rugby supporters together!

SOCIAL EVENTS - DIGWYDDIADAU CYMDEITHASOL

Apart from the occasional bi-lingual Noson Lawen and the St David's Day entertainment, there has been relatively little entertainment solely in the Welsh Language. In January 2002 however, a Welsh Night was advertised and very quickly became a complete sell-out. Hogia'r Wyddfa, a close harmony group specialising in Welsh folk music, together with Annette Bryn-Parry (Piano) and Comedian John Ogwen gave us an evening of Welsh Entertainment at its very best.

[In July 2007, 'Mynediad am Ddim' similarly sold out within days and gave us another wonderful evening of Welsh language folk-music. (See Photo in Centenary Events)]

June 2002: Great increase in the use of Clubhouse, with increased takings due to 'pleasant environment' created by the arrival of Pip Settle and Phil Shakespeare [Caterer and Assistant Barman]

Pip and Phil's appointment and success coincided with a highly conscientious effort from Ian Cooper to inject life into the social side of the Club. By 2003, the Club was witnessing sights it had never seen before.

Our cartoonist, Tony, takes his creative talent to another level and dresses as a tramp at the 2005 ragball

Members dress up for a Hot August Night (60s style) in 2003

SOCIAL EVENTS - DIGWYDDIADAU CYMDEITHASOL

Members dress up for the 2nd Hot August Night in 2004. The Captain, H E Jones Left, was un-recognisable as he dyed his hair during his year of office in support of his named charity.

A serious 'Gloria in Excelsis' Duet at the first Christmas Sing-a-long in 2003.

Members and friends join in with the 2006 Christmas sing-a-long, complete with percussion instruments. Over £500 for Charity is raised on these Carol Evenings.

A fun rendering of 'Jingle Bells' by the Club's Comb Choir, at the first Christmas Sing-a-long in 2003.

The Bridge Enthusiasts at a Christmas Party in 2004, with Lady Captain Janet Ellwood, front row left.

SOCIAL EVENTS - DIGWYDDIADAU CYMDEITHASOL

The original Tailor Maid Band, formed by Ian Cooper, Captain 2006. The Band played in his Captain's Day Evening Entertainment. **Pictured are: Front:** Jack Dobson (Lead Vocalist) **1st Row: Left to Right,** Helen Gwent (Cornet), Siân Teleri Hughes (Vocalist), Ian Cooper (Drums), Louise and daughter Victoria Gaskell (Vocalists) **2nd Row: Left to Right,** Sam Humphreys (Lead Guitar), Lee Coppin (Rhythm Guitar and Percussion), Alwyn Williams (Rhythm Guitar) **3rd Row: Left to Right,** Doug Lear (Saxophone), Mark Jones (Bass Guitar), Tony Connolly (Keyboard) and Aron Williams (Trombone).

Members ponder over questions on the rules of golf in a Rules Quiz in 2006.

The Ladies' Captain, Megan Roberts, (right) leads Members in a Barn Dance on her Farewell Evening, March 2007.

In 2006, Ian Cooper provided the customary Captain's Day half-way house drinks at the 'Shankers' Arms' on the 16th Tee. Some Competitors however were seen taking refreshments as early as the adjacent 6th Tee!

Jazz also became popular and was a 'first' for the Club in 2005. Several bands have played at Nefyn since then and the Blue Magnolia Jass Orchestra, who play in major jazz festivals, have appeared regularly at the Club.

SOCIAL EVENTS - DIGWYDDIADAU CYMDEITHASOL

Outings - Teithiau

OUTINGS
TEITHIAU

Isod, cawn ddetholiad o ymweliadau Adran y Merched ac Adran y Dynion â Chlybiau yng Nghymru a Lloegr dros y degawdau diwethaf. Cyfeirir at deithiau undydd a theithiau aros mewn cyfres o ffotograffau.

LADIES' SECTION

Ladies frequently played in the Union Meetings and from the early 1950s, if there were much travelling involved, they stayed overnight in a local hotel.

> *May 1951: Sec to write to Castle Hotel Deganwy for 7 single rooms and dinner in the evening.*
>
> *Mar 1952: St David's Hotel, Harlech, to be booked for 10 single rooms and dinner.*

The actual outings for Nefyn Ladies began in 1966, with an outing to Conwy. [Rumour has attempted to date the first ever outing to Holyhead in 1972 but this is incorrect.] That first outing to Conwy was not particularly well supported by Nefyn Ladies:

> *Oct 1966: [Ladies' First Ever Outing] It was reported that as only 11 were going on an outing to Conway, Pwllheli and Caernarvon Clubs should be invited to join the outing. [Sic] [This number then increased to 20!]*

Some other outings followed but they were spasmodic. In 1972, Lady Captain, Enid Evans, organised the outing to Holyhead and continued to organise outings annually for the next 20 years.

Ladies' Outing to Aberdyfi, 1986.
Lady Captain, Joan Kilner, is kneeling centre front row with Marian Grace, Lady Secretary. [Aberdyfi, always a popular venue, had been first visited in 1974.]

Ladies' Outing to Holyhead Golf Club in September 1972.
Lady Captain Enid Evans is seen in the picture, centre of the middle row.

Ladies at Menai Court Hotel, Bangor after their outing in 1988 to Bull Bay. *Pictured centre is Lady Captain, Anne Thomas with her arm around Nell Hughes. [Until fairly recently it was always a tradition to dine at a hotel on the way home from the outing.]*

OUTINGS - TEITHIAU

Ladies' Outing to Chirk, 1993.
Lady Captain, Jacqui Wilcox is seated fourth from the Left.

The Ladies' Outing to Chirk is one the ladies will remember for a very long time. The Course was relatively new, very long and extremely wet on the day of their visit. Scoring was difficult and the winning score was a mere 18 points by Shirley Roulston! Dilys Ll Owen remembers the occasion more than most. It was her very first outing with the Ladies and she recalls a horrendous game... when she failed to score even one point! On her return home, husband Gwilym asked her how she had got on and when she related her tale of woe, he flatly refused to believe her – maintaining that surely no-one could fail to score even one point in 18 holes!

Ladies' First Golfing Weekend Away, September 2006

The Ladies' Captain, Megan Roberts, planned a weekend away for the Ladies of the Club in September 2006 at Patshull Park Hotel and Golf Club, near Wolverhampton. In the region of 30 ladies participated in the 2 day event.

Pictured Left to Right: *the Ladies' Captain, Megan Roberts with the winners of the Team Event, Dilys Ll Owen, Megan M Williams, Rhiannon Ingman and Louise Rowley.*

The Centenary Year and The Spring Outing

The 2007 Ladies' Spring Outing to Llanymynech was a great success. For once, the weather was kind and the scoring impressive with the Ladies' Captain, playing off a handicap of 2, winning with 37 pts!

The arrival at Llanymynech had been quite dramatic! The coach had got stuck on the very narrow hill up to the Golf Club and the Ladies began to panic wondering how on earth they would be able to carry golf bags, trolleys, batteries and change of clothes! However the Club's Greens' Staff, complete with tractor and trailer and some of our own Ladies, who had already arrived by car, took it in turns to shuttle Members and their belongings up the steep hill to the Clubhouse!!

01.06.07 *"..panic and dismay when the coach got stuck."*

Some of the Ladies treat coach driver O G Evans to a non-alcoholic drink after his ordeal with the bus on the lane up to Llanymynech Golf Club, Spring 2007. [It was the same OG who had presented the Ladies' Section with the O G Evans Autumn Outing Shield in October, 1997.]

Visit to Mottrom Hall, Prestbury, Cheshire

The Ladies' Captain organised a weekend away in September 2007. 32 Ladies stayed at the Hotel and another 10 who lived locally joined daily for the golf and the socialising!

From Left to Right, enjoying dinner at Mottram Hall are Deirdre Allinson, Angela Rimmington, The Ladies' Captain, Kate Norbury and Sue Gray.

MEN'S SECTION

The Men have had outings and overnight visits since the early 70s but sadly, there is very little photographic evidence of these occasions.

Members recall visiting Hawkstone Park, near Wem, Shropshire on a couple of occasions in the 70s and staying overnight.

Veterans Outing to Trearddur Bay Golf Club 1970
Standing Left to Right: *Unknown, Val Leigh-Morgan, Tom Poole, Ivor Williams, Peter Lane, Harry Parry, Robert Thomas, G I Pritchard Ellis, Captain W Parry, Captain Dan W Jones, Unknown, Captain Richard Griffith and Unknown.*
Front Row, Left to Right: *Cyril Davies, Alf Whalley, George Ensor, Owen Roberts, Unknown and John Ty Gongl.*

Annual Outings

Louise Rowley, Left, loses on a card play off to partner Fiona Vaughan Thomas at Llanymynech 2007.

Men's Outing to Bull Bay, mid 70s. Left to Right (Front Row): Peter Lane, Gordon Smith, Robin Griffith
Standing, Left to Right, *Stephen Lane, James Bentley, T Gareth Gruffydd, Rhys Griffith, W R Hughes, R M Williams, Captain Will Roberts, Geraint Hughes and G I Jones.*

6 Members on the Outing to Rhuddlan in June 1990. Clockwise from centre: Edward Jones, Huw Merfyn Williams, G Ivor Jones, John Blore, Edric Williams and Ellis Roberts.

Exchanges

In 1989, the seed was planted for exchange visits with other Clubs. Prenton Golf Club was the first to be involved and the exchanges with them continued for a number of years.

[See Captain's Chapter 2003 for photo of visit to Wilpshire in 1990.]

Trips to Spain and Portugal

In 2001, Pete D'Aoust organised what was to be the first of regular biennial trips to Spain and Portugal. The first three visits, 2001, 2003 and 2005 were to Benalmadena, near Malaga and the 2007 Portugal trip was to Alvafera.

(Above): The Men's Trip to Spain 2003.

(Below): The last night in Spain, 2003.
What happened next? Captain J Davison and Vice-Captain H E Jones are presented with gateaux and are wholly unprepared for having them thrown into their faces!

Trip to Florida

Eight Gentlemen Members planned a trip to Florida in February, 1993. (One member withdrew because of illness).

Pictured Left to Right: Will Ll Jones, Alwyn Williams, Lt Col Robin Parry, Emyr L Evans, Ioi Williams, Paul Farrow and Patrick McAteer.

The Seniors

The Seniors' Inter-Club Matches began in the early 90s and the inaugural organiser was Bob Entwistle. The first Seniors' Match was played against Royal St David's Golf Club at Harlech. In 1998, Dennis Humpherson took over as Organiser passing the reins to Tony Connolly in 2005.

The Seniors at Aberdyfi, April 2006.

In 2007, the Seniors played, home and away, against Aberdyfi, Abersoch, Bull Bay, Caernarfon, Conwy, Criccieth, Holyhead, North Wales, Porthmadog, Pwllheli and Harlech.

The Irish Trips

Nefyn Seniors' first visit to Ireland October 2005.

Ireland 2005. Pictured Left and Right are Duncan Smith and Tony Connolly, Trip Organisers, with the Captain of Coollattin Golf Club and Nefyn Golf Club Captain Richard Rimmington.

Taylor's Irish Bar, Dublin, 2005. [Ladies, this is what they get up to when away!]

Ireland Oct 2007. Selection of Nefyn Members and Hosts of Coollattin Club outside the Pro's Shop waiting to tee off the 1st.

The spectacular 10th hole at Hermitage Golf Club, Ireland October 2007.

(Left): The Coollattin Club from Ireland visit Nefyn in September 2006. [Unbelievably, due to some lack of communication, the Bar had run out of Guinness by 6pm!]

OUTINGS – TEITHIAU

PHOTOS COMMEMORATING CENTENARY EVENTS
LLUNIAU O DDIGWYDDIADAU'R CANMLWYDDIANT

Ar Ddydd Sadwrn, Ebrill 7fed 2007, dathlwyd dechreuad y Canmlwyddiant gyda Chyfarfod Cyffredinol Blynyddol y Clwb. Yn dilyn, ceir crynodeb o'r prif ddigwyddiadau yn ystod y flwyddyn mewn ffotograffau.

The Centenary Year began on Saturday April 7th 2007, with the AGM and continued to the AGM of 2008, held on Saturday, March 22nd. There follows a pictorial account of the main events of the year. The Golfing Centenary Presentations are presented in another section.

April 2007

The Centenary Captains unveil the Centenary Commemorative Stone *prior to the Captains' Drive-in on Easter Sunday, April 8th 2007*

The Captains' Drive-in, Easter Sunday 2007. Pictured from Left to Right: *Vice-Captain Gordon Smith, Captain Emyr L Evans, Ladies' Captain Fiona Vaughan Thomas and Ladies' Vice-Captain Janet Brown.*
Photo: Dewi Wyn, Pwllheli

May 2007

The Captain's Good Lady, Mrs Marian Evans (Left) and the Ladies' Vice-Captain Janet Brown get in the mood for the **'100 years' Fancy Dress Party'** *on Saturday May 5th, 2007*

The Centenary Birthday Party
Monday May 7th 2007

The Centenary Birthday Cake. *Members were invited to celebrate the 100th Birthday with a Champagne Reception in the Clubhouse on Monday, May 7th, exactly 100 years to the day the Club was formed.*

Members at the Centenary Celebratory Birthday Party, May 7th 2007

August 2007

The Officers of the Ladies' Committee get a soaking supporting the Captain at the crack of dawn on his **Sponsored** 100 **Holes of Golf. Left to Right:** *Ladies' Captain Fiona Vaughan Thomas, Ladies' Secretary Shan Gruffydd, Ladies' President Carys Wyn Jones and Ladies' Vice-Captain Janet Brown, August 2007*

July 2007

'Mynediad am Ddim' *at an evening of Welsh Folk Music on July 13th 2007.* **Left to Right:** *Rhys Ifans, Geraint Davies, Emyr Wyn, Robin Evans, Peter Jones and Graham Pritchard*

'Youngsters' [1] *Nellie Trenholme and* [2] *Dorothy Roberts, both of them Past Lady Captains and Lady Presidents, show the way on the dance floor at the Centenary Concert featuring 'Mynediad am Ddim'*

CENTENARY EVENTS - DIGWYDDIADAU'R CANMLWYDDIANT

The Centenary Ball, August 11th 2007

Four hundred and seventy people attended the Ball. Marc Macauley Catering from Rhyl were the outside caterers and the magnificent marquee was hired from Tents and Events in Mold. The Golf Club ran the Bar.

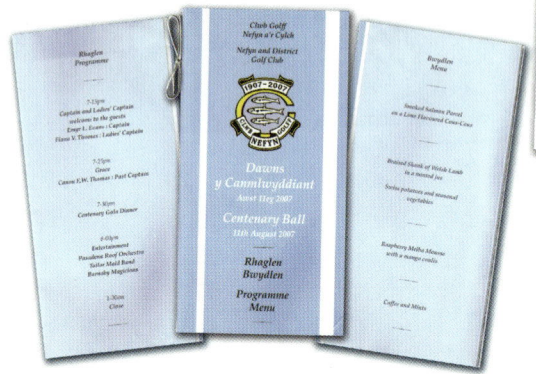

Members and Their Guests Arrive at The Centenary Ball

Left to Right: *Chairman of Greens' Committee Richard Harris Roberts with his wife, Iona, together with Shirley Ellis and Club Trustee, Ieuan M Ellis*

The Gaskell Family **Left to Right:** *Robert, Helen, Anthony, Victoria, Club Chairman Chris Gaskell and wife, Louise*

The Programme and Menu for the Centenary Ball

The Marquee which stood on the Practice Ground

Members and Guests seated for the banquet at the Centenary Ball

CENTENARY EVENTS - DIGWYDDIADAU'R CANMLWYDDIANT

Left to Right: Chairman Match and Handicap Committee Ian Hamilton, Assistant Junior Organiser Carol Smith, Karen Hamilton, Christine Smith and Club Vice-Captain Gordon Smith

Clockwise: Megan Roberts, County Captain Laura Wyn Roberts, Meinir Roberts, Gwilym Owen, Griff Roberts, Dilys Ll Owen, Fred and Dorothy Barton and Captain H E Roberts

Clockwise: Marion and Stuart Hall, Barbara and Graham Moss, Janet and Roger Ellwood, and Ladies' Vice-Captain, Janet Brown

Above, Clockwise: Treasurer Richard Rimmington, Val Moores, Jeff Bissenden, Ladies' Treasurer Angela Rimmington, Roger Smethurst, Hazel Lappin, Rick Moores, Linda Smethurst, Ken Lappin and Heather Bissenden

Left, Clockwise: Head Greenkeeper Patrick McAteer, Gwyneth McAteer, Past Sec/Manager Barry Owens, Sioned Owens, Brian Owens, Menna and Mel Jones, Anwen Owens, Erhard and Linda Nierada

CENTENARY EVENTS - DIGWYDDIADAU'R CANMLWYDDIANT

September 2007

*Some of the Ladies enjoying the **Karaoke on Ladies' President's Evening, Sept 2007**. The Ladies' President, Mrs Carys Wyn Jones, is in the front row, second from the right*

The Centenary Club Invitation
Several clubs, who were also celebrating their Centenary Year in 2007, were invited to Nefyn for a Golf Day and Presentation Dinner. Pictured below with the Officers of Nefyn are representatives of Abersoch, Carmarthen and Welshpool Golf Clubs together with delegates from the Caernarfonshire and District Golf Union and Caernarfonshire and Anglesey Ladies' Golf Association.

November 2007

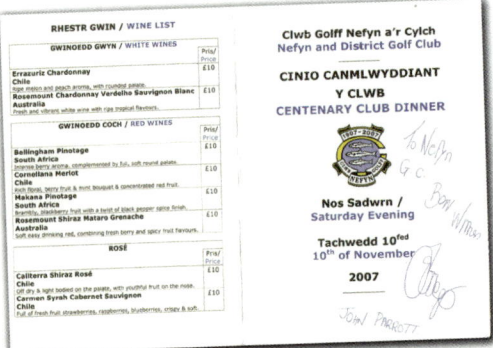

Above and Below: Centenary Dinner Menu, November 2007. Ticket price £20.00 [with John Parrot's autograph]

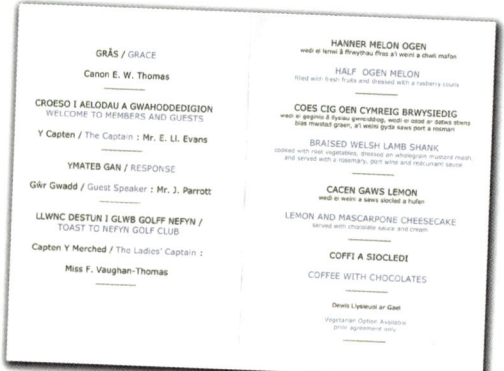

Members and guests await for the speeches at the Centenary Dinner

Distinguished Guests and Officers at the Club's Centenary Dinner. Left to Right: Miss Margaret Worthington (President of the C & A County Ladies' Golf Association), Mr Aled Warren-Rees (President of the Caernarfon & District Golf Union) Mrs Janet Brown (Ladies' Vice Captain), Dr Phil Dixon (President of the Golf Union of Wales), Mr Chris Gaskell (Club Chairman), Mr David Harrison (Captain of the R & A Golf Club), Miss Fiona Vaughan Thomas (Ladies' Captain), Guest Speaker John Parrott (Professional Snooker Player & World Snooker Champion - 1991), Mr Ioi Williams (Club President), Mr Gordon Smith (Club Vice-Captain) and Mr Emyr L Evans (Club Captain)

CENTENARY EVENTS - DIGWYDDIADAU'R CANMLWYDDIANT

Professional Snooker Player John Parrott arrived at 10am, played a round of golf in cold and windy conditions in the morning, challenged some of the Members at snooker in the afternoon and then was Guest Speaker at the Centenary Dinner!

'JP', the golfer

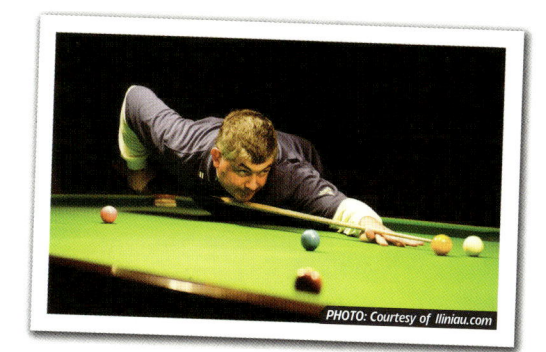

'JP', the snooker-player

'JP', the after dinner speaker

December 2007

Children are entertained by Tom Dawson, Christmas 2007

Some youngsters enjoying the Clown's antics at the 2007 **Children's Christmas Party.** *(Please see Chapter on Juniors for the 2007 Junior Presentation on the same afternoon)*

March 2008 - The End of The Centenary Year

'Côr Glanaethwy' at the St David's Day Dinner, 2008

The Ladies' Captain's Farewell in March 2008 *was a resounding success with Jay Ashton's presentation of 'The Wonder of Elvis' Show*

(Above) *Ladies' Captain sings along on the night with Elvis*

CENTENARY EVENTS - DIGWYDDIADAU'R CANMLWYDDIANT

A SELECTION OF CENTENARY GREETINGS
DETHOLIAD O GYFARCHION Y CANMLWYDDIANT

Cyfarchion Penblwydd gan Mynediad am Ddim.

Mynediad am Ddim (Welsh Folk Group) wish us a Happy Birthday.

Left to Right: Gareth Roberts (S4C Presenter), Huw Llywelyn Davies (Rugby Commentator and Analyst) and Dewi Pws (Welsh Comedian) offer their congratulations on our Centenary.

Llongyfarchiadau ar y Canmlwyddiant! Edrych ymlaen i ddod nôl pan fydd y glaw di mynd.
Gareth Roberts.

Pob hwyl â'r dathlu. Diolch am y croeso. Trueni am y tywydd! Glaw? Never in Nefyn!
Huw Llywelyn Davies.

Roedd y Greens yn fendigedig ond roedd y tato'n oer.
Dewi Pws.

Atgofion Hogia'r Wyddfa

Arwel, yn ôl ei arfer, yn gofyn am gadarnhad dilysrwydd graddnod Myrddin.

Arwel, on the right, in his customary manner makes sure that Myrddin is playing off the correct handicap!

Ar ôl ymlwybro hyd erwau godidog hen gwrs golff Nefyn yn saithdegau'r ganrif olaf, daeth Myrddin a minnau at y deunawfed twll. Roedd golwg digon lluddedig arnom gan i rai o ferched y clwb ddod allan i'n cyfarch a'n cysuro. Roedd gen i saith troedfedd o suddiad i gwblhau fy rownd.

'Arwel', meddai llais o blith y criw oedd wedi ymgynnull, 'os suddi di'r pyt, fi fydd y cynta i dy longyfarch - os fethi di, nei di addo y daw'r Hogia draw i'r clwb i gynnal cyngerdd!' Derbyniais y sialens gan ychwanegu, 'ac mi ddoi am ddim!'

Methu'r pyt wnes i a dyna fynd ati yn y fan a'r lle i drefnu noson yng nghwmni Hogia'r Wyddfa. Yn wir, dyna gysylltiad cynta'r Hogia â Chlwb Golff Nefyn, cysylltiad a barhaodd hyd y cyfnod presennol.

Cafodd Myrddin, Vivs a minnau ddyddiau difyr iawn yn chwarae'r cyrsiau ac yn cynnal cyngherddau yn y Clwb. Byddai'r Clwb yn orlawn bob tro a'r awyrgylch yn drydanol ac yn gwbl Gymreig. Atgofion i'w sawru.

Bu cysylltiad 'Hogia Dydd Mawrth' â'r Clwb yn fodd i'r tri ohonom gael mwy o gemau ar y cyrsiau. Byddai'r croeso'r un mor wresog. Dyma'r unig glwb lle byddai'r Llywydd ei hun yn dod i'n croesawu. Gorchwyl fyddai'n cael ei gwerthfawrogi gan y criw. Gwyddai H D Jones fod pwrpas amgenach i'r gemau Dydd Mawrth yma na phleser yn unig. Bu Nefyn, ymhlith nifer o glybiau eraill yng Ngogledd Cymru, yn gyfrwng i ni allu codi arian, a fyddai erbyn diwedd y flwyddyn yn gyfanswm sylweddol iawn. Pleser o'r mwyaf fydd cyfarfod i rannu'r arian at achosion da.

Mae'r atgofion am gemau Nefyn ar brynhawniau Mawrth yn amrywio o wrando ar Dewi Pws yn dweud jôc ar bob ti, Bryn Terfel yn canu nodyn uchaf yr emyn dôn Calon Lân ar ôl gwneud smonach o'i siot, a John Ogwen bron a chael ei gipio dros y creigiau i'r môr gan gorwynt, a Bryn a finnau yn crefu arno i adael ei glybiau ar ôl! Mae un ystadegaeth yn aros hyd heddiw, sydd yn friw i'm bron - tydw i 'rioed wedi curo Myrddin yn Nefyn!

Llongyfarchiadau ar gyrraedd y cant a phob dymuniad da i'r dyfodol.

Arwel, Hogia'r Wyddfa.

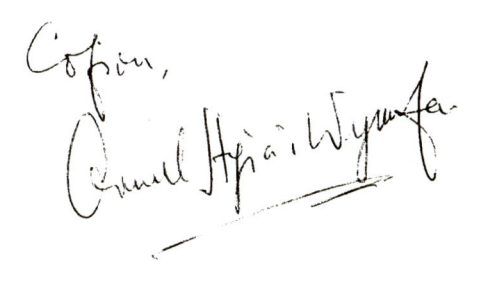

Arwel (Hogia'r Wyddfa - Welsh Folk Group), in sending his congratulatory message, above, recalls many golfing visits to Nefyn and the wonderful sell-out concerts staged at the Club.

A message from Paul Allott, England Cricketer and Sky Sports Cricket Commentator

One word alone sums up Nefyn... **Challenge!** Quite simply, the Golf Course provides the ultimate test of a golfer's ability when tackling the peninsula, so much so that after two holes there is frequently no option but to abandon clubs, caddy and partners and diasappear down the cliff to the Tŷ Coch for a consoling pint or two. Indeed, it was in this very hostel, that the then captain of England, Michael Atherton, imbibed perhaps too much Guinness and was asked to resume his round immediately before he upset anyone else with his ribaldry.

Whatever the conditions, whoever you are with, however you are playing, Nefyn will always be up there in my most challenging of courses, not just in Wales, but worldwide. It is simply that good. Best of luck with your Centenary Celebrations.

Paul Allot (Walt to his mates)

David Llewellyn with Joe Vickery (Newport), Welsh Boys' Champion at Nefyn 2007.

Greetings from David Llewellyn, former Head Welsh Junior Coach.

Congratulations on 100 years of Golf. Always the warmest of welcomes at one of the most spectacular courses I know.

David Llewellyn World Cup 1987.

A message from International Opera Singer, Bryn Terfel

Dim ond gair i ddymuno'r gorau i Glwb Golff Nefyn ar ei ddathladiau. Mae'n bleser pur troedio'r Cwrs arbennig yma ac ymfalchio ym mhrydferthwch ein harfordir godidog.

Tydwi 'rioed wedi cael Par ar y cyntaf ac yn gweddio i beidio taro'r bêl ormod i'r dde ar y pum twll cyntaf! Ond mae o heb os nac onibai, yn Gwrs sydd fel magned yn eich denu yn ôl. Trueni nag ydio yn nes i Bontnewydd. Diolch twym galon hefyd am gefnogi achos y criw Dydd Mawrth.

Yn gywir iawn,

Bryn Terfel's greeting, above, describes the stunning course which is like a magnet drawing people back, time and time again.

Left: *Bryn Terfel (extreme Right) and Mark Hughes, ex-Wales International Footballer and Manager (second from Left), with T G Gruffydd, Moi Parry and Tecs Williams outside the Pro's Shop, August 2003.*

A word from John Ogwen

John Ogwen (renowned Welsh actor, author and entertainer), sends his best wishes and believes the first three letters in Nefyn, spelling 'Nef' (Heaven) in Welsh is no coincidence as the Course, the welcome and the breathtaking scenery are truly heavenly.

Nid cyd-ddigwyddiad mo'r ffaith mai'r union dair llythyren sydd yn cychwyn y gair 'nefoedd' a'r enw Nefyn. Mae Cwrs Golff Nefyn yn sicr o fod yn rhan o'r nefoedd olff sydd i fyny fan'cw yn rhywle. Y Cwrs, y croeso a'r olygfa ryfeddol yn rhoi popeth yn ei le yn berffaith.

Ond mae'r gwynt yn chwythu weithiau. A'r diafol yn cuddio ym mhobman ar ddiwrnod gwyntog. Os bydd y diafol hwnnw'n cael goruchafiaeth arnoch am ddeunaw twll, nid oes golwg ohono yn y Clwb na thrwy'r ffenest lydan sy'n edrych tua'r môr.

Edrychaf ymlaen am ddiwrnod arall yn troedio lawntiau'r nefoedd.

Centenary Greetings - Cyfarchion Y Camlwyddiant

Edrychwn ymlaen yn eiddgar i groniclo hanes y can mlynedd nesa!
The three of us are really looking forward to writing the next hundred years' history!